EVERY DAY WITH THE FATHER

EVERY DAY

WITH THE

ATHER

366
DEVOTIONAL READINGS
FROM
JOHN'S GOSPEL

MARK STIBBE

MONARCH
BOOKS

Oxford, UK & Grand Rapids, Michigan, USA

First published in the UK in 2011 by Monarch Books
(a publishing imprint of Lion Hudson plc)
Wilkinson House, Jordan Hill Road, Oxford OX2 8DR, England
Tel: +44 (0)1865 302750 Fax: +44 (0)1865 302757
Email: monarch@lionhudson.com
www.lionhudson.com

ISBN 978 0 85721 026 5 (print)
ISBN 978 0 85721 234 4 (epub)
ISBN 978 0 85721 233 7 (Kindle)
ISBN 978 0 85721 235 1 (PDF)

Distributed by:
UK: Marston Book Services, PO Box 269, Abingdon, Oxon, OX14 4YN
USA: Kregel Publications, PO Box 2607, Grand Rapids, Michigan 49501

The text paper used in this book has been made from wood independently certified as having come from sustainable forests.

British Library Cataloguing Data
A catalogue record for this book is available from the British Library.

Printed and bound in the UK by MPG Books.

*This book is dedicated with my heartfelt
thanks to Tim Williams
and Anne-Marie Vickers.*

The Father's House Trust

Dr Mark Stibbe is the founder and leader of the Father's House Trust, a charity dedicated to taking the message of the love of the Father all over the world, and to bringing an end to fatherlessness on the earth.

The Father's House Trust seeks to fulfil this vision through five main objectives.

First, the Trust runs schools for leaders that major on the message of the Father's love and the healing of wounded hearts. These are home-based schools in Watford where the Father's House is located. These schools focus on an encounter with the transformative power of God's love.

Second, the Trust runs the same kinds of schools but away from its home base in Watford, and in churches with which the Trust feels a particular partnership. These partner churches are developing all over the world and have a city-changing impact.

Thirdly, the Trust is involved in running annual conferences that serve its vision. These are again based in our own town of Watford. In addition, Mark Stibbe and his team contribute to strategic conferences in the UK and abroad.

Fourthly, the Trust seeks to engage actively with contemporary culture, and specifically to put fatherhood and fatherlessness on the map in realms like government, education, the media, the arts, and family life. The Trust seeks to influence the influencers in these realms.

Fifthly, the Trust is passionate about ministering to the poor and fighting for the cause of the orphan and the widow, in accordance with the biblical mandate to look after those without fathers and those who have lost their husbands (James 1:27).

To find out more about the Trust, please consult the website at www.fathershousetrust.com.

Acknowledgments

This book has been an epic undertaking so there are a few people I want to thank for their support.

First of all, I'd like to thank my family. Writing a book of this size has meant that I have had to use time off to get the project finished. I am so grateful for the understanding and encouragement of my wife, Alie, and our four children – and of course my ever cheerful, ever hopeful labrador, Molly. Living with a writer is not always easy and I am so appreciative of the sacrifices that have been made so that I can do what I do.

Secondly, I want to thank Vicky Akrill and Catriona Reid for going through my text meticulously and pointing out typos and obscurities. Their eagle-eyed attention to detail has helped enormously.

Thirdly, I am so grateful to the Father's House family for their prayers and encouragement throughout. I particularly want to thank Liz Pembroke – whom I forgot to thank when I published *I Am your Father*!

Finally, I am – as ever – grateful to Tony Collins and the Monarch team for their amiable, constructive, and expert advice along the way. Journeys like these are made a great deal easier by such people as this.

Thank you all.

Introduction

If you've never read through a whole Gospel before, then I want to invite you to join me on this journey through one of the greatest stories ever told – the Gospel According to John.

John's Gospel is undoubtedly a book full of spiritual treasure. As we go through its verses day by day, we are going to uncover John's glittering gold and gleaming gems.

We will see that the greatest of these treasures is the Fatherhood of God. John's most memorable achievement is his focus on God as Father – as Papa, Daddy, or Dad. This is the jewel in his crown.

In *Every Day with the Father* I am going to show you how Jesus reveals the Father's love. Everything Jesus says and does in John's Gospel is like a window onto the world's greatest Dad.

In addition, I will try to explain what it means to be an adopted daughter or son of this affectionate Father. Through Jesus (the perfect Son) we will discover what it really means to be a child of God.

So come on a treasure hunt with me. Enjoy the pleasures of each verse but also appreciate the flow of the whole story – from its beginning on the shores of eternity to its ending on the shores of the Sea of Galilee.

You will find as we travel through this Gospel that it truly is a gripping story – a story that builds and builds towards the magnificent drama of the death and resurrection of Jesus.

Once you start on this path, you won't want to stop. John has pearls of wisdom that are more valuable and more profound than any found in even the most celebrated literary masterpieces.

These pearls are the shiny gifts of an extravagant Dad.

They are the love language of the Father that we've all been waiting for.

They are from heaven not earth.

So let's walk together on this journey.

And as we travel, let's pray this prayer:

Dear God, as I read the pages of this book, would you father me. Help me to experience your embrace and encounter your fatherly love. And teach me what it really means to be your child, in Jesus' name, and through the power of your Holy Spirit. Amen.

In the beginning was the Word... .

John 1:1

As we begin these devotional readings, it feels appropriate to look at a verse that deals with beginnings. Here, John flies on eagle's wings to the highest heights to reveal a view that no other Gospel writer gives us. Caught up in the prophetic currents of the Holy Spirit, he takes us back to the start of history and to the origins of the universe. Using words that are very reminiscent of the opening of the book of Genesis, John tells us that at the creation of all things the *Word* existed.

What is this "Word"? The plain answer is that the Word is God's speech. According to the Old Testament, God created all things through his spoken word. During the first six days of creation, God spoke everything into being. This is emphasized in the simple words, "And God said" in Genesis chapter 1.

When John talks about the *Word* he is telling us that God speaks. Accordingly, we should never forget that we worship a Father who reveals his heart and who communicates with his creatures. When the Father speaks, his speech is loving and life-giving.

Aren't you happy that we worship such a Father? There are so many dads today who are either physically or emotionally absent. Our heavenly Father is neither. He is present to us, though we often do not see him, and he speaks to us, though we often don't hear him.

A few verses later John will make it clear that the Word is Jesus. This shows that it is supremely and uniquely through Jesus that our heavenly Father has communicated with his lost and estranged children. If it weren't for Jesus, we would still be groping around in the dark, desperately trying to find God. But in Jesus, the Father has found us. He has come looking for his spiritual orphans and has spoken clearly to us and told us what we must do if we are to become his children and find our heart's true home in him. I am so grateful that Jesus is the Father's Word to us. He is truly the Father's love language.

Devotion: *Dear loving, heavenly Abba, Father, thank you that you have spoken to us through your Son, Jesus, and that we worship a Dad who loves to speak to his children. At the beginning of this book, please help me to make a brand new start in my friendship with you. Amen.*

... and the Word was with God, and the Word was God.

John 1:1

How big is your picture of Jesus? Do you worship a small, finite Jesus? Or do you worship a Jesus who is infinite, glorious, majestic, unlimited, and divine?

John tells us that before the universe was formed and the earth was created, the Word existed with God, and that the Word was at the same time God. If the Word is Jesus then this is momentous! It means that Jesus *was with* God and that Jesus *was* God. It means in fact that Jesus was not just a human being in history; he was and is a divine being in eternity.

Many people today reduce the person of Jesus either by claiming that he is a mythical figure or by saying that he was just a charismatic holy man. But Jesus really did exist and, according to the New Testament writers, he was more than just a man, more than just a prophet or a teacher. He was – and is – God!

John accordingly opens the curtains onto a truly panoramic and other-worldly landscape of revelation in this verse. He tells us that Jesus existed before he was born as a baby and that he was with the Father before creation. He tells us that the Son is separate from the Father and yet mysteriously the same as the Father.

Here of course we run straight into the mystery of the Trinity. Christians believe that God is three persons in one being. God is Father, Son and Holy Spirit – three separate persons yet all one God.

At the very start of all things, John says that the Father and the Son existed. They had always existed (along with the person of the Holy Spirit). Unlike the universe, they never came into being. They are uncreated and eternal. Doesn't that make you want to worship Jesus? He is more than a man and a Messiah, more than a preacher and a prophet. As Thomas will say at the end of John's Gospel, he is both our Lord and our God (John 20:28).

Devotion: *Dear loving, heavenly Abba, Father, your Son Jesus is truly unique. He is the Son who existed before the universe was made, the Son who is everlasting and divine. Help me to declare that Jesus is my Lord and my God. Amen.*

He was with God in the beginning.

John 1:2

The "Word" is one of the titles for Jesus that we find only in John's Gospel. When John writes that Jesus-the-Word was with God in the beginning, he is telling us that the Son was with the Father before all things came into being. Before he created anything, the Son lived with the Father. Before time and space were called into being, Jesus simply enjoyed his Father's presence.

It is important to remember that the Son has existed forever with the Father and will exist forever with the Father. The Son has always been at the Father's side. Before the dawn of history, the Son and the Father laughed, played, and rejoiced together. Before the first sunrise and the first birdsong, the Son was simply *with* the Father, as John the master storyteller reveals.

I have recently come back from a trip to the United States. My twin sister Claire moved out there many years ago. Having not seen her for a long time I felt it was time to go and visit her. I took my youngest son Sam with me. We had a great time travelling together. One of our best times was on a long, seven-hour road trip from Hobbes to Albuquerque. I was driving and Sam was sitting on my right-hand side listening to the music on the radio as we slowly made our way through the long, straight desert roads. For hours we just sat and laughed together, occasionally breaking into song as a familiar hit was played on the radio. It was great fun. I'll never forget it.

What a thing it is for a father to enjoy an affectionate, easy relationship with their son or daughter. What a beautiful thing it is for children and their dads to hang out and simply be together. If you have lacked this from your earthly father, know that you have it in your relationship with your heavenly Father.

John says that Jesus was with the Father "in the beginning". The Son was *with* the Father – simply *being* with his Dad.

Devotion: *Dear loving, heavenly Abba, Father, we thank you that you are the kind of dad that loves to be with us, just as you do with your Son. Thank you that, like Jesus, we can enjoy your company and spend time in the beauty of your presence. Help us to soak in your love today. Amen.*

Through him all things were made; without him nothing was made that has been made.

John 1:3

Genesis chapter 1 is the greatest description of creation you could possibly hope to find this side of eternity. On seven occasions the writer uses the phrase, "And God said". After each occasion, something is created as a result of the Father's life-giving speech – light, the sky, oceans, dry land, vegetation, the sun, moon and stars, the creatures of the sky and sea, animals and, of course, human beings.

Under the anointing of the Holy Spirit, John looks at this phrase "And God said" and identifies this as the Father's "Word", as Jesus. As far as John is concerned, Jesus was present before anything or anyone was made. More than that, Jesus-the-Word was the one through whom everything was created at the beginning of all things. The same Jesus who walked the streets of Jerusalem and the hills of Galilee was present "in the beginning". Jesus sat on the very mountains that he had made and walked on the very sea that he had formed. Everything that has been made by the Father has been made through the agency of his Son and in the power of his Holy Spirit.

So the next time you find yourself looking at the oceans, pause for a moment and say, "Jesus created that!"

The next time you see horses running at the gallop, pause for a moment and reflect, "Jesus made them!"

The next time you look up at the stars in the night sky, pause for a moment and say, "Jesus did that!"

The next time you look at your best friend, your spouse, your child, or your next-door neighbour, pause for a moment and say to yourself, "Jesus created you!"

Planets and people are not the random product of a chain of chance events. They are all the handiwork of Jesus.

Devotion: *Thank you, Jesus, that there isn't a single thing that exists that didn't come into being without you. I worship you for your matchless creativity and your undeniable divinity. Help me to appreciate your artistry in everything and everyone I see today. Amen.*

In him was life, and that life was the light of all people.

John 1:4

John says that there is life and light in Jesus-the-Word. The word translated "life" here is one that John uses time and again in his Gospel. It is the Greek word *zoe* from which we get zoology. Used some thirty-six times in John, it refers to the abundant, spiritual life that Jesus alone can give us. This is in contrast with another Greek word translated "life", which is *bios*, and from which we get biology. If *zoe* is spiritual life, *bios* is physical life. John tells us that in Jesus we receive *zoe* life – a spiritual life that brings a deep sense of fulfilment and which lasts forever!

The word "light" is also used a lot – over twenty times by John. It is the Greek word *phos* from which we get photosynthesis (a word that means literally "putting together with light"). Photosynthesis refers to the process in which rays of light from the sun bring life to plants on the earth. The electromagnetic energy of the sunlight causes a reaction in green plants in which sugar and oxygen are formed. The sugar is then used to make starch, fats and proteins (essential for our diet) and the oxygen enables us to live and breathe.

What a great picture! In John's Gospel, Jesus is presented to us as the "light of the world". Like plants, we depend on the light of the world for everything we need. His light brings us life – life in all its fullness. His energy sweetens and oxygenates our souls.

When I became a Christian on 17 January 1977, it was an utterly life-changing moment for me. One moment I was spiritually dead; the next moment I was more alive than I had ever been. Indeed, I would say that when I woke up the next morning I could hear the birds sing for the first time. It was as if every one of my five senses had been awakened. My spirit had been quickened into life the previous night as I had repented of my sin and put my faith and trust in Jesus. The light of Jesus had filled me with *zoe* life. Jesus truly is the Light and Life Bringer.

Why not stretch out your hands to the Son today?

Devotion: *Jesus, light of the world, I thank you so much that you are the source of real life and spiritual light. I choose life today. I choose to walk in your light. As I receive from you, help me to be a life-bringer to others and to brighten up their lives. Amen.*

The light shines in the darkness, and the darkness has not understood it.

John 1:5

There is nothing quite like the sight of bright pinpricks of light against a backdrop of pitch-black darkness. The darker the night, the more resolutely the lights seem to shine.

I remember one time I was preaching in Sweden. I was there for about three weeks in November and on one of the Sundays I travelled by train to Stockholm to speak at a church there. It was Advent Sunday.

On the way back it grew very dark in the late afternoon. As the train sped through the now invisible landscape I began to see lights everywhere. The Scandinavians are particularly fond of seven-branched lights, and these were shining from hundreds of windows in the houses dotted across the snowy landscape. Even though the darkness seemed to be very deep, the lights were strong and inextinguishable. I remember staring at the window and the Holy Spirit saying to me, "The light shines in the darkness, and the darkness has not understood it."

One of the things you quickly understand when you become a Christian is that there is an intense spiritual battle taking place between light and darkness. This battle is very evident in John's Gospel. Jesus comes into the world as the Father's light but he is opposed by many. This is because many human beings prefer to live in the darkness rather than the light and feel threatened by the radiance of Jesus. This sense of intimidation is ultimately fuelled by Satan, the adversary of God, who hates anything to do with the light.

We are all of us living on an embattled planet. Darkness surrounds us and some of this darkness is very thick indeed. But John tells us that the light of Jesus shines in the darkness and that the darkness has not understood it. The darkness – and those steeped in it – can neither apprehend nor comprehend the brilliance of Jesus. Only when a person turns from the darkness can they come to the light and become luminous in a world that's hostile to God.

Devotion: *Dear loving, heavenly Abba, Father, I worship you that Jesus is the light of the world and that his light is stronger than the darkness. Help me to be shiny for you as I go about my tasks today. Help me to push back the darkness and draw people to you. Amen.*

There was a man sent from God whose name was John. He came as a witness to testify concerning that light, so that through him all might believe. He himself was not the light; he came only as a witness to the light.

John 1:6–8

John the Baptist was a truly remarkable man. Not everyone would obey the Father's call to go and live in the desert, dress in camel's skin, eat locusts and shout out to people that they needed to repent. John did. Why? The secret is in the words "witness" and "testify" in these verses. These terms are very important in John's Gospel and they occur quite frequently. The original verb translated "witness" is *marturein*, from which we get the word "martyr". John the Baptist was truly a man who died to self. All he cared about was bearing witness to Jesus. He lived and breathed for this and was prepared to embrace a life of total dedication and ruthless self-sacrifice in order to point people to Jesus.

While only a few are called to lay down their lives for the cause of Christ and become martyrs, all of us are called to die to self and testify that Jesus is the light that illuminates our lives. Many of us switch off when we hear things like this. We say, "I'm not an evangelist" and we use this excuse to avoid witnessing to anyone.

John is using the language of the law courts when he talks about "witnessing" so let's use a legal analogy here. In defending a court case today, two types of people are needed: first of all, lawyers or attorneys; secondly, witnesses. The first are professionals and the second are amateurs. While anyone can testify, only a trained professional can really act as a defence attorney.

So it is in the context of evangelism. There are some who are professional evangelists. They are like trained attorneys, if you will. But all of us are called upon to testify. We are like witnesses in a trial. Witnesses may be amateurs, but let me remind you – "amateur" is a French word meaning "lover". Lovers of Jesus make the best witnesses.

Devotion: *Dear loving, heavenly Abba, Father, help me to be a better witness to Jesus. Today in the days ahead, let me be so in love with Jesus that I can't resist talking about him and giving testimony about how much he means to me. Help me to do this out of love not law. Amen.*

He came to that which was his own, but his own did not receive him. Yet to all who did receive him, to those who believed in his name, he gave the right to become children of God – children born not of natural descent, nor of human decision or a husband's will, but born of God.

John 1:11-13

Many people today make a fundamental mistake. They wrongly believe that every person on the planet is a child of God. Sometimes you may even hear a person say, "Of course, we are all God's children."

Verse 12 of the first chapter of John exposes the fallacy of this idea. According to John, we are not born as children of God. In other words, we are not God's children by nature. Rather, we *become* the children of God and this happens when we put our trust in Jesus. Only those who have chosen to follow Jesus can qualify for the term "child of God". We become the Father's children only – and I stress only – when we have had the experience of being "born of God".

The world is accordingly divided into two groups of people: those who have become the Father's children as a result of believing in Jesus, and those who are still spiritual orphans, people who don't know the Father because they haven't yet received his Son in their hearts.

It is a truly miserable thing to miss who Jesus really is. This was tragic in Jesus' day and it is equally as tragic today. John tells us that Jesus came to his own people – the Jewish people of the first century – and they didn't receive him. Others, however, did receive him. They welcomed him and put their trust in him. To those people Jesus gave (and still gives) the right to the title, "child of God".

I can think of no greater privilege than that of being the Father's child. The truth is we were created for love. The Father longs for us to enjoy his presence, to know his affection and to fulfil his destiny for our lives. He longs for us to become his children. But this can only happen if we welcome and receive Jesus as our Saviour. Maybe there is someone you need to help to become a son or a daughter of the Father.

Devotion: *Dear loving, heavenly Abba, Father, I want to pray for all those who think they are your children when in reality they haven't yet become your sons and daughters. Please open the eyes of their hearts. Use me as a vehicle of revelation and invitation in their lives, I pray. Amen.*

> *The Word became flesh and made his dwelling among us. We have seen his glory, the glory of the one and only Son, who came from the Father, full of grace and truth.*
>
> John 1:14

John wrote his Gospel in the ancient city of Ephesus. Six centuries before he started writing, Ephesus had been the home of a Greek philosopher called Heraclitus. Heraclitus used the idea of the Word in his teaching. The Greek word he used is the word *logos* from which we get the word "logic". *Logos* means something like "the reason why". Heraclitus talked about a divine law within all things and claimed this was the reason why everything is the way that it is. Heraclitus and his disciples believed that life is not haphazard but that there is a pattern, a reason why, behind everything.

In verse 14 of chapter 1, John makes perhaps the most sublime statement in the New Testament. He says that the *Logos* became flesh. The Reason Why became a human being, a person, in Jesus of Nazareth. The Word that formed the universe came and pitched his tent among us. The infinite became *an* infinite. Love took on human form and camped out for a while among us.

And all this is not mythical fancy or the stuff of legend. John stresses, "we have seen his glory". John and his friends saw Jesus with their own eyes. They heard, touched, and saw the One and Only Son who came from Abba, Father, full of grace and truth. Furthermore, they came to see that the human body of Jesus was the physical habitation for the glory of God, just as the Tabernacle in the wilderness had been the dwelling place for the glory of God in the time of Moses. They came to see that Jesus is God with skin on.

Whenever we celebrate Christmas, we should always remember that this is the real message of the season. Christmas is not an excuse for indulging the self. It is a time set aside for celebrating the extraordinary mystery of the incarnation – the mystery of God coming to be with us in our place so that one day we might be with him in his. Can there be anything greater than knowing Jesus? He is the human face of Yahweh.

Devotion: *How we worship you, Abba, Father, for being prepared to step down from heaven's throne. How we adore you, Jesus, for taking on human flesh and living your life among us. How we honour you, Holy Spirit, for incarnating this truth in our own hearts. Amen.*

No one has ever seen God, but God the One and Only, who is at the Father's side, has made him known.

John 1:18 (NIV)

How can someone say so much in so few words? Marvel with me for a moment at the extraordinary depth of John's insights.

First of all, John tells us that Jesus is "God the One and Only" (see also John 1:14). There are two great pearls of wisdom here. The first is that Jesus is God. He is not just the greatest man, the greatest teacher, the greatest prophet who has ever lived. Nor is he just the Messiah. He is God himself. He is "God the One and Only One."

The second is that Jesus is God's One and Only Son by nature. Of course, he has millions and millions of sons and daughters who are his by adoption. But Jesus is different. He is the One and Only Son by nature. This means that he is utterly unique – one of a kind.

Secondly, John tells us that Jesus is "at the Father's side". Today, right now, Jesus of Nazareth is at the right hand of the Father, in the place of highest honour and deepest intimacy. He is literally "in the bosom of the Father" (KJV), leaning on his Father's chest, close to his Father's heart.

Thirdly, John emphasizes that Jesus has made the Father known. Another way of putting this is to say that Jesus has revealed the Father to us. He has told us the Father's story. The purpose of Jesus' coming was to show us the limitless vistas of the Father's love.

You see how John says so much in such a few words. No human being has ever seen the Father except Jesus who is the One and Only Son of God, who lives forever at the Father's side, close to his heart. He has revealed the Father to those who have ears to hear.

How blessed we are that Jesus came to earth. If he had not, we would never have known what God is really like. We would never have understood that the one who threw stars into space and makes supernovas for fun is the world's greatest Dad.

Devotion: Lord Jesus, we worship you that you are the One and Only Son. We thank you that you were born to show us the Father's love. We are deeply grateful to you that you have made the Father known to those who accept and believe in you. We can't thank you enough. Amen.

John replied in the words of Isaiah the prophet, "I am the voice of one calling in the wilderness, 'Make straight the way for the Lord.'"

John 1:23

As early as the first chapter of John's Gospel we see the beginnings of conflict. There are Jewish leaders in Jerusalem who are intent on suppressing any person whose activities threaten the political status quo of Israel, which is under Roman occupation. These men become the opponents of Jesus. John simply identifies them as "the Jews" in his Gospel, a shorthand for "hostile Jewish leaders in Jerusalem". It is these authorities who have sent priests and Levites to cross-examine John the Baptist.

John's statement consists of firm "I am nots". It is interesting here to contrast John with Jesus. While Jesus says "I am", John the Baptist says, "I am not." He is adamant that he is not the Messiah. He is determined not to be the focus. His desire is only to make Jesus famous. So he stresses that his role is to be a voice in the wilderness. Notice the word "voice". While Jesus is the Word, John the Baptist is the Voice. Nothing must detract from the priority and supremacy of Jesus.

John goes on to say – quoting Isaiah 40:3 – that he is the voice of "one calling in the wilderness, 'Make straight the way for the Lord'".

Recently I was in Uganda. When I had visited the previous time, I noticed that the road to Kampala from Entebbe airport was full of potholes and extremely hazardous. This time, however, the road couldn't have been smoother. The road had been completely repaired. I asked the driver why and he replied that Queen Elizabeth II had been on a state visit and that the roads that she was going to travel down had been resurfaced and radically upgraded for her coming.

This is really the picture that John the Baptist has in mind when he says that he is making the road straight for the coming of the Lord. His whole purpose in life is not to claim to be the Messiah but rather to prepare a smooth road for the Messiah to make a royal visit. Our purpose in life should be to prepare people for a visitation of the King of Kings.

Devotion: Dear loving, heavenly Abba, Father, thank you for the great example of John the Baptist. Help us to be like him, more concerned about giving Jesus the glory than anything else. Help us to be a people who prepare others to meet Jesus the King. Amen.

"I baptize with water," John replied, *"but among you stands one you do not know. He is the one who comes after me, the thongs of whose sandals I am not worthy to untie."*

John 1:26–27

There are two groups of people who interrogate John the Baptist here. The first is the Levites. These are priests and their concern is to see if John the Baptist is the son of a priest (which he is). The second is the Pharisees. Their agenda is a much larger one. They want to know why John is baptizing people. If he is not the Messiah, or Elijah, or the prophet whose coming Moses prophesied (Deuteronomy 18:15), then why is he baptizing people in the River Jordan? What right has he to do that?

The question is actually an important one because it highlights something unusual about John's ministry. You see, the only people who were baptized in John's day were Gentiles or non-Jews – in other words, pagans who had converted to Judaism. But John defies this tradition. He baptizes Jewish people at the River Jordan. He treats God's chosen people as inherently unclean, just like everyone else.

No wonder the Pharisees question John's authority to baptize. This was going completely against the grain. The message behind John's method was clear, "Everyone needs a wash! Everyone's a sinner." And of course that included the Pharisees as well!

John answers the question about his right to baptize by saying that there is one coming after him whose sandal straps he is not worthy to untie. Untying someone's sandal straps was a task that not even the most menial of slaves was expected to do in John's time. John is therefore saying this: "My authority to baptize comes from Jesus, and he's my Master. Even to say I'm his slave would be too grand a statement."

What a thing it is to note that John the Baptist could only have a slave–Master relationship with God. For those of us who have put our trust in Jesus it is a wholly different matter. We are sons and daughters not slaves, heirs not orphans. We have been given the right to become the children of God!

Devotion: *Thank you, Abba, Father, that I live this side of the Cross and the empty tomb. Thank you that as a result I can enjoy a child–Father relationship with you. Not even John the Baptist was able to experience this. What a privilege! Thank you, Lord. Amen.*

The next day John saw Jesus coming toward him and said,
"Look, the Lamb of God, who takes away the sin of the world!"

John 1:29

John the Baptist continues to point away from himself and to draw attention to Jesus. This is the key characteristic of real prophecy. Genuine prophetic words cause us to love, adore, and thank Jesus even more than we do already. When you next hear or read a prophetic word, ask yourself, "Does this draw my heart towards Jesus?"

John has been waiting for a long time to see the Messiah. Every day he has been alert. "Could this be the day?" he asks himself. Then, out of the crowds, a figure emerges. It is Jesus of Nazareth. And immediately John knows that this is his day of destiny. This is the moment for which he was born. This is the Messiah he is called by the Father to baptize.

As John looks at Jesus the spirit of prophecy rises up in him. He points to the carpenter's son from Nazareth and announces to everyone within earshot, "Look, the Lamb of God, who takes away the sin of the world!"

What an unusual thing to say! John is being approached by a man and he calls this man a lamb! What can this mean? John is saying something really important here. He is probably referring to the lambs that were slaughtered in the Temple in Jerusalem every Passover. This happened in remembrance of the lambs that were killed in ancient Egypt in the time of the Exodus. On that day the blood of the lambs had been daubed on the lintels and doorposts of every Israelite home. When the angel of death came, he passed over the houses marked by the blood of these lambs but visited death upon the homes of those that were not.

John says that Jesus is the true Passover lamb. His blood shed on the cross will be our covering, our protection, our salvation. Thanks to the blood of Jesus shed at Calvary, my sin – which separates me from the Father's love – will be removed. At the Cross, the Father's righteous anger with sin will be satisfied. Anyone who puts their trust in the blood of Jesus can boldly say, "Dad's not mad with me any more!"

Devotion: *Thank you, Jesus, for shedding your blood so that my sin could be taken away. Thank you that even though the penalty for sin is death, you have taken the punishment for me and now I can know for sure that my Father's righteous anger has been turned away. Thank you, my Jesus. Amen.*

> *Then John gave this testimony: "I saw the Spirit come down*
> *from heaven as a dove and remain on him. And I myself did*
> *not know him, but the one who sent me to baptize with water*
> *told me, 'The man on whom you see the Spirit come down and*
> *remain is he who will baptize with the Holy Spirit.'"*
>
> John 1:32–33

John was called John the Baptist because he baptized people in the River Jordan. These people were responding to his call to turn away from sin. As an outward sign that they were doing that, they offered themselves to John in order to be baptized in water.

The word "baptize" in the original language of John's Gospel means literally to "plunge, dunk, drench, saturate, soak, or totally immerse". When John immersed Jesus in the River Jordan, something extraordinary happened – something that didn't happen in the case of every other man, woman, and child he baptized. He says that the Spirit came down from heaven like a dove and settled on Jesus. It was this that caused John to know that Jesus was special. John had been told by the one who sent him to watch out for the coming of the Spirit. The one who sent John was the Father. The Father told John in advance that the descent of the Spirit would mark Jesus out as the Messiah.

We may be tempted to think little of this but the truth is it was an extraordinary event for two reasons: first, because the presence of the Holy Spirit had been invisible in Israel for about 400 years (from the end of the Old Testament era to the beginning of the New); second, because in the Old Testament era the Spirit came and went. He visited but he didn't stay. Here John says that the Spirit of God came upon Jesus and *remained*. This is truly a history-making moment!

And it is history-making because John goes on to add that the Father had told him that this person would be the one who baptized people in the Holy Spirit. Just as John had totally immersed people in water, so Jesus would totally immerse people in the Holy Spirit (a reference to the day of Pentecost). He would drench us in the personal and empowering presence of the Father. We would be dripping with the power of God!

Devotion: *Thank you, Father, for the precious Holy Spirit who came and stayed upon Jesus. Thank you, Jesus, for drenching your followers in the Holy Spirit. Dear Holy Spirit, I ask that you would totally immerse me in the power of the Father's love and presence, in Jesus' name, Amen.*

Turning around, Jesus saw them following and asked, "What do you want?" They said, "Rabbi (which means Teacher), where are you staying?"

John 1:38

John the Baptist is walking with two of his disciples (for John had followers too). John sees Jesus just as he had the day before at the River Jordan, where he had proclaimed that Jesus is the Lamb of God. As John sees Jesus he declares once again that he is the Lamb of God. As soon as John's two disciples hear this, they leave John and begin to follow Jesus. John makes no fuss about this. He is not at all put out that he's lost two disciples to Jesus. John knows that he is only called to prepare the road for the Messiah and he also knows that Jesus is his King. So he releases his followers to leave his own band and to join the embryonic Jesus movement.

It is at this point that Jesus turns around and says to the two new disciples, "What do you want?" Actually this is not a very good translation. The verb translated "want" is the Greek verb *zetein*. It is used a lot by John in his Gospel, some thirty-five times in all, and it means "to seek". When Jesus turns and looks at the two people who are now following him, he asks them the ultimate question, "What are you seeking?"

All of us need to answer this for ourselves. What is the primary quest in our lives? Are we seeking fame and fortune? Are we seeking friends and family? Are we seeking purpose and fulfilment? What is the nature of our life's quest? If life is a journey, what is it the destination that we're longing for?

Jesus' question is the ultimate existential challenge. The two men answer by asking Jesus a question, "Where are you staying?" The word for "stay" is also a key word in John. It means "abide" or "remain" and it is used forty times. The disciples' quest is to dwell where Jesus dwells. Their desire is to be in his presence. I cannot personally think of a higher quest than this – to love, cherish, honour, and live in the presence of God. There is no greater priority than this.

Devotion: *Dear loving, heavenly Abba, Father, I want to live where you live, to dwell where you dwell, to stay where you are staying. Help me to seek after your presence with all of my heart. I long for that sense of your nearness to me. Help me to find it in Jesus. Amen.*

Andrew, Simon Peter's brother, was one of the two who heard what John had said and who had followed Jesus. The first thing Andrew did was to find his brother Simon and tell him, "We have found the Messiah" (that is, the Christ). And he brought him to Jesus.

John 1:40–42

When I became vicar of St Andrew's Chorleywood in 1996 I began to seek the Father's vision for the church. Up to that point the church had been greatly used in bringing renewal to the wider church. Now I sensed the seasons were changing and it was time to make mission our focus. As I prayed, I became aware that the new emphasis was to be on reaching our family, friends, and neighbours with the Father's love.

As I engaged in the task of communicating this vision to the people of St Andrew's I remember coming across this great passage about the original Andrew. As I looked carefully at the text I saw that Andrew was a man who loved bringing other people to Jesus. In fact, John tells us that "the first thing Andrew did" was to witness to his brother Simon Peter. I began to share with the people of St Andrew's that I felt that it was the Father's longing that we should be like St Andrew – a community for whom sharing the Father's love was the first not the last thing we did. I further explained that there were three things that Andrew did – *finding, telling,* and *bringing.* I urged us all to be a people whose highest priority was to find lost people, to tell them about the Father's love, and to bring them to Jesus. I emphasized that this was now the vision and the new focus for the church under my watch. By the time I left St Andrew's, twelve years later, the church had grown considerably through evangelism and we had established over thirty lay-led mission-shaped communities. Hundreds came to Christ during this season.

I wonder if there's someone we need to find, tell about our faith and bring to Jesus. I wonder if there's someone even in our own family with whom we need to share our testimony. I appreciate that our nearest and dearest are often the hardest to reach. But this is where Andrew started – with his own brother, no less. I wonder if it's where some of us need to start as well.

Devotion: *Thank you, Father, for the wonderful example that Andrew was in his own day and is to us today. Help us to hear what you're saying to us about witnessing to others and give us the courage to find, tell and bring others to Jesus, for his glory. Amen.*

Jesus looked at him and said, "You are Simon son of John. You will be called Cephas" (which, when translated, is Peter).

John 1:42

One of the things I love about our heavenly Abba, Father is that he is far more interested in our future potential than in our past failings! All good dads are in fact like this. They don't harp on about the things that their children did that were wrong in the past. Rather, they see the potential that is in their children and they seek to help their children find the God-given dream for their lives. Good dads in this respect are really hope-bringers.

When Jesus met Simon, son of John, he didn't expose all the things that Simon had done wrong in his life. Rather, he looked at Simon and listened to what the Father was saying about Simon's future. What Jesus said was in fact very brief. It essentially amounted to this: "Your name is currently Simon, but in future it's going to be Peter."

Now what does that mean? The name Simon originally comes from a word that means a reed. Reeds are easily swayed by the wind. Peter comes from a word that means "rock". Rocks are not easily swayed. In fact they can take an awful lot to move.

What Jesus is pointing to here is the amazing, personal transformation that Simon is going to experience in his journey with Jesus. Simon will start off being like a reed. He will waver in his faith, as we will see in John chapter 18, where Simon denies that he is a follower of Jesus, not just once but three times. But Simon will not stay like this. He will be radically changed by the outpouring of the Holy Spirit on the day of Pentecost. When the Holy Spirit falls upon him, he will stand and preach the gospel to 3,000 people in Jerusalem, the very place where he showed such timidity. With the fire of the Father's love in his heart, Simon will become Peter – Reedy will become Rocky!

Aren't you glad that your heavenly Dad is more interested in your destiny than your history?

Devotion: *Thank you, Father, that you know the plans you have for me, and they are to prosper me and to give me hope. Help me not to be so hooked into my past that I miss out on my future. Please release me today to embrace my real identity and my true destiny. Amen.*

> *When Jesus saw Nathanael approaching, he said of him, "Here truly is an Israelite, in whom there is no deceit."*
>
> John 1:47

Our passage for today is all about "seeing". The verb "see" occurs frequently in John's Gospel, especially here in John 1:43–51. In John 1:47 Jesus is said to "see" a man by the name of Nathanael. We know little about Nathanael except that he was a man whom Philip brought to Jesus. He seems to have been someone well acquainted with the Torah (the Old Testament books of the Law) because Philip gets his attention by saying that he has found the one that was written about by Moses and the prophets. From this comment we can infer that Nathanael was a man familiar with the Old Testament Scriptures. Jesus now sees Nathanael and announces that Nathanael is a true Israelite and a man in whom there is no deceit. Why does Jesus say this?

I don't think we'll find the answer unless we spot the references to the Old Testament character called Jacob in this encounter with Nathanael. Jacob, son of Isaac (who was in turn son of Abraham) became known as "Israel". He is perhaps best known for two things: for being the man who tricked and deceived his father to give him his brother's inheritance, and for being the man who had a dream about a ladder going up to heaven while he was asleep in a cave. My guess is that Nathanael was a man who loved the story of Jacob. Jesus knows this because he is operating in the gift of prophecy. When he meets Nathanael Jesus tells him that he is a true Israelite because unlike Jacob there is no trickery or guile in him. Later on, in verse 51, he will tell Nathanael that he too will see a ladder to heaven, just like Jacob did.

I wonder if you've ever had an experience like this – where someone gave you a Scripture passage that was the very one that you were most cherishing at that time in your life. They couldn't have known. Only the Father could. When they shared it, you knew without a doubt that the Father loves you, knows you by name, and is intimately involved in your life. This is how Nathanael must have felt.

Devotion: *Dear loving, heavenly Abba, Father, please help me to see more clearly what people around me really need. Help me to see what you're doing in their lives and to hear what you're saying. Please give me a word that goes right to their hearts, in Jesus' name. Amen.*

"How do you know me?" Nathanael asked. Jesus answered, "I saw you while you were still under the fig tree before Philip called you."

John 1:48

Today we continue to study the life-changing encounter that Nathanael had with Jesus. Yesterday we read about how Jesus saw right into the very core of Nathanael's character and gave him a word that only the Father could have known. That word was all about Jacob. Jacob had been called Israel and was a man with deceit in his heart. Jesus looks at Nathanael and tells him he is a true Israelite and that there's no deceit in him. How did Nathanael respond? In this passage we find the answer. He says, "How do you know me?" This is what strangers always say to you when you deliver a prophetic word about their lives. "Who told you?" "Do I know you?"

Jesus gives an intriguing answer. He tells Nathanael that he saw him (notice the verb "see" again here) while he was sitting under the fig tree. What was so special about the fig tree? And what was Nathanael doing in its shade?

There have been many attempts to answer these questions over the last 2,000 years, most of them unsatisfying. The most probable answer is that the fig tree is significant because this is where rabbis traditionally sat to read Torah scrolls while sheltering from the sun's rays. This suggests that Nathanael was a rabbi studying God's Word under a fig tree and that he was all alone when he was doing this. In his quiet time with God that day he was reading about Jacob and reflecting on Jacob's life, maybe even asking the question, "How could someone so deceitful be called 'Israel'?" Jesus then showed up and told him something that only God could have known. "I saw you studying the story of Jacob under the fig tree only this morning."

Wouldn't it be great if more and more of us were able to hear the very precise things that the Father is saying about the people we meet every day? Wouldn't it be great if the church was what it was always meant to be – a family of prophetic sons and daughters?

Devotion: *Dear Father, you have told me in your word that I am eagerly to desire the spiritual gifts, especially the gift of prophecy. I want you to know that I'm hungry for more of the prophetic in my life. Help me to be more like Jesus. Make me a seer in your kingdom. Amen.*

Then Nathanael declared, "Rabbi, you are the Son of God; you are the king of Israel."

John 1:49

I remember a time when I arrived early to speak at a UK conference. I went to my hotel to relax for a few hours before the meetings began. After a while I felt I could do with a cup of coffee so I went to the foyer of the hotel where there was a coffee bar. I was the only person there apart from the young man serving drinks and food.

We got into conversation and as we did so the Father gave me a word for him. He was not a Christian and had no basic biblical knowledge at all. He had been talking about his mother and how she was a clairvoyant who could read peoples' hearts better than anyone else. I had replied that no one had ever read people's hearts better than Jesus and that this same Jesus lived within my heart and that he speaks today. He then said, "Prove it!" Straight away an impression came from left field so I spoke it out. "Your mum and dad split up ten years ago. This has left you with a legacy of pain and a fear of committing to your girlfriend."

My friend practically fell off his seat. He told me that his parents had divorced exactly ten years before and that he had split up with his girlfriend a week ago because he was scared of committing himself to her. He told me he was now saving money through doing bar work to go and live with his father in America, whom he hadn't seen in a very long time. He then said to me, "Wow, Jesus is amazing. He's even more accurate than my mum!" This opened the door for me to talk to him about Jesus and I later sent him a copy of my book, *The Father You've Been Waiting For*, which was especially written for non-Christians. I told him that he'd find the best Dad in the universe through Jesus.

I tell this story because something similar happens to Nathanael when Jesus speaks prophetically into his life. Nathanael suddenly sees who Jesus really is, proclaiming that he is not just a teacher (rabbi), but that he's the Son of God and the messianic King of Israel. This is the purpose of prophecy, to draw people to Jesus and to help people see who Jesus is!

Devotion: *Dear loving, heavenly Abba, Father, I want to grow in the gift of prophecy. So I ask you in Jesus' name to increase the flow of prophetic revelation in my life. Help me to have a divine appointment with someone like Nathanael today – someone open to the gospel. Amen.*

> *"You will see greater things than that."* He then added, *"Very truly I tell you, you will see heaven open, and the angels of God ascending and descending on the Son of Man."*
>
> John 1:50–51

The encounter between Jesus and Nathanael ends with Jesus making a promise about Nathanael's future. Please notice that this is a prophecy. In fact, it is the third of three prophecies that Nathanael has received from Jesus. The first one is to do with the present. Jesus says, "You're a true Israelite and there's no deceit in your heart." The second is to do with the past. "I saw you when you sheltering under the fig tree and like a good rabbi studying a Torah scroll in your quiet time with God." The third one is to do with the future. "Nathanael, you think you've seen a lot already. But you're going to see even greater things. You've seen that I'm the Son of God and the King of Israel. But in the future you're going to see that I'm the stairway to heaven, I'm the ladder between earth and heaven – a causeway across which angels travel."

John does not record how Nathanael reacted, or what he then went on to do with his life. But the truth is that Jesus' promises always come true. Jesus is God and God never lies. That being the case, we can imagine Nathanael becoming a follower of Jesus and a member of one of the earliest Christian churches. It could even be that Nathanael became a prophet or a seer. That is after all what Jesus told him he would be!

How encouraging it is to know that the Father has a plan for each of our lives. How heart-warming it is to know that we all have a unique assignment and destiny from Abba, Father. I wonder what it is in your life that has been prophesied and yet remains unfulfilled. What promises have yet to be completely activated in your life? I believe Jesus wants to say to all of us what he said to Nathanael. We may have seen great things. But there are even greater things ahead.

Why not take that promise, "You will see even greater things", and make it a promise for your life too? Take hold of this and tell your Father in heaven, "I haven't yet seen this. Bring on the greater things!"

Devotion: *Dear loving, heavenly Abba, Father, I thank you so much that you are going to fulfil your purposes for my life. I thank you that I have already seen you at work in the past. I now want to see even greater things in the future, for your glory. Amen.*

On the third day a wedding took place at Cana in Galilee.

John 2:1

In John chapter 2 the action moves to Cana in Galilee. Cana was a small village near Nazareth and John tells us that "on the third day" there was a wedding there.

The expression "the third day" is interesting. If you count the days between John chapter 1 and John chapter 2 you will find there are seven days in total. The first involves John the Baptist being interrogated by the envoys from Jerusalem (1:19–28). The second involves John baptizing Jesus in the River Jordan (1:29–34). The third involves John releasing two of his disciples to follow Jesus (1:35–39). The fourth involves Philip finding Nathanael and Nathanael encountering Jesus (1:40–51). Three days after that, Jesus goes to a wedding in Cana of Galilee (2:1–11).

John's story begins with seven days. Why is this? It is because John is consciously reminding us of the seven days of creation in Genesis chapter 1 and indicating that the coming of Jesus is the start of a new creation. The phrase, "on the third day" highlights this because it points to the resurrection of Jesus, which occurs "on the third day". With the resurrection a new creation truly begins. Death is defeated and the grave begins to lose its sting. The curse of the fall is reversed and the prophecy of Isaiah 43:19 is fulfilled, "See, I am doing a new thing!"

There is a powerful moment in the movie *The Passion of the Christ* when Jesus is carrying his cross through the crowded and clamorous streets of Jerusalem. His mother Mary is running through side streets to try and get to him. She eventually arrives just as Jesus falls to the ground under the heavy weight of the Cross. She is distraught to see her son in such pain. But through blood-soaked eyes Jesus looks into his mother's eyes and says, "I am making all things new."

In Jesus, the new creation has begun. The kingdom of heaven is invading and advancing right now. A brave new world has been made possible. Doesn't this cause your heart to sing?

Devotion: *Abba, Father, I thank you that because of Jesus the old order of things is already passing away and the new has come. I thank you that I am part of a new creation. I thank you that I am a new creation, because Jesus makes all things new, including me. Amen.*

Jesus' mother was there, and Jesus and his disciples had also been invited to the wedding.

John 2:1-2

The first half of John's Gospel contains seven miracles, which is why John 1-12 is often called the "Book of Signs and Wonders", or the "Book of Glory". The miracle that Jesus performs at Cana in Galilee is the first in this sequence of seven mighty works and it involves the miraculous transformation of a large amount of water into vintage wine.

We will come to the miracle itself in a few days' time, but for now I just want to focus on the fact that Jesus was invited to a wedding. In the last of the seven miracles, in John chapter 11, we will find Jesus present at a funeral – the funeral of his dear friend Lazarus in the village of Bethany in Judea. At the first of the miracles he is present at the wedding of a couple in the village of Cana in Galilee.

Why is this important? The answer is because weddings are great opportunities to welcome the presence of Jesus. I have conducted hundreds and hundreds of marriage ceremonies during a quarter of a century as an ordained minister in the Church of England. I have simply lost count of them and forgotten many. But I can remember those weddings where the couple were Christians and invited Jesus into their marriage. In those contexts, there was an altogether different atmosphere. The sense of the presence of God was tangible as the couple and many of their friends and family worshipped the Father in spirit and in truth. In those contexts, a simple message about marriage (with the Gospel included) brought about the transformation of lives. And the wedding receptions afterwards would be full of great conversations. Time and again non-Christian guests would come to me and talk about the amazing sense of peace they felt during the service and ask why it was they felt so close to tears. What wonderful opportunities for sharing the Gospel these occasions brought.

"And Jesus had also been invited." Let's make sure he's always invited today.

Devotion: *Abba, Father, I praise you that when you are invited into a marriage, transformation can truly take place. I pray that I would always make sure that you're welcome in my home, my family, and my friendships. I invite you to come and stay today. Amen.*

When the wine was gone, Jesus' mother said to him, "They have no more wine."

John 2:3

Wedding feasts in the time of Jesus took some organizing and there is reason to believe that Jesus' mother Mary was involved in the catering arrangements. After all, John does say that "Jesus' mother was there" (John 2:1) even before mentioning that Jesus had been invited (John 2:2). It may be that the bride or the bridegroom were in some way related to Mary and had asked her to help with the celebrations.

Most likely the festivities had been underway for at least a day, maybe even more, when the wine ran out. I am not the first to have noticed that the supply of wine only runs out when the disciples arrive. I am not suggesting for a moment that they drank too much but it is an interesting coincidence that they enter and the wine runs out! Whatever the case, this is a very serious situation. The wedding festivities lasted seven days and to have the wine supply go dry would be a disgrace in Middle Eastern culture. It would be a failure of hospitality in a society where hospitality is a highly regarded value.

It is at this point that Mary goes to Jesus and simply tells him, "They have no more wine." She doesn't go to the couple. She doesn't go to the head waiter. She goes to her son. She knows that the only person who can redeem this social disaster is Jesus. So she presents the need to him – and only the need.

For me this is a great picture of intercession. Intercessory prayer is presenting the needs of others to our heavenly Father and praying in the name of Jesus that their lack – whether it's a lack of resources or a lack of health – would be filled by the miracle-working power of the Spirit. This is what Mary does. This is what we can do too.

Is there someone or something you need to bring before the Lord right now? Is there a need that someone else has that you need to spread before the Miracle Worker? Why not take it to the Lord in prayer?

Devotion: *I thank you, Abba, Father, that you are ever present in our joys and in our sorrows. I pray for all those whom I know who are facing a lack in their life – for whom the wine has run out. Please, in your extravagant love, make up the deficit. Amen.*

"Dear woman, why do you involve me?" Jesus replied. "My time has not yet come."

John 2:4 (NIV)

This is the first occasion in John's Gospel where we hear of the "time" of Jesus. The word in the original means the "hour" of Jesus. John wasn't thinking of a literal period of sixty minutes. He was using the word figuratively to refer to the time of Jesus' return to the Father. Jesus had come from heaven and been born on earth as a baby. At the end of his life he would return to heaven having died as a man on a Cross. The hour of Jesus refers to the whole of Jesus' return journey to the Father – a journey that involves his death, resurrection, and ascension.

When Mary comes to Jesus and presents the lack of wine to him he asks her why she is involving him in this matter. She knows that a miracle is needed. He knows that a miracle can be performed. But his concern is that he keeps to his heavenly Father's timetable. In other words, he doesn't want to do anything that will attract undue attention. He doesn't want to provoke any intensification of opposition and he certainly doesn't want any action of his to bring forward the "hour" of his return. For him, timing is everything.

Jesus had a fine-tuned sense of the Father's times and seasons. He knew that this was not yet his "hour". This wasn't the time for his return. But his mother is standing before him, presenting the needs of some newly-weds. How can he resist her? How can he deny them? Will he display his power and glory even though he knows that this is "ahead of time"?

In a sense, every time we pray for a miracle, we are asking the Father to do something ahead of time. We are asking him to do now what he will most certainly do at the return of Jesus at the end of time. We are asking for his kingdom to come right *now*. We are asking for a touch of heaven on earth. We are asking for something of tomorrow's world *today*.

Like Mary, we need to present the need and trust that the Father will do in the present what we know he will do in the future.

Devotion: *Dear loving heavenly Father, there are so many needs that people I love have right now. There are people I care about who desperately need a miracle. I know that you will make all things well at the end of time. But would you please do something today. Amen.*

Nearby stood six stone water jars, the kind used by the Jews for ceremonial washing, each holding from twenty to thirty gallons. Jesus said to the servants, "Fill the jars with water"; so they filled them to the brim. Then he told them, "Now draw some out and take it to the master of the banquet."

John 2:6–8

It is so interesting how the story proceeds. After Mary has presented the needs of the newly married couple to Jesus, he asks her why she is involving him because his time hasn't yet come. Mary doesn't answer this question but now turns to all the waiters who are standing nearby and says to them, "Do whatever he tells you!" She has an unshakable confidence that Jesus is going to act dramatically on behalf of the bride and the bridegroom whether it's time or not! He has given her no grounds for believing this, yet she behaves as if he has.

Now the storyteller points to some earthenware jars that are a few metres away. Note the detail here. We are told how many there are, how much they could contain and what they were for. This is clearly eyewitness reporting. John tells us that there were six of them, that they would have held about 180 gallons of water in total and that they were used by Jewish people at the time for cleansing. In other words, the water was employed to clean the feet of the guests and to wash their hands before and during the meal.

Jesus tells the waiters to fill these six jars with water, which they do to the brim. He then tells them to take some of the water and give it to the master of ceremonies at the wedding reception. To his amazement the master of ceremonies realizes that the water has been turned into wine.

The first miracle Jesus performs in John's Gospel is performed because of the persistent faith of his mother and it is a miracle of abundance. Jesus produces 180 gallons of wine out of 180 gallons of water. That constitutes "abundance" – even if you take into account that many villagers would have been present at the party. Truly, Jesus reveals a Father who is extravagantly generous to his children when they believe.

Devotion: *Loving Father, I thank you for the way you rescued a humble Galilean family from the shame and embarrassment of running out of wine. I thank you for your concern for ordinary people and ordinary things. Please come into my family and bring us your joy. Amen.*

"Everyone brings out the choice wine first and then the cheaper wine after the guests have had too much to drink; but you have saved the best till now."

John 2:10

It was the normal practice for Jewish wedding feasts to last seven days. During that time the newly married couple would be treated like royalty and there would be great celebrations. The couple would be dressed like a king and a queen and seated on makeshift thrones. Children would play party games and there would be the constant sound of music and dancing and the unmistakable smell of burning wood and sizzling meat.

At such events it was normal to serve the best wine at the beginning of the week-long festivities. This was because the guests were most able to tell the difference between vintage wine and ordinary plonk at the start of the week rather than at its middle or end. Their palates and their sense of judgment would be at their most refined at the beginning. However, when Jesus comes to the wedding party in Cana all this is turned on its head. Now, as the party continues, Jesus transforms 180 gallons of water into 180 gallons of wine. The first person to taste it is the head waiter or the master of ceremonies. He is instantly amazed. Not only does he now have 180 gallons of wine that he didn't know he had, he has 180 gallons of the best vintage wine imaginable. This is miraculous wine. It is wine that has been created by the one through whom all things have been made. This is the wine of the Word, the fruit of the true vine. It is the best wine he's ever tasted.

It is for this reason that the master of ceremonies says with such bewilderment, "How come you have reserved the best vintage until now?" He is confused at the breach in protocol and at the same time overwhelmed by the heavenly bouquet in his nostrils.

Here again we see something quite wonderful about our heavenly Father. In this miracle Jesus shows us a Dad who can take hold of the most ordinary things in life – like water – and transform them into the most extraordinary things. If you think about it, he does that with people too.

Devotion: *I worship you, Abba, Father, that you transform insignificant things and people to do significant things for you. Nobody does this like you do. You truly are amazing. Thank you that I am an ordinary person being transformed by an extraordinary Dad! Amen.*

> *What Jesus did here in Cana of Galilee was the first of the signs through which he revealed his glory; and his disciples put their faith in him.*
>
> John 2:11

As John concludes the story of the transformation of water into wine he tells us that this was the first of Jesus' signs. Miracles are usually called "signs" in John. They are called signs because they point to something beyond themselves. According to this verse, they are signposts to the glory – the divine majesty and honour – of Jesus. When Jesus heals the sick, multiplies loaves, walks on water, gives sight to the blind, and raises the dead, these miracles are exhibits that testify to the fact that Jesus is the Son of God. They reveal or unveil his glory. When the disciples saw Jesus turning water into wine they knew that he was more than just a great rabbi. John says they put their faith and trust in him.

Returning for a moment to the miracle in Cana, what more do we learn from it as a result of this concluding comment about signs? If we take the specific instance of the wine running out, we learn that every situation of lack in our lives is an opportunity for Jesus to manifest his glory. The lack of wine at Cana was regarded by the hosts as a difficulty. But Jesus saw it as an opportunity. In the context of their scarcity he performed a miracle that resulted in a manifestation of his glory.

When we go through times when it seems like the wine is running out, we should understand that these are the greatest opportunities for the revelation of the glory of God. When the Father then does what we couldn't do then he is always glorified. We know that only he could have done that. Therefore we boast, but we don't boast about our efforts but we boast about his glory. We say, "Jesus, you are truly amazing. You transformed our water into wine. We had nothing, but you transformed our situation supernaturally. Only you can do this. So we give you all the glory and honour. We give you praise!"

Maybe you have an area of real lack in your life right now. Ask for a sign that will reveal the Father's glory. Ask for a miracle that will release the kind of testimony that truly honours Jesus.

Devotion: *I thank you, loving Father, that you are still doing miracles today. I pray that in my lack you will do such a wonderful work of transformation that Jesus gets all the glory. Even when everything seems to have run out, I will praise you. Amen.*

When it was almost time for the Jewish Passover, Jesus went up to Jerusalem.

John 2:13

Three times a year every Jewish man was required to make a journey to the heart of Jerusalem in order to celebrate one of the three great pilgrim festivals of the Lord: Passover (April/May), Pentecost (May/June), and Tabernacles (September/October). Jesus was a Jewish man and when he started his itinerant ministry in Judea and Galilee he still made time for pilgrimage to Jerusalem for the great feasts. In John 2:13 he makes one of three journeys at Passover time. You can find the other Passover pilgrimages in John 6:4 and John 11:55. As John puts it here, "Jesus went up to Jerusalem."

One of the things I am most happy about in my life is that I was adopted into a family with a very rich Jewish history on my father's side. Stibbe is a Dutch Jewish name and we have Jewish ancestors going back to the seventeenth century in Holland, many of them rabbis. This means that by adoption, I am both a Christian and a person with Jewish roots. So in fact is every Christian!

As we look at John's Gospel through Jewish eyes we begin to see how Jesus fulfils the feasts of the Lord. The classic example is the way in which Jesus becomes the Lamb of God who takes away the sin of the world. When he is crucified Jesus' legs are not broken by the Roman guards. This is to fulfil the requirement in Exodus chapter 12 that an unblemished lamb should be offered for sacrifice. Unblemished means without a single broken bone. Jesus truly fulfils the feasts!

In the story we studied over the last few days we saw that there were six earthenware jars that Jesus had filled with water, which he then transformed into wine. In Judaism, six is the number of imperfection and incompleteness. Seven is the number of perfection and completeness. When Jesus filled the six water jars, he filled what was incomplete and imperfect – which is really what he does with us too! Pray today that the Jewish people will have eyes to see that Jesus is the fulfilment of their Messianic hopes.

Devotion: *Abba, Father, I thank you that Jesus not only attended the Jewish festivals; he also completed and fulfilled them. I pray in his name that you would lift the veil from the minds of your chosen people so that they can truly see that Jesus is the Messiah, the Lamb of God. Amen.*

So he made a whip out of cords, and drove all from the temple courts, both sheep and cattle; he scattered the coins of the money changers and overturned their tables.

John 2:15

The main task I've set myself in this book is to show how Jesus at every turn reveals Abba, Father in John's Gospel. Everything he said and did in some way or another shows us what the Father is really like. Jesus came to reveal the Father and to bring us home to the Father's arms.

That being the case we should note Jesus' behaviour here. He is in the Temple now. He is no longer in the idyllic rural setting of Cana at a wedding. He is now in the bustling metropolis at Passover time. He goes into the Temple and finds people running stalls to change money. Every Jewish man who went into the Temple had to pay a tax worth two days' wages. They brought their own currency which then had to be changed into Temple shekels because their own cash was regarded as too unclean. The money changers who ran this business were onto a tidy earner. They charged a commission on every coin changed and in the process made a lot of money off the visitors, whom they saw as a cash cow.

This made Jesus mad. Not only was he mad because these men were fleecing the poor of Galilee and other areas. He was mad because they were operating in a space in the Temple reserved for Gentile or non-Jewish pilgrims who were looking for the Father's love. This area was known as the Court of the Gentiles and was a space reserved in the Father's house for spiritual seekers from other nations.

Seeing all this Jesus immediately fashions a whip and drives the money changers out of the Temple courts. Indeed he expels everyone else who was exploiting the poor as well, including their animals.

Here we see the righteous anger of the Father against injustice and wickedness. Jesus' anger is a reminder to all of us that our heavenly Dad does get mad with sin. He is a loving, affectionate Father, yes; but he is also a lion who roars against injustice.

Devotion: *Thank you, Father, for reminding me in this story that you are a holy, righteous Dad who gets mad when you see things you hate. Thank you that your anger is an expression of your great love, especially for the poor. Help me to appreciate the fullness of who you are. Amen.*

To those who sold doves he said, "Get these out of here! Stop turning my Father's house into a market!"

John 2:16

Jesus is so radical! I love that about him. How many of us, seeing the poor exploited would have constructed a whip and driven the offenders from the premises! I so admire this about Jesus. He didn't care what other people thought about him. He didn't conform to the religious expectations of people in his own times. He was so free and secure in his identity as the Father's Son that he said and did whatever the Father told him to in every given situation.

In our passage Jesus turns to those selling doves in the Temple. Why were doves for sale? The answer is because the pilgrims at Passover had to make a sacrifice, usually the sacrifice of an ox, a sheep, or a dove. This was to offer thanks for God's blessing on their journey.

Those who sold doves in the Temple fully exploited this custom. If someone hadn't brought with them a pair of doves, they sold these birds for over fifteen times the amount that would be charged elsewhere. Furthermore, if someone did bring their own doves, these birds had to be examined and a fee was charged for this by an inspector. Once again we see how the impoverished pilgrims were being ripped off.

Jesus' anger rages as passionately against the dove sellers as it did against the money changers. He tells them in no uncertain terms that they have turned his Father's house into a market place. Jesus puts an end to this shameless, social injustice and in the process not only liberates the poor, he liberates the animals too.

In the Old Testament the prophets warned that God does not delight in the sacrifice of animals (e.g. Isaiah 1:11–13, Hosea 8:13). Jesus knew that killing an animal could not make a person right with his Father. Only his death would do that. After the Lamb of God was slain there would be no reason to sacrifice an animal again. If you listen hard enough, I'm sure you can hear the animals praising him!

Devotion: *Thank you, Father, that you care not only about the poor but also about all your creatures, including oxen, sheep, and doves. Through Jesus you have revealed your love for human beings and animals. Help us to care about the things you care about. Amen.*

His disciples remembered that it is written: "Zeal for your house will consume me."

John 2:17

As we have seen during our last few studies, there were probably a whole number of reasons why Jesus was so angry with the money changers and those trading in animals for sacrifice in the Court of the Gentiles. But one of the main ones was because Jesus knew that the Temple was his Father's house. Jesus loved and adored his heavenly Father and he couldn't bear to see his Dad's home being so openly desecrated. When he chastised the dove sellers he said, "Stop turning my Father's house into a market!"

It is at this point that John inserts a comment about Jesus' disciples, who witnessed the cleansing of the Temple. John tells us that the disciples looked at Jesus' behaviour and remembered Psalm 69:9, where King David wrote, "Zeal for your house will consume me." They saw this as a Messianic prophecy – as a prophecy of the extraordinary zeal that the Messiah would have for the Temple, for God's house. This verse came to mind as they watched the events unfold and it was another confirmation for them that Jesus was the Messiah.

The word "consume" here is very significant. There are really two types of consumption going on in the Temple. There is the consumption of the people making money off the poor. This was consumerism gone mad. But then there was also the consumption that was going on in Jesus' heart. He was consumed by a passion for his Father's house. That's an altogether different and counter-cultural consumerism.

Which kind do you relate to? For us today it is so easy to bring the wrong kind of consumer mentality into the place of worship. Many turn the worship of God into a consumer item. But true worship – our corporate worship of Abba, Father in spirit and in truth – is not something we consume. It is something that consumes us! If we want to be like Jesus, then we need to be passionate for our Father's house and our Father's presence.

Devotion: *Abba, Father, forgive me for those times in my life when I've been a "consumer" Christian. I don't want you to become something I consume. I want your love, your presence, your glory, to consume me. Help me to be more radical in my passion for you. Amen.*

The Jews then responded to him, "What sign can you show us to prove your authority to do all this?" Jesus answered them, "Destroy this temple, and I will raise it again in three days."

John 2:18–19

Today we come across a common feature in John – misunderstanding. In this Gospel we will frequently see people encountering Jesus. Some understand what he is saying. Others do not. The characters who meet Jesus in this reading emphatically do not.

Just after Jesus has cleansed the Temple he is confronted by some Jewish leaders. They object to Jesus driving out the money changers and the dove sellers and they demand that Jesus performs a miracle in order to prove that he has the divinely given authority to act in such a way. At this, Jesus invites his opponents to destroy "this temple". He then adds that he will raise it up again in three days.

Here Jesus is speaking figuratively of his body. Our bodies are temples of the Holy Spirit. Jesus' body was supremely the temple of the Holy Spirit. As we saw in our reading of John 1:14, Jesus' body is the physical habitation for the glory of God. Jesus is therefore talking about the destruction of his body on the Cross. He is saying, "Destroy this body (my body) and I will resurrect it after three days." In other words, "You will get a sign. It's not going to happen right now. When you kill me, that's when you'll get it. Three days after you've crucified this body of mine, I will raise it up. That will be the greatest miracle of all!"

The Temple authorities completely misunderstand Jesus. They interpret him literally pointing out that it's taken forty-six years for Herod to refurbish the Temple and its precincts. They misinterpret Jesus and completely miss the point. The tragedy in their case is that they are so focused on the Temple of God that they miss the God of the Temple.

What a reminder this is for all of us to pray for spiritual knowledge and understanding so that we don't miss the point of what Jesus is trying to say to each one of us.

Devotion: *Loving Father, I pray that you will give me ears to hear, eyes to see, and a heart and mind to know and understand what you are saying and doing in my life. Please give me greater spiritual wisdom and insight so that I don't miss my moment of visitation. Amen.*

> **He did not need human testimony about them, for he knew what was in them.**
>
> John 2:25

This is the third occasion on which John uses one of his favourite verbs in his gospel, the verb "to know". He will use it fifty-five more times after this. In John's world, what you know and who you know are critical.

In this instance, the word refers to what Jesus knows. John tells us that Jesus didn't need any testimony about another person because he knew what was in them.

How did Jesus know? It would be all too easy to assume that it was because he was God in human flesh. Jesus knew what was in a person because he was God and God is all-knowing. But we need to remember that Jesus was the Word made flesh (John 1:14). Jesus became a human being and while he was fully God he was also fully human. Jesus knew what was in another person's heart because he was a human being filled with the Spirit of God. Jesus was the one on whom the Spirit remained from his baptism onwards. He was the most Spirit-filled man who ever lived. It was through the Holy Spirit that he was given knowledge that was not learned by natural means.

Jesus could read people's hearts because he had the Holy Spirit in his life and the Holy Spirit gave him supernatural revelation about the people he met. He didn't need a report or a brief about other people. He relied on the Spirit who gave him the Father's insights. That is why at the end of John 1 he could look at Nathanael and tell him the deep secrets of his heart. Jesus lived a life of intimacy with the Father and in that place of intimacy he heard the Father's voice.

All this is very significant for us. As followers of Jesus we are human beings filled with the Holy Spirit. We too can live like Jesus did, close to the Father's heart, listening to his whispering voice. Intimacy is the fertile soil in which prophecy grows. So let's fall deeper in love with the Father so we too can know what's in the hearts of others around us.

Devotion: *Abba, Father, I long for more of the gift of prophecy in my life. I too want to depend on your insights more than the reports of others, especially when it comes to understanding other people. Help me to love you more dearly and hear you more clearly. Amen.*

Now there was a Pharisee, a man named Nicodemus who was a member of the Jewish ruling council.

John 3:1

Nicodemus is one of the Jewish leaders in Jerusalem. These leaders are mainly hostile to Jesus as we will see throughout John's Gospel. But among them is a man with a more open mind and a seeking heart. He is Nicodemus. Later in the Gospel he will defend Jesus when his peers are unjustly accusing him (John 7:50–52) and at the end of the Gospel he will make sure that Jesus is given an honourable burial (John 19:38–42). In this respect he will stand out among his fellows.

Who were the Pharisees? The Pharisees numbered around 6,000 men and they were regarded as the most ardent observers of the Jewish Law (the first five books of the Old Testament). Every man who became a Pharisee had to make a vow in the presence of witnesses that they were going to spend the rest of their lives obeying every word of the written Law and all the hundreds of additional rules and regulations that had been inferred from the Law by the scribes. When they had done that they became part of the *chaburah*, the brotherhood.

John tells us here that Nicodemus was a member of the Sanhedrin – the ruling council of the Pharisees. There were seventy men on this council. Nicodemus was accordingly one of the most influential people in Jerusalem. He was a leader of the religious brotherhood of the day yet he came to Jesus because he recognized there was something different about him and he was spiritually curious.

What a tough thing it is to resist the pressure from your peer group and make a stand for Jesus. Maybe you are in a family where you are the only follower of Jesus. Maybe you're at a school or a college where being a Christian causes you to risk isolation and humiliation. Maybe you are in a workplace where the name of Jesus is constantly taken in vain and where being a Christian is belittled. Maybe you're part of a "brotherhood" where other men prefer religious ritual to a personal relationship with Jesus. Look at Nicodemus today and stand out from the crowd.

Devotion: *Abba, Father, I confess that sometimes I am too concerned about what my peers think of me. Help me to have the courage to stand out from the crowd. Help me to be so secure in your love that I only care about your approval, not the approval of others. Amen.*

> *He came to Jesus at night and said, "Rabbi, we know that you are a teacher who has come from God. For no one could perform the signs you are doing if God were not with him."*
>
> John 3:2

As we saw yesterday, Nicodemus was ready to be different from his peers in that he was prepared to concede that Jesus of Nazareth might just have been someone to welcome rather than persecute. In our passage for today we learn that Nicodemus came to Jesus "at night". According to the rabbis of Jesus' day, the optimum time for studying the Law was at night when you were least likely to be disturbed and distracted. So while Nicodemus may have come to Jesus under the cover of darkness in order not to be seen by his peers, it is also possible that he did so because he was genuinely seeking to find out who Jesus really was. He wanted a private and uninterrupted encounter.

Nicodemus comes to Jesus and calls him "Rabbi" and "a teacher come from God". Nicodemus is not acknowledging at this point that Jesus has come down from heaven. He is acknowledging that Jesus is a man "sent by God", an envoy or emissary sent by the Father. In other words, Nicodemus is exhibiting partial not full faith in Jesus. In Nicodemus' heart, Jesus is not divine (God in human form) but he is a divinely inspired teacher. And the basis on which Nicodemus can state this is the fact that Jesus has been performing miracles. These show that "God is with him" – that the empowering presence of God is upon Jesus' life.

What Nicodemus is highlighting here is the fact that Jesus was a man of the Word and the Spirit. Jesus taught the truths of God found in the Scriptures and he also ministered in the power of the Holy Spirit, with signs and wonders confirming his message. I wonder whether this could be said about us? Many believers know the Scriptures but not the power of God. Many operate in the power of God but don't really know the Scriptures. Our heavenly Father wants us to be sons and daughters who love the Word and who operate in the supernatural power of the Holy Spirit. He wants us to be like Jesus – children of both the Word and the Power of God.

Devotion: Loving, heavenly Father, my prayer today is that you would help me to be a student of your written Word and a channel of your miracle-working power. Would you help me to become a person who knows their Bible and who ministers in signs and wonders. Amen.

Jesus replied, "Very truly I tell you, no one can see the kingdom of God without being born again."

John 3:3

This is a remarkable passage because it is one of only two occasions in the entire course of John's story where there is any mention of "the kingdom of God" (here and in John 3:5). Why is this remarkable? In the other three Gospels (the Gospels of Matthew, Mark, and Luke) Jesus talks about "the kingdom of God" all the time. The word "kingdom" is used fifty-seven times in Matthew, twenty-one times in Mark, forty-six times in Luke. In John, Jesus mentions it only twice. The main reason for this is because John's Gospel focuses on the other main theme of Jesus' teaching, "the Fatherhood of God". In John's Gospel, the word "Father" is used 139 times. In the other three Gospels, it is used far less frequently. I believe the reason for this difference is simple: the main audience of Jesus' teaching in Matthew, Mark, and Luke is the crowds. In John, it is the disciples. To the crowds, Jesus says: The kingdom of heaven is near; it's time to repent (Matthew 4:17). To his disciples, Jesus says, "the Father himself loves you dearly" (John 16:27, NLT).

When Nicodemus comes to him by night, Jesus says that people can see the kingdom of God right now if they are prepared to be born again. We will look at the phrase "born again" tomorrow. For now, let's focus on the phrase "kingdom of God". What is the "kingdom of God"? The kingdom is where God the Father rules. Now obviously the Father reigns in heaven but Jesus teaches that this rule has come to earth in and through his words and deeds. This heavenly rule is clearly visible in the fact that Jesus changes water into wine, heals the sick, multiplies food and raises the dead. In Jesus, heaven is invading earth right here, right now. Jesus says, you can *see* it if you are prepared to be born again. You can *see* heaven invading in your own life if you are prepared to experience a radical, spiritual rebirth. If you are prepared to embrace a new beginning, you will *see* heaven come to those who are experiencing hell on earth. So let me ask, how about you? Is the kingdom something you're *seeing* right now in your own life?

Devotion: *Abba, Father, I thank you that the kingdom of heaven has arrived and that it is something very visible to those who have eyes to see. I pray today that I would see signs of the kingdom – of the royal presence of the Father's healing and life-changing presence. Amen.*

"How can anyone be born when they are old?" Nicodemus asked. "Surely they cannot enter a second time into their mother's womb to be born!"

John 3:4

Yesterday we looked at Jesus' use of the phrase "born again". Today, people often distinguish between two types of Christian – regular Christians and reborn Christians. Reborn Christians are often referred to as "born agains" and the tone that is used is usually a cynical one.

However, this distinction is not one that either Jesus or the earliest Christians would have embraced. In the New Testament, a person who becomes a Christian is someone who has been "born again" (John 3:3; 3:5), born anew by God's great mercy (1 Peter 1:3; 1:23), born by the word of truth (James 1:18), and saved by "the washing of rebirth" (Titus 3:5). A Christian is someone who has begun life all over again (Romans 6:1–11). New Christians are people who have experienced such a radical transformation that they can be likened to babies who need spiritual milk (1 Peter 2:2). In the New Testament, all Christians are "born again" Christians. They are people who have turned from a self-centred to a Christ-centred life and who have experienced a new beginning that is so profound it can be compared to a new birth.

Nicodemus should have understood all this because the rabbis had a saying, "A convert who embraces Judaism is like a new born child." But according to John 3:4 Nicodemus did not. He understood Jesus to mean that he had to be born all over again as a baby. He asks how a man like him can be born when he is old. He even adds that it is impossible to enter a second time into your mother's womb – a qualification that just accentuates his confusion.

What all this shows is the massive gulf there is between religion and reality in the Father's eyes. You can be as religious as Nicodemus, but if you're not prepared to be born again then you will never see the Father's reign breaking into your world. Jesus says in John 3:7, "you *must* be born again." Notice the word "must". Being born again is not an optional extra; it is a basic necessity and the bare minimum for all of us.

Devotion: *Dear loving, heavenly Abba, Father, I pray that I would be truly born again. In addition, I pray that you will give me a passion to see other people experience this radical new start in life. Today I renounce religion and I embrace rebirth. Amen.*

Jesus answered, "Very truly I tell you, no one can enter the kingdom of God without being born of water and the Spirit. Flesh gives birth to flesh, but the Spirit gives birth to spirit. You should not be surprised at my saying, 'You must be born again.'"

John 3:5–7

As I said when we looked at John 3:3, the kingdom of God is the Father's heavenly rule on earth. It is the royal presence of the healing and life-transforming power of heaven. Jesus has already said that a person cannot "see" this reality without being reborn. He now tells Nicodemus that a person cannot "enter" this realm unless they are born of water (symbolic of cleansing) and the Spirit (symbolic of power). He says that we cannot enter into the Father's heavenly kingdom unless we receive forgiveness for our past sins and the life of the age to come. The Bible makes it clear that these things can only happen when we come to Jesus and put our faith and trust in him. Only by meeting Jesus can we be born again.

Jesus then adds, "Flesh gives birth to flesh, but the Spirit gives birth to spirit." When we apply this to Nicodemus, the man of religion, we can express this thought as follows. A man-made religion gives birth to a human (i.e. a non-supernatural) way of relating to God. But the Holy Spirit gives birth to a dynamic, spiritual relationship with the Father.

Over the years I have learned this: it is so tempting to run churches and organizations on man-made programmes. But man-made programmes give birth only to man-made results. What we really need is more of the Holy Spirit. Presence not programme should be the priority of our lives. The more of the presence we have in our lives, the more of the prophetic is released in our hearts. When we receive more of the prophetic, we come to know the plans of the Holy Spirit in our lives. When we know these plans, spiritual realities come into being and the kingdom of heaven becomes visible.

So which is it to be – a life of human programmes or a life of Holy Spirit-empowered initiatives? Which kingdom are you going to invest in – the kingdom of man or the kingdom of God?

Devotion: *Abba, Father, I thank you that the Holy Spirit gives birth to spiritual things in my life. I pray that I would always seek to be a person filled with the Spirit and led by the Spirit. I want the things that come into being in my life to be truly born of the Holy Spirit. Amen.*

The wind blows wherever it pleases. You hear its sound, but you cannot tell where it comes from or where it is going. So it is with everyone born of the Spirit.

John 3:8

Have you ever wondered why some people come to Christ while others do not? Have you ever wondered why some people have a dramatic conversion experience while others seem to enter the Christian life in a more gentle way? There is a mystery to the experience that Jesus describes as "being born again". There is mystery in relation to both the "who" and the "how" – *who* experiences it and *how* they experience it.

Knowing this, Jesus compares the ways of the Holy Spirit with the ways of the wind. He says that you may hear the sound of the wind but that doesn't mean you can control it. You have no idea where the wind has come from or where it's heading to next. So it is with the Holy Spirit. You may hear that he is moving, but the rest is a mystery!

My adoptive father Philip Stibbe was a friend of the great C. S. Lewis. For several years before and after World War Two, Dad dined regularly with Lewis and a few other students of English Literature that Lewis was teaching at the time, and in whom he saw tremendous potential. Lewis' conversion to Christianity is a vivid illustration of what Jesus is talking about in John 3:8. Lewis had been wrestling for a long time with whether or not Christianity was true, when he went for a walk in the grounds of Magdalene College, Oxford with his two friends J. R. R. Tolkien and Hugo Dyson. In the early hours of the morning Lewis suddenly began to see that Jesus was the fulfilment of all his (and humankind's) spiritual longings. At that moment, Lewis and his friends heard the sound of a mighty rushing wind that shook the trees. It was quite remarkable and unexpected. The next day Lewis surrendered his life to Christ. In both a literal and a spiritual sense, it was when the wind blew that Lewis was born again.

Oh for the wind of God to shake the trees again! Oh for the majesty and the mystery of the work of the Spirit in the lives of those we know!

Devotion: *Abba, Father, I acknowledge there is mystery when it comes to the ways of the Spirit. But I pray that what you did in Lewis' life you would do in the lives of many people in our day. Let there be the sound of a mighty rushing wind. Send a tornado of revival, Oh Lord, I pray. Amen.*

> *"You are Israel's teacher," said Jesus, "and do you not understand these things? Very truly I tell you, we speak of what we know, and we testify to what we have seen, but still you people do not accept our testimony. I have spoken to you of earthly things and you do not believe; how then will you believe if I speak of heavenly things?"*
>
> John 3:10–12

Jesus' answer to Nicodemus contains something that's not picked up by the English translation I'm using here. He says, "You are *the* teacher of Israel and you don't understand?" The definite article "the" is in the original Greek but for some reason it's not rendered by the NIV translators. Yet it is vital. What Jesus is saying is this: "Nicodemus, you are the premier theologian in Jerusalem and yet you don't understand me. If you don't understand me when I talk to you of earthly things what chance do you have of understanding me when I speak of heavenly realities?"

There is a vital lesson here. We can have all the head knowledge in the world and yet still be blind to the truth of Christianity. We can be a world-class scholar of the Bible and yet still not know who Jesus really is or understand what he is trying to say to us. We may have lots of knowledge *about* God and yet have no real knowledge *of* him. In other words, we may have a great deal of propositional knowledge but lack any real personal knowledge. In the process we fail to see that information doesn't save us. Revelation does.

For a number of years I taught on John's Gospel in one of the finest Biblical Studies departments in the world. It always used to trouble me how many of the lecturers were scholars of the Bible and yet didn't know Jesus and therefore didn't understand the basic truths of Scripture. It has also always fascinated me how uneducated people who are filled with the Holy Spirit understand biblical truths far more clearly than many academics. As Smith Wigglesworth once said, "Some read the Bible in Hebrew, some in Greek. But I read it in the Holy Spirit!"

Nicodemus was the number one theologian in Israel yet he didn't understand Jesus' simple teaching. What a stark warning there is here!

Devotion: O Father, I don't want to be like Nicodemus. I don't want to be a person who knows about you in my head but doesn't know you in my heart. I pray for warmth in my heart not just light in my head. I pray for what C. S. Lewis called "a discipleship of the heart and the mind". Amen.

"No one has ever gone into heaven except the one who came from heaven – the Son of Man."

John 3:13

Jesus has just been speaking to Nicodemus, pointing out that he is trying to explain heavenly things to him in a down-to-earth way. Now Jesus explains why he has the authority to speak about heavenly matters at all. He tells Nicodemus that he has the right to speak about heavenly truths because heaven is his home. It is the realm from which he has come, and it is the realm to which he will return.

On a number of occasions in John's Gospel, Jesus talks about "coming down". The verb translated "come down" is sometimes used of Jesus going down from one geographical location to another (as in John 2:12). Frequently it is used of Jesus "coming down" from heaven. On seven occasions in John 6 it will be used of Jesus, the bread of life, coming down from heaven to earth.

The same is true of the verb translated "going into" in our verse for today. Sometimes it is used in a geographical sense of Jesus going up to Jerusalem (John 2:13). At other times it is used of Jesus ascending or going up to heaven (John 6:62; 20:17). What's interesting about John 3:13 is the way in which Jesus points out that he is the only one who has gone up or ascended to heaven.

What then is "heaven"? Heaven is where the Father is. To be in heaven is to be in the immediate presence of Abba, Father. Jesus says that he can reveal heavenly truths because his home is where the Father is in heaven. He has come from the presence of the Father and will return to the presence of the Father. He has come to the earth as the Son of God and he will return to heaven as the Son of Man.

For those who believe in Jesus and know Abba, Father, heaven is our real home. Today we know the Father's presence through the Holy Spirit. But one day we will be face to face with the Father. I don't know about you, but I long for more of the Father's presence in the here and now.

Devotion: *Abba, Father, I thank you that your Son could communicate heavenly insights because he lived in the atmosphere of the heavenly realms where you dwell. Help me today to be so close to you that I too can understand your ways better. Amen.*

> *"Just as Moses lifted up the snake in the wilderness, so the Son of Man must be lifted up, that everyone who believes may have eternal life in him."*
>
> John 3:14–15

The key to understanding this curious verse is the word translated twice as "lifted up". In the first instance it is used in relation to an incident in the life of the great Old Testament leader, Moses. In Numbers chapter 21, the people begin to complain about Moses leading them out of Egypt. As a punishment, God sends a plague of snakes, which cause havoc. He then tells Moses to create the image of a bronze snake and lift it up in the centre of the Israelite's camp. He instructs everyone to look at the image and those who do are healed of the effects of the snakebites.

In the second instance, the words "lifted up" are used of "the Son of Man". "Son of Man" is a title for Jesus. It is a title that stresses his humanity. Here in our verses for today we learn that Jesus "must be lifted up" and that when he is, those who believe in him will receive eternal life. Just as the lifting up of the serpent in the desert brought life to those who would otherwise have died, so the lifting up of Jesus at the end of his life will bring life to those who put their trust in him. Those who believe will enjoy "eternal life" – abundant, spiritual life that brings salvation and healing.

The word translated "lifted up" is a really powerful one in John. It refers to the elevation of Jesus on the Cross at the end of his life. When Jesus is nailed to a cross beam, and the cross beam is then raised with Jesus hanging in agony upon it, this will be a physical lifting up. At the same time, this "lifting up" is the first stage in a spiritual elevation. Jesus is lifted up from the grave at his resurrection. He is lifted up from the earth at his ascension. Here being lifted up carries the spiritual sense of being exalted. The lifting up of Jesus is therefore a process involving Jesus' crucifixion, resurrection, and ascension.

What blessing there is in the lifting up of Jesus for all who believe in him! There is salvation and healing for all who look up and gaze in believing wonder at the exalted Lord. Look upon him today and ask for all the benefits of the Cross, the resurrection, and the ascension.

Devotion: *Abba, Father, I thank you for the lifting up – the elevation and exaltation – of your Son. As I lift my eyes in adoration to Jesus today, I pray for all the blessings won for me by Jesus. I pray for healing in my body, soul and spirit. Thank you, exalted King of Kings. Amen.*

"For God so loved the world that he gave his one and only Son, that whoever believes in him shall not perish but have eternal life."

John 3:16

Every Christian has a favourite verse in the Bible and I'm guessing that for many readers John 3:16 is number one in the list. This verse has been described as "the gospel in a nutshell". In fact, there is perhaps no finer description of the Father's love in the New Testament.

In order to appreciate this verse more deeply, let's begin by remembering the subject of the verb "love" – it is God. God makes the decision to love. When John says "God", he of course means the Father. It is Abba, Father who takes the initiative to visit and save this fallen planet. He chooses to give up what was most precious to him, his one and only Son. What agony there must have been in the Father's heart when Jesus left heaven for earth. This truly is love. It is not sentimental and superficial. It is costly and self-giving.

Let's now remember the object of this "love" – the "world". The Greek word translated "world" is *kosmos* and it's used seventy-nine times in John's Gospel. It doesn't just encompass one single nation or people group. It encompasses all the lost, spiritual and often hostile orphans of this fallen planet earth. In other words, it embraces everyone.

Does this mean that everyone is now going to heaven? The answer is no. John 3:16 says that we must believe in Jesus. What does that mean? Believing in Jesus is a phrase used often in John's Gospel. It means choosing to put your faith and trust in the person of Jesus now and for the rest of your life. If you do that, then you will not perish – you will not die spiritually – but you will enjoy eternal life both before and after death. The condition for enjoying this life is not good works or great sacrifices. It is active and personal faith in Jesus.

What a great statement John 3:16 is. God is not a tyrannical dictator who coerces us to love him. He is a self-giving Father who woos us into an intimate and life-enhancing relationship with himself. What a Dad!

Devotion: *Thank you, Abba, Father, for giving us your Son, Jesus. Thank you that the gift of Jesus is the greatest demonstration of your love in history. I commit myself to believing in Jesus all the days of my life. And today I simply want to celebrate the Father's love. Amen.*

"For God did not send his Son into the world to condemn the world, but to save the world through him."

John 3:17

When John wrote his Gospel, one of the very interesting contributions he made was the frequent use of the language of the law court. Many of the episodes in John are like a court case in which Jesus is put in the dock and tried. In every situation, the key question is this: What verdict will people pass on Jesus of Nazareth?

In all of this it is vital to remember what John 3:16–17 says that the Father sent Jesus into the world because of his great love for us. The Father's motive for sending Jesus was not one of judgment; it was salvation. If people come under condemnation, it is not because the Father has desired that. It is because their reactions have brought it upon themselves.

How then can Jesus later say that he came into this world for judgment (John 9:39)? Let me try to explain. Whenever a person encounters Jesus in John, their response to him determines whether they come under condemnation or start on the journey of salvation. If they react negatively to Jesus, they bring condemnation upon themselves. If they react positively, they start to receive salvation.

Perhaps I can put it this way. In the first coming of Jesus, the Father's purpose was salvation. If people experienced judgment, then they were themselves responsible for that. In the second coming of Jesus sometime in the future, the Father's purpose will be judgment. When Jesus returns on the clouds in great glory on the last day, he will come to judge the human race. The outcome for all of us will depend on the decisions we have made about Jesus in this life.

The season we're in right now is accordingly a season of grace. In that respect we must pray for our loved ones and others too that they come to believe in Jesus, and we should really do this with urgency.

Devotion: *Abba, Father, I thank you that you sent Jesus into the world because of your love, because you wanted to save and rescue us from our orphan state. I pray for my family and friends that they would come to a positive verdict about your Son while there is still time. Amen.*

"Whoever believes in him is not condemned, but whoever does not believe stands condemned already because they have not believed in the name of God's one and only Son."

John 3:18–19

Let me elaborate a little on what I said in our study of John 3:17. I was trying to explain how the Father sent Jesus into the world in order that we might enter salvation not condemnation. At the same time, even though grace was the Father's motive, people brought condemnation upon themselves because they didn't receive Jesus. That is something that happened then and happens now. When a person chooses not to believe in Jesus, they open the door to judgment.

In John 3:18–19, we learn that believing in Jesus is the way to bring mercy rather than judgment upon ourselves. Believing in Jesus leads to salvation. Refusing to believe in Jesus leads to condemnation. If we choose in this life to reject Jesus, then we have brought judgment upon ourselves. We don't have to wait until the second coming of Jesus and the last judgment. If we do not believe in the name of God's one and only Son, we have brought condemnation upon ourselves today.

The vital word here is the word "condemn". This is the language of the law courts. It means to sentence or judge. John's point is that we sentence ourselves by our own choices in this life, specifically our choice about whether to believe in and receive Jesus. We judge ourselves by refusing to believe in Jesus. The Father's longing is for us to be saved. This is because God is love. But he will not force us to accept Jesus. That choice is ours and ours alone and everything hangs on it.

I wonder if you've ever been struck by the perversity of people's reactions to Jesus. Has it ever occurred to you as strange that some academics will devote endless amounts of time trying to disprove that Jesus Christ existed, while Roman historians never do the same with Julius Caesar, even though there is far greater evidence for Jesus than for any other figure in ancient history! Why is this? It is because Jesus Christ challenges us. He provokes a verdict!

Devotion: *Abba, Father, I confess again today that I believe in the name of your One and Only Son, Jesus Christ. I love Jesus and I exalt his name. Help me never to waver in this matter. While others doubt and question, help me to remain convinced in my faith in Jesus of Nazareth. Amen.*

> *"This is the verdict: Light has come into the world, but people loved darkness instead of light because their deeds were evil. All those who do evil hate the light, and will not come into the light for fear that their deeds will be exposed. But those who live by the truth come into the light, so that it may be seen plainly that what they have done has been done in the sight of God."*
>
> John 3:19–21

I said yesterday that Jesus Christ provokes a verdict. You can't sit on the fence when it comes to Jesus. You either believe in him or you don't. You either confess his name or you don't. Everything depends upon your response to Jesus. Your eternal destiny hangs upon this one thing – do you accept Jesus or not?

Today's reading starts with the words, "This is the verdict." "Verdict" is a legal word. We are in a courtroom drama once again. So what is the verdict? The verdict is that Jesus, light of the world, has entered history but people have chosen to reject rather than accept him because they enjoy the darkness too much.

Why is this? People know deep down that coming to Jesus means coming to the light and that coming into the light exposes our shadows. Our shadows are where our hidden hurts, habits, and hang-ups are. We don't want to deal with these because we are afraid of condemnation. But as a friend of mine is fond of saying, "Jesus didn't come to rub it in. He came to rub it out." He didn't come to condemn us for our sins. He came to save us from them!

I find today's verses helpful for explaining why some people are hostile to Jesus. People who hate Jesus do so because they have a lot to hide. They hate the light because they don't want their shadows disclosed. This is in a strange way reassuring. Next time you have someone reacting angrily to you about Jesus, don't take it personally. It's not you that they hate; it's the light that's shining in you. It's Jesus. Your job, and mine, is to keep walking in the light and living by the truth. Our task is to make sure that we are living authentic, transparent, and consistent lives.

Devotion: *Dear loving, heavenly Abba, Father, help me always to be a person who lives by the truth and walks in the light. Help me to be the real deal, to be the same person in public as in private. If there is any darkness in me, root it out now, in Jesus' name. Amen.*

> *An argument developed between some of John's disciples and a certain Jew over the matter of ceremonial washing. They came to John and said to him, "Rabbi, that man who was with you on the other side of the Jordan – the one you testified about – look, he is baptizing, and everyone is going to him."*
>
> John 3:25–26

Here's something we don't see in the Gospels of Matthew, Mark, and Luke – Jesus baptizing his own followers. The three other Gospels tell us that John the Baptist baptized people in the River Jordan, as does the Fourth Gospel. But only John tells us that Jesus did the same and that many came to Jesus to be baptized on the other side of the same river. In fact, those who come to John the Baptist to tell him about this say, "Everyone is going to him."

One of the greatest tests of our security in the Father's love is our attitude towards other people's successes. If we are threatened by another person doing well, then the chances are we are still living out of an insecure, orphan heart rather than the secure heart of a son or a daughter. If I can put it succinctly I'd say this: orphans hate it when other people thrive; sons and daughters can't help celebrating the achievements of others.

One of the great tests of John the Baptist's character was right here in this incident we are looking at today. While the crowds are beginning to dwindle on John's side of the river, they are evidently increasing on Jesus' side. John responds well as we will see tomorrow. He doesn't get jealous about Jesus' success. He rejoices in it.

In the final analysis we can have plenty of charisma but if our character is lacking then we will eventually be found wanting. We can be the most anointed of prophetic people (as John the Baptist was), but if we are operating out of an unhealed, orphan heart we will sooner or later be found out. Let us never forget that character is just as important as charisma; that the fruit of the spirit is as important as the gifts of the Spirit. How are we doing on the character front? When others do well, do we react like orphans or respond like sons and daughters?

Devotion: *Heavenly Father, help me to be so secure in your love for me that I never get jealous when others succeed, that I never get intimidated when other people prosper. Help me to be so free from the orphan mentality that I am the first to celebrate when others thrive. Amen.*

> *To this John replied, "A person can receive only what is given from heaven. You yourselves can testify that I said, 'I am not the Messiah but am sent ahead of him.' The bride belongs to the bridegroom. The friend who attends the bridegroom waits and listens for him, and is full of joy when he hears the bridegroom's voice. That joy is mine, and it is now complete. He must become greater; I must become less."*
>
> John 3:27–30

One of the secrets of the Christian life is to be so content with who you are and what you're called to do that you never strive to have a position or a purpose that isn't yours. Many of us lack this contentment because we long deep down to be someone or something that our Father has not planned for us. True humility is not only accepting who we are in Christ; it is accepting what we are called to be and do. True maturity is enjoying your identity and destiny, not striving for something that isn't yours.

John the Baptist had two choices when he was presented with the news that there was effectively a revival going on the other side of the same river. He could either get indignant that many of his followers were going over to Jesus, or he could rest in the knowledge that this was his position in the divine scheme of things and that he had fulfilled the Father's purpose for his life. John the Baptist chose the latter.

In every situation like this, we can either react in the flesh or respond in the Spirit. John responds in the Spirit. He tells his listeners that a person cannot be anyone else other than the person the Father intended them to be. John says that he was never called to be the Christ, the Messiah, the Anointed One. He was called to be the forerunner. Put another way, he was called to be the best man at the wedding. He was not called to be the bridegroom. His joy was in announcing the bridegroom and serving the bride – the church. All John ever wanted to do was to make Jesus famous, not himself, and this is what made him truly happy.

What about us? Are we living out of a secure and restful enjoyment of who we are? Or are we striving to be and to do something outside of the Father's plan for our lives?

Devotion: *Abba, Father, I pray that I may be so free from any trace of an orphan mindset that I never want to draw attention to myself, I only want to give Jesus the glory. Help me to embrace true humility in my life and always to resolve to make Jesus famous. Amen.*

"For the one whom God has sent speaks the words of God, for God gives the Spirit without limit."

John 3:34

I love this statement. In the first half of the verse, we learn that Jesus is the one whom the Father has sent. This is one of the most important descriptions of Jesus in the Gospel of John. Jesus is the one sent by God. He is not sent by God in the same way that John the Baptist was – in other words, commissioned to be a prophetic voice. He was sent from heaven to earth to accomplish Abba, Father's unique assignment for his life. This marks Jesus out as different from all the prophets in the Bible and all other religious leaders in history. Jesus is the envoy from heaven called to speak the Father's words. There is no one else like Jesus.

In the second part of the verse, John tells us that God gives the Spirit without limit to Jesus. In the Old Testament era, various people received the Holy Spirit in a partial and temporary way. For example, Gideon received an anointing of the Holy Spirit for particular tasks (Judges 6:34). The anointing came and went in accordance with the need of the hour. With Jesus it is very different. The Father gives the Holy Spirit completely and permanently. In his case, the giving of the Holy Spirit was complete not partial, permanent not transient. Again, there is no one else like Jesus! He stands alone among the world's religions.

I wonder if you've ever seen Niagara Falls, or even a picture of it? It is truly one of the wonders of the world. A seemingly endless supply of water runs down from the heights into a river below, attended by a great and thunderous roar of raw power, and resulting in a misty cloud of vapour.

When I think of Jesus I think of Niagara Falls. Jesus wasn't given the Holy Spirit in a certain measure. He was given the Holy Spirit in complete measure. From the generous heart of the Father, the Holy Spirit is given to Jesus in a continuous and endless flow of power. And from the heart and the hands of Jesus, the Holy Spirit is poured out on the church. In light of this, the best prayer I can think of praying is Jesus, "Pour out your Spirit on us today!"

Devotion: *Abba, Father, I thank you for your extravagant generosity. I thank you that you give the Holy Spirit to your Son in an unlimited and unceasing way. I pray, Lord Jesus, that you would cause the floodgates of heaven to open. Pour out your Spirit in an unprecedented way. Amen.*

"The Father loves the Son and has placed everything in his hands."

John 3:35

In this brief statement we learn something very simple, that "the Father loves the Son". The Father is not some remote monarch who is aloof and indifferent to his Son. The Father isn't like some earthly fathers who are distant from their children, never showing any affection or displaying any love for them. Abba, Father loves his Son. While prophets like John the Baptist were regarded as servants, Jesus is loved as a son. Jesus knows forever that he is the Father's beloved Son, the one in whom the Father delights. The Father "loves" the Son – present tense. That means the Father loves Jesus forever!

The verb translated "loves" in verse 35 is the Greek word *agapao*. It is used often in John's Gospel, some thirty-seven times in fact. It has the connotation of self-giving, self-forgetful love. It is the kind of love that welcomes sacrifice and selflessness. When John says that the Father loves the Son, he means that the Father gives everything of himself to his Son. He gives generously of his Spirit, as we saw yesterday. He gives of himself without holding back.

John adds that the Father has placed everything in his Son's hands. God is not a controlling Father who seeks to hold onto everything himself. He is a releasing Father who entrusts everything to his Son. By giving generously of his Holy Spirit to Jesus, Jesus now reigns as Lord over all. Jesus has authority and power from the Father to speak his words and to perform his deeds. Jesus has the might and the right to confront the darkness of this world and to usher in the light of heaven.

The Father never bypasses his Son. Rather, he first gives everything to his Son Jesus. His Son then puts goods things into our hands. Whatever anointing we receive from the Father, we receive from the Son. If there is anything in our hands – any power to heal, any working of miracles, any grace for mercy – it is because they were first in the hands of Jesus. His hands are the most trustworthy and loving hands of all. They carry the scars of Calvary love.

Devotion: *Abba, Father, you have truly displayed your self-giving love for your Son. You have demonstrated that love in giving everything into his hands. I raise my hands to you today, Lord Jesus. Everything that you have placed there has been given by Jesus. Thank you, Lord. Amen.*

"Whoever believes in the Son has eternal life, but whoever rejects the Son will not see life, for God's wrath remains on them."

John 3:36

All this talk of the Father's love may lull us into a false sense that God is only ever kind and never stern. But while we know that God is love, this love is expressed not only in mercy, but sometimes in judgment. In other words, there are things that make the Father mad. That's why John mentions the Father's wrath in verse 36, and only here.

I remember a few years ago visiting Auschwitz concentration camp. I stood in the building dedicated to the Jews deported from Holland. I went upstairs and I read the names of over 120 members of the Stibbe family who had perished in the death camps. I remember seeing the name of a six-year-old boy, Jonah Stibbe, carved on the wall of remembrance. Part of me wanted to cry. But another part of me was furious. I raged and railed at the sheer injustice of it all.

I believe at that moment I was deeply in touch with Abba, Father's love. You see, anger can be an expression of love. I know that in our world fathers can be abusive in their expression of rage. When that happens, it can never be called love. But our heavenly Father is perfect. He is not like so many dysfunctional, earthly dads. He gets mad because he loves his children, not because he wants to harm them. His anger is an expression of great love not a display of toxic domination.

John says in this verse that if we reject Jesus then the Father's wrath remains on us. What is this wrath? I define the Father's wrath as "his justified and measured anger over human sin, demonic wickedness and social injustice". The greatest sin of all, according to John's Gospel, is to reject the Son. When a person looks into the bleeding face of the crucified Lord and says, "Jesus, you died for me and I don't care", they remain under the justified and measured anger of the Father.

Be sure of this today: if you have chosen to believe in Jesus, then you are no longer under judgment. You are pardoned and free.

Devotion: *Abba, Father, help me to understand that you hate sin, wickedness and injustice. Help me to remember that you get mad with these things and that this too is love. Thank you, Dad, that because of my faith in Jesus, you're not angry with me anymore. Amen.*

Now he had to go through Samaria.

John 4:4

I wonder if you've ever had the experience of being told by the Holy Spirit to go to a certain place because the Father wanted you to have a divine appointment with someone who really needed his love.

John 4:4–42 is a story about precisely this. It all begins with the storyteller informing us that Jesus "had to go" through Samaria. Now this was not the obvious route for a band of Jewish people. Samaria was a region hated by the Jews. The Samaritan people were hated too, mainly because they started as a race when Jews inter-married with pagans hundreds of years before. Jewish people routinely avoided travelling through Samaria when they travelled from Jerusalem to Galilee (or vice versa), even though it doubled the length of their journey from about half a week to a whole week. We read here however that Jesus went through Samaria. Indeed, we read he *had to go*. Why was this?

The answer lies in Jesus' relationship with the Father. Jesus lived in such an immediate and intimate communion with God that he heard what his Father was saying and did what his Father was doing. There was a complete relational and functional unity between the Son and his Father. Jesus "had to go through Samaria" because this was what the Father was saying. This was what the Father was doing on that particular day at that particular moment. Jesus heard and obeyed.

Too many of us – including me – are far too regulated by our own diaries and itineraries. What would happen if more of us were like Jesus in this story? What if more of us were prepared to hear and obey the Father when he said, "go there"? There wouldn't be enough books to contain the testimonies of the miraculous deeds of God.

Many of us install satellite navigation systems in our cars to help us find our destinations. Isn't it time we asked the Father to install a supernatural navigation system in our hearts, even if it means that sometimes we end up going to places we wouldn't normally dream of visiting?

Devotion: *Abba, Father, I thank you for the example of your Son, Jesus. Help me as an adopted son/daughter to be more like your natural Son. Help me to be someone who is steered by your gentle voice to go to places where I can be used by you in remarkable ways. Help me today, I pray. Amen.*

> *So he came to a town in Samaria called Sychar, near the plot of ground Jacob had given to his son Joseph. Jacob's well was there, and Jesus, tired as he was from the journey, sat down by the well. It was about noon.*
>
> John 4:5–6

Having heard the Father say, "You must go through Samaria", Jesus ends up just outside a Samaritan town called Sychar. He is on land that was originally purchased by Jacob (Genesis 33:18–19) and then bequeathed to Joseph (Genesis 48:22). He is exhausted, so he sits down by Jacob's well, the very place where Jacob had first met Rachel, his bride-to-be (Genesis 29).

At this well Jesus is about to have an encounter with a woman from the town of Sychar. This encounter is going to change the woman's life every bit as radically as Rachel's meeting with Jacob hundreds of years before. Rachel of course ended up married to Jacob. The woman of Samaria will end up seeing that Jesus is the most perfect man of all and relating to him as her Saviour.

It has been rightly said that God loves geography. In other words, He honours the geographical locations all over the world where he has done extraordinary and pivotal things in the past. For twelve years I was honoured to be the vicar of St Andrew's Chorleywood, a church where the Holy Spirit had moved dramatically in the 1960s and '70s and then again in the '80s and '90s. When I became vicar there two revivalists came to preach. They were overwhelmed by the Holy Spirit in the parking lot and shouted, "There's a residential anointing over this church!" After that we saw the Holy Spirit moving under my watch too!

Some locations are just especially marked by grace. The ancient Celtic Christians called these "the thin places" – places where the gap between heaven and earth is so thin that it almost doesn't exist at all. These are places of divine encounter and heavenly visitation. Pray for your home, your town, your city to become a thin place. Pray that a spiritual well will be opened up where you live and work.

Devotion: *Abba, Father, I pray in your Son's name that you would open up a spiritual well where I live and where I work. Would you come and honour the locations that I inhabit by visiting them in power. Let me dwell in some thin places, I pray, in Jesus' name. Amen.*

When a Samaritan woman came to draw water, Jesus said to her, "Will you give me a drink?"

John 4:7

Sometimes we are prone to miss the true significance of a Bible verse because we don't have enough knowledge about the culture of the times. Here is a good example of that. From a twenty-first-century Western perspective, there seems nothing strange here. We have just been told that Jesus was tired and thirsty. Here he asks a woman who has come to the well to draw water for a drink. This all seems regulation stuff. But if we think that, we are quite wrong. From a first-century, Jewish perspective, Jesus' behaviour is utterly outrageous.

Why is that? We must remember at this point that Jesus was a Jewish rabbi. Jewish rabbis had very strict rules about relating to women in public. They were not supposed to be seen conversing with a woman they didn't know. That was regarded as shameful. They were even to be very careful not to speak to their own wives in public. When Jesus saw the woman approaching, the protocol of the day dictated that he should have taken twenty steps back from the well. But he doesn't.

We must also remember that Jewish men despised Samaritan women. Samaritan women were regarded as the most unclean of human beings. In fact, Jewish men in Jesus' day had a proverb, the polite version of which went like this: "The daughters of the Samaritans are dirty from the cradle." According to the customs and prejudices of the day, Jesus should have not only withdrawn from the well; he should have avoided the woman at all costs. But he not only stays, he asks her for a drink.

One of the reasons I have written *Every Day with the Father* is because I believe that everything Jesus says and does in John's Gospel points to something of the Father heart of God. In this single moment in John 4:7, we see something truly beautiful about our heavenly Father. We see the extravagantly and relentlessly inclusive nature of his love. Our Father doesn't accept cultural prejudices. He believes in embrace not exclusion. He is the most welcoming of all fathers.

Devotion: *Abba, Father, I love the fact that your heart is open and warm to those whom people in their ignorance despise. Please expose any racial prejudice in my heart. Heal me of all toxic, exclusivist tendencies. Make me more like Jesus, I ask, in his name. Amen.*

> *Jesus answered, "Everyone who drinks this water will be thirsty again, but those who drink the water I give them will never thirst. Indeed, the water I give them will become in them a spring of water welling up to eternal life."*
>
> John 4:13–14

The Samaritan woman is surprised that Jesus – a Jewish man – is conversing with her. In doing so, he is breaking many social conventions of the time. Jesus points out that if she knew who he really was then she would ask him for "living water". At this point she takes him literally and misunderstands what he is saying. But Jesus presses in and makes the wonderful statement that we have in our reading for today. He describes the spiritual water that he has to offer her.

One of the things I love about Jesus is how relevant he is. When he encounters a tax collector he says, "Let's talk about money." When he encounters a fisherman he says, "Let's talk about fishing." When he encounters a water-carrier he says, "Let's talk about water." Jesus finds a way of getting through to those who are thirsty for God.

I remember a leader on my staff team at St Andrew's Chorleywood sharing a remarkable testimony. He knew a man who was not a Christian and yet who was open to talking about spiritual things. One day they met on the street and a conversation began. The man – whose name was John – told my colleague that he had woken up at exactly the same time for the previous four days. The readout on his digital alarm clock said 4:14 each time. He asked my friend why he thought that was happening.

My friend quietly asked for wisdom from the Holy Spirit and then replied, "Well, I believe that 4:14 is a sign for you. Your name is John. John 4:14 says, 'Those who drink the water I give them will never thirst. Indeed, the water I give them will become in them a spring of water welling up to eternal life.' I believe that Jesus is speaking to you, John, out of the Gospel of John, and that it's time to accept his offer!"

What a remarkable Father we have! Pray today that those who are spiritually thirsty would have an extraordinary awakening.

Devotion: *Abba, Father, I praise and worship you that you are speaking to lost people today. I pray that those whom I know and love would hear your voice, especially those who don't know you. May they hear something that speaks to the deepest needs in their hearts. Amen.*

He told her, "Go, call your husband and come back." "I have no
husband," she replied. Jesus said to her, "You are right when
you say you have no husband. The fact is, you have had five
husbands, and the man you now have is not your husband. What
you have just said is quite true."

John 4:16–18

The critical moment in the encounter between Jesus and the Samaritan woman occurs right here. Jesus has offered her the living water that alone will meet the deep spiritual thirst in her life. She replies, "give me some of this water". Jesus then tells her to go fetch her husband, at which point she tells a half-truth. She says that she's isn't married. This is really an example of hiding. She doesn't want to disclose the whole truth about her life. But we have already learned at the end of John 2 that Jesus doesn't need anyone else to tell him what is in a person's life because he knows it by revelation. Here is a great example of that. Jesus reads the woman's heart and tells her that she's been married five times before and that she's now co-habiting with a man out of wedlock.

It is this prophetic insight that changes the whole tenor of the conversation. Up until this moment the woman is quite belligerent. But as soon as the secrets of her heart are exposed she becomes a different person. Suddenly she wants to talk about religious matters and within a few minutes she is running back to her town to tell everyone about Jesus. I think we would call that a dramatic transformation!

A few years ago I wrote a book entitled *Prophetic Evangelism*. It is all about the use of prophecy in witnessing to unbelievers. When we speak out what the Father is saying about the lost people we meet every day, we become far more effective in our outreach. The truth is that there are few things more powerful than prophetic words in evangelism. When they hit the mark they have the power to transform a person's attitude to Jesus instantaneously.

Jesus models prophetic evangelism here. It is a key to the spiritual harvest that follows. We have a lot to learn from him.

Devotion: *Abba, Father, please help me to be very open to what you're saying all the time, not just when I'm with fellow Christians. Help me to hear what you're saying about lost people at work and on the streets. Help me to grow in prophetic evangelism, in Jesus' name. Amen.*

> *"Sir," the woman said, "I can see that you are a prophet. Our ancestors worshipped on this mountain, but you Jews claim that the place where we must worship is in Jerusalem."*
>
> John 4:19

Yesterday we were looking at the importance of the gift of prophecy in witnessing to lost people. It is one of the most powerful and yet underused tools in our utility belts. When we have a word that unveils the secrets of a person's heart it changes their whole attitude to Jesus. It can take them from hostility to receptivity in a matter of seconds.

This is what is happening here. The effect of Jesus' prophetic revelation about the woman's five marriages and current relationship is immediate and striking. She says, "I can see you are a prophet." Now this is revealing. At the start of this story in John 4:9, all the woman can see is that Jesus is a Jewish man. Now something has happened. She sees that he is a prophet. His supernatural knowledge of her life has proved to her that he is more than just an ordinary man; he is a man who can read people's hearts. A little later on in this story she will be asking the question, "Could this be the Christ?" (verse 29) and by the end she will be confessing, along with her fellow townsfolk, that Jesus is "the Saviour of the World" (verse 42). By the end she will have realized that Jesus is more even than a prophet!

Let's develop this thought a bit further. We saw yesterday how Jesus told the woman that she had been married to five men and was now living with a sixth man. Numbers are often significant and symbolic in Jewish thought. For example, as we saw in John 2:13, six is the number of imperfection. Seven is the number of perfection. If the woman has had six men then what does that make Jesus? It makes him the seventh man. It makes him the perfect man. Jesus is the one that she's been looking for. He alone can meet the fundamental need in her life – not by marrying her, but by pointing her to the Father.

Jesus is accordingly not just a prophet. He is perfection itself. For this woman and for all of us, he is truly the answer.

Devotion: *Dear loving, heavenly Abba, Father, I praise and worship you for your Son Jesus. He is the most perfect man who has ever lived. He is the one the world is waiting for. Thank you that Jesus reveals you, Father, and that you are therefore the most perfect Dad there is. Amen.*

"Woman," Jesus replied, "believe me, a time is coming when you will worship the Father..."

John 4:21

As the woman of Samaria realizes that she's in the presence of a prophet, she starts talking about the first religious topic that enters her head. She starts talking about places of worship – Mount Gerazim for the Samaritans and Jerusalem for the Jews. This is very like what happens today. When we say something to a lost person that only God could know they often start talking about church or religion. The important thing in this situation is to do what Jesus did. Jesus allowed her to introduce the subject of worship but then used her words as the springboard for talking about the Father's love for her. This is what we need to do too.

When Jesus spoke to the woman about worship he said something that must have produced an earthquake in her soul. He said, "You're going to worship the Father." The word he would have used for "Father" is a word that would have been heard as "Papa" or "Dad" or "Daddy". The word that he used for worship would have had connotations of profound intimacy. It means something like "to approach the Father to embrace him". Jesus completely redefines what worship is. He says true worship is not restricted to holy sites. True worship can happen anywhere. Anyone who believes in Jesus can worship the Father at any time and in any place.

For the woman of Samaria this must have sounded so good. She had been looking for a long time in men for what she could only find in the Father's love. Heartfelt adoration of Abba, Father is the one thing that is really going to meet the need for intimacy in her life. Jesus effectively says to her, "You've been looking in the wrong place. Only the Father's love can fill the father-shaped hole in your soul. And you're going to meet him and embrace him, and in his arms you're going to find the Father you've been waiting for."

That was Good News for her, and it is the gospel for this fatherless world in which we live today.

Devotion: *Abba, Father I praise and worship you that Jesus didn't come to start a religion; he came to start a relationship. I thank you that you are not a remote God but a relational Dad. Help me to lead other people today towards your arms of love, where true healing is found. Amen.*

Yet a time is coming and has now come when the true worshippers will worship the Father in spirit and truth, for they are the kind of worshippers the Father seeks.

John 4:23 (NIV)

The greatest need that a human being has is the need to love and to be loved. This need is only ultimately met in Jesus. As we encounter Jesus, he then introduces us to the perfect Father. We experience the Father's love through the power of the Holy Spirit – through the one Paul called the Spirit of adoption (Romans 8:15). When that happens, our need for love is fully met and we begin to respond to the divine overtures of love by expressing our praise and thanks to Abba, Father. This is what true worship is. It is not the meaningless recitation of religious jargon. It is the overflow of love from a heart that has been captured by the affection of the world's greatest Dad.

Jesus explains all this to the woman of Samaria in what is the premier passage about Christian worship in the New Testament. He tells the woman that the hour is coming and has now already arrived when true worshippers will worship Abba in spirit and in truth. What does Jesus mean by "spirit and truth"? It could be that he means that we must worship the Father in the Holy Spirit and in the truth (the truth being Jesus, John 14:6). It could also mean "spiritually and authentically". I believe it's both.

True worship is the intimate and affectionate expression of praise to our Father through Jesus and in the power of the Holy Spirit. It is the response of the spiritual core of our being to the Father's matchless display of lavish love and it is an honest, simple and very real expression of our heart's delight that our Father loves us, likes us and is extremely fond of us. In essence, it is our child-like expression of pleasure in the Father's pleasure over us. It is our smile in response to his smile. It is our rejoicing in response to the fact that he rejoices over us with singing (Zephaniah 3:17).

What a revelation of true worship we find in these words!

Devotion: *I thank you so much, Heavenly Dad, that you leap up and down with joy when you think of me. I thank you that I am your happy thought and that you lift up your face to smile at me. Help me to take as much pleasure in you as you do in me today, in Jesus' name. Amen.*

The woman said, "I know that Messiah" (called Christ) "is coming. When he comes, he will explain everything to us." Then Jesus declared, "I, the one speaking to you—I am he."

John 4:25–26

I love this moment in the story. The woman has become deeply intrigued by Jesus' words. As he speaks about God as "Daddy" (*Abba* in the original language), and of worship as an affectionate embrace, something within her heart ignites. She opens her mouth and tells Jesus that she knows that one day the Messiah will come and explain all these things about worship. There is of course great irony here for she is speaking to the Messiah even as she says this. Jesus, however, does not leave her in any doubt. He declares, "I am he."

In the original language Jesus' words should literally be translated, "I, I am." The words are few but the ramifications are many. When Jesus used the phrase "I am" it was electric! She may have recalled the revelation of God's name to Moses in Exodus 3:14: "I am who I am" and the frequent use of the phrase "I am" by Almighty God in the later chapters of the Book of Isaiah. "I am" is God's name. When Jesus says "I, I am he" to the woman of Samaria, he is revealing that he is not just a prophet, not just the Messiah, but God in human flesh.

This woman accordingly becomes the first person in the Gospel of John to whom Jesus reveals his divinity. This is extraordinarily significant. The rabbis of Jesus' day had a very low view of women. They said, "Better that the words of the law should be burned than delivered to women." Jesus does not take this view. He treats women with much greater dignity because he sees that women as well as men are of equal value to his heavenly Abba. So this daughter, in whom faith is so obviously rising, receives a personal revelation of his divinity – the first in John's Gospel.

Jesus came to reveal that God wants to be our Father and that his longing is that we should be his adopted sons and daughters. Our Father doesn't just want boys in his family. He wants girls too. Thank God for the revolutionary nature of Jesus' attitude towards women.

Devotion: *Abba, Father, I thank you for the fact that you love your daughters just as much as you love your sons, and that both are equal in your sight. Please heal me of any hurts that have led me to think otherwise, and help me to be more like Jesus, in his name. Amen.*

> *Then, leaving her water jar, the woman went back to the town and said to the people, "Come, see a man who told me everything I ever did. Could this be the Messiah?" They came out of the town and made their way toward him.*

John 4:28–30

It is an extraordinary thing to reflect on the fact that Jesus never did get the drink he asked for right at the beginning of this story! The main reason for that is because the woman becomes so captivated by what Jesus says to her that she leaves her water jar at the well and goes running into town to tell everyone her testimony. She is breathless with excitement as she goes round Sychar and tells everyone about Jesus and how he knew her heart as if he had access to her innermost secrets! In response they begin to make their way out to the well to see who this man is. Could he indeed be the long awaited Messiah?

It's interesting to ask why the woman became so excited. I think it's because she had come to the well with shame but she left it with honour. Let me explain. When she arrived at the well it was high noon, the hottest time of the day. No one in their right minds drew water at that time of the day. Normally they would do it in the early morning or evening, when it was cooler. But this woman comes at that time because she doesn't want to meet anyone. She is full of shame and wants to hide. If guilt is the negative feeling I have about what I've done, shame is the negative feeling I have about who I am. Shame is essentially an "I am" wound and an "I am" wound needs an "I am" healer.

When Jesus says "I, I am he" to the woman of Samaria in John 4:26 he reveals his divinity to her. That, as we saw yesterday, was an extraordinary honour. Jesus chooses a woman – a Samaritan woman at that – to be the first recipient of the revelation of his divinity. Now she feels worthy, she feels valued, and she feels esteemed. This rabbi has not just given her time, he has given her dignity and honour. In Jesus, she has truly encountered the Father's love and it has caused her heart to sing and her feet to run. No wonder she shares her testimony. She has encountered the "I am" healer and her shame has turned to honour.

Devotion: *Dear loving, heavenly Abba, Father, I thank you so much that when we encounter you our sense of shame goes and honour comes. Thank you that Jesus is in the business of conferring honour and dignity on others. Help me to do the same, in his name. Amen.*

"My food," said Jesus, **"is to do the will of him who sent me and to finish his work."**

John 4:34

After the woman of Samaria leaves, the disciples come back. The disciples have been into Sychar to buy food and eat lunch. It is interesting to note that they don't bring anyone to Jesus. In a few minutes time they will turn around and see the Samaritan woman bringing a crowd to meet Jesus. Who's the real evangelist here, we might ask?

This brings me to my point from this verse in John 4. When the men come back they ask Jesus to eat something. Jesus then says something that really confuses them. He says that he has food that they don't know about. Now Jesus is speaking figuratively here. He is speaking about what nourishes him spiritually. But the men misunderstand. If the woman misunderstands what Jesus meant by water at the start of the story, the men misunderstand what Jesus means by food at the end of it. Jesus is telling them that there is something that satisfies him more even than food. It is what he has just been doing at the well. It is sowing the message of the Father's love into another person's life. It is reaping a great spiritual harvest. This is what feeds Jesus: doing the Father's will and completing the Father's assignment.

Many churches today are at a crossroads. One road leads where the disciples have just been. It leads to the town of "feed me". It is in a territory called "consumerism". The other road leads to the town of "feed them". It is in a territory called "evangelism". This is the road that the woman of Samaria is travelling.

The choice that many churches need to make is between consumerism and evangelism. Jesus wants us to choose evangelism – to choose to be like the woman of Samaria, and indeed Jesus. He wants us to be fed by the exhilarating and epic adventure of mission. He doesn't want us to flit from one church to another with one aim only, "being fed". He wants us to be like the woman of Samaria, sharing the gospel out of love not law in our own town. When that happens, there will truly be a great harvest.

Devotion: *Abba, Father, today I ask that you would help me to confront the idol of consumerism in my life. I choose to be focused on sowing your love into other people's lives and to put that assignment before being fed. Help me to do this out of love not law, in Jesus' name. Amen.*

> **"Don't you have a saying, 'It's still four months until harvest'? I tell you, open your eyes and look at the fields! They are ripe for harvest."**
>
> John 4:35

You have to picture the scene. In the foreground is Jesus, talking to the disciples. He is speaking about harvests. In the background the woman of Samaria is leading many of her town to Jesus. Jesus therefore tells his disciples to open their eyes and take a look at what is happening in the background. It is the most vivid illustration of what he's been teaching them about in the foreground. It is a harvest of souls in which many people are being gathered into the warm arms of the Father and entering his life-transforming kingdom. It is a very dramatic moment.

There are times in our lives when we really need to open our eyes to understand what's taking place in our own field of vision. I remember when I was vicar of St Andrew's Chorleywood we made a momentous decision as a church to move from being an inward-looking to an outward-looking community. In one year we planted something like twenty mission-shaped communities led by members of our congregation. These communities were not large in number; they were not allowed to grow beyond fifty. But they were pioneering groups that met in coffee shops, homeless shelters, and school halls. They went out and rescued the lost and a great number of people were added to us in just a few years. We saw hundreds of salvations and many people healed and set free.

When this had been taking place for a while I remember having dinner with a very prophetic leader from the USA who specializes in church growth consultancy. He asked me what was happening at St Andrew's and I began to share. After just a few minutes he stopped me and said, "Do you realize that you're in the midst of a stunning revival?" That thought had never occurred to me but as soon as he said it I had an awakening. I opened my eyes and I saw how ripe the fields were for harvest. I began to rejoice in what the Father was doing.

Sometimes we just need to look up instead of looking down, and look out instead of looking in.

Devotion: *Loving Dad, I praise you that right now you are doing wonderful things that I need to take note of and celebrate. Help me not to look down but to look up. Help me not to focus on minor issues but on the bigger picture of what you're doing, in Jesus' name. Amen.*

"Even now those who reap draw their wages, even now they harvest the crop for eternal life, so that the sower and the reaper may be glad together. Thus the saying 'One sows and another reaps' is true. I sent you to reap what you have not worked for. Others have done the hard work, and you have reaped the benefits of their labour."

John 4:36–38

I remember when I started my time as vicar of St Andrew's Chorleywood in 1997 I presented a vision for reaching the lost with the Father's love. I talked a lot about evangelism in the process. Some people took offence at this and began to chastise me for using what they called the "'E' word", by which they meant evangelism. Maybe my presentational skills were to blame. Maybe they had had a bad experience of being made to evangelize in the past. Whatever the reason, the "'E' Word" was clearly a very negative one for some.

This is a real shame. Evangelism is not supposed to be hard, miserable or complicated. In John 4:36–38 Jesus explains that much of it is about "sowing" – it is about sowing seeds of Abba, Father's love into lost people's lives through words, works, and wonders. In other words, it is about giving your testimony in a clear and heartfelt way when asked. It is about doing acts of kindness and mercy when others are in distress. It is about believing in the Father's power to heal and praying for the sick when this is invited.

Most of us, if the truth be told, are called to sow – to be those who do the small things that eventually contribute to a person making a big decision. Some, however, are called to reap; they are given a special grace for helping people to be born again. In John 4:36–38, Jesus tells his disciples that they are about to reap what they haven't worked for. Hundreds of Samaritans are pouring out of Sychar to come to Christ. The disciples are about to reap a harvest but they played no part in the sowing process. Jesus did all that. He sowed; they are reaping.

Jesus says there is joy when the harvest comes. When the church starts sowing and reaping out of love not law, there is great gladness.

Devotion: *Abba, Father, I pray today for an outpouring of your affection in my heart. Fill me to overflowing with your divine kindness so that I sow your love into the lives of lost people all around me. Help me to do this supernaturally, effectively and joyfully, in Jesus' name. Amen.*

> *Many of the Samaritans from that town believed in him because of the woman's testimony, "He told me everything I ever did." So when the Samaritans came to him, they urged him to stay with them, and he stayed two days. And because of his words many more became believers.*
>
> John 4:39–41

One of the remarkable things about John's Gospel is the very positive, active, and pioneering role that is played by the women in his story. This is especially true of the woman of Samaria. John says here that many of the people in the town believed in Jesus because of the woman's testimony. The word translated as "testimony" is the Greek word *logos*, which can also be translated as "word". The Samaritans believed because of her "word".

This is significant because in John 17:20 Jesus prays this to the Father: "My prayer is not for them alone. I pray also for those who will believe in me through their message". The word translated "message" here is *logos*. This should remind us of the woman of Samaria. She leads people to believe in Jesus because of her "word", her "message". Her testimony leads to a spiritual harvest, to a great awakening, in Sychar.

The woman of Samaria is therefore no negative stereotype. She is not a servile, passive, cardboard female. She is full of life and colour. She engages in a theological debate with Jesus about worship. When she hears the message of the Father's love she goes running into her town to invite everyone to "come and see". She is one of the first people to become an ambassador of the Father's love in John's Gospel!

One of the most interesting things about this woman is that she is given no name. I used to think this was regrettable but now I am quite glad. Her anonymity is actually inspirational. This woman kick starts a revival in her town yet we don't even know her name. That, I believe, is prophetic for our times. Revivals in the past have been led by great preachers like Wesley and Finney. In the future they will be led by an army of nameless, faceless heroes – women as well as men.

The age of celebrity is over. The age of the heroes has begun.

Devotion: *Abba, Father, my prayer today is that you would help me to be one of your anonymous heroes. I want to be a catalyst for a spiritual awakening among my family, friends and colleagues. I thank you that you know my name. That's all that matters. Amen.*

> *They said to the woman, "We no longer believe just because of what you said; now we have heard for ourselves, and we know that this man really is the Saviour of the world."*
>
> John 4:42

I wonder whether we realize just how big a thing it was to call Jesus "Saviour of the World" in the New Testament era. This is what the Samaritans are doing in John 4:42. It was political dynamite!

This confession of faith is extraordinary enough at the spiritual level. Here is a town of Samaritans confessing that the Jewish rabbi at the well is not just the Saviour of the Jewish people but the Saviour of the Samaritans too. In fact he is the Saviour of every person, whatever their nationality. He is the Saviour of the World.

This is stunning in itself. But there's more. You see, in the ancient world, the title "Saviour of the World" was already in use. It was used of the most powerful political leader on the planet at that time, the Roman emperor. He alone was addressed as the world's Saviour. Yet now, in John 4:42, the Samaritans are using this title to describe a humble Galilean carpenter! They are effectively saying, "The emperor in Rome thinks he is the Saviour of the World. He is not. The rabbi Jesus is the world's Saviour. While the emperor conquers the world through the love of power, the carpenter from Nazareth will conquer the world through the power of love."

When people became believers in the first century they applied to Jesus titles that were politically explosive. Titles like "Son of God", "Saviour of the World", and "Lord" were used of the Roman emperor. By the first century, the ruler of the Roman empire had acquired the status of a god. When people started to confess Jesus as Son of God, Saviour of the World, and Lord, this had huge implications. They could not confess Caesar as lord any more and that would often cost them everything.

Let's pray today for all our brothers and sisters in Christ all over the world whose confession of Jesus puts them in direct conflict with oppressive, political forces. Let's remember the suffering church today.

Devotion: *Dear loving, heavenly Abba, Father, I pray that you would give great courage and comfort to all your sons and daughters worldwide who are facing persecution for their faith in Jesus. Enfold them in your arms and embolden their witness, in Jesus' name. Amen.*

Once more he visited Cana in Galilee, where he had turned the water into wine. And there was a certain royal official whose son lay sick at Capernaum. When this man heard that Jesus had arrived in Galilee from Judea, he went to him and begged him to come and heal his son, who was close to death.

John 4:46–47

It would not be at all surprising that news of the great miracle that had happened at Cana earlier in the Gospel had spread around the town and the region like wildfire. It would not have been easy to keep secret when so many had tasted the heavenly wine that Jesus had miraculously produced, especially when there was 180 gallons of it!

One of the people who had obviously heard is described here as "a certain royal official". He was probably a courtier in the palace of Herod Antipas, the tetrarch of Galilee. This courtier was the father of a son who was close to death. When this dad hears that Jesus has returned to Galilee, he takes time off work to travel the twenty-five miles from his home town of Capernaum to Cana to see him. Here is a father who puts his family first.

I have often said over the years that "the kingdom of God is for the desperate". In other words, if you and I want to see heaven invading and lives being changed then we must be prepared to be passionate for that. A visitation of God happens amidst hungry not apathetic believers. Miracles break out among those who are desperate not among those who are self-sufficient.

Here is a father who is desperate. He is so desperate that he is prepared to travel all this way to implore Jesus for help. Not only that, he is so desperate that he is prepared to humble himself before a rabbi from Nazareth. In this poignant cameo, a courtier comes to a carpenter for help.

Maybe you're a parent reading this, and perhaps you have a great concern for one of your children. Be inspired by this devoted dad from Capernaum and believe that help is on the way.

Devotion: *Dear loving, heavenly Abba, Father, help me to be more desperate to see you move in my life and in my family. Stir up in me a deep hunger for the in-breaking of the kingdom of heaven here on earth. I want to come to you with simple faith and deep desire today. Amen.*

"Unless you people see signs and wonders," Jesus told him, "you will never believe."

John 4:48

Let's spend a few moments looking carefully at this verse today because at first sight it looks like a very strange statement. A desperate father has come to Jesus, travelling from Capernaum to Cana, to implore him to come and heal his sick boy who is dying. Jesus' response to this request is to utter a rebuke. Why does he do this?

It is important to start by noting that Jesus is not specifically addressing the father in verse 48. His comments are addressed to "you people". The Greek verb that is used for "see" here is "you plural" not "you singular". The TNIV is therefore right to translate it as "you people". But who are these people?

I think the best explanation is that Jesus is criticizing those who have come with the father. The father was a royal official in the court of Herod the tetrarch of Galilee. It is very likely that an entourage came with him, many of whom were only interested in one thing – seeing Jesus do signs and wonders. Notice that this is the only time in John's Gospel where the phrase "signs and wonders" is used. John's preferred word for miracles is just the word "signs" on its own. This I think is crucial. The people who have come with the courtier are only interested in a bit of sensational, wonder-working ministry. Jesus rounds on them, not the father, and says, "You're the sort of people that will only ever believe in me if you see something supernatural and spectacular. You're not here like this father, who is desperate. You're here because you want a show."

If this is correct then John 4:48 cannot and must not be used (as it sometimes is) to teach the church not to expect or desire the miraculous. It is not an unqualified condemnation of signs and wonders. It is a critique of those who need miracles in order to have faith, not those who have faith (like the father) and who need a miracle.

Let's always make sure we approach signs and wonders like the father. Miracles are for the desperate.

Devotion: *Abba, Father, please help me always to keep miracles in perspective. Help me never to want them for their own sake, or for show or for entertainment. Help me to pray for signs and wonders not in order to believe in you but because I already believe in you. Amen.*

> **The royal official said, "Sir, come down before my child dies."
> "Go," Jesus replied, "your son will live." The man took Jesus at
> his word and departed.**
>
> John 4:49–50

Last time we were in Cana (in John chapter 2) events unfolded in the following order. A request was made to Jesus by his mother in the form of a statement about the wine running out. This was followed by a rebuke from Jesus, which took the form of a comment about this having nothing to do with him. In spite of this rebuke, there followed a response in the form of a miracle, because Jesus' mother wouldn't take no for an answer!

Here we are again in Cana at the end of John chapter 4 and events proceed in exactly the same way. A father makes a request to Jesus about his son's healing. Jesus replies with a rebuke to those who have a wrong attitude towards signs and wonders. In spite of this rebuke, there follows a response from Jesus in the form of a miracle, because the father wont take no for an answer. He's a desperate dad.

Let's look at what the courtier says. He says "Sir, come down before my child dies." The verb "come down" is the same that is used in John's Gospel for Jesus coming down from heaven. That may or may not be significant. What is definitely of interest is the way the father refers to his son as a "little child" here. Up until this moment he has called him "my son". Now it is *paidion*, the diminutive form of *pais*, child.

We know from our study of the previous verse that Jesus was reluctant to pander to those in the father's entourage who were after a display of signs and wonders. Yet, in the end, Jesus does perform a miracle and he does so for two reasons: first because the father has been prepared to press in with faith past the rebuke; secondly, because the father's plea for his "little boy" has appealed to his compassion.

In this story an earthly father's love releases a demonstration of our heavenly Father's love. Jesus says, "Your son will live" and the royal official believes because he has heard, not because he has seen.

Devotion: *Heavenly Father, I pray today for all those who need a miracle. Would you please reveal your great love by releasing your power to save, heal and deliver those in distress. Thank you for your heart of compassion. Please pour out your Spirit, in Jesus' name. Amen.*

While he was still on the way, his servants met him with the news that his boy was living. When he inquired as to the time when his son got better, they said to him, "The fever left him yesterday at the seventh hour." Then the father realized that this was the exact time at which Jesus had said to him, "Your son will live." So he and all his household believed.

John 4:51–53 (NIV)

In the end, Jesus does perform a miracle, but he does so at a distance. Jesus stays in Cana and says to the man, "Your son will live." The official, who is used to taking important people at their word, believes what Jesus has just said and returns to his home. As he does so he is met by his servants who tell him that his little boy is now alive and well. On enquiring about the time of his son's recovery, he discovers that the fever left the previous day at the "seventh hour" (about 1 p.m.), the very time that Jesus had spoken to the father. As a result of this great healing, the father and all of his family and household come to faith in Christ.

Not long ago, a friend of mine was speaking at a conference on healing. The pastor hosting the event informed him that there was a man in his church suffering from terminal cancer and who was at death's door. The pastor drove him to the man's bedside. When my friend got there he found the man's family members around the bed saying goodbye. Not one of them was a Christian but they asked my friend to pray for their loved one. He agreed but before he did so he asked some questions. "If I pray for this man and he is healed, would that confirm to you that Jesus is real?" They all said yes. "If Jesus is real will you all put your faith and trust in him?" They said yes. So my friend prayed and within a few minutes the emaciated man was sitting up in bed, completely healed, and eating a good healthy meal. All his family saw the miracle and became Christians. The man made a full recovery.

What a great thing it is when something miraculous happens in someone's life and their whole family, seeing that only Jesus could have done this, comes to faith! Perhaps there is someone you know who needs a miracle, someone whose family is not saved. Pray for the Father to do something so miraculous that they and their whole household believe in Jesus.

Devotion: Dear loving, heavenly Abba, Father, I pray that you would move so powerfully in non-Christian homes on my street and in my town that whole families would come to believe in Jesus. Do today what you did in Cana 2,000 years ago, I pray, in Jesus' name. Amen.

> *Some time later, Jesus went up to Jerusalem for one of the*
> *Jewish festivals. Now there is in Jerusalem near the Sheep*
> *Gate a pool, which in Aramaic is called Bethesda and which is*
> *surrounded by five covered colonnades. Here a great number of*
> *disabled people used to lie – the blind, the lame, the paralyzed.*
>
> John 5:1–3

We now move from the rural settings of Samaria and Galilee to the bustling metropolis in Jerusalem. Jesus has gone up to the city for one of the Jewish feasts. This is very likely one of the three major annual festivals – Passover, Pentecost, or Tabernacles – which observant Jews would attend. John doesn't say which particular one it was. He is actually more interested in the specific place than the time. He locates the action that is about to follow at a pool near one of the city gates (the Sheep Gate). This he identifies as the Pool of Bethesda and he mentions a very precise detail – that the pool was surrounded by five colonnades. He adds that the sick used to lie around this pool, and he highlights three groups of people, the blind, the lame and the paralyzed.

Notice how detailed the description is here. It used to be said of this account that the place described didn't actually exist and that the author was simply writing fiction. But this sceptical view was completely rebuffed by the discovery of a pool answering this description by archaeologists in the nineteenth century. It was found – five colonnades and all – about 100 feet north-west of St Anne's church. This proved beyond doubt that the Pool of Bethesda was not a creation of the author but an actual, historical site.

Why am I mentioning this? It's because so many people have been sold the lie that the Gospel of John is a work of fiction that contains no valuable historical data. This is wrong. The findings of archaeology have consistently confirmed the reliability of John's reporting, and I believe will continue to do so.

So spend a few moments celebrating the great and glorious truth that the Christian faith is an historical faith. The story we are about to read really happened. The place existed and so did the people.

Devotion: *I worship you, Abba, Father, because you have made yourself known in a specific time and place in human history. You have come to us in Jesus – a real man who lived at a real time in a real place. Thank you that my faith is based on solid facts, in Jesus' name. Amen.*

One who was there had been an invalid for thirty-eight years.

John 5:5

You will notice in the NIV translation that a verse is missing between verse 3 and verse 5. The King James Version of the Bible, however, contains verse 4: "For an angel went down at a certain season into the pool, and troubled the water: whosoever then first after the troubling of the water stepped in was made whole of whatsoever disease he had." This gives the reason why so many blind, lame, and paralyzed people used to lie around the Pool of Bethesda.

Now at this pool there was a man who had been disabled for thirty-eight years. He was lying at a healing spa called "Bethesda" which means literally "House of Mercy" or "House of Grace". He is about to meet the source of all mercy and grace. He was seeking healing near the Sheep Gate in Jerusalem. He is about to be healed by the one who will later call himself the Gate through which his sheep, his followers, go in and out (John 10:7–9). He is hoping for an angel to bring about his healing. But he is about to meet the one to whom angels bow their knees and raise their voices in praise: Jesus, the Son of God and Word made flesh.

If you go to any high-street bookstore today you will find large numbers of non-Christian books on angels and other spiritual subjects. They are usually found in what are called the MBS section of a shop – Mind, Body, Spirit. Many non-Christians are searching for spiritual answers to life's questions and buy large numbers of these books. Indeed, MBS is now the best-selling genre of books after fiction. Some also attend spiritual workshops and retreats that promise them spiritual rebirth and healing. There is a profound longing for spiritual answers and spiritual experience among many today.

What people need more than any of these things is an encounter with Jesus. It is in Jesus alone that we find grace and mercy. It is in him that we find the true gateway to another world. It is in him that we find salvation, healing, and freedom. Don't seek an angel; seek Jesus. Don't seek the bling; seek the King!

Devotion: *Loving Father, I pray that you would help seekers to find in Jesus all that they are looking for. In the modern equivalents of Bethesda, wherever they are, I pray that seeking people would encounter Jesus and that they would find in you, Abba, their heart's true home. Amen.*

> **When Jesus saw him lying there and learned that he had been in this condition for a long time, he asked him, "Do you want to get well?"**
>
> John 5:6

The man who has been disabled for thirty-eight years is in for a surprise. For him it was just another day at the spa in Jerusalem. He was waiting for the waters to stir and hoping that somehow, in spite of his handicap, he would manage to dive into the water first. What he hadn't counted on was meeting Jesus.

Jesus looks around the pool and sees all the blind, lame, and paralyzed people lying within the colonnades that surrounded it. It is a sight of overwhelming need. Yet one man – and only one man – catches his attention. It is the man who has been paralyzed for nearly four decades. Jesus learns about his condition (John doesn't tell us how) and he goes to the man and asks him whether he wants to get well.

Now this at first sight is a very strange question. If the man has been waiting nearly forty years to be healed, surely he *wants* to get well. On the surface of things, that seems obvious. But Jesus sees beyond the surface of things. At the end of John chapter 2 we learned that Jesus didn't need anyone else's testimony about a person because he knew by divine revelation what was in each person. That applies here also.

What did Jesus see in this man's heart that led him to ask such a question? I believe he saw that the man had become dependant on his disability; that his disability had become so much a part of his life that his identity was now inextricably tied up with it. In a strange way maybe even his security was too. Jesus saw all this and therefore asked, "Do you actually *want* to be healed?"

I have met people like this – people who are deeply ambivalent about being healed. They hang out where healing prayer is offered but there is a part of them that has grown accustomed to their condition and so they won't let go of it. Maybe you are like this too. Maybe Jesus is asking, "Do you really want to get well?"

Devotion: *Abba, Father, I pray that I may always answer yes to the question, 'Do you want to be healed?' Whether this healing is spiritual, emotional, mental, or physical, my answer to your overtures of love is a resounding, "Yes, Lord. Make me well!" in Jesus' name. Amen.*

"Sir," the invalid replied, "I have no one to help me into the pool when the water is stirred. While I am trying to get in, someone else goes down ahead of me." Then Jesus said to him, "Get up! Pick up your mat and walk." At once the man was cured; he picked up his mat and walked.

John 5:7–9

Today is an extraordinary day as I write this. One of our best-selling, secular newspapers in the UK (The Daily Mail) has an article about a miracle that occurred this year in a church in the USA. The lady who was healed is called Delia Knox. She was badly hurt in a car accident over twenty years ago and has had no feeling in her legs since. She has been in a wheelchair for that time and thought that she would never walk again. Then, at a meeting this year in a church in Alabama, she received prayer for healing and while she was being prayed for she heard the Holy Spirit say to her, "Get up." For the first time in over two decades, feeling came back into her legs and she had the faith to get up and walk around the auditorium. Now she can walk. Her husband said, "What has happened to my wife has changed our lives." The headline in the newspaper read, "It's a miracle! After twenty-three years in a wheelchair, woman walks again and says it's all down to spiritual healing" (22 December 2010).

The Bible tells us that Jesus is "the same yesterday, today and forever" (Hebrews 13:8). Two thousand years ago he came to a man who had been paralyzed for thirty-eight years and told him to get up and walk. And he did. In the year 2010, Jesus spoke to a woman who had been in a wheelchair for twenty-three years and said, "Get up and walk." And she did. Tomorrow, as the sick are prayed for all over the world and Jesus says, "Get up and walk," people will be rising up and walking.

Our reading today tells us that when Jesus spoke the words, "Get up! Pick up your mat and walk", that the man's disability was completely and instantly healed and that he picked up his mat and walked.

Maybe Jesus is saying this to you today. Maybe he is speaking a word of great authority and freedom of your life. "It's time to get up. It's time to walk again. Be healed. Be free."

Devotion: *Abba, Father, I pray that right now you would remove whatever is afflicting me in my life. Whether it is a physical or a non-physical ailment, I don't want it any longer. I want to rise up and be free from it. So I pray in faith for your freedom, in Jesus' name. Amen.*

> *The day on which this took place was a Sabbath, and so the Jews said to the man who had been healed, "It is the Sabbath; the law forbids you to carry your mat."*
>
> John 5:9–10 (NIV)

We might expect there to have been a great celebration when the man was healed of his thirty-eight-year disability. Not a bit of it! As soon as he starts walking around with his mat in his hand some Jewish people start criticizing him. They tell him that he is breaking the rules of the sabbath by carrying his bed in public.

Who were "the Jews" that chastised the healed man? Most likely "the Jews" is shorthand for Jewish leaders in Jerusalem who were hostile to Jesus. They were almost certainly the Pharisees who prided themselves on being the people who observed the requirements of the Law more faithfully than anyone else. These same Pharisees had developed the biblical commandment about keeping the sabbath day holy into hundreds of minute rules that were never intended by the Father. In particular, they had taken some words from Jeremiah 17:21–22 about not bearing a burden on the sabbath day and had created many very precise religious regulations out of it. Some of these were nothing short of nit-picking in the extreme. For example, they argued that it was even unlawful for a man to carry a needle in his robe on the sabbath day. That being the case, carrying a mat would have been a very obvious infringement of the laws of the sabbath for people with such a mindset.

It is people of this kind who pick on the newly healed man. It is not Jews in general because Jesus is Jewish, as is the man who has just been miraculously healed. It is Pharisees whose religion decreed that this man should be stoned to death because he was carrying something from a public place to a private home. Now the poor man is in a worse state than before! Up to the point he met Jesus he was disabled at the pool. Now he's met Jesus he could be stoned to death!

Who ever said that meeting Jesus was a passport to a life of ease? In many cases it is a passport to controversy.

Devotion: *Dear loving, heavenly Abba, Father, I want to thank you so much that knowing Jesus is infinitely worthwhile. I want you to know that even though at times this means I have to face difficulty and controversy, this is better than living without you, in Jesus' name. Amen.*

> *So, because Jesus was doing these things on the Sabbath, the Jewish leaders began to persecute him. In his defence Jesus said to them, "My Father is always at his work to this very day, and I too am working." For this reason the Jews tried all the harder to kill him; not only was he breaking the Sabbath, but he was even calling God his own Father, making himself equal with God.*

> John 5:16–18

In John 5, opposition to Jesus intensifies as some Jews in Jerusalem begin to persecute him. John has already told us in his prologue that Jesus came to his own people (i.e. the Jewish people) and that they did not receive him (John 1:11). Now we see this vividly demonstrated as some of his contemporaries begin to attack him. In fact, it says in our passage for today that they tried even harder to kill him. Why was this?

The answer lies in the statement that Jesus makes when he justifies his healing of the man on a sabbath day. He says, "My Father is always at his work to this very day, and I, too, am working." This is an absolutely momentous claim. Not only is he calling God "My Father" (the first of twenty-four occasions in John's Gospel when he does this). He is also effectively saying, "God didn't stop working on the sabbath day; I am working on the sabbath day; therefore God and I are one."

It seems that one of the things that really angered the opponents of Jesus was his claim that God was his Father. The word Jesus would have used was *Abba*, an intimate term that can be translated "Dad", "Daddy", or "Papa". Jesus was claiming to have a special filial relationship with God. He was claiming by implication to be the Father's Son. This was the reason for him defending his healing of the paralyzed man; he healed the man on the sabbath day because this was what his Father was doing.

What we see in this passage is the utter irreconcilability of relationship and religion. Jesus stands for those who want to call God "My Abba", who want to relate to God in a child–Father way. Jesus' enemies stand for those who want to worship a remote God and relate to him in a slave–Master way. Relationship and religion are incompatible. We must learn to relate to God as Abba's child.

Devotion: *I thank you, Abba, Father, that Jesus came to this earth to lead us away from lifeless religion into an intimate relationship with the world's greatest Dad. I want to stand for relationship over religion. Draw me close to you today. Help me to know you as "My Abba". Amen.*

Jesus gave them this answer: "Very truly I tell you, the Son can do nothing by himself; he can do only what he sees his Father doing, because whatever the Father does the Son also does. For the Father loves the Son and shows him all he does."

John 5:19–20

One of the most life-changing experiences I have had as a Christian was in 1985 when I went to hear John Wimber speak at the City Hall in Sheffield. One of the things that he taught us there was the central importance of John 5:19 for understanding the ministry of Jesus. Here Jesus says that he only ever does what he sees Abba, Father doing. The healing of the man at the pool of Bethesda immediately precedes this statement. Wimber showed us that there were many people who were ill at the spa in Jerusalem but that Jesus only healed one of them. This was because Jesus did what the Father was doing and the Father restricted his healing to this one man. Wimber then went on to say that this was the keynote of Jesus' life and it should be the keynote of ours too. We should only seek to do what Abba Father is doing, especially when it comes to praying for the sick.

John Wimber highlighted the wellspring of Jesus' life – intimacy with the Father. The relational unity between the Father and the Son was so profound that the Son only ever said what he heard his Father saying; he only ever did what he saw his Father doing. Indeed, Jesus said that the Son couldn't do anything without his Father. He said that his Father loved him as his Son and showed him everything that he did.

Many of us spend our whole lives asking our Father to bless the thing that we have found ourselves doing. Jesus shows us a different way. Jesus shows us the importance of finding out what the Father is doing and blessing that.

Those of us who are adopted sons and daughters need to be more like the natural Son. We need to be a people who give up trying to show the Father our ministry, and instead let the Father show us his.

Devotion: *Dear loving, heavenly Abba, Father, today I want to say something quite simple but very heartfelt. It is this. I want to be more like Jesus. I want to live in such an intimate relationship with you that I can truly say that I only do what you're doing, in Jesus' name. Amen.*

"Very truly I tell you, whoever hears my word and believes him who sent me has eternal life and will not be judged but has crossed over from death to life."

John 5:24

After the healing of the man at the pool of Bethesda, the remainder of John chapter 5 is taken up with Jesus' response to his questioners. This response takes the form of a long discourse or section of teaching. This is one of the distinctive features of John's Gospel – the way some episodes are followed by long teaching. If you look at John chapter 5 you will see how this works. The chapter begins with the healing at the pool (verses 1–15). The rest of the chapter concentrates on the words of Jesus, mainly in response to his relentless and aggressive questioners.

In the run-up to John 5:24, Jesus tells his listeners that the Father has entrusted the task of judgment to his Son. Now, in verse 24, he tells his opponents what they must do if they want to escape condemnation. He begins with the words "I tell you the truth" (or "Very truly I tell you" in the TNIV). In the original, this is "Amen, Amen", an expression that Jesus uses fifty-one times during the course of this Gospel. Whenever Jesus begins a statement with this phrase it is intended to add emphasis and gravitas to what follows.

Jesus tells his listeners that they will only escape judgment if they listen to what he says and believe in him who sent him. The one who sent Jesus is the Father. Jesus' challenge to his listeners is to put their trust in the one whom Jesus reveals, Abba Father. If they do this they will receive eternal life. Indeed, they will have crossed over from death to life.

I became a Christian in 1977. My testimony is that I was walking down a street when I heard these words in my heart: "Mark Stibbe, if you died tonight, where would you stand before the judgment seat of God?" At that moment I knew that I stood condemned because of my rebellious, sinful life so I knelt down with a friend, repented of my sins, and put my trust in Jesus. When I did that, I was no longer under judgment; I was pardoned. I was no longer spiritually dead; I was alive! That was the best thing that ever happened to me.

Devotion: *Loving Father, I thank you so much that you have made a bridge from death to life. Thank you that all we have to do to cross it is to believe in Jesus and then we will avoid condemnation and live forever with you. I reaffirm my faith in you today, in Jesus' name. Amen.*

"I seek not to please myself but him who sent me."

John 5:30

This is one of those little remarks with big meaning. They come thick and fast in the long teaching sections of John's Gospel and you can easily miss them if you read too quickly.

Here Jesus tells his listeners that he isn't at all concerned about what they think of him or indeed about their expectations of him. He doesn't live for their approval. He lives to please the one who sent him.

This phrase "the one who sent me" is another way of saying "My Father". Jesus seeks only to please the Father – his Abba in heaven, his Daddy. He is not a man pleaser. He doesn't seek the acceptance and applause of those around him. His only desire is to ensure that he lives his life in such a way that his Father is always pleased with him. Living under the Father's smile and enjoying his Father's pleasure is the great goal of Jesus' life. All lesser ambitions are eclipsed by this one supreme, over-riding dream – to bring pride and joy to the heart of Abba, Father.

I don't know about you, but one of the things I have found hardest during my life is combating the tendency to please people. All this probably stems from an insecurity that in turn has its roots in being abandoned by my biological father. Too often in my life, especially in the days when I was leading churches, I tried to keep everyone happy. Pretty quickly I learned the truth of the old cliché that you can only please some of the people some of the time; you can never please all the people all the time. How liberating it has been to change my focus and to live to please my Father rather than the people I've been called to influence.

This was how Jesus was living as he said these words in John 5:30 and he is modelling it even as he is saying it. He is not seeking to please them. He is only seeking to please his Father by sticking to what his Father wants him to say! His focus is the will, desire, pleasure and longing of his Abba. Ours needs to be too.

Devotion: *Abba, Father, I ask that you would set me free from any insecurities in my life that make me want to please people rather than please you. Heal the wounds at the core of this tendency and help me to care only about what brings you pleasure, in Jesus' name. Amen.*

"... he has given him authority to judge because he is the Son of Man."

John 5:27

Hundreds of years before Jesus was born, God raised up a man called Daniel in Babylon (modern Iraq). Along with 50,000 other Jewish people, Daniel was in exile. Jerusalem had been sacked and the Temple destroyed by the Babylonians. God's people were now languishing in a foreign land, desperate to go home to Judah.

While Daniel was serving the kings of Babylon, he had many visions and dreams. One of his most powerful is described in Daniel 7:13–14: "In my vision at night I looked, and there before me was one like a son of man, coming with the clouds of heaven. He approached the Ancient of Days and was led into his presence. He was given authority, glory and sovereign power; all peoples, nations and men of every language worshiped him. His dominion is an everlasting dominion that will not pass away, and his kingdom is one that will never be destroyed."

Six hundred years later, the Jewish people are back in Judah and Jerusalem. Jesus of Nazareth is walking among them and is now engaged in heated debate with those who will not believe in him. He warns them that his Father in heaven has given him authority to judge because he is "the Son of Man".

It seems most likely that Jesus understood himself to be the one like a son of man mentioned in Daniel 7:13, who is given authority to rule over the nations by the "Ancient of Days" (i.e. by his Father). Jesus knew that one day all the peoples of the earth will worship him and that his kingdom will go on forever.

This is so encouraging for those who have put their trust in Christ. Religious leaders come and go but Jesus remains forever. They are sons of men. He is the Son of Man.

Human institutions come and go but what Jesus began will last for eternity. This is because human institutions are human inventions. What Jesus inaugurated was the kingdom of God!

Devotion: *I thank you, Abba, Father, for giving your Son authority to judge. I thank you that Jesus is the Son of Man who has authority to rule the nations. I thank you that one day every knee will bow before him and confess that Jesus Christ is Lord! Amen.*

"If I testify about myself, my testimony is not valid. There is another who testifies in my favour, and I know that his testimony about me is valid."

John 5:31–32 (NIV)

Jesus now begins to talk about those who testify on his behalf. Right at the start of the list he mentions another who testifies in his favour, whose testimony about him is impeccable. He is referring here to his Father in heaven. Jesus' Father is the first to defend his Son's integrity.

One of my favourite theologians was a man called John McLeod Campbell. I love his writings not because everything he said was flawless but because he was a man who really understood the Father heart of God. He was a man who knew the vital importance of helping believers to leave their orphan state behind and to enter into their position as sons and daughters through the Spirit of adoption.

Sadly, Campbell was harassed by the church denomination into which he had been ordained. They wanted him to preach and write about a far more severe and angry God. They wanted him to be more legal in his language and less relational. But he refused and so was brought before an ecclesiastical court where he was tried and then stripped of his ordination and his ministry.

Perhaps the most moving moment in his trial was when his father turned up to bear witness to his son's character. John had been brought up by a devoted and very loving father. Indeed, looking back on this childhood, he said that it was his father's love that had made him so acutely aware of the love of his heavenly Father. As John's father stood in the court, he declared, "While I live, I will never be ashamed to be the father of so holy and blameless a son. Indeed, in this respect, I challenge anyone in this house to bring forward anyone who can come into competition with him." What a dad! No wonder John McLeod Campbell had such a unique understanding of Abba, Father's love!

Jesus says that the first person to come and testify on behalf of his character and credentials is his Father. The same is true for us as well.

Devotion: *Dear loving, heavenly Father, I thank you that we do not face the trials of life alone, but that you are with us. You are by our side and you are on our side, especially when the forces of this world are raging against us. Thank you for your supportive, protective love. Amen.*

"John was a lamp that burned and gave light, and you chose for a time to enjoy his light."

John 5:35

In Jesus' list of those who testify in his defence he adds the name of John the Baptist. As he does so he uses this magnificent picture of John as a burning lamp which illuminated his surroundings. He tells his accusers that they basked in the Baptist's light while it was shining.

I can't think of any better description of a child of God than "a lamp that burns and gives light". This should be the ambition and the dream for our whole lives: that we would be filled with the holy flame of Abba, Father's love and that we would light up the lives of the people around us.

I don't know about you, but this verse challenges me. It challenges me to ask the question, "How bright am I shining for Jesus?" I think every one of us needs to take a luminosity test from time to time. We should honestly assess the impact of our lives on others.

The origin of the Olympic Games gives us a helpful picture. In its earliest form the Games consisted of a very long race in which the competitors had to run over fields, through valleys, across rivers, and up and down mountains. The race was called the *milos* – from which we get the word "mile".

The most interesting thing about the race was that every runner had to carry a lit torch. The person who won the race was not necessarily the first person to get to the finishing line. The winner was the first person to cross the line with their torch still burning.

John the Baptist was a torchbearer for Jesus. He shone right up to the end of his life, which may have been imminent when Jesus uttered these words in John 5:35. John the Baptist ran the race and finished well. His torch was still burning as he crossed the line.

Let's be so filled with the fire of Abba's love that we are both inextinguishable and irrepressible. Don't let your heart grow cold. Ask the Father to light the fire again in your heart today.

Devotion: *Abba, Father, I pray for the holy flame of your love today. I don't want to be a flickering candle. I want to be a burning lamp. I don't want to shed a little light. I want to spread your light far and wide. I want others to be drawn to the light of Jesus in me. Amen.*

> **"For the works that the Father has given me to finish – the very works that I am doing – testify that the Father has sent me."**
>
> John 5:36

Jesus was acutely aware that he had been given a unique assignment by his Father in heaven. This assignment he referred to as the work that Abba had given him to finish. In the story of the woman of Samaria in John 4, Jesus had used this phrase when the disciples had returned from Sychar and asked him to eat something. He said "My food is to do the will of him who sent me and to finish his work" (John 4:34).

The word "work" is used twenty-seven times in John's Gospel. Sometimes it refers to the works or the deeds of human beings (as in John 3:19–21). Sometimes it refers to the miraculous works that Jesus performed during his ministry (as in John 14:10–12). On other occasions it is used to refer to the work or the purpose that the Father had given Jesus – the work of coming into the world to save human beings. John 5:36 and 4:34 are examples of this use of the word.

Each one of us has a unique assignment given to us by our heavenly Father and we are all called to find this overarching plan for our lives. Sometimes the work the Father is calling us to is something that we are meant to embrace within our paid work, whatever that may be. Sometimes our paid work becomes the means by which we can achieve the greater purpose for our lives. Our work (small "w") can be either the vehicle or the support for our Work (big "W").

Whether the Father's assignment is within our work or funded and facilitated by our work the important thing is for us to embrace our mandate and indeed to complete it. Finishing well should be one of the great objectives of our lives. It is of course one thing to start. It is quite another thing to finish. And the old saying is true – the world is full of good starters but not as full of good finishers.

Why not ask today for greater revelation concerning your unique assignment? And in addition, for the motivation to finish well.

Devotion: *Abba, Father, I thank you that your Son knew very clearly the assignment that you had entrusted to him. Help me to understand better the nature of your entrustment to me and help me not to be distracted by enticements but to stay the course and finish the task. Amen.*

"You have never heard his voice nor seen his form, nor does his word dwell in you, for you do not believe the one he sent."

John 5:37–38

Jesus now gets confrontational with his accusers. He tells them that they have never heard the Father's voice nor seen the Father's form. They have never heard God speak to them as a loving Father nor have they ever seen his face. He, on the other hand, has both heard and seen. He has come from heaven, and heaven, as I shared in a previous study, is the atmosphere of the Father's presence and love. Jesus had lived in that realm from before the foundation of the world and in that realm he had always heard the Father speaking directly to him and had gazed upon the beauty of his face. Even now, in his incarnate life as a human being, Jesus hears his Father's voice and sees his Father's form. Jesus lives in such an intimate relationship with the Father that he knows what the Father is saying and he even knows what the Father looks like. To use the beautiful phrase of John Owen, the "Prince of the Puritans", Jesus enjoys "immediate communion with the Father in love". His accusers, on the other hand, do not.

Jesus says that the proof that they don't know the Father is the fact that his word does not dwell in them and they have failed to believe the one he sent. If the Father's word had made its home in their hearts they would have responded positively to Jesus. They would have known immediately that he was the Father's Son and they would have chosen to believe in him. But they did not. They reacted in a hostile way and they refused to put their trust in Jesus.

There are two key words in John 5:37–38 – "voice" and "word". Word is *logos* in the original. Voice is *phonē*, from which we get the word phonetic. Jesus teaches in this passage that it is possible to hear the Father's voice and to know the Father's word. Put another way, we can enjoy "immediate communion with the Father in love" by positioning ourselves to hear him speak to us through both prophecy and Scripture. By eagerly desiring the gift of prophecy, and faithfully reading the Bible, we can hear the Father speaking to us today.

Devotion: *Abba, Father, I don't want to be like the enemies of Jesus. I want to be a friend of Jesus. I want to be someone who hears you prophetically and who knows what you're saying to me in the Scriptures. Open my ears today, I pray, in Jesus' name. Amen.*

> *You study the Scriptures diligently because you think that in them you possess eternal life. These are the very Scriptures that testify about me, yet you refuse to come to me to have life.*
>
> John 5:39–40

It is one thing to read the Bible. It is quite another thing to understand it. For most people, the Bible is a dusty old book with printed words on a page. But to those who have been born again, the words on the pages of the Bible are luminous. To those who have eyes to see, the Bible is the Father's illuminating truth. It is revelation not just information.

The people Jesus was talking to in John 5 searched the Scriptures diligently. They worked very hard at investigating the Old Testament in its original language but in spite of all this industry they didn't understand the Scriptures because they didn't accept Jesus. The words of the Old Testament pointed to Jesus. The prophecies of the coming Messiah in the Old Testament are fulfilled in Jesus and in him alone. Jesus is accordingly the key that unlocks the treasures of the Hebrew Bible. Without Jesus, the treasures remain hidden in the darkness. With Jesus, everything begins to make sense because the Scriptures testify to him.

This book, *Every Day with the Father* was published in 2011. The year 2011 was very special one for the Bible because it was the 400th anniversary of the publication of the King James Version of the Bible in 1611. This translation of the Scriptures has had an immense and incalculable impact on Western culture. Many people are celebrating its influence.

While this is welcome, it is important to help people to see that you cannot truly understand the Bible unless you believe in Jesus. When you are born again you fall in love with the one who is the author and the subject of the Bible. When that happens, you find that the Scriptures speak to you personally not just academically.

Studying the Scriptures is a vital spiritual discipline. More of us need to take it seriously. But our study only really benefits us when we know the Lord of the Book, not just the Book of the Lord.

Devotion: *Abba, Father, give me a fresh love for your written Word, the Bible. Help me to be someone who studies it faithfully and enable me always to do this relationally not just intellectually. Help me to hear you speaking to me personally through its pages, in Jesus' name. Amen.*

"I do not accept praise from men... "

John 5:41 (NIV)

I remember when I was helping to lead a church in the north of England. I was very involved in the Sunday evening service, which was attended by 500 to 600 people. I worked so hard to impress them during my early days there. I slaved away on my sermon preparation and did everything I could in my presentation to make them like me. I was extremely driven by the need for their approval and applause.

Then one Sunday evening I was in the middle of my talk when I suddenly had to stop. It was like a cone of light had come down from the ceiling and enveloped me. I was literally bathing in a golden glow for several seconds. While there I heard my heavenly Father speak to me – not audibly but in my heart. He told me that he really loved me and that he also really liked me.

That experience completely transformed my perspective. When I eventually realized that there were a lot of people wondering why I had stopped speaking, I said something like this: "Oh, I'm really sorry about that. I've just had the most amazing experience of the Father's unconditional acceptance of me and I now realize that I'm completely free of the need for your praise." With that there was an eruption of applause. Everyone cheered and clapped. At the very moment when I didn't need their praise any more, they gave it!

In John 5:41 Jesus tells his listeners that he does not accept man's praise. What he means by that is that he simply doesn't accept, receive or welcome the flattery or adulation of human beings. He is totally free from either the need or the desire for that. The only praise he loves is his Father's praise.

As the adopted children of a perfect Father we need to be free from the need to be praised and applauded. The only thing that really matters is that the Father loves us, likes us and is proud of us. May this be more than enough for us today.

Devotion: *Abba, Father, I thank you that it is quite simply enough to know that you are proud of me and that you love me dearly. Help me not to be driven by the need to succeed, the need to be needed, the need to be valued. Help me to find all I need in you, in Jesus' name. Amen.*

"I know that you do not have the love of God in your hearts."

John 5:42

Jesus tells his listeners that the reason they are being so hostile to him is because they don't have God's love in their hearts.

How does a person come to the point where they have the Father's love in them?

There are two main steps: believing and receiving.

The first step is to believe that Jesus is the Father's Son and that through his death on the Cross our sins can be forgiven and our hearts can find their true home in God's love. This step involves admitting that you are a sinner and confessing that Jesus has come to save you from your sins.

The second step is to receive the Holy Spirit. Now it's important to understand that the Holy Spirit must already be at work within your heart if you have repented of your sins and put your trust in Jesus. It is simply not possible to do these things without the help of the Holy Spirit. At the same time, believing in Jesus leads to us receiving the Holy Spirit and this is not just something that we acknowledge in our heads. It is something we experience in our hearts. God's love is shed abroad in our hearts by the power of the Holy Spirit when we choose to believe in Jesus. The Holy Spirit gives us the right to become the adopted children of God. The Spirit of adoption wells up within our hearts as we cry *Abba, Father* to God. And the Holy Spirit bears witness to our spirits that we are the adopted children of God.

If you have never done either of these things, can I recommend that you do that now? Choose to believe that Jesus died for your sins. Then ask for your Father to fill your heart with his divine love. Ask for your heart to be captured by the Father's extraordinary affection. Pray for an experiential not just an intellectual faith.

Jesus told his contemporaries in John 5 that the Father's love was not in their hearts. May he never say that of us.

Devotion: *Abba, Father, I choose today to reaffirm my faith in your Son Jesus Christ as the Saviour of the World and the Lord of all. Please pour out your Spirit afresh and help me to receive a new measure of the Spirit of adoption in my heart, in Jesus' name I pray. Amen.*

Then Jesus went up on a mountainside and sat down with his disciples. The Jewish Passover Feast was near.

John 6:3–4

At the end of John chapter 5 we were in Jerusalem and Jesus was defending himself against religious leaders who were accusing him of making himself equal with the Father. Now in John 6 Jesus has gone north into the Galilean countryside. He goes up a mountain and sits down with his disciples. After the hurry, noise, and crowds of the city he makes room for some down time with his closest followers and friends.

John tells us that it is Passover time. There are hundreds of thousands of people making their way to Jerusalem to celebrate the festival. Passover takes place in spring, usually April time, and so the winter rains are over. Flowers are beginning to emerge and the sun is shining again. Jesus relaxes with his disciples away from the demands of the people and breathes in the clean air on the mountaintop.

We can learn so much from Jesus here. He models the Father's blueprint for a healthy life. No one else in history has had the responsibilities, mandate, and pressures that Jesus of Nazareth had. Yet he never at any point comes across as anything or anyone else than the Prince of Peace. Jesus lives from a serene centre. He enjoys and exhibits the Father's *shalom*.

If we are to emulate Jesus we will need to develop boundaries in our lives. It is essential that you and I learn to work from a place of rest, as Jesus did. For that to happen we need to do what Jesus did – spend time taking in the great outdoors, hanging out with friends who energize rather than enervate us, and give ourselves permission to dial down and have fun.

If it was important for the Son of God to do these things, then it is important for the adopted sons and daughters too.

We are not called human *doings*; we are called human *beings*. Perhaps today you need to learn to *be* not just *do*.

Devotion: *Loving heavenly Father, I pray that you will teach me the rhythms of life as you understand them. Help me to take time aside to walk up mountains and sit down with friends. Keep me from living a frenetic and unhealthy life. Enable me to walk at a different pace. Amen.*

When Jesus looked up and saw a great crowd coming toward him, he said to Philip, "Where shall we buy bread for these people to eat?" He asked this only to test him, for he already had in mind what he was going to do.

John 6:5–6

One of my dearest friends is fond of saying this: "When God asks you a question, it's not because he wants information!"

That's so true if you think about it for a moment. There are three things we can say about Abba, Father. First, he is omnipotent – which means he's all-powerful. Second, he is omnipresent – he is present everywhere in his creation. Third, he is omniscient – he knows everything and he sees everything.

One of the things that John is clear about is this: Jesus of Nazareth is not just a great teacher and a great prophet. He is also God. Jesus is God in human flesh. He is the human face of *Yahweh*, the I am. Those who see Jesus, see the Father.

That being the case, when Jesus asks Philip where they are going to get enough food to feed the thousands, he doesn't ask because he doesn't know! John makes this plain. He adds an aside to the reader to say that Jesus already knew the answer. He was asking in order to see how Philip would respond.

I expect at this point Philip was baffled. He came from this same region (Bethsaida) and would have known where the local shops were. But this is a huge number of people and it's very short notice! There doesn't seem to be any obvious, practical, immediate solution.

There are times when the Father asks us things and when he does it is not for information. Very often it is to test us to see whether we will try and fall back on the flesh or rely totally on the Spirit. In these situations we need to remember that our comprehension is not a prerequisite for our cooperation. We simply need to make sure that our response is one of faith not unbelief.

Devotion: *Abba, Father, I worship you because you are all-knowing; you see and understand all things. When you ask something of me, help me to remember that you are looking for a faith response not for information. Help me to respond well in these life-defining moments. Amen.*

Philip answered him, "It would take almost a year's wages to buy enough bread for each one to have a bite!"

John 6:7

I wonder if you have bad memories, as I do, of giving a foolish answer to a question put to you by a teacher at school. It is not a very pleasant experience when you find that you've missed the point entirely. You can feel embarrassed. You can even feel foolish.

I am sure that Jesus never intended that Philip would feel this way, but I am equally certain that Philip did feel foolish when he answered Jesus' question about where the lunch was coming from with a lame comment about the bill for the picnic.

What was Jesus looking for from Philip here? He was looking for a response of faith. Faith is believing in something even when you can't see it. Faith is believing that something is coming to you *before* you see it.

If faith is choosing to believe even when you cannot see something, the reward of faith is eventually seeing what you've chosen to believe. The world says, "I'll believe it when I see it." The follower of Jesus says, "I'll see it when I believe it."

Philip couldn't see with his human eyes how food could be bought at a moment's notice to feed a multitude of 5,000 men (and probably a greater number of women and children too). Instead of responding with faith, he reacted with folly.

It is all too easy to look at the size of a challenge and default to a fleshly perspective. But what Jesus is looking for in us is faith. He doesn't want us to go to the Father and tell him how big our problem is. He wants us to go the problem and declare how big our Father is.

Maybe you have a great challenge today. Remember what Jesus was seeking to find in Philip. Don't react with folly. Respond with faith. Believe that God is bigger than your biggest problem and that you'll be able to find in him the answer to what you're facing.

Devotion: *Dearest Father, whenever I am faced with a seemingly impossible challenge, I want to commit today to responding with faith not reacting with folly. Thank you that you are far bigger than my greatest difficulty and that nothing is too hard for you, in Jesus' name. Amen.*

> *Another of his disciples, Andrew, Simon Peter's brother, spoke up, "Here is a boy with five small barley loaves and two small fish, but how far will they go among so many?"*
>
> John 6:8-9

Of all the disciples who followed Jesus, Andrew is one of my favourites. He first appears in John chapter 1. When we encounter him there we see him finding his brother Simon, telling him about Jesus, then bringing him to meet Jesus. When we studied that passage earlier in this book we celebrated the way Andrew brought someone to Jesus.

Here in the story of the feeding of the 5,000 we see Andrew doing the same thing again. Jesus has asked Philip where they are going to buy food to feed the multitude. Philip has not answered that question well, as we saw yesterday. Now Andrew steps in and brings a boy to Jesus. Once again Andrew is the man who brings people to Jesus.

In this instant, the boy has his packed lunch of five barley loaves and two small fish. John is very specific here. The bread was made of barley. This was the cheapest kind of bread in Israel. It was bought and eaten by the poor and was disdained by the rich. In addition, the boy has two fish – small pickled fish from the Sea of Galilee.

The boy has brought his packed lunch (no doubt lovingly supplied by his mother) in his long walk to meet Jesus. Now this same boy willingly hands over his meal. He doesn't hold on tightly to what he has but gives it all away.

There is a lot we could say about this one moment in the story but I'd like to focus on this one thought – that it was a young person who became the catalyst to the great miracle that followed.

In John 4 it was the woman of Samaria who kick-started a mighty move of God. Here in Galilee it is a young person. See how the Father takes hold of ordinary and unlikely people and uses them to bring about his mighty purposes. Pray for young people today to rise up with their loaves and fishes to see miracles and feed the hungry.

Devotion: *Abba, Father, I thank you for the willingness of this boy to let go of the little that he had so that you could do a great miracle. Raise up a revival generation of children and young people who will be agents of a mighty move of God in the world, in Jesus' name. Amen.*

Jesus said, "Have the people sit down." There was plenty of grass in that place, and they sat down (about five thousand men were there). Jesus then took the loaves, gave thanks, and distributed to those who were seated as much as they wanted. He did the same with the fish.

John 6:10–11

One of the great joys of being a dad is sitting down with your family, giving thanks to God for the gift of food, and then seeing everyone fed and satisfied.

This is exactly what happens here. Jesus behaves like a dad at a Jewish meal. He sets up a huge, metaphorical table out in the open air under the spring sunshine. He asks everyone to sit. He then takes hold of the five barley loaves and the two pickled fish from the boy's picnic basket and gives thanks using the traditional *berakah* or prayer of blessing: "Blessed are you, O Lord our God, King of the universe, who brings forth bread from the earth for us to eat." He then shares the food around and everyone is miraculously fed – 5,000 men and many women and children too (as the boy's presence here confirms). John tells us that they all have as much as they want.

I remember a long time ago watching a film called *Viva Christo Rey*, which means "Christ the King lives!". It was a true story about a charismatic church situated near the poorest of the poor in a city on the border of Mexico and Texas. The leader of the church was very challenged by reading some words of Jesus in Luke's Gospel about hospitality. Jesus teaches in Luke 14:12–14 that his followers are called to be very radical in this area. They are called to have meals for people who could never invite them back.

Reading this, the pastor and his people took a truck to the rubbish dumps. They didn't have enough food to give to the 300 hungry people that came. But Abba, Father multiplied what they had so that everyone had as much as they wanted.

What a generous, caring, miracle-working Dad we have!

Devotion: *Abba, Father, I thank you for all that I see of you in Jesus' feeding of the 5,000. I thank you for all I see of you in the church that went and fed the hungry on a rubbish dump. Help me to excel in mercy so that I too will see miracles of provision for the poor. Amen.*

> *When they had all had enough to eat, he said to his disciples,*
> *"Gather the pieces that are left over. Let nothing be wasted." So*
> *they gathered them and filled twelve baskets with the pieces of*
> *the five barley loaves left over by those who had eaten.*
>
> John 6:12–13

The bread and the fish have been miraculously multiplied and now the thousands of people are satisfied. Actually, the word translated "had enough" is one that should really be rendered "eaten until they were completely full". It is the word used in Luke 1:53 of the one who "filled the hungry with good things". Now Jesus tells his disciples to gather up all the remaining food so that nothing is wasted. When they do so, they fill twelve baskets.

Now you have to ask the question, where did the twelve baskets come from? There can only really be one answer. They came from the twelve disciples. These twelve men had come to the mountain carrying their own picnics. Jewish men always travelled with baskets. They were bottle-necked in shape. The sight of them was so common that the Roman writer Juvenal talked of "the Jew with his basket". The twelve baskets must have originally belonged to the twelve disciples.

If that is the case, then the disciples must have eaten their lunches before Jesus asked Philip where they were going to get the money to buy enough food to feed the crowd. In the event, the disciples were guilty of putting their own needs before the needs of others. Maybe they even sensed what was coming and that they might be asked to share their meals. The folly of this way of thinking is exposed by the sight of their baskets being filled after everyone has been fed.

How does a person live in a constant state of abundance? The answer is supplied by this hypothetical reconstruction of the mystery of the twelve baskets. If this is right then the key to living under the ongoing and extreme generosity of the Father is to keep giving away what he gives you! If we empty our baskets in the service of others, then Abba, Father will make sure that our baskets are constantly full!

Devotion: *Loving, generous Father, my prayer today is that you would help me not to hold on like an orphan to what I have but rather to be like a trusting child of the King of Kings, to give away generously what I have received from you, in Jesus' name. Amen.*

After the people saw the sign that Jesus performed, they began to say, "Surely this is the Prophet who is to come into the world." Jesus, knowing that they intended to come and make him king by force, withdrew again to a mountain by himself.

John 6:14–15

In Deuteronomy 18:15, Moses had said this to the Israelites: "The Lord your God will raise up for you a prophet like me from among your own brothers. You must listen to him." By the time Jesus began his ministry, there was a longing among many first-century Jews for the appearance of a prophet who would be like Moses. He would deliver them from the oppression of Roman rule in the land of Israel.

When Jesus multiplied the loaves and the fishes, the people began to discuss who he really was. They decided that he must be the prophet foretold in Deuteronomy 18:15. If they could crown Jesus king, then he would gain a strong enough following to mount a real challenge to the occupying army of Rome. Finally they would be delivered from the yoke of the unclean *goyim,* the pagans.

But this was not Jesus' way. He had come to save his people, yes. Even his name – *Yeshua* – hinted at that, for it means salvation. But the manner of this salvation was not through the use of violence and force. Quite the opposite, in fact; Jesus would eventually save his people by absorbing violence and force on the Cross. Jesus would deliver us not by being a perpetrator of violence but by being the victim of it – not by killing but by being killed.

Jesus withdraws from the crowd here because his way is not the way of the zealot or the bandit. It is not the way of the general or the gladiator. His way is the Father's way.

There is a warning to all of us in this: we must always take great care that we don't try to harness Jesus to our own schemes and methods. Our task is not to try and force him to do our will. Rather it is to do his will in his way, and all because we love him.

Devotion: *Loving Father, I thank you that your ways are not my ways, and that your thoughts are not my thoughts. You act and think differently from me. Help me to be so in touch with your heart that I know rightly how to challenge the ways of the world, in Jesus' name. Amen.*

> **When they had rowed about three or three and a half miles, they saw Jesus approaching the boat, walking on the water; and they were frightened. But he said to them, "It is I; don't be afraid."**
>
> John 6:19–20

Jesus withdraws from the crowds who are clamouring to make him king and he sits on top of a mountain alone to commune with his Father. His disciples have gone ahead of him in a boat across the Sea of Galilee. As they make their way over the four mile stretch of water a fierce storm appears from nowhere (as it sometimes can on this particular lake) and the boat is now in danger about half a mile from the shoreline. Jesus, seeing his followers in difficulty, comes down from the mountain and walks on the water towards them.

The disciples are now terrified. In fact, if they were scared before by the storm, they are now even more scared by Jesus walking on the water. The Greek verb is *phobeo*, from which we get the word *phobia*. The disciples already knew that Jesus was a miracle-worker; he had turned 180 gallons of water into vintage wine, healed the sick, and multiplied the loaves and fishes. They had just grown used to Jesus as miracle-worker. But now he appears to them as a water-walker. That was altogether a new revelation and it terrified them.

As Jesus approaches, he says two things: "Be not afraid", using the same word *phobeo*; but he also says, "It is I." Literally, "I am" – the divine name. Jesus discloses his divinity to his disciples in the midst of the storm.

It is said that sometimes the darkness is darkest just before the dawn. There are times in our Christian lives when we don't think we're going to make it and when quitting seems like the best option. We don't have any more energy or motivation to row any longer. Maybe we are crossing over some lake of transition and there is turbulence all around us (as there so often is in times of major change in our lives). In such times we must remember that Jesus is watching over us and that sooner or later we will have our own revelation of his glory and greatness, even if we have to wait until the darkest hour before his light appears.

Devotion: *Abba, Father, in the turbulent trials of life, I pray that you would help me not to be scared but prepared – prepared to have an encounter with you that will comfort me in my time of trouble and empower me in my time of transition, in Jesus' name. Amen.*

Then they were willing to take him into the boat, and immediately the boat reached the shore where they were heading.

John 6:21

It is so interesting to me that John records the disciples were *willing* to take Jesus into their boat. Remember that up to this point they have been struggling to make the last half or mile or so across the lake to reach the seashore. The storm is holding them up and putting them all in danger. Jesus walks on the water towards them and they are terrified. At this point they have a choice to make. Are they going to row on without him? Or are they going to welcome him on board, even though he has terrified them? In the end, they "receive" him – a Greek word that is used some forty-six times in John's Gospel, including its very first use in John 1:12: "To all who received him, to those who believed in his name, he gave the right to become children of God." The disciples *received* him because they knew that it really was Jesus, not a ghost.

John now says something very striking. He says that as soon as Jesus was on board, the boat *immediately* arrived at the shoreline. The Greek word is *eutheos* and it means "straight away, without delay, instantly, forthwith". John uses it sparingly in his Gospel. He has used it in John 5:9 of the man at the Pool of Bethesda *immediately* being made whole. He will use it only two more times after this, in John 13:30 and 18:27. Its appearance here in John 6:21 is very revealing. It means that as soon as Jesus was on board the boat, the disciples accelerated to their destination supernaturally.

Sometimes we are tempted to achieve the Father's plan for our lives in our own strength. We rely on programmes rather than presence – on the flesh rather than the fire. When this happens it is amazing how slow and painful our progress can be. But when we renounce our self-reliance and rely on the Holy Spirit, suddenly we find the going so much easier and our pace so much faster. *Acceleration* comes to those who reach the end of themselves and find the beginning of God. It comes to those who realize that it is much better to welcome Jesus on board our boat than to try and row on without him.

Devotion: *Abba, Father, I want to repent of my tendency to fulfil your goals for my life without your help. I renounce self-reliance and striving, in Jesus' name. I welcome you on board my boat and pray for you to take over. Let acceleration kick in, in Jesus' name. Amen.*

> *"Do not work for food that spoils, but for food that endures to eternal life, which the Son of Man will give you."*
>
> John 6:27

In John 5 the chapter started with a miracle (the healing of the man at Bethesda) and then went into a long section of teaching. A work was followed by words – words that were in response to the work. If you want the technical terms, *narrative* was followed by *discourse*; *showing* by *telling*. Here in John chapter 6 we find the same thing. The chapter begins with a miracle (the feeding of the five thousand) and then proceeds to a very long section of teaching related to that miracle. Since the miracle itself had involved food (and specifically bread), we find that most of John 6 is devoted to what really nourishes human beings – food that endures to eternal life and bread from heaven.

In our passage for today Jesus is interacting with the crowds that have followed him. He challenges them concerning their motivation for "seeking" him. In John 6:26 he tells them that they are only pursuing him because they ate the loaves and were filled. The word translated "filled" is the word people used of animals that ate hay until they were completely full. Jesus effectively tells them, "You're only following me because you troughed out on the bread. You're not spiritually hungry; you're just physically hungry."

I remember sitting next to a man at a dinner party who was extremely well off materially and felt no need for God in his life. He started to challenge me about my faith so I asked him if he had been hungry before the meal. He replied yes. I asked him if his physical hunger presupposed something that would satisfy it – namely food. He said yes. I then reminded him that ever since the dawn of time most human beings have had a different kind of hunger – a spiritual hunger. I added, just as physical hunger presupposes the existence of something that will satisfy it, so spiritual hunger does too. I encouraged him to become hungry for food that doesn't spoil but which lasts forever – food that only Jesus, the Son of Man, can provide. He became very quiet and reflective after that. My prayer is still that he would find the Bread of Heaven.

Devotion: *Loving Father, I don't want to be like the crowds – hungry for those things that don't last. I want to be hungry for the things of God, which never die. Intensify my spiritual hunger, I pray. Help me to be as hungry for your presence as I am for food, in Jesus' name. Amen.*

"On him God the Father has placed his seal of approval."
John 6:27

What a great thing for Jesus to say! This is one of my favourite sayings in the whole Bible. Jesus, talking about himself, says some very simple but quite wonderful words; he says that Abba, Father has placed his seal of approval on him.

The verb translated "placed his seal" occurs twenty-five times in the New Testament. For example, it is used of the Roman soldiers who placed Pilate's seal on the stone covering the entrance to the tomb of Jesus (Matthew 27:66). This told everyone who saw the tomb that it was now the property of Pontius Pilate, the Roman governor, and that no one was to touch it without his express permission.

In our day, it is our signature that authenticates something. In Jesus' day it was a seal, which usually involved the imprinting of a signet ring using hot wax. Seals were indicative of ownership, authenticity, and authority. They told you that the object was someone's property, that it was real and not fake, and that the owner had the authority, the right to decide what to do with it.

In John 6:27 Jesus says that Abba, Father has placed his seal on him. He has made it known that Jesus belongs to him as his Son, that Jesus is the real deal, and that Jesus is under the Father's authority, acting on the Father's behalf. This sealing happened at Jesus' baptism where the Father declared that Jesus was his beloved Son, his chosen one, the delight of his life. That seal remained on Jesus and is on his life forever.

The good news is this: the same is true for those who follow Jesus! We too are sealed – sealed in the Holy Spirit (2 Corinthians 1:22; Ephesians 1:13 and 4:30). We too have the Father's seal of ownership and approval on our lives. We too can hear the words, "You are my beloved child, the pride of my life." What a great liberation that is! We belong to the Father. We really are his children. From now on, we don't need to live *for* approval. We can live *from* approval. Hallelujah!

Devotion: *Abba, Father, I thank you that you sealed your Son with the enduring sign of your approval and authority. Thank you that you seal your adopted children too. Today I want to promise to live from your approval, not for the approval of others, in Jesus' name. Amen.*

> **Then Jesus declared, "I am the bread of life. Whoever comes to me will never go hungry, and whoever believes in me will never be thirsty."**
>
> John 6:35

Previously in our readings of John's Gospel I have pointed out the importance of the number seven in Judaism. Seven is the number that signifies perfection. If there are said to be seven of something, then they're perfect. Six signifies imperfection (remember the six jars in John 2?). Seven implies wholeness and completion.

In our verse today Jesus utters the first of seven sayings about himself that begin with the words "I am". The list as a whole is

I am the bread of life (John 6:35)
I am the light of the world (John 8:12)
I am the door, or gate (John 10:7)
I am the good shepherd (John 10:11)
I am the resurrection and the life (John 11:25)
I am the way and the truth and the life (John 14:6)
I am the true vine (John 15:1)

There is something here for everyone! To the cook, Jesus is the bread; to the electrician, he is the light; to the builder, he is the door; to the farmer, he is the good shepherd; to the funeral director, he is the resurrection; to the road builder, he is the way; to the gardener, he is the vine. Jesus is for everyone and he is absolutely perfect.

In John 6:35, Jesus speaks to the crowds that he fed with the loaves and fishes and he tells them to look for food that satisfies them spiritually. Now he announces that he is the bread of life and that they will never be spiritually hungry or thirsty again when they come to him. The meaning then is clear: only Jesus can satisfy our longing for the Father's love. There is no other way to Abba, Father other than Jesus.

Devotion: *Abba, Father, I want to praise you for Jesus. He really is perfection. And I thank you that he is the bread from heaven that truly and uniquely satisfies those who are spiritually hungry. Thank you so much, Jesus, for meeting my need for God, in your name. Amen.*

"All whom the Father gives me will come to me, and whoever comes to me I will never drive away."

John 6:37

Here we learn some deeply revealing truths about what happens when a person is born again and becomes a Christian.

First of all, we learn that whenever anyone comes to Jesus and commits their lives to him, it is because Abba, Father has already been working in their hearts. When I became a Christian, it wasn't just because I made a choice; it was because my Father made a choice. He chose me. As it says in Ephesians 1:5–6, he chose me before the foundation of the world and predestined me in love to become one of his adopted children – something which brought him great pleasure. When I came to Christ in 1977 it was because the Father wanted to give me as a gift to Jesus and no power of hell could stop this from happening. As Jesus says, "All whom the Father gives me will come to me".

Secondly, we learn that Jesus will never "drive away" the person who comes to him. The words "drive away" are strong ones. They mean "to throw out, cast aside, reject". Jesus here makes a promise. He tells us that if we come to him, then he will never reject us. To those of us who have been rejected by those we love in the past, this is a great and stunning promise for our future. The Father revealed in Jesus does not abandon or reject his children. He remains committed and present to them for eternity. When I became a Christian, I discovered a Father who is the complete opposite of my biological dad. My biological father left my birth mother before I was born. My heavenly Father has promised never to cast me aside.

In light of all this, we need to pray for our unsaved family and friends that they would be among those whom the Father wants to give to Jesus. There are great mysteries here, of course – not least the mystery of why the Father chooses to work in some but not in others. But this should not prevent us from praying that other people would come to Jesus and find the unconditional love of the Father.

Devotion: *Abba, Father, I pray for all my family and friends who don't yet know you. Would you move powerfully in their hearts today? Let them be numbered among those you have appointed for salvation. Draw them to Jesus and help them to find the love that will never let them go. Amen.*

At this the Jews there began to grumble about him because he said, "I am the bread that came down from heaven."

John 6:41

John chapter 6 begins with events unfolding at Passover time. The Passover festival commemorated the great escape of the Israelites from captivity in Egypt hundreds of years before. This mass exodus resulted in a journey of four decades through the wilderness. As Moses led the people, they became hungry when the food ran out. In Exodus 16:2–3 we read, "In the desert the whole community grumbled against Moses and Aaron. The Israelites said to them, 'If only we had died by the Lord's hand in Egypt! There we sat around pots of meat and ate all the food we wanted, but you have brought us out into this desert to starve this entire assembly to death.'" Moses went to God with the people's complaint and received this answer: "I will rain down bread from heaven for you" (Exodus 16:4). Thereafter, manna began to fall from the sky and the people had enough to eat each day.

This is the background for all that follows the multiplication of the loaves and the fish in John 6. As the chapter progresses, some of Jesus' Jewish contemporaries begin to grumble. The word John uses for "grumble" is *goguzzo*, which sounds like what it describes! These people were moaning about Jesus' words that he was the bread that comes down from heaven, the bread that gives life to those who are spiritually hungry and who eat it. They couldn't understand how a man who was the son of a carpenter from Nazareth could possibly have come from heaven. What they failed to see was that Jesus was speaking of spiritual not earthly matters. He was making a claim to be like the heavenly bread of Exodus 16. In the process they failed to notice that their grumbling equated them with the moaning masses in the same chapter.

I have served as a leader in four churches and spent a large portion of my life visiting churches all over the world. I can safely say that most of my experiences have been immensely positive. But just occasionally I have encountered "murmuring". It is tragic when the people of God start grumbling in a church. Let's resolve not to grumble.

Devotion: *Abba, Father, I know that it is right to complain if someone teaches something that contradicts the Bible. But it is not right to grumble when I'm being legitimately challenged. Help me to know the difference and to be a positive influence, in Jesus' name. Amen.*

"No one can come to me unless the Father who sent me draws them...".

John 6:44

Most Christians have favourite passages or verses in John's Gospel. I guess if we were to take a poll, there would be quite a few that would choose John 6:44. Here Jesus teaches that no one can ever believe in him without the Father first working in their hearts. No one can become a Christian without Abba, Father first making Jesus attractive to their souls. At every point in the process of being born again, the Father is involved. He is supernaturally at work in the power of his Holy Spirit drawing people's hearts towards his Son Jesus Christ. When I became a Christian, the whole of the Trinity was actively engaged in my transformation. That is some thought!

Jesus tells us here that the Father draws people. The word translated "draw" is the same word that is used in John 21 of Simon Peter drawing in the nets when he goes fishing. When the risen Jesus tells Peter to cast his nets over the other side of his boat, we learn that they caught so many fish that they couldn't draw in the nets (John 21:6). When Peter eventually got back to the shore, we read in John 21:11 that Peter drew the nets that were full of fish onto the beach. In both verses the verb "draw" is the same word as is used here in John 6.

I became a Christian because my heavenly Father cast out his net and caught me. He then drew me to the person of his Son Jesus who died for me at Calvary. Gazing upon the crucified Saviour I repented of my sins and put my trust in him. Looking at Jesus accordingly brought me life. As Jesus puts it in John 6:40: "my Father's will is that everyone who looks to the Son and believes in him shall have eternal life".

Drawn to the Son of Man, lifted up on the Cross, I was born again and received abundant life. This is what Jesus promised would happen in John 12:32, where exactly the same verb – "to draw" – is used again. "I, when I am lifted up from the earth, will draw all people to myself." Whenever a person experiences the amazing grace of salvation, they only do so because the Father has first drawn them to his Son.

Devotion: *Abba, Father, I thank you for the drawing power of your love, for the magnetic attraction of your amazing grace. Thank you for drawing me in the net of your mercy towards the person of Jesus. Draw me closer and closer to him I pray, in his name. Amen.*

> **"Whoever eats my flesh and drinks my blood has eternal life, and I will raise them up at the last day."**
>
> John 6:54

At the beginning of John 6, Jesus took bread, gave thanks and distributed it on the mountain. That should have reminded us of the Holy Communion service. At the Last Supper the night before he died, Jesus had a Passover meal with his disciples. He broke bread and told them that this was his body, broken for them. He then poured wine and told them that this was his blood which was shed for them. When he did that he instituted the Lord's Supper for the whole of history.

In John 6 Jesus starts the chapter breaking and giving bread to the crowds. By the end he has explained that he is the bread from heaven and they must eat his flesh and must drink his blood. This sounds strange to our ears now and it was evidently strange to many of their ears then. But Jesus was pointing to his death on the Cross. He was telling his listeners that they needed to receive by faith the full benefits of the Cross if they were to experience eternal life.

Today, we eat bread and drink wine at the Lord's Supper because Jesus commands us to do these things in remembrance of him. When we do, we are nourished by what was achieved in his crucified flesh and his outpoured blood. By faith we receive the blessings of the Cross as we eat and drink in community together. First and foremost we receive more of his life. This life keeps on flowing into our hearts until the last day, when Jesus returns and he resurrects us to new life.

I have always loved the Holy Communion service, whether it is in a traditional church with patens and chalices or in a person's home with a plate and a cup. There is something about it that brings me into the atmosphere of the Father's love. I know I'm not alone in this. Many of my brothers and sisters in Christ feel the same way, whatever their denomination. Many are nourished by the life of the Spirit in this simple act of remembrance. It is something we need to cherish.

Devotion: *Dear Father, thank you so much for the Lord's Supper. Thank you for the simple elements of bread and wine and how they remind me of the body and blood of your Son. Help me to receive more of your life every time I partake of this great meal, in Jesus' name. Amen.*

> *"Just as the living Father sent me and I live because of the Father, so the one who feeds on me will live because of me."*
>
> John 6:57

I want to tell you about my adoptive father, Philip Stibbe. He was a truly wonderful man. He had a statesmanlike quality that meant that heads would turn to look at him when he came into a room. He was a man who loved telling stories to his children, especially those of C. S. Lewis and J. R. R. Tolkien whom he had known at Oxford University. He was the kindest man I ever met. And he was a father to the fatherless, an earthly reflection of the Father heart of God. He adopted my twin sister and me, taking us from an orphanage in London to his own home, where he and his wife Joy brought us up. He was a remarkable man.

But you will notice that I have written this in the past tense. I have consistently said "he was", not "he is". In 1997 my father died after a long illness. My brother Giles and I were by his bedside at the Norfolk and Norwich hospital. It was a cold and bleak January afternoon and we held Dad's hand as his breathing became shallower and quieter. I had been told that a person's hearing is the last thing to go so I read Psalm 23 to him, emphasizing with my faltering voice that goodness and mercy will follow us all the days of our lives, and that we will dwell in the Father's house forever.

And then he went. My father was no longer alive. He was dead. He was gone. The conversations that he and I had had would happen no more. His favourite chair at home was empty. There would be no reassuring voice at the other end of a telephone, no comforting hand upon the shoulder, no smile – oh, how I miss that smile.

And so it is that I want to pick just three words from today's passage and leave them with you. They are Jesus' description of God as "the living Father". Our heavenly Father is not dead; he is alive forever. He is not a dead God to whom we can never speak. He is the living Abba, Father who loves to commune with us through his Word and Spirit and through bread and wine. When we find Jesus, we find "the living Father".

Devotion: *Dear heavenly Abba, Father, I thank you that you are alive, that you are full of life. I worship you that you don't die and leave us as earthly fathers do. You live forever and you stay close by our side. I praise you with all my heart for being "the living Father". Amen.*

"The Spirit gives life; the flesh counts for nothing. The words I have spoken to you – they are full of the Spirit and life."

John 6:63

At this stage there were many people following Jesus. But when he began to speak about eating his flesh and drinking his blood many of them began to complain that this was really tough teaching. They couldn't stomach the implications of what Jesus was saying because they were interpreting him in an earthly rather than a heavenly way. Bound by a crude literalism, they couldn't penetrate beyond these symbols to the realities to which they pointed. And so they grumbled. "This is hard to take in. In fact, it's hard to take."

In response Jesus asks whether his listeners are offended by his talk of flesh and blood. Then, instead of reassuring them, he says something even more offensive. He asks them what they would do if they saw him – the Son of Man – ascending to the place in heaven from which he had come. Well, the flesh and the blood were bad enough. That sounded like cannibalism. But now he was talking as if he was divine. And that in their ears sounded like blasphemy. It sounded as if Jesus was saying that his home was in the glory of heaven!

It is at this point that Jesus makes his comment about the power of his words. He says that if his hearers can push past the offence and embrace the truth of what he says, then they will understand that his words are vehicles of spiritual life. Jesus' words, while appearing offensive to some, are really the channels of the Father's love and life to all those who remain faithful to him. Jesus' words are words born of the Spirit, not born of the flesh. They do not derive from human ingenuity; they come from the Father heart of God.

There is a message here and the message is this. Jesus sometimes offends our minds to expose our hearts. When that happens it is really important that we push through to the place where we can hear what the Father is saying, because that is where we find new life.

Devotion: *Abba, Father, sometimes I have to admit that I am offended by the things I hear you saying through your Word and by your Spirit, mostly because they disturb my comfort zone. Please help me to push past the offence to the life that comes from obeying you. Amen.*

Simon Peter answered him, "Lord, to whom shall we go? You have the words of eternal life. We have come to believe and to know that you are the Holy One of God."

John 6:68-69

As Jesus concludes his challenging message about his flesh and his blood, we see two responses. The first is defection. John tells us in verse 66 that many of his disciples at this point turned back to their homes and would not walk with him as their rabbi any longer. They couldn't cope with the offensive nature of some of Jesus' words. They wanted a Jesus that multiplied loaves and healed the sick. They wanted a master who would comfort the afflicted not afflict the comfortable. So they left him. That was a defection.

The second response we see is one of declaration. We can imagine hundreds leaving at this point. The twelve disciples however remain. Jesus turns to them and says, "Aren't you going too?" Peter now makes this wonderful comment about Jesus' words. He tells his master that there is nowhere else for them to go. There is no one else for them to follow. He alone has the words of eternal life. Only his words give revelation that leads to transformation. Only his words carry the very power of heaven, conveying the life of the age to come.

And then Peter adds, "We believe and know that you are the Holy One of God!" What a declaration this is. Peter confesses Jesus publicly as the Messiah. It is interesting to note that the demons that Jesus confronted recognized him as this. In Mark 1:24, a man who is possessed by an evil spirit shouts out, "What do you want with us, Jesus of Nazareth? Have you come to destroy us? I know who you are – the Holy One of God!" Even unclean spirits recognized the clean, pure, and holy spirit of Jesus and recognized him as God's "Holy One".

Peter and the Twelve choose the path of declaration rather than defection. It would have been easy to follow the crowd and leave. But Peter, speaking on behalf of the Twelve, says that they know and believe as a group that Jesus has the words of eternal life. So they stay.

Devotion: *Abba, Father, when I hear things that aren't easy to understand or accept, help me to be one who chooses to declare my love for you, not one who falls away. Increase in me a steadfast spirit so that I may remain true to you and your Son, Jesus Christ. Amen.*

> **"No one who wants to become a public figure acts in secret.
> Since you are doing these things, show yourself to the world."**
>
> John 7:4

John chapter 7 begins with Jesus staying in the north, in Galilee, where the action of John 6 has unfolded. For the next five or six months Jesus remains here up until the time of the Feast of Tabernacles in September or October. This seven-day feast was a harvest festival in which the people of Israel gathered in their crops before the long winter months and celebrated God's goodness to them. It was also a time when they looked back at their history and thanked God for preserving them when they were living in makeshift tabernacles or booths in their wilderness wanderings after the Exodus. It was finally a festival in which they looked forward to the future and prayed for rain – not just literal rain for their crops but spiritual rain, the rain of the Holy Spirit. John chapter 7 will describe events in Jerusalem during this feast.

While he is still in Galilee, Jesus' brothers come to him. Who were these brothers? Some say they were sons of Joseph by a previous marriage. Others say they were cousins or close associates. Another view is that they were sons that Joseph and Mary had after Jesus had been born. These were Jesus' biological younger brothers and, according to Matthew 13:54–56, their names were James, Joseph, Simon and Judas.

Whoever these men were they get things horribly wrong. They have seen Jesus doing miracles in Galilee. They now tell him that he should go to Jerusalem and do miracles there (John 7:3). According to them, Jesus has disciples in Judea and they need to see his miracles too. They then make this extraordinary statement: "No one who wants to become a public figure acts in secret" before finally adding, "show yourself to the world".

What these brothers don't understand is the way in which Jesus has embraced the value of the hidden life at this point in his ministry. They value celebrity. He values invisibility. He knows that there will be a time when his glory will be shown to the world, but it isn't yet and it will be shown through his death, not through his miracles.

Devotion: *Abba, Father, I thank you that Jesus had the courage to stand against those who were pushing him to go public and become famous, even in his own family. Help me not to collude with a celebrity mindset, whatever form it takes, in Jesus' name. Amen.*

Jesus told them, "My time is not yet here; for you any time will do."

John 7:6

Jesus' reply to his unbelieving brothers reveals some very interesting things about time. I don't know about you, but I find time fascinating. The Greeks of Jesus' day did as well, and some of this interest is reflected in the two Greek words they used. The first of these words was *chronos*, from which we get the word chronology. It refers to ordinary, ongoing, mundane time. It is the kind of time that someone is very conscious of when they're employed in doing a quite boring job. They watch the minute hand of their watch slowly moving around the dial as they wait for the end of the day. Such people have become preoccupied with *chronos*. They are clock-watchers – and the irony is that having watched the clock all their working lives, they are often given a clock as a retirement gift when they leave their work behind!

The other Greek word used for time was *kairos*. If *chronos* meant ordinary, regular time, *kairos* denoted extraordinary, unique time. This is the word Jesus used at the very beginning of his ministry when he announced in Mark 1:15 that the "time" had been fulfilled and that the kingdom of God was now at hand. *Kairos* here refers to a moment of great opportunity, a moment that can either be seized or missed. This is the kind of time that lies behind the following maxim: the opportunity of a lifetime needs to be seized in the lifetime of the opportunity.

Jesus is talking to his unbelieving brothers about the *kairos* principle. He tells them that for them, any time is right. They could go to Jerusalem to the Feast on any day. It would make no difference. No one will notice them. But for him it is an entirely different matter. He can only go when his Father tells him to go. He can only go when his Father determines that it is a *kairos* moment – the perfect time of opportunity.

Jesus lived with an awareness of *kairos*. His brothers only knew about *chronos*. As sons and daughters of the same Father, we need to become more adept at discerning the seasons and the times.

Devotion: *Abba, Father, I appreciate that much of my life is lived in ordinary,* chronos *time. But I also know there are moments of opportunity in which you present me with an invitation to enter* kairos *time. Help me to seize these moments when they come, in Jesus' name. Amen.*

However, after his brothers had left for the festival, he went also, not publicly, but in secret.

John 7:10

Yesterday we looked at the difference between *chronos* and *kairos*. The brothers were interested only in *chronos*, in ordinary time. Jesus was also interested in *kairos*, in unique moments of God-given opportunity. The brothers wanted Jesus to go to Jerusalem now. Jesus waited until the moment of maximum opportunity.

Winston Churchill famously remarked, "To every man there comes in his lifetime that special moment when he is figuratively tapped on the shoulder and offered a chance to do a very special thing, unique to him and fitted to his talents. What a tragedy if that moment finds him unprepared or unqualified for that which would be his finest hour."

Churchill understood the importance of the *kairos* moment. Jesus did as well. Great leaders have an unusual sense of the importance of timing. Jesus had this gift more than anyone who has ever lived.

The brothers, bound by chronology alone, travel to Jerusalem. Jesus, living in the light of what we might call *kairology*, stays behind in Galilee. He waits until halfway through the seven-day feast. Then we read that he also made the journey, not publicly but in secret.

Now here once again we see a great difference between two ways of living. The brothers of Jesus live in *chronos*. Jesus lives in *kairos*. Not only that, but the brothers live with a desire for Jesus to go public. Jesus lives with a love for secrecy and invisibility.

John says in our verse today that Jesus went up to the Feast at the *kairos* moment of greatest opportunity but that he made his pilgrimage secretly not publicly. Jesus knew when it was right to do things openly and visibly. He also knew when to do things privately and invisibly.

I wonder which of these two we identify with. Do we live with a finely tuned sense of *kairos*? Or do we live only with a sense of *chronos*? Do we welcome times and seasons of invisibility? Or do we long only for publicity and celebrity?

Devotion: *Abba, Father, I thank you so much for what I learn about true sonship from Jesus. Help me not only to be sensitive to my kairos moments. Help me also to value those times when you call me to embrace invisibility, in Jesus' name. Amen.*

Among the crowds there was widespread whispering about him. Some said, "He is a good man." Others replied, "No, he deceives the people." But no one would say anything publicly about him for fear of the leaders.

John 7:12–13

Jesus has now arrived in Jerusalem for the Feast of Tabernacles. He has travelled secretly because everyone is looking for him. According to John 7:11, the Jewish leaders were asking, "Where is that man?"

Jesus arrives and goes to the Temple. Among the pilgrims there, people are giving voice to all sorts of views about him. John says there was "widespread whispering". The word in Greek is *goggusmos* (pronounced *gongusmos*), which means "murmuring". It is the noun form of the verb that is used three times in John 6 and which we translated there as "grumbling". The crowds in the Temple area were whispering, yes, but they were murmuring in a negative not a positive way.

The reason why they were murmuring was twofold. First they couldn't decide whether Jesus was a good man or a deceiver. Secondly, they were reluctant to discuss these things openly because they were afraid of being reprimanded by the religious authorities.

It was C. S. Lewis who invented what has come to be known as the great "trilemma". If a "dilemma" is a situation in which a person has to choose between two alternatives, a "trilemma" is a situation in which a person has to choose between three options.

Lewis argued that all human beings are faced with three options when it comes to Jesus of Nazareth, and they must make their choice. They must choose to believe that Jesus was bad, he was mad, or he was God. They must decide whether he was a liar, a lunatic, or the Lord.

It is fair to say that orphans live in fear; sons and daughters live by faith. All of us have a choice whether to live out of an orphan mindset or the mindset of a son or a daughter. Let's choose to live out of faith not fear. Let's be confident in our declaration that Jesus is Lord and let's also be unafraid of what others may say.

Devotion: *Abba, Father, I come to you asking for your strength to be unafraid to say what I believe about Jesus. Give me greater boldness to confess that Jesus is my Lord. In the choice that I have to live in fear or in faith, I choose faith, in Jesus' name. Amen.*

"Stop judging by mere appearances, but instead judge correctly."

John 7:24

Jesus is engaged in an intense debate with the religious leaders in the Temple in Jerusalem. These leaders are still mad with Jesus because he healed the man at the pool of Bethesda. That was on the sabbath day and the Law as the Jewish leaders interpreted it had decreed that no work should be done on the "queen of days". Healing is work, therefore Jesus is a lawbreaker. Therefore he cannot be the Messiah.

Jesus answers by saying that *they* are the ones who are the lawbreakers. To prove the point he brings up the subject of circumcision. The Law says that on the eighth day of his life a boy shall be circumcised (Leviticus 12:3). Sometimes the eighth day would inevitably fall on a sabbath. In that situation, the Law determined that the boy could be circumcised on a sabbath day, even though it was technically work.

Jesus takes hold of this and rounds on his accusers. He tells them that they have interpreted the law of Moses to mean that no healing can be done on the sabbath. All medical attention – other than life-saving attention – is forbidden. Yet circumcision is a form of medical procedure that is not life-threatening. The Jewish leaders are guilty of hypocrisy. They permit what they themselves forbid.

And what's more, circumcision involves doing a measure of damage to the flesh but Jesus has brought health to the man at Bethesda. He has given him his mobility back. The man has been made whole. How can it be wrong to give a man his health and right to take away a piece of a boy's flesh? Jesus says, "Stop looking at life superficially. Go beneath the surface and judge matters more fairly."

Now that answer was brilliant! Jesus outwits some of the cleverest people of his day. He understands not just the letter of the Law but the spirit of the Law. He knows the heart of the one who gave the Law, his loving Father, and he knows that this Law was given to liberate not to oppress us. We must make sure that we are like Jesus in this regard.

Devotion: *Abba, Father, I don't want to be a person who knows your laws but not your love. I want to be like Jesus and have the kind of intimacy with you that brings deep insights about you. Help me to look at life more deeply and through your eyes, in Jesus' name. Amen.*

"... when the Messiah comes, no one will know where he is from."

John 7:27

Some of the crowd in John 7 have been asking if the religious leaders have concluded that Jesus is the Messiah; they are doing this because they are curious as to why the authorities are allowing him to speak so openly in the Temple. Perhaps it is because they have come to the conclusion that Jesus is the Christ and they are giving him a platform. But the people in the crowd reason that this cannot be true. According to their beliefs, no one would know where the Messiah would come from. Jesus is from Nazareth. Indeed, he is called Jesus of Nazareth to distinguish him from the many other men called Jesus at the time. If everyone knows Jesus' home address, then he can't be the Messiah.

The problem here is that the people have a wrong view that the Messiah would simply appear out of nowhere. They thought no one would know where he had come from and there would be a veil of mystery over him. One minute he would be concealed from the world, the next he would emerge onto the stage of history. As the rabbis were fond of saying, "Three things come completely without warning – the Messiah, a godsend and a scorpion"! They could never accept that the Messiah would come from a known address, and especially that the Messiah would come from a despised place like Nazareth in Galilee. Didn't Nathanael say in John 1:46, "Can anything good come from Nazareth?"

One of the reasons why I know that Christianity must be based on solid historical facts is because of details like this. It would have been all too easy for the Gospel writers to have cut out embarrassing details. But they choose to record them simply because they are true.

Another reason why I love the Christian faith is because its founder did not appear like a religious celebrity or mythical superhero but he grew up in an ordinary place. This shows that our Father is present in the mundane parts of our lives and that he transforms ordinary things with his beautifying love. If we expect to find him only in the sensational, we may well miss him.

Devotion: *Abba, Father, I thank you that your Son didn't just suddenly appear but that everyone knew him as Jesus from Nazareth. They knew where he had grown up. They knew his parents and his father's trade. Thank you that the dust of Nazareth is on the throne of heaven. Amen.*

At this they tried to seize him, but no one laid a hand on him, because his time had not yet come.

John 7:30 (NIV)

In our verse for today Jesus is still teaching in the Temple in Jerusalem. He has just told the crowds of pilgrims something that has provoked a very hostile reaction. He says in verses 28–29: "I am not here on my own authority, but he who sent me is true. You do not know him, but I know him because I am from him and he sent me." Notice those five words, "You do not know him". In their own sacred house, Jesus tells his Jewish contemporaries (especially the religious leaders in Jerusalem), that they do not know the Father. They do not know the one whose presence was said to reside in the Temple. The chosen people didn't know the one who chose them.

That of course was a very hard thing to hear and the response was immediate. John tells us some people tried to seize Jesus. The word means to apprehend someone. However, they failed to throw themselves upon him (that's the force of the words translated "laid a hand on him"). John explains that this was because Jesus' "time" had not yet come. The time that's being referred to is the time of Jesus' return to the Father, which involves his death, resurrection, and ascension to heaven. Jesus wasn't seized by anyone in the Temple because it wasn't his time to be seized. Jesus' times were in the Father's hands and the Father's timing is always perfect. He is never too early, never too late. He is always right "on time" because he is the Lord of time.

This is an encouraging thought for us too. Our lives are in the Father's hands. The time for our homecoming has already been set because all the days ordained for us are written in his book of life (Psalm 139:16). The time for our departure from this world is not decided by us or by others. It is only determined by Abba, Father. It is he who has numbered our days. It is he who brought us into this world and it is he who will carry us out of it. Aren't you grateful that your life is in the tender hands of the most loving, perfect Father in the universe? You can trust him today. You can trust him all the days of your life.

Devotion: *Thank you, Abba, Father, that my life is in your hands. You determined when and where I was born. You have determined when and where I shall die. My days are under your watchful and caring gaze. I praise you that I can trust you now and every day, in Jesus' name. Amen.*

> *Still, many in the crowd put their faith in him. They said, "When the Messiah comes, will he perform more signs than this man?"*
>
> John 7:31

One of the things that we can be in absolutely no doubt about is the fact that Jesus performed many miracles. All four of the Gospels witness to this fact. The historical traditions behind this are so strong that they are hard to deny. Jesus of Nazareth did extraordinary supernatural works. He turned water into wine, healed the sick, multiplied loaves and fishes, walked on water, and many other things besides.

One of the reasons why there were some in the crowd in Jerusalem who chose to believe in Jesus is because everyone knew about the quantity and quality of his miracles. There was at least one man walking around the city who had once been disabled and who had now been healed by Jesus (John 5). He may even have been in the Temple precincts as Jesus taught the people now. Consequently, some of the people knew that Jesus had healed the sick and they figured that he had to be someone special. They asked a very insightful question. "When the Messiah comes, will he do more miracles than this man Jesus?"

This is an example of what's called a rhetorical question – a question expecting the answer "no". No, the Messiah when he comes will not do more, because the Messiah has already come and his name is Jesus. Many therefore choose to believe in him. They believe he is the Anointed One of God because of the evidence of his miracles.

In this they were doing something that Jesus himself encouraged. He taught his own disciples to believe in him on the basis of his miracles (John 14:12). In Matthew's Gospel, when John the Baptist is in prison and doubting whether Jesus is the Messiah, Jesus sends him a message. He tells two men, "Go back and report to John what you hear and see: The blind receive sight, the lame walk, those who have leprosy are cured, the deaf hear, the dead are raised, and the good news is preached to the poor" (Matthew 11:4–5). How we need to pray for this kind of evidence in today's church. Miracles testify to who Jesus really is.

Devotion: *Abba, Father, I thank you that you are still healing the sick today. You have declared in your Word, "I Am the God who heals." You didn't say, "I was", or "I will be." You said, "I am." Please pour out your Spirit upon us and anoint us to do the works of Jesus. Amen.*

> *Jesus said, "I am with you for only a short time, and then I go to the one who sent me. You will look for me, but you will not find me; and where I am, you cannot come."*
>
> John 7:33–34

I have often tried to imagine what it must have been like to have been alive at the time of Jesus. What must it have been like to listen to Jesus as he taught here in the Temple in Jerusalem, or on the mountains of Galilee? What must it have been like to have seen him heal the sick and raise the dead? How much would I have understood?

I like to think of myself as a person who would have known that Jesus was very special. I picture myself discerning that he was unique, that he was more than a teacher or a prophet, that he was the Father's only Son. I like to think I would have seen who he really was and been numbered among those who chose to believe in him.

But in my honest moments, I am not so sure that this is completely true. In all likelihood I would have been part of the crowd, swayed by this view and that, carried along by the seductive power of peer pressure, and all too easily I may have missed who Jesus was in the fleeting moments when he crossed my path, or I crossed his.

Jesus tells the crowds in the Temple that he is only with them for a short time and that he will have left to return to his Father before they even know it. He is only present with them in human flesh for a while and when he has gone they will no longer be able to look for him in the way they are now. And they won't be able to follow him either. The road he is taking is a road never travelled – a road that will never be walked by anyone else again. It is the road home to glory via the Cross and the empty tomb. Only he can take that route, no one else.

If we had been in Jerusalem during the events recorded in John 7, would we have seized the day and followed Jesus? Or would we have missed who he was and lived the rest of our lives in the half-light of regret? Would we have sought the Lord while he could be found (Isaiah 55:6)?

Devotion: *Abba, Father, I appreciate after reading this that time is very short. We only have a certain number of minutes and hours in which to seek and then to find your Son. Give me a new sense of urgency in my own seeking, and help those I love to seek you too. Amen.*

On the last and greatest day of the festival, Jesus stood and said in a loud voice, "Let anyone who is thirsty come to me and drink."

John 7:37

Jesus is at the Feast of Tabernacles in Jerusalem. This was one of the three major festivals in the Jewish year and every adult male within a fifteen-mile radius of Jerusalem was required to come to the city and celebrate the feast. Consequently, the city's population must have swelled by about a quarter of a million people as the crowds of pilgrims flocked to the Temple for the seven days of festivities.

On the last of these seven days – a day known as the Great Hosanna – Jesus stands up in the crowd and shouts very loudly, "Let anyone who is thirsty come to me and drink."

In order to understand why Jesus said this, we must know about one of the daily rituals of this feast. Each day a number of priests in white robes went to the pool of Siloam in Jerusalem and filled a golden pitcher with its water. They then processed back to the Temple courts through the Water Gate, all the while singing the words, "With joy you will draw water from the wells of salvation" (Isaiah 12:3). On arrival they would pour out the water as an offering, praying for rain as they did so. It would be September or October and after a dry summer, rain would be much needed if the crops were to grow and the future harvests gathered. At the same time, as they poured the water over the altar of sacrifice, the priests would pray for the fulfilment of Ezekiel 47. They prayed that the Messiah would come and that the river of God (the Holy Spirit) would flow from the altar of sacrifice in the Temple out into the land, bringing life wherever it went.

Jesus hears the priests returning and singing, "With joy you will draw water from the wells of salvation." The word "salvation" in Hebrew is the word *yeshua*. That's Jesus' name! When the priests sing Isaiah 12:3, Jesus stands and declares, "If you're looking for water – living, spiritual water – come to me. The river of God is going to flow from a new altar of sacrifice – from the Cross." What an amazing synchronicity! Don't you just love it when a plan comes together?

Devotion: *Abba, Father, I worship you that your Son fulfils the Feast of Tabernacles. As this feast is still celebrated in years to come, may many of your chosen people draw spiritual water from the wells of your Son, and may they do it with joy, in his name. Amen.*

> *"Whoever believes in me, as Scripture has said, rivers of living water will flow from within them." By this he meant the Spirit, whom those who believed in him were later to receive.*
>
> John 7:38–39

There has always been uncertainty about how to interpret verse 38. Some argue that Jesus is referring to himself when he speaks these words. In effect, he is saying that streams of living water will flow from within his own body. They point to the water that pours from the wounded side of the crucified Jesus to endorse their claim (John 19:34). Others argue that Jesus is talking about those who will come to faith in him. Out of them, the Holy Spirit will flow like streams of living water.

Earlier in these devotional readings in John I spoke about how the author often leaves it uncertain which of two interpretations the reader should embrace. I think that's true here. There are compelling arguments for both views – the view that the Holy Spirit flows out of Jesus at the Cross and the view that the Holy Spirit flows out of those who believe in Jesus. By not telling us which view he intended he leaves it open to us to embrace both.

Tomorrow I will consider how this verse applies to Jesus. Today let's think about how it applies to us.

Jesus says that it is out of our "belly" that the Spirit flows. The NIV doesn't include this but it is there in the original Greek and it refers to the womb (see John 3:4). The Holy Spirit is meant to overflow from the deepest part of us. From the place where life springs forth in the natural, the river of life is meant to flow in the spiritual. This means that liquid waves of life-giving love are meant to pour from the believer's life.

Notice John also talks about this as "streams". The word translated "streams" is *potamoi*. It can be translated "stream", "flood", or "river". This means that we are not just to leak a little but to overflow a lot! We are supposed to be reservoirs that release a flood of the Father's love to the world. We are not supposed to exude a trickle but a river!

Devotion: Abba, Father, I welcome a greater release of the Holy Spirit within my life today. I thank you that your Spirit is in me but I want to pray that I will become a fountain that overflows with your divine love to this fatherless world. Release your power, I pray, in Jesus' name. Amen.

Up to that time the Spirit had not been given, since Jesus had not yet been glorified.

John 7:39

One of the things I do is I write books. It is interesting looking back to reflect on which books have done well and why. It is also interesting to look back and think about which have done poorly – and why!

One of the books I most enjoyed writing was *Fire and Blood*. It was about the relationship between the work of the Cross and the work of the Spirit. I saw that there were many Christians who celebrated the Cross but didn't really welcome the dynamic presence of the Holy Spirit. I also saw that there were many who celebrated the dynamic presence of the Holy Spirit but who didn't really welcome the message and lifestyle of the Cross. I wrote *Fire and Blood* to help those who preach the Cross to embrace the power of the Spirit, and those who welcome the power of the Spirit to embrace the Cross. In the end, the book didn't sell at all well. It seemed that many wanted to have the Cross without the Spirit, or the Spirit without the Cross.

In John 7 Jesus has been speaking about the Holy Spirit during the Feast of Tabernacles in Jerusalem. In verse 37 John adds that at this time the Holy Spirit had not been given to the people. That was to happen at the end of Jesus' life when he had been glorified – when he had been lifted up on the Cross, raised from the dead, and elevated to the glory of heaven. After Jesus had been crucified, the Spirit would be given. Until then, people had to wait until after the death of Jesus until the gift of the Spirit would become available.

What John is highlighting here is the inseparability of the work of the Cross and the work of the Spirit. He is underlining the truth that there is no Pentecost without Calvary, no Calvary without Pentecost. The work of the Cross leads to the experience of the Holy Spirit. The experience of the Holy Spirit leads us back to the work of the Cross. In the final analysis, authentic Christians understand and proclaim the power of the blood and welcome the fire of the Holy Spirit.

Devotion: *Abba, Father, help me to embrace the marriage of the Cross and the Spirit. Help me to discover even greater depths to the work of the Cross in Jesus' life and my own. Help me to learn about and experience even more of the fire of your Spirit, in Jesus' name. Amen.*

The people were divided because of Jesus.

John 7:43

I have met many different views about Jesus over the course of my life. In my own extended family I have heard the view that Jesus of Nazareth never really existed; that he is no more historical than the Robin Hood of English legend. In the universities I have encountered the view that Jesus was a charismatic, Jewish holy man but not the Son of God. In talking with Jewish and Muslim people I have heard the view that Jesus was more than just a teacher but less than the Messiah; that he was a prophet who spoke divine truth. I have come across these and many other views besides.

There has never been – and will never be – a person in history who provokes more varied reactions than Jesus. The crowds in the precincts of the Jerusalem Temple came up with all sorts of different views about him – that he was a good man, a possessed man, a deluded man, an anointed man, and even a prophetic man. Everyone had a view. When Jesus is the focus of discussion, people find it very hard to sit on the fence. Even saying, "I'm not bothered" is a reaction!

In John 7:43 we hear that there was a division in the crowds about Jesus. The word translated division is the Greek word *schism*. It derives from a root meaning a tear, a split, or a gap. In fact, the verb form is used in John 19:24 of the untorn garment of Jesus and in John 21:11 of the unbroken nets of Peter. In modern English "schism" is a word used to describe the splits that sometimes tragically occur between groups of Christian believers.

The best way to prevent division in the church is to remain united and confident about Jesus. Jesus is not just a figure in history. He is not just a great religious teacher. He is not just a prophet. He is not even just the Messiah. Jesus is God made flesh, the Son of God, the human face of the Father. He was Lord and is Lord, now and forever. When we truly know that Jesus is the Son of God – and not just intellectually but relationally – then we are truly united (Ephesians 4:13).

Devotion: *Abba, Father, please unite your people around the truth that Jesus Christ is the Word made flesh, the Son of God, and the Holy One. Help us never to allow our confidence in Jesus to be eroded by scepticism or ignorance. Give us a clearer voice about your Son, in his name. Amen.*

Finally the temple guards went back to the chief priests and the Pharisees, who asked them, "Why didn't you bring him in?" "No one ever spoke the way this man does," the guards replied.

John 7:45–46

I love this moment in the unfolding drama of John chapter 7. The religious leaders in Jerusalem have sent their own temple guards to go and arrest Jesus. When these officers return they come back empty-handed. When they are asked why, they reply that they have never heard a person like Jesus! They testify to the fact that Jesus is someone very special indeed – so special that they felt they didn't have any right to lay their hands on him.

What is it I wonder that impressed these men? At the very beginning of John's Gospel we learn that Jesus came from the Father and that he came as one "full of grace and truth" (John 1:14). Those two words – grace and truth – are a key to why the temple guards were so amazed.

Let me elaborate. First of all, they highlight the *manner* of Jesus' teaching. Jesus taught with "grace". He didn't teach in a harsh and aloof way. He taught in a way that commended the Father's love. Even when he had to get angry with some of his contemporaries, his anger was an expression of his love. It was his way of trying to awaken the hard-hearted people of his day to move from Law to love and from religion to reality. Jesus' teaching style exhibited the Father's grace.

Secondly, these words underline the *content* of Jesus' teaching. Jesus' teaching was full of truth. It wasn't learning derived from religious gurus before or during his era. It was truth that came straight from the Father heart of God (John 7:15–16). Many people noticed this and were astonished by it. Jesus' teaching contained the Father's truth.

If people examined what came out of our mouths, would they be impressed? The sad fact is that there are too many believers who speak truth without grace, or grace without truth. We need to be more like Jesus and speak the Father's truth in a gracious way.

Devotion: *Abba, Father, I thank you once again for the example of your Son. As one of your adopted children, I want to learn to think like Jesus and speak like Jesus. Help me to communicate your message in a way that embodies your mercy, in Jesus' name. Amen.*

"Have any of the rulers or of the Pharisees believed in him?"

John 7:48

There are a number of different responses to Jesus in John chapter 7.

There is first of all the response of outright unbelief. The chapter begins and ends with this theme. At the start, we learn that Jesus' brothers do not believe in him (verse 5). Now we find that the Jewish leaders and the Pharisees don't believe in him either (verse 48).

There is secondly the response of hostility. Some people in the crowds take a very antagonistic view of Jesus. Their anger is aroused by his teaching and they accuse him of a being a deceiver (verse 12) and demon-possessed (verse 20). Some even try and seize him (verse 30).

Then there is thirdly the response of curiosity. Some members of the crowd in the Temple embody this attitude. They are curious about Jesus' history and identity. Some of them are even prepared to concede that he is a good man (verse 12) and a prophet (verse 40).

Fourthly, there is the response of belief. There are people who listen to Jesus' teaching in the Temple precincts and who confess that Jesus is the Christ (verse 41). Many in the crowd put their faith in him (verse 30). However, fear of the Jewish leaders keeps this faith quite hidden (verse 13).

There is a spectrum of responses to Jesus described in John 7 as a whole. It seems that Jesus' very presence provokes a reaction. His words certainly do. Every time he speaks there is a response.

Some of the crowd – no doubt the poor people of the land – have greater faith in Jesus than the religious elite in the city. The Pharisees had all the theology but no understanding. They had the Law but no love. They had religion but no recognition.

It is a truly tragic thing to see the response of the religious leaders here in verse 48. It is a clear reminder that the Father isn't interested in whether we know ecclesiastical law or religious doctrine. He is only interested in whether we truly believe in his Son.

Devotion: *Abba, Father, there are many ways that people react to your Son. I want to say today that I believe in Jesus and that I intend to make this faith a public not just a private reality. Let your perfect love drive out all my fear, in Jesus' name. Amen.*

The teachers of the law and the Pharisees brought in a woman caught in adultery. They made her stand before the group and said to Jesus, "Teacher, this woman was caught in the act of adultery. In the Law Moses commanded us to stone such women. Now what do you say?"

John 8:3–5

John chapter 8 begins with a story that doesn't appear in many of the earliest manuscripts of the New Testament, a story about Jesus' conduct towards a woman caught in the act of adultery. I'm not going to go into the reasons why the best, oldest manuscripts don't have this story. You can consult almost any commentary on John to examine the issues. Suffice it to say that I believe this is a story about something that actually happened, that it is therefore history, and that it is a fitting episode within John's account of the ministry of Jesus.

The action begins with the teachers of the Law and the Pharisees bringing a woman to Jesus who has been caught red-handed in the act of adultery. It seems that they had already decided that they wanted to do this and had been watching out for someone to fall sexually so they could publicly expose Jesus in some way. What they were doing hunting for a couple committing adultery is a question that's worth asking. It must have involved a measure of voyeurism that suggests more than a little hypocrisy. But we will let that go.

Now they bring the woman who's been a partner in this act to Jesus. Notice that the man is not brought. When a man commits adultery, he is regarded by his peers as macho. When a woman commits the same offence, she is often regarded by the men as loose. These men make her stand before Jesus and the people that he's with. As a rabbi, he would now be expected to tell everyone what the Law says and then to enforce it. The Law regarded adultery as one of the gravest sins and the punishment in this instance should have been death. What will Jesus say?

We shall see in the days to come. In the meantime, there's a warning here. The Scribes and the Pharisees don't treat the woman as a person; they treated her in a completely loveless way.

Devotion: Abba, Father, help me never to treat people like cases. Please prevent me from becoming like the Scribes and the Pharisees, who preferred Law to love. Keep reminding me that you are kind as well as holy, in Jesus' name. Amen.

Jesus bent down and started to write on the ground with his finger.

John 8:6

As Jesus is presented with a woman caught in the very act of adultery, he is now in a moral dilemma. If he says that the woman should be stoned to death, then he will be accused of lacking compassion. If he says that she should be released, then he will be accused of moral compromise. What is he to say?

The text tells us that Jesus bends down and starts to write with his finger in the dust at his feet. The verb translated here as "write" is *katagrapho*, which suggests that Jesus was writing actual words. The word translated 'ground' is the noun *ge*, which can be translated earth, land and even world. Jesus doesn't reply immediately. He bides his time.

Why did Jesus do this? One quite plausible suggestion is that Jesus was writing in the sand a list of the sins that the accusers had themselves committed. This suggestion comes from the use of the verb *katagrapho*, which doesn't just mean "to write" (which would be the verb *grapho*); it means to write down a record against someone.

Whatever the correct interpretation, Jesus took his time over answering the woman's accusers. He knew that he was really the one on trial, not her. He spent a few moments seeking the Father's wisdom in this situation. Jesus writes in the sand while he waits for his Father's words.

It is so easy when we are cornered in an argument to look for the wisdom of words to help us out. In these situations we so often answer too quickly and reveal our lack of wisdom. How much better it is to wait upon the Father and listen to what he is saying. His words of wisdom are so much more succinct and telling than our wisdom of words.

Jesus excelled in a spiritual gift that the apostle Paul mentions in 1 Corinthians 12:1–11: "the word of wisdom". This is a gift that we can ask the Father for as well.

Devotion: *Abba, Father, teach me to bide my time when I'm asked a question that's hard to answer, as your Son did here. Help me to pause and listen to you for your words of wisdom. Help me to trust in you, Abba, and not to lean on my own understanding, in Jesus' name. Amen.*

When they kept on questioning him, he straightened up and said to them, "Let any one of you who is without sin be the first to throw a stone at her." Again he stooped down and wrote on the ground.

John 8:7–8

I wonder if you've ever been in a situation where you've been really put on the spot and you don't know what to say. Jesus was in that predicament here. He has been presented with a woman caught in the act of adultery and according to the Law she should now be stoned to death. Her accusers have asked him what to do. He stoops and writes in the sand. Then he straightens up and says, "Let any one of you who is without sin be the first to throw a stone at her."

Jesus stands up to the Scribes and the Pharisees and gives the perfect answer; he says, "Okay, you can go ahead and stone her. But the sinless person must go first." Interestingly, the Greek word translated "without sin" here is *anarmatetos*, which means, "without a sinful desire". Jesus is therefore saying, "Let the person who has never had a sinful sexual desire throw the first stone." If any of the men had tried to punish the woman after that they would have been exposed as the ultimate hypocrite.

One of the most challenging areas for a Christian to be truly authentic is the area of human sexuality. What Jesus reveals here is the Father's longing for us to walk in sexual purity as sons and daughters, not as slaves. Sons and daughters know they are flawed and therefore will not conduct witch-hunts against others who are sexually broken. Pharisees do the opposite. They hold themselves to a standard that they are not really keeping and then judge others for falling short.

Our task is not to approach human sexuality with the mindset of the Pharisees. Our task is to approach it with the mindset of Jesus. This is the difference between slavery and sonship. Sons and daughters understand that wrong sexual choices are substitute affections. They also understand that such choices never satisfy the deep need for love that lies at the core of our being. Only one thing can do that – the Father's love. Tomorrow we will discover that this is what the woman is about to receive from Jesus.

Devotion: Abba, Father, I ask you to forgive me for those times when I have lived like a slave in the area of my sexuality. Help me to walk in purity in this aspect of my life. Help me to do this out of love not out of law. Empower me to live like a son, not a slave, in Jesus' name. Amen.

> *Jesus straightened up and asked her, "Woman, where are they? Has no one condemned you?" "No one, sir," she said. "Then neither do I condemn you," Jesus declared. "Go now and leave your life of sin."*
>
> John 8:10–11

As this story of the woman caught in the act of adultery reaches its conclusion we wait to see how Jesus will respond. Everyone else has left the scene after Jesus' words, "Let any one of you who is without sin throw the first stone." All the men who had sought to accuse her have left, beginning with the old men first. Presumably the older men were more in touch with their sinful humanity than the younger ones. They knew that Jesus' words had left them looking exposed and foolish on the moral high ground they'd been occupying. Now they have climbed down and retreated, the younger men following sheepishly in their wake.

So now it's just Jesus and the poor, hounded, and dishevelled woman. He says two things to her. First he tells her that he does not condemn her. Second he tells her to sin no more.

Once again we see the glorious balance of those two qualities that John has told us were the chief attributes of Jesus. In John 1:14 he revealed that Jesus was full of "grace and truth". These words point to two great virtues: compassion and confrontation. Jesus was first of all compassionate and merciful with the people he met. He was secondly confrontational when people needed to hear the truth. In his communication of truth he was merciful. In his exercise of mercy he was truthful. Authentic discipleship involves imitating Jesus; it means exhibiting non-judgmental compassion and honest confrontation.

One of the great insights of John's Gospel is this: that Jesus' words and actions reveal the Father heart of God. In his treatment of the woman caught in the act of adultery, we see a beautiful and memorable example of this. Jesus treats the woman with a fatherly compassion. He says, "I don't judge or condemn you." But he also reveals the Father's challenge. He says, "Don't commit adultery again. Restrict the joyful expression of your sexuality to the covenant of marriage."

Devotion: *Abba, Father, I praise you for what I see in the example of your Son in this story. Help me to grow in compassion for others. But help me not to collude with compromise by remaining silent when you call me to challenge others in love. Amen.*

When Jesus spoke again to the people, he said, "I am the light of the world. Whoever follows me will never walk in darkness, but will have the light of life."

John 8:12

After the story of the woman taken in adultery, we are still in the Temple precincts during the Feast of Tabernacles. Most likely the story we have been studying for the last few days took place in the Court of the Women, which was just beyond the Court of the Gentiles (where the non-Jewish pilgrims were allowed), and was the only part of the Temple a woman was permitted to enter.

In the Court of the Women there were four enormous candelabras. They were known collectively as *menorhot* and were made of gold. Each *menorah* was composed of seven branches and together these twenty-eight lights illuminated the Temple courts. Indeed, it was said that the light created by these four *menorhot* radiated so brightly that they illuminated the city of Jerusalem for miles around.

On each evening, the priests lit the *menorah*. They replenished the oil in the branches and replaced the wicks. They had to climb ladders to do this because the candelabras were so tall. As the candles blazed throughout each night, all the pilgrims camping out in their Tabernacles or booths would see the light and remember how their ancestors were led by a pillar of fire by night in the wilderness.

It was during the lighting of these *menorhot* on an evening towards the end of the Feast that Jesus uttered the words, "I am the light of the world." Jesus once again announced that he was fulfilling the Feast of Tabernacles. Just as he had invited the thirsty to come to him when the priests brought water into the Temple, so now he tells everyone he is the light of the world as the candles are lit.

In saying this Jesus again uses the divine name ("I am") and reveals his divinity. In Psalm 27:1 we read "The Lord is my light." Jesus is the Lord who lights up our lives.

Devotion: *Abba, Father, thank you that your Son Jesus is the light of the world who entered the darkness of our world. As your Son, he shone the light on your character and revealed you as our Father. This is the source of our life and we thank you so much. Amen.*

"I am not alone. I stand with the Father, who sent me."

John 8:16

There are many signs and symptoms of what I call the orphan heart condition. The orphan heart is the heart that feels separated from its father's love. It is the heart that has never felt loved, valued, protected, and provided for. It is the heart that doesn't know a father's love and feels like it belongs nowhere.

The orphan heart condition is very common today, both inside and outside the church. This is because much of the world is now in the grip of a pandemic of fatherlessness. So many children today are growing up without the love of a father – so many, in fact, that it is possible to speak of this generation as "the orphan generation".

There are many signs and symptoms of the orphan heart condition. Orphans tend to be people who feel sad and unsafe. They strive to earn people's affection and value through performance. They mistrust others and are often secretive. They feel a deep sense of rejection and shame and they feel all alone.

The only person who can heal this orphan heart is Jesus. Jesus was the exact opposite of an insecure and striving orphan; Jesus was the Son who knew with certainty the love of his heavenly Father. Jesus rested in a deep sense of security about his Father's love. Even under pressure, Jesus lived out of a sense of his Sonship.

Here in the Temple in Jerusalem, when so many people in the crowd are accusing and intimidating him, Jesus rests in his position as the Father's Son. He is not looking for their affirmation and acceptance; he rests in the knowledge that his Father already affirms and accepts him. He doesn't need their love; he already has his Father's love.

In the midst of the crowd, Jesus says, "I am not alone. My dad and I stand together." Jesus was not an orphan; he was the Son. He didn't feel isolated in the universe; he felt encircled by his Father's love. He didn't stand alone; he stood with his Dad. What an example for us!

Devotion: Abba, Father, help me always to know that I don't stand alone but that you stand with me. Heal me of any orphan-hearted feelings of isolation. I know that the devil isolates but I also know that Jesus integrates. Let me be integrated today, in Jesus' name. Amen.

Then they asked him, "Where is your father?" "You do not know me or my Father," Jesus replied. "If you knew me, you would know my Father also."

John 8:19–20

The people in the crowd in the Temple were not used to relating to God as "Father". This was very strange to their ears. The Jews in Jesus' day commonly related to God as "Lord" and "King", not Father and Friend. Their God was a transcendent reality – the God of the faraway place, wholly other, beyond our reach. The God of Jesus was this too, but he was also the God of the near-at-hand, within the reach of thirsty souls. For Jesus, God was and is Abba, Father.

As Jesus continues to speak about his "Father", his contemporaries are baffled. They ask, "Where is your father?" They interpret Jesus literally and ask him where Joseph is. Jesus replies that they do not know his Father. If they had recognized who Jesus was then they would know the Father. Jesus is the Father's only Son by nature. Acknowledging the Son should lead to acknowledging the Father because the Son reveals the Father in everything he says and does.

Let's pause and reflect on Jesus' words, "If you knew me, you would know the Father." Let me ask you, "Do you know the Father?" Many believers have come to know Jesus and have put their trust in him. This is the most important decision that a person can make; it is the decision that saves a person from being eternally separated from the Father. Knowing Jesus is the most critical thing in your life and mine.

But knowing Jesus isn't the end game. Jesus came not only so that we might enter into a relationship with him by faith; he came to lead us to the perfect Father. Jesus was our mediator in this. He closed the gap between earth and heaven on the Cross and he did this to provide the way to the Father (John 14:6). To know Jesus personally without knowing Abba relationally is to live in an incomplete reality.

The truth is: we were always meant to become Abba's children (2 Corinthians 6:18). Isn't it time to fall in love with the Father?

Devotion: Almighty God, I thank you for the simplicity and the challenge of Jesus' teaching about knowing you as Abba, Father especially here in John 8. Release more of your Spirit of adoption into my heart today so that I might not only know Jesus, but know you too. Amen.

They did not understand that he was telling them about his Father.

John 8:27

Jesus has just been teaching the crowds about his authority. He tells them that they are from below while he is from above. They are earth-bound creatures while he is the man from heaven. He warns them to listen to him because if they don't believe in him they will die in their sins. They reply, "Who are you to say such things?" Jesus adds that the one who has sent him is reliable and true and that he has only spoken what he was told to say.

It is at this point that John tells us that the people did not understand that Jesus was speaking to them about his Abba, his Father. They simply weren't used to this way of relating to God. Their way was the way of religion. In the religious mindset, God is a master and the believer is a slave. In Jesus' mind, God is a Father and the believer is a son or a daughter. In the religious mindset, God is remote. In Jesus' life, God is relational. Jesus stands for the very opposite of religion.

The people in the crowds simply didn't understand the way Jesus was speaking. They didn't have any personal experience of God as a Father who speaks to his children personally. As a result, they couldn't tune in to his wavelength of spiritual intimacy. Jesus knew God as his Abba – his Daddy, Papa, and his dearest Dad. This was the reality in which he lived all the time. He knew the Father's heart and he heard the Father's voice. They, on the other hand, did not understand these things.

One of the greatest needs in the church today is a revelation of the Father heart of God. There is far too much religion and not enough reality. Jesus didn't come to start a religion; he came to start a relationship. Through his death and resurrection, he opened up the way to his Father's house so that lost spiritual orphans could come running home like the prodigal into his welcoming arms of love. That's what Christianity is all about.

The church needs the revelation of the Father. Maybe you need that too. Maybe you need more of that today.

Devotion: *Abba, Father, I thank you for the example of your Son Jesus who lived in the reality of your love. I pray that I too would learn to live like a son or a daughter. Help me to enjoy intimacy with you and to hear your voice. Take me further up and further in to your heart. Amen.*

> *"When you have lifted up the Son of Man, then you will know that I am he and that I do nothing on my own but speak just what the Father has taught me."*
>
> John 8:28

Christians have traditionally understood the Cross in many different ways. They have understood Jesus' death in a commercial way – as a redemption in which people are bought out of slavery by the power of Christ's blood. They have understood it in a sacrificial way – as the slaughter of the Lamb of God for our sins, once and for all. They have understood it in a martial way – as the defeat of the devil in the war against darkness. They have understood it in a legal way – as the pardon won for guilty sinners by the substitutionary death of Jesus.

John's greatest contribution to our understanding of the crucifixion is to see it as revelation. In John, the lifting up of Jesus at Calvary (and subsequently in his resurrection and ascension) is an event that unveils heavenly truth. It tells us that Jesus loved us more than any other man who has ever lived. It tells us that Jesus lived out of a greater love – the love that lays down its life for its friends. It tells us that God is a Father who loves us so much that he would even give up his one and only Son so that we might experience his divine embrace.

John's contribution to our understanding of the Cross is immense. John sees the Cross as revelatory. The crucifixion and exaltation of Jesus confirms that he is the divine "I am". It reveals that he is truly the Son of the Father. It underlines the fact that Jesus only ever said what the Father said; he only ever did what the Father did. And if the Son only ever did what the Father was doing, then the Father was involved in the Calvary event too. He suffered as his Son suffered.

In John's eyes, the Cross is the Father's loudest shout in history – a passionate and echoing cry of "I love you" to a deaf world. While others see the Cross in a legal way, John sees it in a relational way. In John's understanding, Jesus' death is the ultimate revelation of divine love. Let's respond to his love with our love.

Devotion: *Abba, Father, I thank you that the lifting up of the Son of Man was the most revelatory event in history. Help me to delve more deeply into its rich meaning and continuing significance. Help me to respond to your overtures of self-giving love today, in Jesus' name. Amen.*

> **"The one who sent me is with me; he has not left me alone, for I always do what pleases him."**
>
> John 8:29

I love these words, "he has not left me alone". Jesus is talking about his heavenly Abba. He's saying, "Even though I've come from heaven to earth, my Abba is still with me. Even though I'm now a human being, my heavenly Father has not left me. He never leaves me because I'm his Son and he loves me."

That's a great thing to say about any dad. Dads are supposed to be there for you. Abba, Father was always there for Jesus and still is. This is an indisputable fact and an unchanging reality.

If you've had a father who deserted you or left you when he didn't want to, then it's a heart-warming revelation to find that you have a Father who will never forsake you. All of us should know this. Once we have made a decision to follow Jesus we receive the Spirit of adoption and we know God as our Father and indeed cry out, "Abba, Father" (Romans 8:15). We are unconditionally loved by a dad who has promised that he will never forsake us (Hebrews 13:5).

I have to admit that it took me a long time before I could say with confidence that I knew this to be true. Having had a biological father who left before I was born, whose name I don't even know, I found it easy to relate to Jesus but not to the Father. I thought fathers were people who deserted you. But then one day I had an encounter with the Father's love. I had a direct, personal revelation that my heavenly Father had adopted me and that I would never be alone again because my Abba, Father is always there beside me.

Jesus said, "he has not left me alone". The word he uses for "leave" is the same he will use in John 14:18 when he tells his disciples, "I will not *leave* you as orphans." Orphans feel fatherless and all alone. Sons and daughters know that the Father will never leave them. Let's move from the orphan state to the state of the son or the daughter.

Devotion: *Abba, Father, I pray that you will help me to know by personal revelation that you will never leave nor forsake me. Thank you that you are faithful not an abandoning Father. Heal my orphan heart so that I may know with confidence that you are always with me. Amen.*

To the Jews who had believed him, Jesus said, "If you hold to my teaching, you are really my disciples. Then you will know the truth, and the truth will set you free."

John 8:31–32

I want to point something out today that I believe is of immense significance if we are to interpret the rest of John chapter 8 in a responsible way. I say this because parts of this chapter have been used to abuse the Jewish people. Some have taken hold of Jesus' words – such as, "Your father is the devil" (John 8:44) – and said that they are a description of the Jewish people in general. This has a fuelled an anti-Semitism which has, in turn, led to the most appalling atrocities against the Jewish people. Tragically this has derived ultimately from the church's own wrong understanding of both Scripture and the heart of the Father.

As we come to verse 31 of John 8, let it be noted that Jesus is not talking to or about Jewish people in general. He is talking to and about Jewish people "who had believed him" – people who had come to faith but then rejected it. The harsh language of John 8 is therefore not a condemnation of the Jewish people as a whole. How could it when Jesus was a Jew and his disciples were Jewish? It is a condemnation of what is called "apostasy", of starting out on a journey of faith with Jesus and then consciously rejecting everything to do with him. John 8 is not about ethnicity; it's about apostasy. Like Hebrews 6:4–6, these alarming words are directed at those who have fallen away.

We know from the end of John chapter 6 that there were Jewish disciples who fell away because they found Jesus' teaching too difficult. Here in John 8:31–32 and the rest of the chapter Jesus makes one final, urgent, and passionate plea to those who used to be his followers in Jerusalem. He tells them to hold onto his teaching. He tells these former disciples not to be deceived by the devil who is the father of lies. If they stick with his teaching then they will know the truth. If they know the truth then they will be free from deception and no longer vulnerable to defection. These words should be taken to heart by all Christians today.

Devotion: *Abba, Father, I want to pray for your forgiveness for the way the church has misinterpreted this chapter and used it to foster hatred against the Jewish people. I renounce anti-Semitism in Jesus' name, and I pray for more of your heart for the chosen people. Amen.*

> **"Now a slave has no permanent place in the family, but a son belongs to it forever."**
>
> John 8:35

This is one of those verses that you can easily pass over too quickly and miss. Here Jesus uses a very simple word picture from the family as it was understood in his time. Speaking to people who don't realize how enslaved they are, he says that slaves don't belong in the family and have no place in the home where they serve. In stark contrast, a son belongs to his family and knows that he has a place not only in his home but in his father's heart. Slaves live in a constant state of insecurity. Sons live in the opposite spirit – secure in their daddy's love.

Jesus contrasts two different kinds of spirituality here. The first is the spirituality of slavery. This is really the heart attitude of spiritual orphans. They are constantly striving to earn other people's love and value, especially God's. They don't really feel as if they belong anywhere and live in a profound sense of loneliness – both at a human and a spiritual level. They are deeply insecure about whether they are loved and at the same time prone to anger because of what they lack. Their whole lives are lived out of a sense of "ought and must". It is a life of religious servitude.

The son or the daughter lives in the entirely opposite spirit. Their spirituality is one of position not performance. They know that they are loved unconditionally by their Father and live from approval not for approval. They feel a very strong sense of belonging, both in relationship to their heavenly Dad and in relationship to their brothers and sisters. They know that they will never be alone and that their Father loves them dearly and is always by their side. They are completely at peace about their Father's acceptance and also their place in his family. They live only to please him by doing his will and living by faith.

Jesus says to people who are religious slaves that they can stay as slaves or choose to live as sons and daughters. Slaves come and go in the household. Sons and daughters remain. Put like that it's amazing that anyone would want anything to do with slavery.

Devotion: *Abba, Father, I thank you for those like William Wilberforce whom you raised up to abolish slavery. We pray that you will continue to set free those who are literally enslaved. But we also pray that you would bring many people out of spiritual slavery too, in Jesus' name. Amen.*

"If the Son sets you free, you will be free indeed."

John 8:36

I have a good friend who often says this when he preaches: "I want to get everything that Jesus paid for." In other words, he wants to receive every benefit of the finished work of the Cross. Forgiveness and pardon for sin are a great blessing. No one should ever underestimate or trivialize these great gifts. But if there's more that was achieved at Calvary, then he wants those blessings too. And I have to say, I'm with him on that. I too want everything that Jesus paid for.

In John 8:36, Jesus introduces a blessing that I believe we need to emphasize far more than we do. It is the blessing of freedom. Jesus says to his accusers that they are effectively living out of slavery. He tells his enemies that they can be set free from their slavery. They can be set free from the orphan-hearted rebellion that he calls sin. Freedom is theirs in Jesus if they want it. They can be sons not slaves but to do that they need to come to the Son.

One of the main characteristics of those who have truly come to love Jesus and know God as their Abba, Father is freedom. They are no longer bound to a legalistic drive to earn God's love through performance. They rest secure in their Daddy's unconditional affection. Furthermore, they are no longer enslaved by the desires of their human flesh. Rather they have had their hearts seized by the love of all loves and infinitely prefer the love of the Father to the love of this world.

Jesus says to those who think they are sons when in fact they are slaves, "I can set you free, and if I set you free, this will be real, lasting freedom not fake, religious freedom."

Today it is said that there are many believers within the church who are forgiven but not free. Forgiveness of sins is a great blessing of the Cross. Freedom from slavery is as well. Our destiny as sons and daughters of the Father is to be free as well as forgiven.

So come to the Son today and ask to be "free indeed"!

Devotion: *Abba, Father, I come to you in Jesus' name to ask for a revelation of your love that breaks every chain of slavery in my life, whether these are chains of sin or chains of legalism. I want to experience the blessing of freedom and enjoy being Abba's child. Amen.*

"I am telling you what I have seen in the Father's presence...".
John 8:38

Let's celebrate for a moment the relationship that Jesus enjoyed with his heavenly Father. Jesus says that he reports what he has seen and heard in the presence of the Father. Jesus lived out of an immediate intimacy with Abba, Father. In heaven, Jesus enjoyed – and indeed enjoys today – a face-to-face communion of love with his Daddy. He is forever so close to his Father's heart that he hears what his Father is saying and he knows what his Father was doing. When he was born on earth as a human being, Jesus didn't lose this intimacy. He still enjoyed the Father's presence. In fact, everything that he said came from this unhindered and perfect union with Abba, Father. Everything he did came from this source of divine love. That is why he can say quite simply and boldly to his accusers, "I am telling you what I have seen in the Father's presence."

Is it possible for us as believers to have this kind of relationship with the Father? The answer is, "yes, and no". Let's deal with the "no" part first. What we cannot enjoy in this life is the same kind of face-to-face intimacy with the Father that Jesus enjoyed in heaven and indeed on earth. Jesus could say that he "saw" the Father and that he "heard" the Father. His intimacy with Abba was immediate. There was no need of any kind of mediator. It was indeed "face to face".

With us it is different. We cannot behold the Father's face with this kind of immediacy. We can relate to the Father, yes, but our relationship is a mediated rather than an immediate one. We need a mediator to enjoy the Father's presence and this mediator is Jesus. We have access to Abba only through Jesus and in the power of the Spirit (Ephesians 2:18). We cannot know the Father without knowing the Son, and we cannot know the Son without the help of the Holy Spirit.

One day we will see the Father face to face and he will wipe away every tear from our eyes (Revelation 21:3–4). In the meantime, we relate to the Father through Jesus, and we experience the Father's love through the indwelling presence of his Holy Spirit (Romans 5:5).

Devotion: *Dear Father, I am looking forward to the day when I'm going to see you face to face. I pray that you would help me to draw closer to Jesus and to be more filled with your Spirit that I might dwell in your presence and hear your voice today, in Jesus' name. Amen.*

"We are not illegitimate children," they protested. "The only Father we have is God himself."

John 8:41

When my twin sister Claire and I were born in 1960, we were born to a single mother. Our biological father had left our mum before she gave birth to us. They were not married. When Claire and I were growing up as children we became aware of a difference between us and other children whose parents were married. We were "illegitimate" because our parents had never married. They were "legitimate". The colloquial term for this illegitimacy is of course "bastard", a word that was used of me on at least one occasion as an insult. It produced a root of shame in my life that was only removed when I came to know the Father I had been waiting for – the Abba, Father revealed by Jesus.

Jesus' enemies in John 8 say, "We are not illegitimate children". Actually, the phrase is slightly different in the original. In the Greek language there is a word for "illegitimate child". It is the word *nothos*, which the writer to the Hebrews uses in Hebrews 12:8 for the person who will not accept the loving discipline of their Heavenly Father. Here in John 8:41, the word is not *nothos* but a phrase that should be translated "born of fornication". Jesus' opponents claim that they have not been born as a result of sexual immorality (sexual intercourse outside wedlock). They have been born within the covenant marriage between Yahweh and his people. They are therefore the legitimate children of the Father.

Here again we see how Jesus' enemies have renounced love for Law. They are falling back on the fact that they can trace their ancestry back to Abraham and that they're part of God's covenant people. What they fail to see is that it isn't enough just to say that they're in the family whose Father is ultimately God. That is merely to state a legal fact. Jesus reveals that there's much more to it than that. You can be in the family and have no intimate relationship with the Father. You can be a child by law but not a child in love. The Jews who are talking to their fellow Jew, Jesus of Nazareth, fail to see this. The issue for them is legitimacy not intimacy. The issue for Jesus is simply this: do you love Abba, Father?

Devotion: *Dear loving, heavenly Father, help me never to get into a mindset that believes I am your child because of my family tree or my blood line. Help me to understand that legitimacy is about intimacy. Help me to fall deeper in love with you, in Jesus' name. Amen.*

> *Jesus said to them, "If God were your Father, you would love me, for I came from God and now am here."*
>
> John 8:42

On thirteen occasions in the Old Testament there are glimpses of the Fatherhood of God. For example, in Deuteronomy 1:31 Moses tells the Israelites that God has led them through the wilderness as a father carries his young son upon his shoulders. In Psalm 68:5 King David declares that God is "A father to the fatherless". In 2 Samuel 7:14, God says of David's son Solomon, "I will be his father and he will be my son." In Isaiah 63:16 and 64:8 the people of Israel declare, "you are our Father". In these and other places God reveals himself as "Father" to his chosen people. This was his desire from the beginning. He always wanted his people to relate to him as Abba.

But the tragic fact was this: God's children rejected him. They went after foreign gods and worshipped idols. They forgot the Lord and abandoned his ways. Even though God had treated his people as a firstborn, much loved son (Exodus 4:22), his people sinned and in the process rebelled against love itself. You can hear something of the agony in the Father's heart over this in Hosea 11:1–3 and especially in Jeremiah 3:19–20, where he says: "How gladly would I treat you like my children and give you a pleasant land, the most beautiful inheritance of any nation. I thought you would call me 'Father' and not turn away from following me. But like a woman unfaithful to her husband, so you have been unfaithful to me, O house of Israel, declares the Lord."

In John chapter 8, Jesus talks to fellow Jews who call God "Father" but do so out of religion not relationship. The proof of this is the fact that they fail to love Jesus. If they really did know God as Father, then they would recognize that Jesus was his Son and welcome, honour and adore him. But they do none of these things. They accuse him and try to kill him.

The lesson is this: it is not enough to know God as Father conceptually. We must know the Father affectionately. This can only happen through an encounter with Jesus and an experience of the Holy Spirit.

Devotion: *Dear God, I don't want to be one of those who uses the word "Father" of you but has no real experience of what that means. I want to know you relationally. Religion is simply not enough for me. Help me to enjoy intimacy with the world's greatest Dad, in Jesus' name. Amen.*

"You belong to your father, the devil, and you want to carry out your father's desires."

John 8:44

We are going to have to tackle these difficult verses in John chapter 8. It is really important that we interpret this passage responsibly because they have so often been taken out of context. For example, in the 1930s, the Nazis produced a children's book that was designed to foster hatred of the Jews. On the first page were the words, "The father of the Jews is the devil", a direct quote from John 8:44. Do we need any more evidence than this that John 8 has been abused in atrocious ways?

Let's remember what I wrote about John 8:21–32. Jesus is not addressing Jewish people in general. He is talking to those who had believed in him but who have fallen away. Far from slipping away into silent anonymity, they are now accusing and threatening Jesus in a very vocal way and even trying to kill him. John 8:44 is accordingly not directed against the Jewish people as whole. It is directed against those Jews who were formerly pro-Christ but who are now anti-Christ.

Why did John choose to include these verses? Surely they are out of place in a story where the primary theme is the Father's love? Perhaps I should say something here about my understanding of the original context of John's Gospel. I have become persuaded that this Gospel was published in a situation where Jewish believers in Jesus were being persecuted by fellow Jews who did not believe in Jesus, and worse still, by fellow Jews who had once believed in him.

John decided to include Jesus' challenging words in John 8 because he wanted to encourage his own readers not to become like those Jews who had believed but now did not, but to hold fast to the teaching of Jesus and remain in relationship with the Messiah.

What a lesson. All of us who confess Jesus as Lord need to stay true. We must always remain loyal to Jesus even if it means that our own people reject us, as they did Jesus.

Devotion: *Abba, Father, help me to be faithful to Jesus to the very end of my life. Don't ever let me turn against you or your Son. I renounce the spirit of anti-Christ in the mighty name of Jesus and I resolve to remain a loyal child of yours and disciple of his all my days. Amen.*

"Whoever belongs to God hears what God says."

John 8:47

One of the hallmarks of being an adopted son or a daughter of God is that we can hear what the Father is saying. This is what Jesus is driving at here in his heated debate with those who had once followed him but are now defecting, and indeed rejecting him. Jesus tells them that those who belong to the Father hear the Father. Those who do not are deaf to the Father's voice.

This point is made also by the apostle Paul in Romans 8:14 when he says that those who are led by the Spirit of God are the sons of God. The adopted children of God know the leading of the Holy Spirit. They have learned to listen to the promptings of the Spirit in all situations. Their ears are fine-tuned to Abba's voice.

How in practice do we hear God speak? I have an acrostic that I use which may help here. In the days before radar, sailors navigated by the stars. I use the word *stars* to sum up the primary ways in which the Father speaks to us.

S is for Scripture. The Father speaks first and foremost to us through his Word. The Bible is our Father's book. Through it Abba speaks to us.

T is for Testimony. By testimony I mean the inner witness of the Holy Spirit. We know the Father's voice in our hearts.

A is for Advice. The Father speaks to us through the advice and wisdom of other believers in the church.

R is for Revelation. The Father communicates through prophetic phenomena such as dreams, visions, pictures, and so on.

S is for Situation. Abba, Father often speaks to us through our circumstances.

Hearing the Father's voice is an art that all his adopted children need to cultivate. If we belong to him, we will hear him.

Devotion: *Abba, Father, I thank you that you still speak to us today. Help me to learn the unique ways in which you communicate with me. Make me more receptive to the whisperings of your Spirit. Help me to know better the mind of Christ in all things, in his name. Amen.*

"Very truly I tell you, whoever obeys my word will never see death."

John 8:51

What did Jesus mean when he promised that those who obey him, "will never see death"?

The answer will be found if we first define the word "death". Was Jesus referring to literal, physical death here? If so, was he claiming that the person who is consistently and unwaveringly obedient to his teaching will never die? Clearly this cannot be the case. If it was then there would be some believers who would have gone straight to heaven without having to endure the process of dying and death itself. This self-evidently has not occurred. So what did Jesus mean?

When Jesus was talking about death here he was talking about a second, spiritual death, not our first, physical death. The New Testament talks about death in two ways. There is first of all the death that we must all one day die. As the poet Robert Frost once said, we all have a "rendezvous with death". This is one form of death. However, the New Testament talks about a second death. This is a death that occurs after the last judgment at the end of time.

What kind of death is this? According to the Scriptures, Jesus is going to return on the clouds in great glory on the last day of history. When he does everyone will be raised from the dead, both the good and the bad, and all people will be judged. When they are, those who have chosen to believe in Jesus will live forever. Those who have wilfully rejected Jesus will experience a second, spiritual and eternal death. It is this death that Jesus is referring to in John 8:51.

Jesus tells his Jewish peers in Jerusalem that the only way they can guarantee living forever is by believing in him and keeping his word. The word "keep" here means "guard", "watch over", and "hold fast to". It is the word used in John 12:7 of Mary "keeping" her jar of aromatic oil for Jesus' burial. Jesus says that guarding and holding fast to his teaching is absolutely critical if we are to avoid the second death. We must keep on believing in Jesus and guarding his words in our hearts.

Devotion: Abba, Father, I want to thank you for the words of your Son, Jesus Christ. They are the most precious words in history – more costly than gold and more beautiful than diamonds. Help me to guard, cherish, and hold fast to them all the days of my life, in Jesus' name. Amen.

> *"You are not yet fifty years old,"* [the Jews] said to him,
> *"and you have seen Abraham!"* *"Very truly I tell you,"* Jesus
> answered, *"before Abraham was born, I am!"*
>
> John 8:57–58

Jesus' enemies have earlier claimed that Abraham is their father. The name "Abraham" contains the Hebrew word for father ("Ab", pronounced "Av") and the word *hamon* (multitudes of people) and can be translated "father of the multitudes". The word *hamon* is related to the verb *hama* which means to make a loud noise.

That seems extremely appropriate in the case of John 8. Here are some Jews who are now becoming extremely vocal towards Jesus. They claim to be the descendants of Abraham. In fact, they seek refuge in this idea, as if this inoculated them against spiritual blindness and death. These children of Abraham are indeed part of a noisy crowd.

Now once again I want to underline that this passage is not about all Jews in general. It is about a group who have become hostile to Jesus. And they are hostile because Jesus is saying that he is greater than Abraham. They point out that Jesus isn't yet fifty years old so how could he have even seen him.

Jesus says, "before Abraham was born, I existed". Here is the clearest claim we have on the lips of Jesus that he existed in history before he was born as a human being. Jesus says, "before Abraham was, I am". Jesus calls himself the "I am" here. "I am" is God's name in the Old Testament. Jesus is not just the "I was" or the "I will be". He is the "I am!"

So Jesus was alive before Abraham. Indeed, many would say that Jesus actually met Abraham, that he was one of the three men who visited Abraham at the oaks of Mamre in Genesis 18. Abraham was visited by the Trinity – by the Father, the Son, and the Holy Spirit! Jesus was one of the three that came and had fellowship with him.

Let's worship Jesus, the eternal I am and ask him to visit us today.

Devotion: *Abba, Father, I want to worship you because there is no one greater than Jesus. At his name every knee is going to bow and every tongue confess that he is Lord, to your glory, Father. I thank you for honouring your Son so. I give him all the honour today. Amen.*

As he went along, he saw a man blind from birth. His disciples asked him, "Rabbi, who sinned, this man or his parents, that he was born blind?"

John 9:1–2

At the end of John chapter 8, Jesus slips out of the Temple courts before his enemies have a chance to seize him. Now he is walking with his disciples in Jerusalem and we read that he sees a blind man. We should note the use of the word "see" here. If ever there was a Bible story about "seeing", John chapter 9 is it.

And so the story begins with Jesus seeing a man who has been blind from birth. This is the only time in John's Gospel – or any of the Gospels – that we come across a person whose physical affliction has been with him since birth. Seeing him, the disciples ask Jesus whose sin was responsible for the man's condition – his or his parents.

This question may seem a little strange to our ears. After all, how could the man's sin have caused his blindness when he has been blind since birth? But the Jews of Jesus' day had a firm belief in the connection between sin and sickness. If someone was sick or disabled, then either they had sinned or their parents had sinned.

There is a hint of truth here because sickness is ultimately caused by sin, the sin of Adam and Eve. It was their primal disobedience that opened the door to disease and disability. So sickness is indeed *ultimately* caused by sin. But whether it is *immediately* caused by it is a different matter. Often it is simply a consequence of living in a fallen world.

As the disciples look at the blind man, they see him as a theological puzzle rather than a person in need. The disciples approach the blind man with theological curiosity. Jesus approaches him with touching compassion. While the disciples see him as a philosophical enigma, Jesus sees him as someone in need of the Father's love.

What will we do when we next see a sick or disabled person? Will we be clinical or will we be compassionate? Will we be like the disciples? Or will we be like Jesus?

Devotion: *Abba, Father, I want to pray for those I know who are sick and suffering. Please help me to approach them in the way that Jesus would. Fill me with your heavenly compassion so that I can be a channel of your love and a minister of your healing, in Jesus' name. Amen.*

> **"Neither this man nor his parents sinned," Jesus said, "but this happened so that the works of God might be displayed in him."**
>
> John 9:3

Yesterday we saw how the disciples approached the man born blind. They didn't go to Jesus and say, "Can we help this poor guy? Can you pray for his healing?" They treat him as a test case in a theological debate. They ask, "Who's to blame for this? Is it him or his parents?"

It is fascinating to see how Jesus responds. What will he say? He is the source of divine wisdom, the human incarnation of the all-knowing God, and the fount of all knowledge. What enlightenment will he offer on the greatest puzzle of all – the causes of human suffering?

Jesus avoids the issue altogether. He doesn't offer any explanation, other than to say what it isn't! He tells the disciples that the man's blindness has neither a generational nor a personal cause. Neither his parents nor the man himself were to blame for this condition.

Jesus' answer is all about the purpose of this sickness, not its origin. He says that the ultimate purpose is that the miracle-working power of God will be put on display in the events that follow. Jesus speaks only about the consequences not the causes here.

Does this mean that God caused the man's blindness in the first place? Not at all, we must distinguish between the Father's causative will and his permissive will here. There are things that he causes to happen and there are things that he allows to happen.

This is the latter. The Father permits the man to be born blind because he is absolutely brilliant at turning situations around for his glory. There is no one like Abba, Father. What the enemy intends for harm in our lives, he can turn to good. This is what he's going to do here.

Maybe some of us need to adopt a similar view in relation to sickness and suffering. This side of heaven's shores, we may have to learn to be content with knowing about purposes rather than causes – with knowing what may come out of sickness, rather than where it's from.

Devotion: Abba, Father, thank you for helping me to see there are limits to what my finite mind may be able to understand. In relation to sickness, my focus is so often on "Why has this happened?" From now on, may it be on "How may you be glorified through this?" in Jesus' name. Amen.

> **"As long as it is day, we must do the works of him who sent me.
> Night is coming, when no one can work. While I am in the world,
> I am the light of the world."**
>
> John 9:4–5

This is at first sight a hard saying to understand. What does Jesus mean by "day" and "night" in these verses? Why does he say that he is the light of the world only while he is in the world? Is he not the light of the world forever, not just during his earthly life?

Here, in a chapter of John's Gospel where we have already started to grapple with some of the deepest mysteries of human existence, Jesus now speaks in very enigmatic terms about the sense of urgency that he has about completing his Father's assignment.

Jesus begins by drawing a distinction between day and night. Day is the time for working. Night is the time for resting from work. Speaking figuratively, he is describing his two to three-year ministry as the daytime. It's the time for him to do the Father's work. But night-time is coming. This is the time of his departure. When night comes, the opportunities for him to minister miracles in his incarnate body will be over. The time for him working on the earth as a human being will have concluded and the time for him to go home will have come.

It is for this reason that Jesus says, "While I am in the world, I am the light of the world." While it is daytime, and he is ministering in Israel, his light shines for those who get a chance to see or to hear him in the flesh. But when night-time comes, and Jesus returns to Abba to sit and rest at his right hand in heaven, then the opportunity for enjoying this light in its present form will have gone.

So Jesus tells his disciples that there is a sense of urgency. It's daylight now, but night-time is coming. We too should live with this urgency. As sons and daughters, our lives are an opportunity to shine. We will not have this opportunity again so let's make the most of every day until the night-time comes and we can rest and sleep from our labours.

Devotion: Abba, Father, I thank you for giving your Son Jesus to this fallen, sinful world and for the radiant way in which he did your work. Thank you that you allowed such a bright light to burn for a while. Help me to be radiant for you every day, in Jesus' name. Amen.

> *Having said this, he spit on the ground, made some mud with*
> *the saliva, and put it on the man's eyes. "Go," he told him,*
> *"wash in the Pool of Siloam" (this word means "Sent"). So the*
> *man went and washed, and came home seeing.*

John 9:6–7

Many believers, confronted by the challenge of human sickness and suffering, are presented with a choice and the choice is this: Will they adopt a view that says that this is the Father's will and do nothing? Or will they see this situation as an opportunity for God's glory to be displayed and pray for an intervention from heaven?

Many Christians, when confronted by human tragedy, tend to default to mystery. They say, "This is tragic and it's unexplainable. Somehow we will get through this. But we're just going to have to learn to suffer in silence." They assume that suffering is part of the Father's will for their lives and they adopt a melancholic philosophy of resignation.

Other Christians, in the face of the same kind of difficulties, default to a very different mindset. Instead of saying, "This is to be endured", they say, "This may be tragic and unexplainable but we're going to believe God in spite of our circumstances. We are going to use this difficulty as an opportunity for Abba, Father to demonstrate his mighty power."

In the story of the man born blind, Jesus adopts the second way of thinking. He has already told his disciples that the purpose of the man's condition is to display the work of God. Now he spits on the ground, makes mud from the dirt and saliva, rubs it on the man's eyes, and tells him to go and wash in the Pool of Siloam.

In the context of a great need, Jesus doesn't default to mystery, he defaults to miracles. He doesn't adopt a theological view that says the man must accept his condition. He performs a creative miracle. He mixes his saliva (the DNA of heaven) with the clay beneath his feet (the stuff of the earth) and creates brand new eyes for the man!

Let's make sure that we don't forget to contend for miracles.

Devotion: *Abba, Father, I want to have the mind of Christ when it comes to sickness and suffering. Help me to be more active in my faith and to believe that you will display your work through my life. Help me to believe that you still do creative miracles today, in Jesus' name. Amen.*

"The man they call Jesus made some mud and put it on my eyes. He told me to go to Siloam and wash. So I went and washed, and then I could see."

John 9:11

Nothing is ever accidental in the kingdom of God. Let me give you an example of that. On 17 January 1977, I was walking down a street in Winchester in the south of England. I was far away from God but I was also living in the middle of a remarkable revival.

While walking towards my boarding house late at night, God began to speak into my rebellious heart. Nowhere near a church or a preacher, God pursued me in his love and utterly transformed my life. That street was where I was born again.

That street was – and indeed still is – called Kingsgate Street. The place where I encountered the King of Kings was called Kingsgate. It was a portal, a gateway, to the royal presence of God. I can't think of a more appropriately named road on which to get saved!

In the story of the man born blind, the critical moment comes when Jesus sends him off to a pool in Jerusalem called Siloam. The Pool of Siloam was a well-known site in the city. It was a large open-air pool (twenty by thirty feet), which was fed by a tunnel that King Hezekiah had built.

The name Siloam meant "sent" and referred to the fact that the water was sent via the tunnel into the city. It was from this pool that the priests took water for the Feast of Tabernacles, as we saw in our study of John 7:37. The blind man washed his eyes in this pool and came home seeing.

The blind man was "sent" to the pool called "sent" by the man who was "sent" by God. John clearly sees this as an example of divinely ordained synchronicity. We should too.

So nothing is accidental in the kingdom of God. And by the way, this pool did exist. Archaeologists discovered it in 1880, with an inscription revealing its name.

Devotion: *Abba, Father, thank you that even details like place names are significant to you. Help me to hear what you're saying about the places that I inhabit. Give me an expectation that heaven might invade my street, in Jesus' name. Amen.*

Some of the Pharisees said, "This man is not from God, for he does not keep the Sabbath."

John 9:16

If you're feeling right now, "Haven't we been here before?", then the answer is "yes"! In John chapter 5, the Pharisees rose up against Jesus for healing a man on the sabbath day, at a pool in Jerusalem (the Pool of Bethesda). Here they criticize Jesus for healing a man born blind at the Pool of Siloam in Jerusalem, also on the sabbath day.

The Pharisees in this story remind us of the toxic power of religion. Let's identify some characteristics of religious people from John 9.

First of all, religious people are defined by what they are against rather than by what they are for. Here the Pharisees are very negative people. They are clearly against Jesus healing the sick on the sabbath.

Secondly, religious people delight in witch-hunts. They stalk Jesus, or those whose lives have been changed by Jesus (like the man here in John 9) and they put them on public trial.

Thirdly, religious people are belligerent people who are always spoiling for a fight. In John chapter 9 they pick on an innocent man who's been healed on the sabbath and they use him to get at Jesus.

Fourthly, religious people manipulate others through fear and control. In John 9 they manage to bully the parents of the man who's been miraculously healed so that they won't give evidence.

Finally, religious people are single-issue people. In John 5 and here in John 9, their only concern is sabbath violation as understood not by Scripture but by their traditions and teachers.

We must take great care not to fall into religion. We are called to be like Jesus and to behave as sons and daughters not as orphans and slaves. We are called to be open-handed and compassionate like Jesus, not to stand with a fist like the Pharisees.

Devotion: *Dear loving Father, please keep me from moving from reality to religion and from love to law. I ask that you would make me very vigilant in this area. Enable me by your Holy Spirit to resist the impulse to become religious and to be like your Son Jesus, in his name. Amen.*

He replied, "Whether he is a sinner or not, I don't know. One thing I do know. I was blind but now I see!"

John 9:25

It has been rightly said that the man with a theology is at the mercy of the man with an experience. In other words, the person who has a testimony of what the Father has done in their lives has much greater credibility and authority than a person with just a theory.

The man who was formerly blind but now can see has a great testimony here in John chapter 9. The Pharisees have already questioned him once about his healing. They now summon him a second time and declare that Jesus is a sinner.

What does the man say? He tells the Pharisees that he doesn't know if Jesus qualifies as a sinner, as a law-breaker, in their terms. That's an issue of theology and is their concern. But what he does know is that he had been blind from birth, but that now he can see.

The man who has been healed is the real hero of John chapter 9. He is the one character who remains in focus from the story's beginning to its end. Jesus appears at the beginning and the end but not in the longest section, the middle of the episode. As far as John is concerned, the man giving his testimony in the presence of these intimidating Jewish leaders is an example for all believers.

This man teaches all of us that we must have an up-to-date story of what the Father has been doing in our lives. The man's story was a "now" story. It wasn't a story about what had happened decades before, although that is sometimes valuable as well. In addition, this courageous man teaches us that we must ensure that when we have a story we share it. We must never be afraid of giving verbal testimony to authentic experiences of the Father's love in action, however arrogant our listeners may be.

Let's always remember, testimony is the most powerful form of theology. Our story is more commanding than a theory.

Devotion: *Abba, Father, I pray today for a testimony of your love and power in my life that is real and compelling. And help me to have the confidence to say to even the most intimidating people, "Once I was blind, but now I can see", in Jesus' name. Amen.*

And they threw him out.

John 9:34

The story of the man born blind (but who has been wonderfully healed) is now coming to a crescendo. The Pharisees who have been interrogating him reach a fever pitch. Having hurled all manner of insults at the poor man, they now throw him out. The verb in the original Greek language is a violent one. It means that they drove him out with force. It is a word that can be translated "pluck out", "expel", or "eject".

What exactly are these Jewish leaders doing here? John has told us in verse 22 that the man's parents would not stand up for him because they were afraid that their Jewish leaders would throw them out of the synagogue. When John reports very tersely that "they threw him out", he means us to understand that they ejected him from the local synagogue and that this man was now excommunicated.

It is often very challenging for people of other faiths when they meet Jesus. Sometimes this can mean that their own family ostracizes them. It can also result in them becoming isolated from their community as a whole, especially from their faith community. Many Christians have had to suffer rejection from their family and excommunication from their former religion as a result of becoming followers of Jesus.

I am thinking right now of a man who was born a Muslim and who had a miraculous encounter with Jesus in a London hotel room after reading a Gideon Bible and having had a dream of Jesus. His family rejected him and his own people persecuted him because of his newfound faith in Christ. He was thrown out of his home and had to flee from his country.

The man born blind has gained his sight but has lost his family – both his literal and his spiritual family. For him, encountering the supernatural power of Jesus has cost him everything.

To those in the suffering church throughout the world today he is a great comfort. To those whose Christian lives are free from persecution, he is a great challenge.

Devotion: Abba, Father, I want to bring before you today the suffering church. I pray for all those I know who have paid a heavy price for confessing Jesus as their Lord. I pray that you will give them the boldness of the man in John 9, to keep standing for Jesus, in his name. Amen.

Jesus heard that they had thrown him out, and when he found him, he said, "Do you believe in the Son of Man?"

John 9:35

What a poignant and moving moment this is in the developing drama of John chapter 9. We read yesterday that the man had been cast or driven out of the synagogue by the Pharisees. What is to happen to him? Where will he go? Even his own family fails to rally round and pick him up. They are now nowhere to be seen. He is all alone, an outcast in a city that has been his home for decades.

John says that Jesus hears that the Pharisees have thrown the man out of the synagogue and that he finds him. The word "find" is used nineteen times in John and often of people finding Jesus. For example, in 7:34–36 it is used three times in the statement, "You will seek me and you will not find me". In John chapter 9 it is interesting to note that it is Jesus who seeks and finds. He takes the initiative to locate the man.

Why does Jesus bother to come back and find him? The answer is because Jesus doesn't just want a person to receive healing. He wants them to become a disciple as a result of their healing. In John 5:14, Jesus finds the man whom he's healed at the Pool of Bethesda. That man doesn't appear to become a disciple. Here he finds the man whom he's healed at the Pool of Siloam. This man does become a disciple.

The main point in today's verse, however, is really the contrast between the Pharisees and Jesus. The Pharisees drive the man out. Jesus, on the other hand, does not. As Jesus says in John 6:37, "All whom the Father gives me will come to me, and whoever comes to me I will never drive away." Here Jesus uses the same verb as is used of the man in John 9 – "to drive out". While the Pharisees expel people, Jesus welcomes them.

One of the greatest needs we all have is the need to belong. This poor man no longer belongs anywhere. He is a lost orphan in a now hostile world. But Jesus comes looking for him and in so doing the man receives not only a healing but also a home – a home in the Father's arms of love.

Devotion: Abba, Father, I thank you for your great compassion for those who feel rejected and alone in the world. I praise you that you want your church to go looking for the lost and to show them your merciful and inclusive love. Help me to partner with you in this, in Jesus' name. Amen.

Then the man said, "Lord, I believe," and he worshipped him.

John 9:38

Jesus has found the man who has been expelled from the synagogue. In looking for him he exhibits so much of the Father heart of God. His seeking of this lonely outcast highlights the pursuant and relentless love of God towards those who feel cast adrift on the sea of life. The man must have marvelled at this in subsequent years and thought often to himself, "He came looking for *me*."

When Jesus finds the man he presents him with a question, "Do you believe in the Son of Man?" Son of Man is a messianic title in John's Gospel. The man replies, "Sir, who is he that I may believe in him?" Jesus answers, "You have already seen him. In fact, he is the one speaking to you right now." At this the man responds with a confession of faith and says to Jesus, "Lord, I believe" and worships him.

What an extraordinary journey this man has been on. Look at the development of his faith. At the start of the story, the man refers to him as "the man they call Jesus" (verse 11). In the middle of the story he refers to Jesus as "a prophet" (verse 17). By the end he is calling Jesus "Lord" and acknowledging him as "the Son of Man". John brilliantly describes this person's increasing insight into who Jesus is.

The journey this man makes is a metaphor for the journey of every soul. All of us have to make our choice concerning Jesus. Is he just a man? Is he just a prophet? Or is he the Son of Man and the Lord? Maybe you agree that Jesus lived as a human being but was nothing more. Maybe you agree that he was a prophet but nothing more. Abba, Father wants you to see that Jesus is Lord and come to believe in him.

The man of Siloam not only regains his physical sight. He also learns to see with the eyes of his heart and confesses with his mouth that he believes in Jesus and worships him. In the process, his spiritual eyes become as clear as his physical eyes. The man who could see nothing before can see everything now.

Devotion: *Abba, Father, I pray that you would enlighten the eyes of my heart with revelation in the Holy Spirit so that I might know Jesus, and so that I might know you, much better than I do now. I want to see you as you really are. Help me to see you more clearly, in Jesus' name. Amen.*

Jesus said, "For judgment I have come into this world, so that the blind will see and those who see will become blind."

John 9:39

There seems to be a contradiction here. Earlier in John's Gospel we heard that Jesus came into the world not to judge it but to save it. Yet here we hear him declaring that he has come into the world "for judgment". How can we reconcile these two apparently opposite truths?

When we read in John 3:17 that God did not send Jesus to condemn the world but to save it, this is the truth. The Father's purpose in sending Jesus was not to judge human beings. That is going to happen at the end of time. The purpose of Christ's first coming was salvation. The purpose of his second coming will be judgment.

Nevertheless, people *were* judged in Jesus' lifetime but people brought judgment and condemnation upon themselves by their reactions to Jesus. According to John, some believed in him openly. Others believed in him secretly, for fear of the Jewish leaders. Others were confused and divided. Still others rejected him and even opposed him. In all of this Jesus did not judge those who opposed him. Those who refused to believe in Jesus brought judgment upon themselves.

This then explains the verse for today. Jesus came to save the world not to judge it, but people's negative verdict about him meant that they placed themselves under judgment. In rejecting Jesus, they rebelled against the Father's love, and in rebelling against the love of all loves, they condemned themselves.

The result is that the blind ended up seeing and those who had sight ended up being blind. Those who were spiritually blind ended up seeing, because they admitted their blindness. This is the story of the man born blind. Those who thought they saw spiritually ended up becoming spiritually blind. This is the story of the Pharisees.

The behaviour of the Pharisees in John 9 reminds us that spiritual pride is the greatest blockage to prophetic perception.

Devotion: *Abba, Father, help me to remain humble before you and always desperate for your help in seeing things as they really are. Banish every trace of a religious spirit from my life in Jesus' name, and help me to develop 20/20 spiritual vision, in Jesus' name. Amen.*

> **"I tell you the truth, the man who does not enter the sheep pen by the gate, but climbs in by some other way, is a thief and a robber."**
>
> John 10:1 (NIV)

As John chapter 10 begins we are still in Jerusalem. Jesus now begins to teach about sheep and sheep pens. These are word pictures that would have been very familiar in the agricultural world of the first century in Israel. They are images that point to the community of those who truly belong to the Father.

There is only one true way into this community and that is through Jesus. All through John's Gospel Jesus teaches that the only way to become a child of God and a member of the Father's family is through believing in him. A person can only enter the sheepfold through Jesus. As we will see in a few days' time, Jesus alone is the gate.

Why does Jesus move to this teaching about shepherds and sheep in John 10? The answer is because the Pharisees in John 9 had clearly revealed themselves to be false and harmful shepherds. When a poor, blind man had been healed they did not rejoice in his miracle nor did they welcome him into their fold. They interrogated him and to all intents and purposes put him on trial and sentenced him. They robbed him of his dignity and stripped him of his membership of the synagogue. In this respect, their behaviour couldn't have been less pastoral or shepherd-like. They were bad shepherds not good shepherds.

Jesus starts speaking of sheep and shepherds at the start of John 10 because he wants to make it very clear that the Pharisees are indeed spiritually blind. They have failed to see that all attempts to experience true spiritual light and life that seek to bypass Jesus are false and ultimately harmful. People who teach a Christ-less way into the Father's presence are thieves and robbers. They deceive people into thinking that they can become a child of God without believing in Jesus and in the process they deprive people of all the blessings of their salvation. Jesus is adamant; if you want to become part of the fold you have to entrust yourself to him.

Devotion: *Father, I pray that you would help me to be bolder when I meet people who deceive others spiritually, especially those that teach that people can know you without faith in your Son. Help me to speak the truth to them in a gracious and clear way, in Jesus' name. Amen.*

... his sheep follow him because they know his voice.

John 10:4

I want to introduce you to my older brother. He's called Giles. You don't know him, but I have known him for over fifty years. When my twin sister and I were adopted by Philip and Joy Stibbe, we were welcomed into a family of three people. My adoptive parents had a son of their own. Giles is their biological son. We were embraced and welcomed into a family with new parents and a wonderful older brother.

Having known Giles for a long time, I don't need him to introduce himself to me. When he phones me, he doesn't need to let me know, "It's Giles, your brother, speaking." When he's in the same room as me and I hear his voice, I know instantly that it's him because I have grown used to the specific intonations in the way he speaks, and the very distinctive turns of phrase that he uses. He is not just my brother; he's my friend.

In John 10:4, Jesus says of his followers that the "sheep follow him because *they know his voice*". I wonder: have you learned yet to hear his voice? Do you recognize the unique way in which Jesus addresses you? Remember that you are an adopted child of God and that Jesus is the Son by nature. You are part of a family in which Jesus is your perfect older brother. Jesus wants to communicate with you.

How do we know his voice? It's interesting that whenever Giles speaks to me I can recognize Dad's voice in both what he says and the way he says it. It's like my adoptive father is still alive and speaking to me. This may be a helpful picture for us. When our older brother Jesus is speaking to us we should be able to hear the voice of our heavenly Abba. The Son's voice sounds the same as the Father's.

This is important. Sometimes we may find ourselves listening to the words of someone who claims to have heard Jesus. If their words don't sound like the kind of thing the Father would say, we should ignore them. As sheep, we know the shepherd's voice. As the adopted children of God, we learn to recognize the voice of our perfect older Brother.

Devotion: *Dear Lord and loving Father, I pray that you will help me to grow in my relationship with Jesus. Give me ears to hear what he is saying to me as my friendship with him develops. Enable me to hear my Father in the words of my perfect Brother, in his name. Amen.*

"I am the gate; whoever enters through me will be saved. They will come in and go out, and find pasture."

John 10:9

Jesus has already uttered a number of sayings beginning with the phrase "I am". In John chapter 6 he says "I am the bread of life". In John chapter 8 he says, "I am the light of the world." Here in John chapter 10 (in both verses 7 and 9) he says, "I am the gate." Other translations render this as, "I am the door." In each of these cases Jesus is reminding us that he is the God-Man. "I am" is God's name in the Old Testament.

What did Jesus mean here? He meant that he is the one through whom we find salvation for our souls. He is the entrance, the portal, the gateway into the presence of the Father. He is like the gate at the entrance to a walled sheepfold in front of a shepherd's house in Jesus' day. Through him the sheep go into the fold at night and come out of the fold in the morning. Through him, the sheep find "pasture".

Let's unpack this. First of all, please note that Jesus says, "I am *the* gate", not "*a* gate". In a world of religious pluralism – where people believe in many ways to God – Jesus makes an exclusive claim. He resists the idea of plurality and emphasizes singularity. He says that he alone is the gate.

Secondly, let's notice the metaphor itself. The idea of a door is one that has timeless appeal. Many stories dwell on doors. C. S. Lewis's *The Lion, the Witch and the Wardrobe* describes a door to another world. That's fiction. This is fact. Jesus is a real portal to a real world.

Thirdly, we might dwell on what it is this door opens up to. Jesus describes this as "pasture". He is referring to the open hills. This shows that we are not destined to be cooped up in a place of restriction. We are meant to live and thrive in the spacious place of the Father's love.

If you've never gone through the door, go through it today. If you have, enjoy the open field that is the all-sufficient and sustaining presence of the Father's love.

Devotion: *Dear Abba, Father, thank you that in Jesus I can enter into the unrestricted and beautiful vistas of your love. Help me to enjoy the open pastures of your presence today, and help me to lead others to the Door that opens out onto a landscape of hope, in Jesus' name. Amen.*

> **"The thief comes only to steal and kill and destroy; I have come that they may have life, and have it to the full."**
>
> John 10:10

A friend of mine was once asked, "Do you believe in the devil?" He replied, "I don't believe *in* the devil. I believe *against* the devil."

In our verse for today, Jesus continues to teach using the picture of sheep in the sheepfold. He draws a stark contrast between the devil and himself. He speaks of the devil as a thief who comes to steal, kill, and destroy the sheep. He, on the other hand, has come to earth in order to do the exact opposite – to give wayward sheep the abundant life they've been longing for, a life that can be lived to the full.

I am not one for giving the devil any undue attention. But I am also not one who ignores him altogether or who regards him as a fictitious or mythical figure. C. S. Lewis warned about two extremes when he said that people tend to veer towards becoming materialists or magicians when it comes to thinking about the devil. They either don't believe he exists or they become preoccupied with him.

I believe that there is an organizing intelligence behind all the evil that's in the world today and that this "person" is the one whom the Bible calls "the devil", "Satan", "the destroyer", and so on. He was once an angel in heaven but he chose to rebel against the Father's love and became the original and ultimate orphan. Since then he has been trying to destroy what's precious to the Father. He is the ultimate robber.

Today, this original orphan is hard at work trying to bring human beings into the same spiritual state that he experiences – the state of spiritual fatherlessness. He is desperately trying to keep unbelievers from coming to Jesus. He is also trying to keep believers from enjoying the full life that comes from knowing God as Abba, Daddy, Papa, Dad and Father. In this sense he truly is a robber.

The devil is an orphan and an orphan maker. We don't believe *in* him. We believe *against* him. We don't ignore him but we also don't focus on him.

Devotion: *Dear loving Abba, Father, I thank you that in Jesus we can enjoy the superabundant life – the life of a son or a daughter. Help us to resist the enemy's attempts to rob us and our loved ones of this freedom. Help us to close all our doors to the thief, in Jesus' name. Amen.*

> **"I am the good shepherd. The good shepherd lays down his life for the sheep."**
>
> John 10:11

There are perhaps few more attractive pictures of Jesus of Nazareth than this one of him as a loving shepherd who gives his life for his sheep.

The word "good" in the title "good shepherd" is the Greek word *kalos*. This can mean two things. It can mean good in the sense of efficient, hard working, capable, and faithful. It can also mean good in the sense of noble, kind, beautiful, and attractive.

I think Jesus means both. He is a good shepherd in that he does everything that a spiritual shepherd would be expected to do and he does it really well. In other words, he is efficient and faithful. He is also a good shepherd in that he puts the concerns of his sheep first and he is prepared to sacrifice everything – including his own life – on behalf of his sheep. In other words, he is noble and kind.

To understand this word-picture we need to remember that a shepherd in the ancient world was in constant danger from all sorts of threats, not least the wolves and the robbers that stalked the sheep. Indeed, shepherds would sometimes lose their lives defending the safety of their sheep. Whenever that happened it was truly the case that they had done something *kalos* – something faithful and noble.

Why does Jesus use this picture? The answer is because Israel had known many bad shepherds. It had been led astray and exploited by selfish rather than selfless leaders. In Ezekiel 34:7–10 God condemns those who have cared for themselves rather than their flocks. In verses 11–16 of Ezekiel 34 he promises to come as a shepherd himself and look after his sheep in person. Jesus is the fulfilment of this promise.

The proof of this is in John 18 when Jesus stands outside a walled garden and stands between the Temple guards and his disciples. We will see him protecting his sheep and in John 19 laying down his life for them. Truly, Jesus is the good shepherd. He reveals the Father's pastoral heart.

Devotion: *Dear Abba, Father, I thank you for the shepherd-like love that you reveal in Jesus. I pray for pastors and leaders in your church today. May they truly reflect your protective and selfless love and may they be greatly blessed in all that they do, in Jesus' name. Amen.*

> *"The hired hand is not the shepherd and does not own the sheep. So when he sees the wolf coming, he abandons the sheep and runs away. Then the wolf attacks the flock and scatters it. The man runs away because he is a hired hand and cares nothing for the sheep."*

John 10:12–13

There are many signs and symptoms of what I call the "orphan heart condition", which I mentioned in the discussion on John 8:16. This is the condition of someone who has not been brought up by a loving, faithful father and who has consequently developed the characteristics of an orphan. One of these signs or symptoms is a poverty mentality – the mentality that hoards as much as possible because of a fear that there's never going to be enough. Another sign or symptom is greed – the desire to accumulate money and possessions in the hope that having more will take away the pain within the soul.

In our passage today Jesus draws a contrast between the hired hand and the shepherd. The shepherd puts the lives of the sheep before his own life and is willing to sacrifice his security and indeed his life for his sheep. The hired hand is the entire opposite. The hired hand is just that – a hand hired to look after the sheep. If the shepherd is doing what he does because he loves the sheep, the hired hand is doing what he does because he is paid to do so. Put another way, the shepherd is in it for the sheep; the hired hand is in it for the money.

In all of this, the shepherd behaves like a son while the hired hand behaves like an orphan. When it comes to the needs of others, the shepherd is open-handed and open-hearted, trusting and faithful. The hired hand is tight-fisted and cold-hearted, mistrustful and fearful. When the wolves come for the sheep, the shepherd stands his ground and protects the sheep. The hired hand abandons the sheep and lets the wolves attack and scatter the sheep. This is because the hired hand is only concerned about receiving, not giving.

When we are called to any kind of leadership role we can either behave like a son or an orphan, like a shepherd or a hired hand. When the wolves start to growl, what is your response? Is it fight or flight?

Devotion: *Dear loving Abba, Father, help me always to put the needs of other people first. When I am called to look after others in an organization or a family, I ask that you would help me to put giving before receiving. Deal with any orphan tendencies in my life and set me free. Amen.*

> *"The reason my Father loves me is that I lay down my life – only to take it up again. No one takes it from me, but I lay it down of my own accord. I have authority to lay it down and authority to take it up again. This command I received from my Father."*
>
> John 10:17–18

One thing we can say with absolute certainty is that Jesus knew that he was loved by his heavenly Abba. He lived in a constant and immediate intimacy with his Father and he knew from his baptism onwards that his Father was delighted in him. Jesus knew his Father's affection and acceptance, and he knew that his Father's love was based on his position as the Father's Son.

We too can learn to say with Jesus those simple words, "my Father loves me". We too can come to a place where we rest in our position as adopted sons and daughters of the Father. This is a place of great freedom and security. It is the place where all striving has to cease and where all our fears are washed away. It is a great place to be and it is the secret to working from rest.

Does all this mean that we can now do whatever we like? Not at all! We are called to a life of obedience – a life of doing what the Father wants us to do. Knowing the Father's unconditional love is not a passport into a life of compromise. It is rather the wellspring of a truly obedient, consecrated Christian life. Having experienced Abba's pleasure we long to please him all the more through our obedience.

This is really what lies behind Jesus' words here. Jesus knows that he is loved unconditionally by his Father, but he also knows that his obedience causes his Father to love him all the more. Jesus had choices, just as we do. He chose to obey his Father's will. He chose voluntarily to lay down his life and then take it up again. He chose to embrace the Cross and the empty tomb. He said yes to the Father.

Knowing the extravagant affirmation of the Father's love should lead us to become obedient to the Father's commands, just as Jesus was.

Devotion: *Abba, Father, I praise and thank you for your Son's example. He knew he was already loved and yet he chose to obey your will and lay down his life. This caused you to love him all the more. Help me to remember that my obedience releases more of your pleasure. Amen.*

"My sheep listen to my voice; I know them, and they follow me. I give them eternal life, and they shall never perish; no one will snatch them out of my hand."

John 10:27–28

This is one of the most beautiful and reassuring statements in the Bible. There are four great truths for you to treasure today as you reflect with me on the great benefits of being a follower of Jesus.

The first is that Jesus knows us. He doesn't just know about us. He knows us. If I tell you about my amazing wife Alie, you will know about her. That's called propositional knowledge. But it's not the same as actually knowing her. I know her directly, relationally, daily. That's personal knowledge. Jesus says here that he knows us. There are nearly two billion people who know Jesus Christ on the earth today. Yet he knows each and every one of us personally. That's amazing!

Secondly, Jesus says that he gives us eternal life. Knowing Jesus personally leads to great rewards. The best of all is that we enjoy today, right now, a quality of life that is superabundant and everlasting. If you're a Christian, then you are full of life – real, heavenly, mighty, and eternal. You are full of the same life-giving power that raised Jesus from the dead. That's grave-busting, death-defeating life!

Thirdly, Jesus says that we will never perish. Even though we will die physically, we will not perish spiritually. We have eternal life. That means there's no spiritual death for us. We are going to live forever in the Father's house with Jesus!

Fourthly, Jesus says that no one can snatch us out of his hand. Our names are written on his hand. We are under his loving, all-powerful hand every day. There is no power of hell or force on earth that can ever remove us from the protective and omnipotent hand of the Son of God. Our lives are truly in his hands and that's the safest place to be.

So let's keep listening to the shepherd and following him. That way we can be sure of always enjoying these immense privileges.

Devotion: *Dear Abba, I thank you that you know me personally, that you fill me with your heavenly life, that you have promised I will not have to endure spiritual death, and that nothing can ever separate me from your love. I am so grateful to you, in Jesus' name. Amen.*

"My Father... is greater than all."

John 10:29

I love this statement. Here is Jesus, surrounded by antagonistic religious accusers, and his response to all their perverse interrogations is to state quite simply that his Abba is greater than all.

What a thing to be able to say! Whenever we are under pressure from the world, the flesh and the devil, we too can say, "My Abba is greater than all!" My Dad is greater and bigger than any other force at work in this universe! He is truly mighty to save.

Maybe you're facing a tough situation right now. You feel hemmed in and under great pressure. There's opposition to who you are and what you represent as a Christian and right now it feels like you're under siege from constant enemy attack.

If you are, you have a choice. You can either react in your flesh and complain about your situation and allow it to weigh you down and defeat you. Or you can respond in the Spirit and declare that your God is bigger, greater, and mightier than all that you're facing.

Someone once said that circumstances are like mattresses. You're not supposed to be under them. You're supposed to be on top of them! We can either say, "This is too heavy for me", or we can say, "My Abba is greater than all this!"

Jesus was being accused by some of his peers in Jerusalem in John 10. His response in this situation was to focus on his Father not on his enemies. In the midst of a demonic onslaught of interrogation and intimidation, Jesus made a wonderful declaration of faith. He said, "My Daddy is greater, bigger, stronger...". He is greater than even the most angry and aggressive person. He is greater than an entire army of accusers. He is greater than unclean spirits. He is greater than the father of lies, the devil. Our Daddy is simply greater. In fact he deserves superlative praise. Our Dad is the greatest!

Devotion *Dear loving, heavenly Father, I want to make my own decree today that you are far stronger, mightier, greater, and bigger than even the most antagonistic forces at work against me. I proclaim that Jesus is Lord and my Daddy is greater! Amen.*

"I and the Father are one."

John 10:30

Not long ago I was speaking at a conference on the theme of the Father's Love. During the weekend I had the privilege of meeting some of the leaders who were hosting the event. One of them shared a testimony of how she came to discover that God is her perfect, heavenly Father.

She began by telling us that she had been brought up as one of seven children. Her dad had had a very demanding job and so all she could really remember from her earliest years was her mum frequently telling her to be quiet so as not to wake dad up. Consequently she grew up with the feeling that her dad was not there for her.

When she became an adult she gave her life to Jesus. She told me that she found it very easy to relate to Jesus because he was her best friend as well as her Saviour. She couldn't ,however, relate to God as Father. Like so many people, she projected the face of her earthly father onto the face of her heavenly Father. As a result, for many years she saw God as a sleeping dad who was too tired to be interested – as a Father whom she was not to bother.

This lasted quite a while, until one day she sensed Jesus speaking to her out of the words of John 10:30, "I and the Father are one." As she pondered these momentous words, she had the impression that Jesus was saying the following, specifically to her:

"You know, I and the Father are one. If you want me, you're going to have to have the Father too."

All of a sudden she saw that Jesus came to reveal that God is a dad who is always awake, always interested, always available, always engaged. For her, this was a moment of great revelation and breakthrough which began a deep work of healing in her life. Today I can confidently testify that she knows God as her Abba and helps others to know this too.

Let's never forget that through John 10:30, Jesus wants to tell us, "if you want me, you're going to have to have the Father too!"

Devotion: Dear perfect, loving heavenly Father, I thank you so much that Jesus and you are one. I thank you that when we come to Jesus, we come to the perfect dad. Thank you that you are never too tired or busy to engage with me in affectionate love, in Jesus' name. Amen.

"I and the Father are one."

John 10:30

What kind of "oneness" is Jesus referring to here? He is referring first of all to oneness in the sense of doing. Jesus does exactly the same things as his Father does. In fact, he only ever does what he sees his Father is doing (John 5:19). When Jesus proclaims that he and his Father are one he means that they do the same things. There is complete unity in the things that they do.

But the word means more than that, which is incidentally why his accusers are mad at him. The word denotes being not just doing. When Jesus says that he and his Father are one, he means not only that they do the same things but also that they are one and the same "being". He is therefore making a clear statement of his divinity. He is saying that there is no difference between him and God.

What this teaches us is that Jesus and the Father are two separate persons and yet one in substance and being. This much was stated right at the beginning of the Gospel when John tells us that Jesus-the-Word was with God (i.e. separate) and at the same time was God (i.e. the same). Jesus and his Father have their own personalities and yet are one and the same in nature.

Notice that Jesus is not saying that he and his Father are two separate divinities or gods. That would mean violating one of the greatest tenets of the faith – that the Lord our God is one (Deuteronomy 6:4). Jesus says here that he and his Father are still one in being though they have different names and distinct identities. They are related within the Godhead in a way that is profound and mysterious.

If you are a follower of Jesus, you are not just following a great teacher or a prophet. You are following a person who is completely one with the Father, both in doing and being. There is no one greater than the God-Man Jesus. He is truly both fully human and fully divine. He alone could say, "I and the Father are one." Hallelujah!

Devotion: *Abba, Father, I thank you so much again for the uniqueness and the supremacy of Jesus. There has never been anyone like him, nor will there ever be again. Help me to be bold about Jesus' divinity, even if it is sometimes unpopular, in his name. Amen.*

"...the one whom the Father set apart as his very own...".

John 10:36

This is a most beautiful description by Jesus of himself. His accusers are rounding on him, livid that he has just claimed in John 10:30 that he and the Father are one. As far as they are concerned, Jesus has committed the sin of blasphemy. He has made himself equal with God when he is nothing more than a man in their eyes. In reply Jesus tells his opponents that he is "the one whom the Father set apart as his very own". From the Father's perspective, he is one of a kind.

The word translated "set apart" is the Greek verb *hagiazo*. It can be translated as "hallowed". The New King James version of the Bible uses the word "sanctified" at this point. The New Living Translation turns this into a title and has Jesus describing himself as "the Holy One". The word is used twenty-nine times in the New Testament, including in Matthew 6:9 when Jesus teaches his disciples how to pray, saying, "Our Abba in the heavens, *hallowed* be your name."

What is Jesus saying here? He is saying that he is a man who has been set apart by his Father in heaven and uniquely consecrated to perform a task on the earth. Jesus is declaring to his contemporaries that he is a man on a mission – a mission that is divine in origin and cosmic in impact. He is giving voice to his sense of destiny as the Son of the Father. He is decreeing that he has an ambassador from heaven and that he alone has come to fulfil the Father's purpose for his life.

What a thing it is to know your special destiny in God. Do you realize that as a Christian you too can declare that you are a person with a special assignment on the earth, that your life is not an accident but a life of special purpose? You and I have been consecrated by a loving heavenly Father and set apart to fulfil a task and a responsibility that no one else has. Sooner or later you will come to know what that is by the revelation of the Holy Spirit. When you do, realize that only you can fulfil it.

So don't miss your destiny. Seize it.

Devotion: *Loving Father, I thank you that you consecrated your Son for a unique purpose in this world. As your adopted child, I am so grateful that you have given me a special assignment as well. Help me to know the plans you have for me and to fulfil them, in Jesus' name. Amen.*

"I am God's Son."

John 10:36

It was the pop singer George Harrison who once said that there are three questions that everyone deep down wants answering. Who am I? Where am I from? And where am I going? These three questions relate to three fundamental needs that every human being has – the need to know our identity, our history and our destiny.

Yesterday we heard Jesus talking about his destiny and his history. He declared that he has been set apart by the Father to fulfil a unique assignment on the earth – an assignment that he has come from heaven to fulfil. He knows where he is heading and he knows where he is from. He is clear about his destiny and his history.

In today's very short reading, Jesus sums up his sense of who he is in four words. He proclaims that he is God's Son. If his history is that he's come from his Father in heaven, and his destiny is to fulfil the work the Father has given him on the earth, his identity is simply that he is the Father's Son.

Many of us are tempted to derive our sense of who we are from what we do. We define ourselves by our occupation or our role. In John 10:36 Jesus states simply that he is the Father's Son. This is his identity. It is not derived from what he does or what he is called to do in the future. It is derived from his position not from performance.

Many of us can easily fall into the trap of making our identity dependent upon our work or ministry. We need to disentangle these two things. Our identity is not in what we do but in who we are. My personal identity is not derived from the fact that I'm a writer. My identity is derived simply from the fact that I'm an adopted son of my heavenly Father. This is who I am now. This is who I will be forever.

Your identity is in the fact that you are Abba's child, not in what you do. Let go of the old, false self that is tied up with status, task and role. Take hold of your new true self as a son or a daughter of the king.

Devotion: Abba, Father, I thank you for the sense of identity that Jesus had as your Son. Help me to be equally clear and confident about who I am in Christ. Don't let me define who I am by my performance. Let it all be to do with my position as your child, in Jesus' name. Amen.

Again they tried to seize him, but he escaped their grasp.

John 10:39

One of the most telling characteristics of Jesus in John's Gospel is his dramatic elusiveness. Those who are trying to capture him always find that he escapes their grasp. Throughout John's report of Jesus' three-year ministry there are a number of attempts by people to arrest or kill him. Some of his contemporaries, angered by the clear claims that he makes that God is his Abba, attempt to do him harm but he always slips away. Truly the light shines in the darkness but the darkness cannot grasp him (John 1:5).

Here his opponents in Jerusalem – probably the Jewish leaders who have been harassing him throughout John chapters 7–9 – *seek* to seize him. The word "seek" is one of John's favourites. Those who seek Jesus for noble reasons always manage to find him (John 1:38). Those who seek to find him for the wrong reasons fail every time (John 5:16). The word translated "seize" has also been used before, in John 7:30, 7:32, 7:44, and 8:20. In those instances it refers to the hostile Jewish authorities who try to arrest him. It will be used in the same way in John 11:57.

Interestingly, when we reach John 21 – a story about a fishing expedition – the same verb will be used twice of catching fish (verse 3 and verse 10). In John 10:39, Jesus will not be caught in the net of his accusers. He escapes every time until the designated hour of his passion. Only then does he allow himself to be taken into custody, tried, and sentenced to death. In all other situations he will not and cannot be seized. His Father in heaven protects and hides him until the pre-ordained moment when at last his enemies are allowed to catch up with him.

Many followers of Jesus today can take comfort from this. Our loving heavenly Abba is in sovereign control of our lives. If we find ourselves in situations where people are trying to do us harm, we can take solace in the thought that this can never happen unless the Father permits it. Our lives are in his hands. He knows where we are and his angels are all around us. When we need to be hidden, he will conceal us.

Devotion: *Dear heavenly Father, I pray today for the suffering church throughout the world and especially for my brothers and sisters who are being persecuted and pursued. Shelter them under your wings. Release your angels to protect them, I pray, in Jesus' name. Amen.*

And in that place many believed in Jesus.

John 10:42

In the final part of John chapter 10 Jesus moves away from the hostile environment of the city to the far more receptive people of the countryside, to the area where John the Baptist had been baptizing in the River Jordan. The crowds who had heard John preach about Jesus now hear Jesus for themselves. They acknowledge that everything John had said about Jesus is true. The chapter ends with this glorious final flourish: many people came to faith in Jesus in that place.

Don't you just long for a move of God like that today? I don't know where you live but wherever it is I hope that you are praying and trusting for a work of the Holy Spirit in which many people experience a spiritual awakening and confess Jesus as Saviour. This happened here in John 10:42. It happened earlier in John's Gospel in the town of Sychar (John 4:42). These seasons are very precious indeed. They are times of great grace in which many become Christians.

One of the key characteristics of a genuine move of God is acceleration. Jonathan Edwards, when he witnessed the revival that sparked the first Great Awakening in New England in the eighteenth century, said that more was achieved in seven days than in seven years. The number of people that were swept into the kingdom of God in a very short space of time was far greater than the number who had come to faith over many years. Don't you long to see that in your village, town, or city?

One of the things we can do in our own location is pray for a season of accelerated grace in which more happens in a week than in a decade before. Start praying today – if you are not already – that hundreds, no thousands, of people will come to know Jesus where you live, where you work. Pray that Jesus will pay you a visit where you are and that one day a news reporter will say, "and in that place many believed in Jesus". It has happened before. Why not at your address?

Devotion: *Abba, Father, I thank you that many people came to faith in the location that Jesus visited here. I pray for a visitation of the Spirit of Jesus to where I live. Let there be a great awakening and let it be said that many people believed in Jesus, in his name. Amen.*

Now a man named Lazarus was sick. He was from Bethany, the village of Mary and her sister Martha.

John 11:1

We left Jesus at the end of chapter 10 staying across the River Jordan where John had formerly been baptizing people. Jesus has relocated there from Jerusalem during the Feast of Hanukkah or Dedication (John 10:22). This was during winter. Now it is springtime and the Feast of Passover is drawing near. This will be the last Passover of Jesus' life. It will be the "hour" of his return to Abba, Father.

As the hour draws near, there is time for one last miracle. This miracle involves a man called Lazarus. We don't know much about this man except that his name – Eleazar in Hebrew – means "God helps". It was a very common name for Jewish priests during the time of Jesus so it's just possible that Lazarus was a priest who served in the Temple in Jerusalem. He lived just outside Jerusalem, in the village of Bethany.

Lazarus lived with his two sisters, Martha and Mary. He doesn't seem to have been married because there's no mention of a wife or of children. We can assume that the two sisters were single too. The fact that Lazarus becomes seriously sick is accordingly bad news for them. Lazarus is the man in the house; he is the provider. His sickness is therefore potentially devastating for them, not just emotionally but economically.

It is into this small family that Jesus of Nazareth is about to walk and perform a miracle. In fact, John chapter 11 is the most moving and compelling of all Jesus' miracles. No other miracle is told in such detail or such depth. John takes his time in this story, relating many of the human emotions associated with sickness and death.

There is an encouraging and consoling message here. Jesus is intimately concerned about all the details of our families, whatever their makeup. He is deeply involved in all the moments of our lives – the good times when we laugh and rejoice, and the bad times when we suffer and cry. Jesus reveals that the Father cares.

Devotion: *Abba, Father, I thank you that my family concerns do not go unnoticed by you. You see everything and are acquainted with my sorrows and very aware of my challenges. I ask you to make your presence felt in the lives of family members who need you. Amen.*

... the sisters sent word to Jesus, "Lord, the one you love is sick."

John 11:3

Isn't it fascinating how the sisters don't mention the name Lazarus in the message that they send to Jesus? They describe their brother as "the one you love". Jesus immediately knows that this is Lazarus who is sick because Lazarus was clearly a much-loved friend.

When we look at John's Gospel we see that there are, broadly speaking, three types of people that relate to Jesus. There are first of all the fans of Jesus. These are people who laud and applaud Jesus and treat him like a celebrity. The crowd of people that wanted to make Jesus a king in John 6:15 would come into this category. They are people who love Jesus' miracles and who treat him as a folk hero in Israel.

Then secondly there are the foes. These are the enemies of Jesus, usually the Jewish religious leaders in Jerusalem (including the Sadducees) and of course the Pharisees. We will meet some of these characters at the end of this chapter (John 11). They will start plotting to kill Jesus because they are frightened that he is threatening their national security as well as their own position and influence.

Finally, there's a much smaller third group and this is composed of the *friends* of Jesus. Lazarus and his two sisters – Martha and Mary – fall into this category. They are people who love Jesus simply for who he is and not for what they can get from him. They are friends with whom Jesus can feel totally relaxed. They have a home that is open to him and a guest room that is always reserved for him.

It is clear from the opening of John 11 (and indeed from the first episode in John 12) that Lazarus was one of Jesus' closest friends and that Lazarus' home was a safe house for Jesus on his itinerary. What a great thing it is to have friends like this – friends with whom you can dial down and be yourself; homes where you don't have to try and where you know you're going to be royally dined and wonderfully rested.

Don't just aim to be a friend of Jesus; aim to make friends like Jesus did.

Devotion: *Abba, Father, I want to thank you for the friends that you've given me in my life. Thank you so much for those people who accept me for who I am and in whose presence I find recreation. Strengthen these friendships and please add more to my life, in Jesus' name. Amen.*

When he heard this, Jesus said, "This sickness will not end in death. No, it is for God's glory so that God's Son may be glorified through it."

John 11:4

When Jesus hears the message sent from Martha and Mary – that their brother Lazarus is seriously ill – he tells his disciples that this is not going to be the end of Lazarus. In fact, this sickness is going to be the occasion for the Father's glory to be revealed to many people. As the Father's glory is made manifest, the Son of God will be glorified as well. The name of Jesus will be exalted and magnified.

How did Jesus know that this sickness was not going to end in Lazarus' death? The answer is because he listened very carefully to what his Father was saying. In every situation of sickness and suffering, Jesus asked his Father, "Abba, what are you saying here? What are you doing in this particular instance?" And whatever the Father said, Jesus said. Whatever the Father did, Jesus did too.

I have a friend who has been praying for the sick for decades and who is mightily anointed by God in this area. He has seen countless signs and wonders but he has also seen some people die. When I asked him how he coped with this he said, "I always ask the sick person what the Father is saying to them personally. If they reply that they think the Father wants them to be healed, I pray for a miracle. If they reply that they don't know, I pray for a miracle. But if they say that they think it's time for them to go home, then I release them to go home."

I have learned a lot from this. We need to begin with the Father's will in every situation of sickness. If we start there, then God will get the glory every time. If a person is prayed for and recovers, then God gets the glory and the name of Jesus becomes even more famous. If the person dies well and goes home to the Father, then God again gets the glory because their homecoming is often the opportunity for a memorable witness to lost people, especially those who come to the funeral service. So let's always ask the Father, "Abba, what are you saying here?"

Devotion: *Dear loving, heavenly Father, I ask that you would give me a greater awareness of when you are saying, 'this sickness is not going to end in death', and when you're saying, 'it's time to go home'. Help me to hear you much more clearly as I pray, in Jesus' name. Amen.*

Jesus loved Martha and her sister and Lazarus. Yet when he heard that Lazarus was sick, he stayed where he was two more days.

John 11:5–6 (NIV)

Isn't this a curious moment in the story of Lazarus? Jesus has just heard that the one whom he loves is sick. As we have seen earlier on in this chapter, the two sisters don't name Lazarus when they send their message to Jesus. They simply refer to their brother as "the one whom you love". Clearly Lazarus was a very dear and special friend to Jesus. Jesus probably spent many days and nights at Lazarus' house in Bethany, enjoying good food and great fun with his friend. Yet when he hears the news that this same man is very sick, he doesn't drop everything to go immediately to his sick bed. Rather, he stays the other side of the River Jordan for another two days. In essence, he delays the miracle.

One of the hardest things to cope with as a Christian is what I call the delays of God. When we pray earnestly about a situation in our lives, we hope and believe God will answer as soon as possible. In some cases we find that God answers immediately and powerfully, even to the point where we can say, "Before I even called, you answered." But then there are times where the opposite seems to happen, and we see a situation where there is seemingly no answer to prayer. Finally, there are situations where the Father does grant us our heartfelt request but it takes much longer to happen than we expected or wanted.

It seems that when we pray for a supernatural intervention of God there are at least three possible responses, "yes", "no" and "later". In the case of Lazarus' sickness, the answer was "later". Jesus delays going to Lazarus' house in Bethany. In fact, he delays it until after Lazarus has actually died, as we will see.

If the Father has made a promise that you haven't yet seen fulfilled, don't lose heart. I know the delays of God can be the occasion of much concern and many tears, but hang on in there. Keep trusting, keep praying, and keep on believing God even though you don't yet see what you long for. Understand that help is on the way. It's just a matter of time.

Devotion: *Dear Father, there are situations in my life where I would love to have a breakthrough right now. I pray that even if I have to wait, you will help me to persevere. Help me to remember that you are a loving Dad who knows what's best for me, in Jesus' name. Amen.*

"Our friend Lazarus has fallen asleep; but I am going there to wake him up."

John 11:11

I remember when my first child was very young. My wife and I used to put him to bed in his cot every night. In the morning we would go into his room, sometimes very early, to comfort him when he was crying.

When he was about eighteen months old, and now fully understood that I was his dad, I recall going into his bedroom one morning. It was summer time and the sunlight was pouring through the cracks between the curtains. He had slept a little late and when I walked in he stirred from his sleep, blinking and rubbing his eyes. He started to cry a little. When he saw I was there, he didn't say anything. He just got to his little feet, stretched out his arms towards me, and grabbed hold of my shoulders as I picked him up. I can still remember to this day the lovely smell of his head and the softness of his cheek against mine. I can remember how he calmed down in his father's embrace and how his crying turned to chuckling.

When the Bible talks about death it often uses the metaphor of sleep. Jesus does that here. He comes to a point where he knows that Lazarus is no longer sick, he has died. So he tells his disciples that "Our friend Lazarus has fallen asleep". Notice he says "our friend". Clearly it wasn't just Jesus who enjoyed fun times at Lazarus' house. His disciples did too. Jesus says that Lazarus has gone to sleep and he then adds, "We're going to his house to wake him up."

The Bible teaches us that one day we will all fall asleep in death, unless we are alive when Jesus returns. But the Bible also promises that Jesus is coming back to planet earth. When he does, there will be a sound loud enough to wake the dead – quite literally. There will be the sound of a great trumpet call and those of us who died in Christ will wake up from our slumber and meet the Lord. When that happens we will meet our heavenly Abba face to face and we will enjoy the rapture of his embrace. Our crying will turn to rejoicing as he wipes away every tear from our eyes – just as a father does with his child.

Devotion: Dear loving, heavenly Father, teach me to see death as you see it, not as the end of my life but as its beginning. Help me to remember that I will one day wake up from this sleep at the dawn of a new day and that you will hold me close and heal my heart. Amen.

> **Then Thomas (also known as Didymus) said to the rest of the disciples, "Let us also go, that we may die with him."**
>
> John 11:16

I'll be honest with you. I'm fascinated by Thomas. There has been so much bad-mouthing of him over the centuries. He has always been known as "Doubting Thomas" and has been the subject of many negative portrayals in both preaching and paintings. But I often wonder whether we've been a little hard on him.

Please notice here that John tells us that Thomas was known in his own mother tongue as *Didymus*, which means "the twin". Thomas is the Greek translation of Didymus and it also means "twin". I have thought a lot about that over the years, not least because I am a twin too. I have a lovely twin sister called Claire. When Claire and I were growing up, it was easier for people to refer to us not by our individual names but simply by the term, "the twins". I always flinched at this subsuming of both of our identities into this term, "the twins".

What happens when a person's identity is undermined in this way? They can go in one of two ways. They can accept the situation and lose all sense of individuality, or they can rebel against it and go to extreme lengths to be noticed.

Maybe I'm reading too much into Thomas, but I believe there may have been something of this in him. When Jesus resolves to go back to Judea (a place of danger for him personally), Thomas blurts out, "Let's go with him so we can die with him." Thomas, of course, will do no such thing. But it's not what he says that's important here. It's why he says it. Thomas just wants to be different. He wants to be unique. He doesn't want to be swallowed up by the phrase "the twins" or for that matter by the term "the Twelve". He just wants to be himself!

Let's be careful about labels. Even something as apparently harmless as "the twin" can cause someone to slip into insecurity and to forget their identity. Let's celebrate people's uniqueness and let's ditch the labels.

Devotion: *Abba, Father, I thank you that you have made me a unique individual and that you know me by name. Thank you that my name is written on your hand and engraved upon your heart. Tear every label off me today and help me never to label others, in Jesus' name. Amen.*

On his arrival, Jesus found that Lazarus had already been in the tomb for four days.

John 11:17

Why does John take the trouble to mention that Lazarus had been dead for "four days"? The answer is because the Jews of Jesus' time believed that the soul of a dead person hovered over their body for three days and then left forever on day four. If there was any chance of resuscitation it was in this three-day timeframe but once that was over there was no possibility of that person coming back to life.

Jesus postpones his arrival to the fourth day after Lazarus' death and he does this entirely on purpose. He knows that the Father is going to raise Lazarus from death but he also knows that timing is everything. To do the right thing at the wrong time is to do the wrong thing. So he waits until the moment when it would have been regarded as absolutely impossible for Lazarus to come back to life before he performs a miracle.

To understand the reason behind this divine delay we must go back to the beginning of John 11 where Jesus had promised that the glory of God would be seen in what was to come. I can think of no better place for God to get the glory than at a funeral. At the moment where the word "impossible" is now on everyone's lips, God does what's beyond human understanding and capability.

We need always to remember that the word "impossible" is not in heaven's dictionary. Nothing is too hard for the Father. Nothing is too difficult for the Dad who is greater than all things, including death. Our God is greater, stronger, and mightier than the worst situations and the most threatening dangers. There is nothing beyond his power or capabilities. Our God is a great big God.

Whatever storms you are facing right now, don't go to God and tell him big your storm is. Go to the storm and tell it how big your God is.

Remember, with him all things are possible.

Devotion: *Abba, Father, when I have to face various storms, help me to lift my eyes above the turbulence and remember how great you are. I pray for the gift of faith today – an unshakable confidence that you are greater than my most difficult circumstances, in Jesus' name. Amen.*

When Martha heard that Jesus was coming, she went out to meet him, but Mary stayed at home.

John 11:20

When we meet Martha and Mary in Luke's Gospel, we find that they have very different personalities. According to Luke 10:38–42, Mary is a contemplative while Martha is an activist. Mary sits at Jesus' feet, in the position of a rabbi's disciple, listening to Jesus' words. Martha meanwhile gets hot and bothered in the kitchen, trying desperately to organize the catering for the visit of Jesus and his disciples. Martha becomes indignant about her sister's apparent laziness and tells Jesus so. Jesus lovingly challenges Martha about her focus, saying that Mary has not sacrificed the best for the good. Martha has been distracted by many things while Mary has been focused on just one.

Here in John 11 we meet the two sisters once again. They hear that Jesus has arrived at Bethany and it is Martha who rushes out first while Mary stays at home. Maybe once again there is a hint of the differences that we see in Luke 10. Martha reacts to the news of Jesus' arrival by doing, Mary by being. Martha runs out to Jesus in a great fit of anxiety. Mary stays at home, more content just to wait.

History has not been very kind to Martha. Most preachers have tended to paint her in a negative light. But the truth is, if the world was full of Marys, nothing would ever get done. So the world needs Marthas, but it needs Marthas who have been healed of a mindset that says "I do therefore I am." It needs people with Mary's heart and Martha's hands.

If we are to live as the true children of our perfect Abba, Father, then we must learn to *be* first and to *do* second. We need to begin in Mary mode, worshipping the Father. Then we need to move to Martha mode, working from a place of loving adoration.

In the final analysis, Abba, Father is looking for working lovers more than loving workers. He is looking for people whose service flows out of intimate communion with him.

Devotion: *Dear heavenly Father, I pray that you will help me to combine the best of both Mary and Martha in my life. Help me to put first things first and sit at your feet in restful adoration. But help me to move from that place of loving acceptance to serving others, in Jesus' name. Amen.*

"Lord," Martha said to Jesus, "if you had been here, my brother would not have died. But I know that even now God will give you whatever you ask."

John 11:21–22

You've got to love Martha. She has come out of her home to meet Jesus. She is overjoyed that he has arrived because he meant everything to Lazarus and he means everything to her and her sister. She knows what he is capable of. Living this close to Jerusalem she would have known about the healing of the paralyzed man at the Pool of Bethesda and the healing of the blind man at the Pool of Siloam. She would have heard stories of how Jesus transformed water into wine and fed the multitudes through a miracle of multiplication. She would have listened to the disciples relating how he had walked upon the waves of the sea and many other things besides. But now this is the ultimate challenge. This is death.

Martha looks at Jesus through teary eyes and tells him that if only he had come sooner her brother would have lived. What faith is this! She knows that Jesus could have healed this sickness. But her faith doesn't stop there. Her faith is not just about what might have been. Her faith is about what still could be. So she tells Jesus that even now God can do something amazing through him. She understands that the man standing before her has a special, indeed unique, relationship with God. That what Jesus asks for, he receives from God. So she says, "even now". "Even now when we are past the point of no return... even now, when my brother's body is in the tomb... even now, the impossible is possible."

Martha's level of faith is extraordinary. She truly believes in Jesus. No wonder Jesus loved hanging out in this home in Bethany. No wonder he loved having down time with Lazarus and his sisters. Their level of faith must have thrilled him.

How important it is to look beyond the realms of what is practically and scientifically possible and to believe in what is supernaturally achievable. It is our faith that brings pleasure to the Father.

Devotion: Abba, Father, I thank you for Martha's astonishing faith. Thank you that she truly believed that Jesus could do a miracle at her brother's funeral. Help me to grow in my faith and to be one like Martha who believes in you in the tough times not just the good. Amen.

Jesus said to her, "Your brother will rise again."

John 11:23

What would you prefer to settle for in the face of adversity and tragedy? Would you prefer to settle for theological truths or for a supernatural encounter?

This is what our passage for today encourages us to ask. Jesus has just heard Martha utter some amazing words of faith. She has told him that if he had come earlier her brother would not have died. That's faith in the power of Jesus to heal sickness – even terminal illnesses. She has gone on to say that even now Jesus can do something miraculous. That's faith in the power of Jesus to conquer death, even her brother's death. Now Jesus replies by reassuring her that one day her dearly loved brother will rise from the dead. One day, on the last day of history, there will be a resurrection of the dead and Lazarus will be included in that. This is what I would call a theological truth.

The question now is whether Martha will settle for a theological truth when she can have a supernatural encounter. Will she be content with the pastoral comfort of knowing that her brother will live again in the distant future? Or will she press in beyond this and have an encounter that radically redefines her understanding of truth?

Too often as Christians – and I'm speaking for myself here – we default to pastoral words about heaven in the future when we could be praying for an invasion of heaven right now. What would happen if every single person reading this book were suddenly to rise up with active and unusual faith and say, "It's not enough to know that sometime in the future all will be well; I believe it can be well right now"? What would happen if all of us were to rise up and say, "It's not enough to wait until heaven before we see the sick healed and the dead raised; I believe we can see these heavenly realities today"?

Our Father is waiting and looking for children who don't just settle for theological truths but who are agents of heaven-on-earth encounters.

Devotion: *Dear loving, heavenly Father, when I'm faced with seemingly impossible situations, give me faith to see a miracle. Help me to believe in your supernatural power. Help me not to wait for a future heaven for healing. Help me to bring heaven to earth today. Amen.*

Jesus said to her, "I am the resurrection and the life. Anyone who believes in me will live, even though they die; and whoever lives by believing in me will never die."

John 11:25–26

When Jesus tells Martha that her brother Lazarus will rise again, Martha agrees and says that she knows he will be resurrected from death on the last day of history. With this, Jesus says something truly astounding. He looks at her and says, "Martha, you're looking at the resurrection right now."

Here in these verses we see Jesus once again using the phrase "I am", which, as we have seen, in the Old Testament is the name for God. If it wasn't enough to be using God's name, Jesus adds "I am the resurrection and the life." In other words, "Everything you're waiting for on the last day you can find in me, right now. The resurrection of the dead, living forever in the joyful presence of the Father, all this you can have right now because I am the divine Dead-Raiser and I am the divine Life-Giver, in person."

And there's more! Jesus adds, "whoever who believes in me will live". He means here, "live spiritually, live forever". He then says, "even though they die". He means here, "die physically". He continues, "and whoever lives" (he means in this physical life) by believing in me (in this life, while they have an opportunity to live by faith), "will never die". He means here "die spiritually", as in eternal death, sometimes referred to as the "second death" that follows the last judgment.

Putting it all together, Jesus tells Martha that those who believe in him will live forever spiritually, even though they die physically in this mortal life. Those who believe in him while they live in this mortal life will never suffer eternal spiritual death when Jesus returns on the last day of history. They will live forever in Abba, Father's house, with new, resurrected, spiritual, and glorified bodies that will never wear out and never experience death again.

Hallelujah! What a promise!

Devotion: *Dear Father, I worship you that your Son Jesus Christ is the resurrection and the life. I pray that more and more people would come to believe in your Son and then understand that death is not a hopeless end but the gateway to an endless hope, in his name. Amen.*

"I believe that you are the Christ, the Son of God, who was to come into the world."

John 11:27 (NIV)

It's one thing to say that you believe in Jesus when everything is going well in your life. But to say it when a loved one has died, a funeral is in full swing, and there's the sound of mourning in the air, that's a very different matter. When you're on your way to the tomb of a person you adored, it's not as easy to say, "Jesus, I truly believe in you."

Yet this is precisely what Martha does.

As she speaks with Jesus near her brother's tomb, she hears Jesus say that he is the resurrection and the life and that the one who believes in him will live forever spiritually. As he finishes speaking he asks her, "Do you believe this?" Martha answers in the affirmative and tells Jesus that she believes three things about him.

First of all, Martha says she believes that Jesus is the Christ. Not *a* Christ but *the* Christ. There had been many men pretending to be the Messiah in Israel in the first century. They were false Messiahs. Martha says quite emphatically, "You are *the* Christ", "You are the Anointed One", "You are the one we have all been waiting for."

She secondly adds, "You are the Son of God." Again, she doesn't say "a son of God", but "*the* Son of God". On her lips this means more than Jesus is in some nebulous sense a child of God or a son adopted by God. It means that Jesus is the Father's unique and precious Son by nature, from eternity to eternity.

Finally, she adds "who was to come into the world". Martha sees what so few see in John's Gospel, that Jesus is the one whom the Father had purposed to send to this earth to save us from our sins. She recognizes Jesus as a divine envoy from the realms of heaven. She knows that in Jesus, God has visited this planet.

Oh for a bold and unswerving faith like Martha's!

Devotion: *Dear Father, I thank you once again for Martha's faith in Jesus. Help me to be bolder in my confession of Jesus. When times are tough and when the circumstances aren't easy, help me to keep believing and confessing that Jesus is Messiah and Lord, in his name. Amen.*

When Mary reached the place where Jesus was and saw him, she fell at his feet and said, "Lord, if you had been here, my brother would not have died."

John 11:32

I wonder if you've noticed that there's something about Mary. I'm talking about Mary of Bethany, not Mary of Magdala or Mary the mother of Jesus. There are a number of Marys in the Gospels as you can see. The one whom John is writing about here is Mary the sister of Lazarus.

This Mary of Bethany is like her sister and yet at the same time unlike her. She is like Martha in the sense that she says exactly the same thing to Jesus that her sister had. She tells Jesus that her brother would not have died had Jesus arrived earlier. But she's different as well. While Martha stands and engages in theological debate with Jesus when he arrives, Mary falls at Jesus' feet.

This is the thing we notice about Mary of Bethany. When we meet her in the Gospels, she is usually found at Jesus' feet.

In Luke's Gospel, Jesus comes to the home of Martha and Mary. Martha is busy doing many things while Jesus is in the house. Mary on the other hands sits at Jesus' feet and listens to his teaching (Luke 10:39).

Here in John chapter 11 we find Mary of Bethany weeping at Jesus' feet as she mourns her brother's death and Jesus' delayed arrival.

In John chapter 12, Mary of Bethany will be seen again at Jesus' feet, this time anointing them with the fragrant and extremely expensive oil that she has been saving for his burial (John 12:1–8). She wipes the ointment on his feet with her hair and the whole house is filled with the scent of the perfume.

It seems then that this Mary spent her time at Jesus' feet. Whenever Jesus appeared in her life, she either listened adoringly to his teaching, or interceded with her tears, or brought a sacrifice of praise and worship to him. There truly is something about this Mary.

Devotion: Dear loving heavenly Father, I thank you for the example of Mary of Bethany. Help me to be a more passionate intercessor. Give me that same longing to sit at your feet and bring my prayers to you. Help me to offer you the gift of my tears, in Jesus' name. Amen.

When Jesus saw her weeping, and the Jews who had come along with her also weeping, he was deeply moved in spirit and troubled.

John 11:33

John reports that Jesus had a very strong emotional reaction when he saw Mary weeping over her brother at his feet. He tells us that Jesus was deeply moved in spirit and troubled.

We will meet the word "troubled" again at a later date but today I want to concentrate on this phrase "deeply moved in spirit". This could also be translated "groaned in his spirit". It was a word used of a horse snorting with rage. It signifies a deep and passionate response of anger.

What was it that Jesus was so angry about here? My view is that Jesus is angry because he is confronting the devil's work. It is the devil who causes suffering and robs people of health, life and loved ones. Jesus is mad with the enemy.

I remember a time when my wife and I were ministering in a Norwegian Lutheran church where there had not been any healing ministry before. We asked people to come forward to receive prayer for healing if they were sick. An elderly couple walked forward. The man had his arm locked in a position that had completely disabled him. This was the legacy of a stroke from a number of years before. His wife was directly behind him weeping with desperation for her husband. I remember looking at Alie and saying, "This is not right. I'm cross about what the enemy has done here." We prayed with a passion that came straight from the Father's heart and he was immediately healed. I'll never forget his wife's tears of joy or his reaction – he went round all his fellow church members in the coffee time waving his arm in the air and saying, "Look what the Lord has done for me."

There are times when the Holy Spirit stirs up a holy rage in us about what the devil has done to people. This is what's happening here. One look at Mary weeping at his feet, and the mourners weeping at the tomb, and Jesus groans with rage at the devil's work. Maybe we could do with more of this kind of righteous rage.

Devotion: *Abba, Father, my prayer is a simple one today. When I am faced by clear evidence of the enemy's destructive work, please stir up in me a holy rage against the darkness. May this godly passion lead to an end to suffering and injustice, in Jesus' name. Amen.*

Jesus wept.

John 11:35

As is very well known, this is the shortest verse in the Bible, just two words. John tells us that after Jesus has groaned with anger at the devil's work, he now weeps. This is a strong word in the original Greek. It really means "sobs" and is a different verb from the one used to describe the crying of the mourners at Lazarus' tomb. When Jesus sees the suffering of the grieving people at his friend's tomb, he breaks down in convulsive sobs and weeps unashamedly and publicly before everyone who has come to the tomb with him.

There is so much we could say here but let's just remember today that one of the main objectives of this Gospel is to show how Jesus' words and actions point to the Father. If everything Jesus says and does reveals what God the Father is like, then his sobbing at Lazarus' tomb speaks volumes. It shows us that Abba, Father is not remote from our suffering – he is not another emotionally distant father like the ones we so often meet in the world today. Rather, our heavenly Abba suffers with us when we suffer. He weeps when we weep.

This is a very different picture of God from what we find in other religions. Most religions find it impossible to answer the question, "What is God doing when we suffer?" Some portray God as apathetic – as far removed from our suffering and incapable of pain. With Christianity, it's a different matter altogether. In Jesus we see that God is compassionate. He suffers with us when we suffer. He sobs with us when we sob. He knows what it's like to lose a loved one in death. He even knows what it's like to experience death itself.

Whenever we have to suffer the sharp pain of loss, let's remember what Corrie Ten Boom's sister said when she was imprisoned during World War Two in a Nazi concentration camp. Before she died, Betsi said to Corrie, "Go tell the world that there is no pit of suffering so deep that Jesus Christ isn't deeper still."

Devotion: *Dear Lord Jesus, I love the fact that you sobbed at your friend's tomb, even though it must have cost you dearly. I love it because it teaches me that God isn't detached from my pain. When I am crying, help me to remember the tears of my Father, in your name. Amen.*

Some of them said, "Could not he who opened the eyes of the blind man have kept this man from dying?"

John 11:37

The mourners ask a question which, if we're really honest, many of us have asked at times as well. "Why, when we hear so many stories of other people being healed, has my loved one died?"

I remember when I was quite a new Christian, in the late 1970s and very early 1980s, being a very strong admirer of a man called David Watson. David was a man of the Word and the Spirit who had seen his church grow phenomenally from very humble beginnings. He was a remarkable preacher of the gospel who relied on the power of the Holy Spirit and saw countless conversions. He also prayed for the sick and saw many healed. I can remember hearing him speak when I was a student at the University of Cambridge and being immensely impressed, especially when the guest I had brought made a first-time commitment to Jesus Christ at the end of his message. He was a most remarkable man.

But David was diagnosed in his late forties with terminal cancer. Everyone prayed for him. The great and mightily anointed men and women of God prayed for him with the laying on of hands. People all over the country and indeed the world interceded for his healing. But in the end, at a relatively young age, he went home to be with the Lord.

I recall visiting Holy Trinity Church Brompton in London on the morning the news broke that David had gone home. This was a church that loved David and there was an audible gasp of shock. It was as if everyone was deep down saying what the mourners were saying in John 11: "Couldn't Jesus have healed David, when through David he healed so many others?"

In the year before he died, David wrote a magnificent book called *Fear No Evil*. In it he addressed this issue and he came to rest in a word of wisdom that the Father gave him. When it comes to the mystery of suffering, he said that "There are no easy answers, only good responses." I have never found anything more helpful than that.

Devotion: *Abba, Father, there are many things that you have revealed to us and that I do understand but there are also some things that you have concealed from us that I don't. Help me not to seek easy answers but rather to embrace good responses, in Jesus' name. Amen.*

Then Jesus looked up and said, "Father, I thank you that you have heard me."

John 11:41

Jesus is now standing outside Lazarus' tomb. Everything seems utterly hopeless. The mourners are wailing and Lazarus lies dead behind the great stone that blocks the entrance to where he lies. How will Jesus respond in this dark and dire situation?

We should note two things. First of all, Jesus doesn't look down; he looks up. He doesn't look down into the place of death and become preoccupied with the problem at hand. He looks up to his heavenly Father whom he has said before is "greater than all". There is a real word of encouragement to all of us here. In every trying and tragic circumstance, we have a choice. We can either choose to look down into the pit of despair or look up into the source of our hope. We can either look down at the work of the enemy or we can look up and gaze into the beauty of our Father's eyes. Jesus chose to look up.

Secondly, Jesus didn't pray as if the Father hadn't yet heard him. He prayed knowing that the Father had already heard him. Jesus in fact prayed as if the thing he was requesting had already been granted. What a great lesson there is here. We can either beg God to send help or we can thank him that help is already on the way. A true child of the Father prays as if the request has already been granted, even if that answer comes in unexpected ways.

I remember in our first year running the Father's House Trust coming to the month of August. We didn't have enough money to get through to September and I didn't have enough to pay my staff or the bills. On a Tuesday morning I started to pray about this. I was looking down and begging God to do something. Then I sensed the Holy Spirit saying, "Look up and thank your Dad." So I did that. When I arrived at work there was a cheque on my desk for exactly the amount we needed. It had been sent by a church that had taken up an offering for our work two weeks before! Help had already been on the way before I got praying!

Devotion: *Dear loving, heavenly Father, I pray that you will help me to be a person who looks up, not down – a person who thanks you that you have already answered, not begging you to answer. Help me to be more like Jesus in this respect, in his name. Amen.*

Jesus called in a loud voice, "Lazarus, come out!"

John 11:43

Now is the climactic moment of this great story. Everything has been building up to this denouement. Jesus has started the story outside Judea, then he has stood outside Bethany, before finally he stands outside the tomb of Lazarus. Everything has been homing in on this one extraordinary moment in time when Jesus shouts out in a loud voice, "Lazarus, come out of the tomb!" And of course Lazarus comes out, resuscitated and alive.

I remember once hearing a brilliant Pentecostal preacher say that it was a really good thing that Jesus mentioned Lazarus' name at this point. If Jesus hadn't been specific about who he meant, then every dead person in every tomb within the range of his voice would have come walking out of their tombs too! There was such divine authority in the command of Jesus that a general resurrection could have taken place. It was a good job Jesus was precise about who he meant!

I have often said that Jesus was the worst funeral director in history. Every funeral he went to he messed up because he raised the dead person. He raised the daughter of Jairus at her funeral. He raised the son of the widow of Nain at his. Here he raises Lazarus from the dead even while the mourners are in full swing. Jesus messed up every funeral he ever went to, including his own. He couldn't stop raising the dead and when it came to his own death, he raised himself up too!

Back in John 5:21, Jesus says this, "Just as the Father raises the dead and gives them life, even so the Son gives life to whom he is pleased to give it." He then goes on to add in verse 25, "Very truly I tell you, a time is coming and has now come when the dead will hear the voice of the Son of God and those who hear will live." Here in John 11 is the fulfilment of these words. We see Jesus exercising the Father's power over death itself and we watch as Lazarus hears the voice of the Son of God and lives.

There is no one like Jesus. He is truly Lord of all.

Devotion: *Abba, Father, I worship you that you have the right and the might to raise the dead and bring life to the lifeless. You are truly an awesome and glorious God. Your power is a death-defeating, grave-busting power. Help me always to remember how great you are. Amen.*

The dead man came out, his hands and feet wrapped with strips of linen, and a cloth around his face. Jesus said to them, "Take off the grave clothes and let him go."

John 11:44

How did Lazarus feel at this point? The last thing he probably remembers is drifting in and out of consciousness shortly before his death. Now he is alive. He's somehow got to his feet. And in spite of the restrictive effects of the grave cloths around his feet and his face, he has stumbled out of the tomb into the bright light of a new day. How does he feel as he stands before Jesus and the crowds?

I'll tell you how he feels. He feels alive but he also feels bound. He has come back to life but he is now fettered by the burial clothes in which he has been tightly wrapped. Understanding this perfectly, Jesus utters a second command. If the first one is to Lazarus, "Come forth", the second one is to the bystanders, "Untie him and let him go."

I have always seen this as a great picture of what Jesus wants to do for all of us. First of all, he wants to call us out of a place of death. The Bible teaches that until we are born again we are dead in our sins. However, as soon as we put our trust in Jesus this all changes. Resurrection life causes our spirits to be quickened. We are suddenly alive to God.

But there is more. Having received new life, we secondly need to be set free. Like Lazarus emerging from the tomb, we are still bound by the trappings of our former life. Accordingly, we need a community of people who are dedicated to removing our grave clothes so we can run through life rather than stumble and fall.

When I first became a Christian, I was saved but I was still sick. I was born again, but I was still very bound. I have been so grateful over the years to those who have removed the grave clothes of abandonment, insecurity, sadness, loneliness, mistrust, anger and many other things besides. My inheritance is to be free indeed and so is yours!

So receive more freedom today!

Devotion: *Dear loving Abba, Father, thank you that when I was born again I received new life. Today I pray that you will help me to be a part of a community of your children who can help me to be released from anything that still binds me. Set me free I pray, in Jesus' name. Amen.*

Then one of them, named Caiaphas, who was high priest that year, spoke up, "You know nothing at all! You do not realize that it is better for you that one man die for the people than that the whole nation perish."

John 11:49–50

The news about Lazarus' return to life has spread like wildfire. Some people believe in Jesus as a result but others go to the Jewish leaders in Jerusalem to tell them what Jesus has done.

With that the chief priests and the Pharisees call a meeting of the Sanhedrin. The main topic on their agenda is this: What are we going to do about Jesus? Their problem is this. If Jesus carries on doing the kinds of things that he's just done at Bethany, then the whole world will start believing in him. If that happens then the Roman forces occupying Israel will start to become very nervous. Seeing everyone following Jesus will be a major threat to the stability of the region. The chief priests and the Pharisees will very likely lose their grip on power as the Romans seek to reassert control.

At this point the high priest that year, a man named Caiaphas, pipes up. He accuses his peers of ignorance. He tells them they should understand that it is expedient for one man to perish rather than the whole nation. That person is Jesus. Accordingly, he must die if the nation is to continue living. John adds that Caiaphas was in fact uttering a prophecy when he made this political statement. He didn't know he was prophesying about the necessity of Jesus' sacrificial death. But in fact he was.

Caiaphas was a most unpleasant man. As a Sadducee he was fiercely protective of his power under Roman rule and concerned only with guarding against civil disorder. He was also very rude to his peers, calling them "ignorant". Yet the Father chooses to speak even through this man. Caiaphas tells everyone that Jesus has to die on behalf of the nation. While he means that in a political way, John understands it spiritually.

Sometimes the Father speaks through strange mouthpieces. We must learn to be like John – discerning enough to hear his voice.

Devotion: *Abba, Father, sometimes I am guilty of thinking that you only speak through people whose hearts are completely given over to you. Help me to remember from this story that you can speak through anyone, however imperfect. Give me more attentive ears, I pray. Amen.*

So from that day on they plotted to take his life.

John 11:53

John tells us here that the members of the specially convened Sanhedrin began from this time on to plot to kill Jesus. In other words, the raising of Lazarus from the dead becomes the catalyst for crucifying Jesus. And here's the irony. The act of giving life results in an act of taking life. Giving life to Lazarus leads to Jesus' life being taken from him. The seventh and final miracle that Jesus performs in John's story results in his martyrdom.

There is a little signal to this effect in John 11:43 where John reports that Jesus shouted out in a loud voice, "Lazarus, come forth". The verb translated "shouted" is the Greek word *kraugazo*. It is used here and then on three other occasions, all in the crucifixion narrative (John 18:40; 19:6; 19:15). There it will be used of the crowds clamouring for Barabbas to be released and for Jesus to be crucified. Jesus' shout for life accordingly results in a shout for his death.

Sometimes some of us may be guilty of praying for miracles because we think they will lead to a more comfortable and successful life. We think that signs and wonders will result in the alleviation of pain and spectacular church growth. Often they do. But sometimes they also act as a catalyst for opposition. An increase in power sometimes leads to an increase in persecution. A greater manifestation of heaven can lead to a greater conflict between kingdoms.

There are two very revealing sentences in Acts chapter 6. The first is in Acts 6:8 and it describes an increase in miracles through Stephen's ministry: "Now Stephen, a man full of God's grace and power, performed great wonders and signs among the people." In the very next verse we read the following sentence: "Opposition arose, however, from members of the Synagogue of the Freedmen". In Stephen's case, an increase in power led to an increase in persecution.

We all need to be prepared to pay the price for more of the glory of God.

Devotion: *Abba, Father, I thank you that Jesus was prepared to raise Lazarus from death even though he knew that this would be the catalyst for his own death. Help me to embrace a theology of the Cross not just a theology of glory, in Jesus' name. Amen.*

> **Therefore Jesus no longer moved about publicly among the Jews. Instead he withdrew to a region near the wilderness, to a village called Ephraim, where he stayed with his disciples.**
>
> John 11:54

There are times when it's important to make a public stand and there are times when it is important to withdraw from the public eye and to recuperate.

Here Jesus disengages from his controversies with the hostile religious leaders in Jerusalem and moves to the secluded village of Ephraim, near the desert. There Jesus stays with his disciples, away from the heat of the battle, resting before his final, momentous journey to Jerusalem. In Ephraim, Jesus retreats in order to advance.

There are times in our Christian lives when we are called to make a public stand. Once we are called to do that, we must take great care to do so only in the timeframe that the Father decrees. If we move outside that timeframe we will find that we court unnecessary pain and aggravation. But if we make our stand only as long as the Father asks us to, and then withdraw when he tells us too, we will be able to hold our ground even when it feels like there is a great darkness rallied against us.

I remember a time in my Christian life when I clearly sensed the Father asking me to make a public stand against an issue that was particularly dark within our culture. After a number of months of intense warfare and opposition, I sensed the Father saying that I had done what he required and that it was now time to withdraw from the battle and recuperate. Sensibly I agreed and after a while the storm clouds lifted and I began to feel less battle-weary and more refreshed.

I learned a lot from this experience. I learned that there are seasons for engagement and there are seasons for disengagement. The important thing is to listen to Abba Father as Jesus did and to understand that there are some battles that we are called to fight right now, some that we are not called to fight at all, and some which we may be called to fight later.

Devotion: *Dear Father, I thank you for this picture of Jesus withdrawing for a while from the battlefield in order to recuperate with his disciples. Help me to listen to you more attentively so that I get the right balance between engagement and withdrawal, in Jesus' name. Amen.*

And the house was filled with the fragrance of the perfume.

John 12:3

And so, after the great miracle of the raising of Lazarus, we now find ourselves back at Bethany. Jesus has made the journey with his disciples from Ephraim near the desert back to the precincts of Jerusalem in time for Passover. Now he is at the house of Lazarus and his two sisters where a special dinner has been cooked in his honour. Lazarus is there reclining next to Jesus and Martha is busy serving her Rabbi and Lord. Her sister Mary, meanwhile, brings a jar of extremely expensive perfume to the table. She has been reserving this for Jesus' death but now she takes it and anoints Jesus' feet with it, wiping it over his skin with her hair. As she does so the whole house is filled with the fragrance.

What a great example Mary is! She takes her most precious possession and she "wastes" it on Jesus. Having seen Jesus restore her brother to life, she now expresses her heartfelt thanks and praise by engaging in an action that expresses the unbridled extravagance of her love. She gives her all to Jesus and in the process reveals not just extraordinary devotion but also extraordinary humility. For in Mary's day you would sometimes anoint someone's head with oil as a mark of honour. But here Mary anoints Jesus' feet. And she doesn't care what anybody else thinks of her. She is so enraptured with joy at what Jesus has done for her that she is totally free from worrying about how this all looks.

John reports that when Mary made this unself-conscious gesture that the whole of Lazarus' home was filled with the fragrance. Everyone was affected by this solitary act of self-forgetful adoration. Just one heart given completely over to Jesus produced a transformation of the atmosphere in the house. One act of love changed everything.

Whenever we go to the house of the Lord to worship our heavenly Abba, we are called to bring a sacrifice of praise. When just one person chooses to express their gratitude and devotion in an extravagant, humble and selfless way, the fragrance of this fills the whole house. Let's choose to be like Mary and give the Lord our passionate devotion.

Devotion: *Abba, Father, I thank you for Mary's love for you. I pray that you will help me to respond to your generosity with a deeper and more selfless adoration. May my love for you be extravagant and may the effect of it be felt by others, in Jesus' name. Amen.*

> *... one of his disciples, Judas Iscariot, who was later to betray him, objected,... "It was worth a year's wages."*

John 12:4–5

We are still in Lazarus' house, where a dinner is being held in Jesus' honour. It is just before the Passover festival in April (about AD 30) and Jesus is preparing for the hour of his death and resurrection. Everyone at the dinner is still breathless with excitement that Lazarus is alive and well. No doubt many of the disciples are looking at him eating his food and watching him laugh with joy.

Within this little cameo of domestic bliss, John highlights a number of different characters and their responses. Lazarus reclines next to Jesus, no doubt leaning on his friend from time to time. His response is one of affection. Then there is Martha, as usual busily waiting at the table and making sure everyone has what they need. Her response is one of service. Then there is Mary, who pours her most expensive possession on Jesus' feet. Her response is one of worship. And finally there is Judas, who complains when he sees Mary wasting such a gift on Jesus. His response is one of greed.

What is Judas's problem? John tells us that Judas was in charge of the common purse. He was tasked by Jesus to account for all the income and expenditure for the group. Judas takes offence at Mary's gesture and says that the perfume should have been sold and the money given to the poor, because it was worth a working person's wages for a whole year. This sounds like a noble statement but it isn't. John tells us that Judas had been embezzling the funds. So he was not concerned about the poor at all. He was angry about a missed opportunity for lining his own pocket. His was the response of an orphan not a son.

When someone takes the moral high ground on an issue to do with money or other matters, we should not always assume that their motives are pure. Sometimes, as in Judas's case, the apparent nobility of their cause is a smokescreen for an orphan heart.

Devotion: *Abba, Father, please give me greater discernment not only about the hearts of others but also about my own heart, especially when it comes to the issue of money. Give me a greater integrity in my financial stewardship and help me to be generous not greedy. Amen.*

They took palm branches and went out to meet him, shouting, "Hosanna!" "Blessed is he who comes in the name of the Lord!" "Blessed is the king of Israel!"

John 12:13

John tells us at the beginning of chapter 12 that it was six days before the start of the Passover festival that the dinner at Bethany was held at Lazarus's house. That dinner is over and now it's the following day. Hundreds of thousands of pilgrims have already converged upon Jerusalem and are filling the streets. Something in the region of 2.5 million visitors would have arrived during the run-up to this feast. News is now spreading that the celebrated miracle-worker, Jesus of Nazareth, is on the outskirts of the city. The man who has raised a dead person is on his way. Expectation is running very high.

As the swelling crowd greets Jesus at the gates of the city, the people do something that must have caused the Jewish authorities in the city great alarm. At the end of John 11, the leaders of the Sanhedrin had expressed their anxiety that the whole world will soon be following Jesus. Now they see the masses declaring "Hosanna" as Jesus arrives. The word means "God saves!" Furthermore, they hear them proclaim him as the one who comes in the name of the Lord and as "the King of Israel!" They must have been choking with rage and quaking with fear.

And they would have reacted like this because the crowds are quoting the Scriptures, specifically Psalm 118:25–26. A century before this, the crowds had welcomed Simon Maccabeus with these words when he returned to Jerusalem. They had waved palm branches as he entered Jerusalem after his victory at Acra.

Jesus is being greeted here as a conquering, military hero when of course he is nothing of the sort. He is the suffering servant who saves through the power of love not through the love of power. We must always take great care not to paint Jesus as a military conqueror, nor to use him to justify aggressive crusades.

Devotion: *Dear Abba, Father, I praise you that you are a God of love not a God of violence. I thank you that you want to transform the world through sacrificial compassion not through military domination. Help me to be a person of peace not a person of war, in Jesus' name. Amen.*

Jesus found a young donkey and sat on it, as it is written: "Do not be afraid, Daughter Zion; see, your king is coming, seated on a donkey's colt."

My beloved adoptive father would never tolerate a bad word about donkeys. In World War Two, he had been part of a daring group of soldiers behind enemy lines in the jungle in the Far East. For him and his colleagues, their donkeys were their best friends. They carried heavy loads and bore extreme hardship for their masters. My father was always keen to praise an animal that is so often the object of scorn.

Francis of Assisi was a great lover of animals and his donkey was perhaps the most loved of all. When Francis died, his donkey was at his bedside. Those who witnessed Francis's passing reported that his donkey wept when his master went home.

Donkeys are indeed precious creatures.

And they have been made so supremely by this act that Jesus performed as he entered Jerusalem. The crowds wanted him to enter on a horse as a military conqueror. They wanted him to wield a sword and kill the Romans. But he arrived on a young donkey's back, and he came to die on a Cross at the Romans' hands.

In making this gesture, Jesus was preaching a message without words. In all probability he would not have been heard had he tried to speak. So, in fulfilment of Zechariah 9:9, Jesus makes a stunning statement. He comes to Jerusalem as the Prince of Peace not as the God of War.

What amazing courage Jesus shows. In returning to the city he knew that he would be arrested and put to death. The Jewish authorities have been threatening and indeed plotting to kill him. That is why he withdrew to Ephraim at the end of chapter 11. Now he returns understanding that his hour has come. But he does so making it clear for those who have eyes to see that he saves through dying not through killing; he saves through being a victim not a victor.

Devotion: *Abba, Father, I thank you for the donkey that carried your Son. Help me to be a carrier of the presence of Jesus – not a false Jesus that incites hawks but the real Jesus who inspires doves. Help me to be one who brings the Prince of Peace to others, in his name. Amen.*

Now there were some Greeks among those who went up to worship at the festival. They came to Philip, who was from Bethsaida in Galilee, with a request. "Sir," they said, "we would like to see Jesus."

John 12:20–21

This is another one of those episodes that you will only find in John's Gospel. Here, at Passover time, John reports that there are some Greeks in the city of Jerusalem. Who are these Greeks and what are they doing? There are two possible answers to this. The first is that they are restless Greek people who are travelling far and wide searching for the truth. The Greek mindset in those days was the mindset of what we might call "the seeker". Ancient Greece had been the cradle of philosophy and philosophy means literally "the love of wisdom". It is possible that these Greeks were people searching for answers to the deepest questions of life and who felt irresistibly drawn to Jesus, the fount of true wisdom.

It is also possible that they were Greek converts to Judaism. The Temple contained a court reserved for those who were not Jewish called the Court of the Gentiles. This was constructed as a space for non-Jews who were invited into the Father's embrace. As it says in Isaiah 56:6–7: "foreigners who bind themselves to the Lord to minister to him, to love the name of the Lord, and to serve him, all who keep the Sabbath without desecrating it and who hold fast to my covenant – these I will bring to my holy mountain and give them joy in my house of prayer. Their burnt offerings and sacrifices will be accepted on my altar; for my house will be called a house of prayer for all nations."

John doesn't tell us which of these two possibilities is correct but either way the Greeks in John 12 stand for "foreigners" to the covenant who were seeking Jesus. They come to Philip asking for an introduction (perhaps because Philip is a Greek-sounding name). Philip passes them on to Andrew who, as so often, leads them to Jesus.

Sometimes the people who most want to find Jesus aren't who we expect them to be. We need to look at others with the Father's eyes, seeing the seeking hearts that lie beneath unlikely appearances.

Devotion: *Dear loving, heavenly Abba, I pray that you will help me to look at others through your eyes. Help me to discern who is genuinely seeking Jesus among all those that I'm surrounded by every day. Help me to lead them to Jesus, as Andrew did. Amen.*

"Very truly I tell you, unless a kernel of wheat falls to the ground and dies, it remains only a single seed. But if it dies, it produces many seeds."

John 12:24

One of my greatest heroes of the faith was Smith Wigglesworth (1859–1947). Smith was a plumber and a preacher. He had no theological training but he was one of the most anointed men of God who ever walked the earth. Hundreds of thousands were converted as a result of his gospel preaching ministry, and countless people were healed as he prayed for the sick. Smith saw more miracles in a week than most of us witness in a lifetime. He even raised the dead, including on one occasion his wife. He was an extraordinary man who once said, "Some read the Bible in Hebrew, others in Greek. But I read it in the Holy Ghost!"

During his lifetime Smith prayed for 100 people that he knew who had never made a commitment to Jesus Christ. Just before Smith died in 1947, he became troubled that only ninety-eight of these had become Christians. What about the remaining two – why had the Father not saved them? Well, the remaining two attended Smith's funeral service. As they heard story after story of Smith's remarkable faith in Christ, their hearts melted and they surrendered their lives to the Lord. The final two came to Christ only after Smith had died.

In John 12:24 Jesus tells us that a grain of wheat will only be fruitful if it's buried in the soil and dies. It is only when the seed dies that it can produce many other seeds. Here of course Jesus was primarily referring to his own death. He was telling his listeners that it wouldn't be until he was dead and buried that his life would really start to bear fruit. His real legacy would be activated once he had left.

And so it is with those who follow Jesus. If we have lived lives yielded to Jesus, we will leave a lasting mark when we die and our homecomings will be the occasion for more lives to be changed. As one seed dies, many others are born. Let's therefore live lives that really count. And let's leave a lasting legacy on planet earth.

Devotion: *Dear loving Abba, Father, help me to make it my aim to finish my life well. Thank you for people like Smith Wigglesworth whose deaths have produced so much life. Thank you that the death of your saints is precious in your sight, in Jesus' name. Amen.*

> *"Those who love their life will lose it, while those who hate their life in this world will keep it for eternal life."*
>
> John 12:25

I doubt if there is a Christian missionary anywhere in the world who hasn't heard the name Jim Elliot. Jim was one of five men who felt called to take the Good News about Jesus to the people of Ecuador and especially to the Acua tribe in the jungle. They began their mission to the Acua Indians by dropping gifts from an airplane, hoping that these would show their good intent. Eventually they decided to land and meet members of the tribe. Having established a base, they made first contact. There were five men in all – Jim Elliot, Ed McCully, Nate Saint, Roger Youderin, and Peter Fleming. None of them lived to describe what happened. They were all killed by members of the tribe who used their spears to murder them.

At first sight it might seem that the men had died in vain. But the wives of two of the men found an open door into the tribe as a result of a miraculous turn of events and began to live with the very people who had killed their husbands. Before very long the tribe was to turn to Jesus Christ. One of the tribesmen who had been involved in the killing of the five men was later to give his testimony. Counting his fingers he would say, "I have killed twelve people with my spear. But I did that when my heart was black. Now Jesus' blood has washed my heart clean, so I don't live like that anymore."

Yesterday's reading was all about a kingdom principle. Just as in the natural world a seed has to die and be buried before it bears much fruit, so in the spiritual world there has to be death before there can be life. Sometimes this is self-death – dying to self. Occasionally it can be actual, physical death – as in Jim Elliot's case.

Jesus said the one who dies to self in this life will truly live forever in heaven. As Jim Elliot once said, "He is no fool who gives what he cannot keep to gain what he cannot lose." Following Jesus is often hard, but it is always infinitely worthwhile.

Devotion: *Dear Abba, Father, I thank you for the example of your Son, who was prepared to lose his life in serving you. Thank you for the example of Jim Elliot. Help me to cultivate a greater selflessness in my service of you and of others, for the honour of Jesus' name. Amen.*

"My Father will honour the one who serves me."

John 12:26

One of the greatest problems in today's world is shame. Many people today suffer from a deep sense of shame. They believe the lie that they are worthless and hopeless.

Where does this shame come from? Ultimately it comes from the devil who is the father of lies. But the emotional or psychological root is very often the absence of an affirming father. So many children today grow up without a loving, accepting and encouraging dad. This creates the fertile soil in which shame can grow.

An ancient Jewish sage called Ben Sira once remarked that, "A person's honour comes from their father." When a father speaks words of affirmation over his daughter or son, it releases honour into their lives. When a father is absent in the home, then honour is very often absent too, and shame starts to breed within the child's soul.

If you have lacked a good, encouraging, and honouring father, be assured that you can have one today. Jesus says here that anyone who chooses to believe in him, to follow him, and indeed to *serve* him, will receive the honour of the greatest Father of all. They will hear their heavenly Father's words of affirmation and approval.

When do we hear these words? Some say it is only when we have faithfully served Jesus all our lives and gone to heaven that we will hear the Father's words of honour over us. Only then will we hear our Abba in heaven saying, "Well done, my good and faithful servant."

But it's not just in heaven but here on earth that we can know the Father's honour. Even now we can hear our Abba saying, "You're my child, my chosen one; I delight in you." Today we can hear our Father rejoicing over us with singing and telling us that he's proud of us.

So let's keep serving Jesus. Our dedication to the Son is the path to our affirmation as a son.

Devotion: *Dear Lord and heavenly Father, I pray that you will help me to keep serving your Son Jesus Christ. And in serving him I pray that you will continue to make up the honour deficit in my life by speaking your loving words of honour over my soul, in Jesus' name. Amen.*

"Now my soul is troubled, and what shall I say? 'Father, save me from this hour'? No, it was for this very reason I came to this hour."

John 12:27

It's often said of the Jesus we meet in John's Gospel that he is very divine but not at all human. I don't happen to agree with this. The Jesus that I meet in John is fully human as well as fully divine. For example, in the previous chapter we saw Jesus at the tomb of Lazarus exhibiting very human emotions. He groaned with rage at what the devil had done to his friend and he sobbed at the sight and the sound of all those who were grieving at the funeral. Clearly, the same Jesus who can make divine claims like "I am the resurrection" also manifests emotional responses such as anger and grief.

When Jesus stood outside the tomb of Lazarus, John reports that he was "troubled" (John 11:33). This same word is used again in John 12:27 where we hear Jesus saying "Now my soul is troubled". The word translated "soul" is the word *psyche*, from which we get the word "psychology". As Jesus approaches his agonizing death on the Cross, he gives voice to the emotional turbulence within his human soul. He uses the word *tarasso* to describe his agitation – a word that stirs up an image of the rolling seas. It is the word used for the angel "troubling" the waters in John 5:4 and 5:7.

As Jesus experiences this inner emotional turmoil, he considers whether he should ask Abba to rescue him from this terrifying ordeal. He then dismisses that thought as he remembers that it was precisely in order to embrace this hour that his Abba sent him to the earth. As he remembers his assignment, he overrides his anxiety.

It has often been said that courage isn't the absence of fear but the ability to master fear. Jesus overcomes his fears by realigning his thoughts to the mission that he has from his Father. He overcomes his agitation by reminding himself that his Father's plan is perfect and that he can trust in his heavenly Abba. That is a truly comforting thought.

Devotion: *Abba, Father, I confess that from time to time my soul is troubled by the prospect of great trials. Thank you that your Son Jesus felt these emotions too. I pray that my trust in your perfect plan will prove stronger than my deepest fears, in Jesus' name. Amen.*

"Father, glorify your name!"

John 12:28

I think many of us tend to forget that there are two really important names in the New Testament. There is first of all the name of Jesus. This is the name that the Father honours. We read in Philippians 2 that the Father has highly exalted his Son and given him the name above every other name, that at the name of Jesus every knee shall bow and every tongue confess that "Jesus Christ is Lord", to the glory of God the Father. The Father accordingly loves to glorify the name of his Son.

But the opposite is also true. The Son loves to glorify the name of his Father. During his three-year ministry, Jesus was constantly seeking to promote the name of his Father. He revealed that God is known as Abba, Father. When he taught his disciples how to pray, he stressed the importance of beginning with the words "Our Daddy in the heavens". He then added that we should say, "hallowed be your name". What name should we hold sacred? It is the name "Abba", "Papa", "Daddy", "Dad".

As Jesus approaches the very end of his earthly life, he now sees the shadow of the Cross before him. This is the hour of his crucifixion, resurrection, and ascension. It is the hour of his return to his Father. As this hour approaches, Jesus is troubled. He asks out loud whether he should pray, "Father, save me from this hour", and concludes that it was for this hour that he came into the world. He then adds these words, "Father, glorify your name!"

What Jesus is asking here is that the Father's name will be exalted and made famous because of his obedience. Jesus' obedience to the Father's call won't just lead to the Father glorifying the name of his Son. It will result in the Son glorifying the name of the Father. It will do this because countless people will come to see that the Cross of Christ is the ultimate demonstration of the Father's love. People will come to say, "See how much the Father loves us that he gave up his only Son for us."

Let's give more honour to the name "Abba, Father".

Devotion: *Dear Lord and heavenly Father, forgive me that I have sometimes forgotten that your name is supremely important, like your Son's. Help me to hold sacred the name "Abba". Make your name even more famous on the earth, I pray. Amen.*

> *"Now is the time for judgment on this world; now the prince of this world will be driven out."*
>
> John 12:31

I don't know if you've ever noticed this, but there are no deliverance miracles in John's Gospel. In Matthew, Mark, and Luke, there are many stories of Jesus driving out unclean spirits from those who were being afflicted and oppressed by the devil. Miracles of deliverance were perhaps the most common and obvious of Jesus' works of power according to these Gospel writers. When it comes to John's Gospel, there are none. Is this because John didn't know of any of these incidents? Or is it because he deliberately chose to leave them out?

The answer is because John decided to omit them. John would have known about Jesus' exorcisms from his own historical traditions but he chose to leave them out because he wanted all the focus to fall on something else – on the Cross. Here in John 12:31, Jesus uses the language of deliverance to describe his imminent death. He says "now the prince of this world will be driven out". The words "driven out" are how Matthew, Mark, and Luke describe Jesus delivering people from demons. When Jesus prays for the oppressed, their devils are "driven out".

John chooses not to include deliverance miracles in his Gospel because he wants us to see the Cross of Christ as the greatest act of deliverance in human history. John knows that the cosmos has been under the control and influence of the prince of this world (i.e. the devil). But he also knows that Jesus drove the devil out at Calvary. The devil's downfall was secured when Jesus was lifted up. When Jesus died, he didn't die as a victim; he died as a victor. He died a death that dealt the decisive blow to the devil's power on planet earth.

There are many ways to look at the blessings of the Cross – as redemption, as satisfaction, as substitution, and so on. But in John 12:31 we see another angle. The Cross is the place of our liberation. The death of Jesus is therefore not a tragedy; it's a triumph!

Devotion: *Dear Father, I worship you that in Jesus we have the victory over the enemy of our souls. I thank you that through his shed blood, Jesus drove out the prince of this world. Jesus, you are truly our victor, our champion and our king. We worship you today. Amen.*

> **"I, when I am lifted up from the earth, will draw all people to myself."**
>
> John 12:32

Jesus speaks now about being lifted up from the earth. He is referring to the death that he is about to die at Calvary. There his wrists will be nailed to a wooden *patibulum* or cross beam, which will then be fixed to a *stipes* or post. This post will be lifted up, causing Jesus' body to be elevated above the earth. There he will spend his last hours of life, struggling for breath, and bleeding from his wounds. It will be a horrible and ugly sight and yet it will also be the revelation of the most beautiful thing in the universe – the Father's love.

As Jesus prepares for the ordeal of his passion and death, he declares that his elevation on the Cross is going to have a magnetic, drawing power on human beings for the whole of history. Whenever the Cross is portrayed and preached in the future, it will have a powerful appeal for everyone and anyone who acknowledges their sin and their need for forgiveness. It will draw spiritual orphans into the arms of their loving Abba, Father.

I remember the first time I began to understand this. I had been ordained as a Christian minister for about a year and I was at that time leading a youth group for fourteen- to eighteen-year-olds. I used to meet with them every Sunday night at 8 p.m. in an old church hall.

One Sunday evening I decided to speak about the Cross. I asked a carpenter to make a large wooden cross. I encouraged all the teenagers to invite their friends. The following Sunday night we had over sixty young people crammed into the room listening attentively as I described what Jesus had done for them and why. At the end of my message, twelve teenagers went to the Cross to kneel in repentance. All of them made first-time commitments to Jesus Christ. They were irresistibly drawn to the love of the Father that night and their lives profoundly changed.

The Cross has a drawing power greater than anything else in creation.

We can't and mustn't bypass the Cross.

Devotion: *Abba, Father, I thank you that the Cross is the greatest revelation of your love in history. Thank you for its incomparable power to draw people to Jesus. Thank you for its pull in my life. Help me to share the message of the Cross more often. Amen.*

... at the same time many even among the leaders believed in him. But because of the Pharisees they would not confess their faith for fear they would be put out of the synagogue; for they loved praise from men more than praise from God.

John 12:42–43 (NIV)

At the moment I'm marvelling at one of my sons who's going on strongly with the Lord. He is doing a job working with men who are not Christians. Every evening when he comes home from work he reads books by Christian thinkers who are very good at making hard things simple. He listens to talks by speakers who know how to explain the deeper issues of life in ways that everyone can access, whether they are churchgoers or not. He is hungry to learn.

Right now my son is taking C. S. Lewis's book, *The Four Loves*, into work with him. During the breaks he is reading passages to his colleagues. They are genuinely eager to learn and wonderful opportunities for talking about the Christian faith are being opened up as a result. It's so encouraging to see how my son is so secure in his heavenly Father's love that he is not intimidated by his peers nor is he afraid or ashamed about talking to others about his faith.

In our passage for today we read about some of the Jewish leaders in Jerusalem. Not all of them were hostile to Jesus. We learn here that some of them actually believed in him but they did so secretly. They were crypto-believers because they were afraid of being censured and ostracized by their peers. John informs us that they cared more about being rejected by their colleagues than being accepted by the Father. They loved praise from men more than praise from God.

The Bible teaches us that the fear of man is like a snare or a trap. It is something that obstructs us and binds us. It prevents us from becoming who we are truly meant to be and it delays us from embracing where we are truly meant to be heading. The fear of man obscures our identity and inhibits our destiny. The only antidote to this fear of man is the love of the Father. Abba's love drives out our fear (1 John 4:18).

Devotion: *Dear loving, heavenly Father, I ask that you would make me so secure in who you are and who I am that I no longer feel intimidated by others, especially by my non-Christian peers. Help me to be open about my faith and ready to share when asked, in Jesus' name. Amen.*

Jesus cried out, "Those who believe in me do not believe in me only, but in the one who sent me."

John 12:44

I have the privilege of travelling all over the UK and indeed the world. I have visited countless churches and Christian conferences in my work at the Father's House Trust. My message is primarily about the Father's love, which I believe is the premier message of Jesus.

As I visit many different churches, I have to admit that I sometimes become a little discouraged and the main reason for this is because so many Christians relate to Jesus but they don't relate to the Father. They worship Jesus, sing to Jesus, and pray to Jesus, but they don't mention Abba, Father. In many places, people speak to God as everything but Father, calling him Lord, God, Creator, King, but never Father, let alone Abba, Daddy, Papa, or Dad. I think one of the things that New Testament Christians would be most shocked about in contemporary churches is the lack of affectionate attention given to the Father. It's as if Jesus only came to reveal himself. It's as if we have forgotten that it is our ability to call God "Abba" that marks us out as different from all other religions in history.

In our verse for today Jesus couldn't be clearer. He makes it abundantly plain that when a person truly comes to faith in him, it's not just Jesus who they now believe in; it's the Father who sent him they believe in as well. Jesus came to reveal the Father and he went to hell and back (quite literally) so that we could be reconciled to the Father. Jesus accordingly doesn't just want us to worship him alone. He wants us to worship his Abba, Father in spirit and in truth. Isn't it time we restored the forgotten Father to his rightful place in our adoration?

The number one reason why so many Christians don't relate to Abba, Father is not just bad theology and teaching but also because they have been poorly fathered by their earthly dads. If that's true of you too, then ask Jesus to heal the wounds from your father so you can call God your heavenly "'Dad".

Devotion: Abba, Father, I thank you that Jesus wants me to believe in you, pray to you and worship you. This is what he came for. Please restore the Father's song in my life. Help me to give you my most heartfelt and affectionate praise, in Jesus' name. Amen.

"When they look at me, they see the one who sent me."

John 12:45

Yesterday we heard Jesus stress that believing in him means believing in the Father as well. When a person comes to faith in Jesus Christ, they are not only meant to relate to Jesus as their Saviour but they are supposed to start relating to God as their Abba, Father. Faith in Christ is supposed to lead to faith in God as your Abba, your Daddy.

In today's passage we hear Jesus stating that anyone who looks at him sees the Father. Jesus is, as it were, a window onto the Father. If we want to know what God the Father is like, then we need to look at his Son. Jesus is an exact and unerring picture of the God who wants to be known and loved as Abba, Father.

So, when we see Jesus transforming 180 gallons of water into wine at Cana, we see the Father. In fact, we see an extravagant Father.

When we see Jesus driving out the money changers in the Temple, we see the Father. In fact, we see a chastising and holy Father.

When we see Jesus relating to and helping a despised Samaritan woman, we see the Father. In fact, we see an inclusive Father.

When we see Jesus feeding the 5,000 hungry people, we see the Father. In fact, we see a practical and providing Father.

When we see Jesus helping the woman caught in adultery, we see the Father. In fact, we see a merciful Father.

When we see Jesus healing the man born blind, we see the Father. In fact, we see a mighty, powerful Father.

When we see Jesus weeping at the tomb of his friend Lazarus, we see the Father. In fact, we see a weeping Father.

Jesus is the only one in history who has truly shown us what Abba is like.

We can't say anything about this Father that isn't first seen in Jesus.

Devotion: *Abba, Father, I thank you that you have revealed yourself as the world's greatest Dad, and I also thank you that when I look at Jesus I see you as a Father who loves us like no earthly father ever could. Help me to see more of your Fatherly love in Jesus, in his name I ask. Amen.*

> *"I did not speak of my own accord, but the Father who sent me commanded me what to say and how to say it."*
>
> John 12:49 (NIV)

It's one thing to understand the content of what you need to say to someone. It's another thing altogether to understand the form in which that message needs to be communicated. Jesus was the greatest communicator who has ever lived. No one has ever attained the heights of wisdom and truth that he achieved. Jesus was and is the best teacher who has ever graced the stage of history. And he was the best because he knew how to express divine revelation with divine wisdom. Jesus understood that truth has to be allied to grace if it's to be heard and lived. He knew better than anyone that how you say something is just as important as what you say.

And so Jesus tells us here that he lived so close to his Abba's heart that he heard not only what needed to be said to people; he also heard how Abba, Father wanted this truth to be conveyed.

So, when Jesus was with Nicodemus, the Father not only told Jesus what to say to him (that Nicodemus needed more than religion), he also told Jesus how to put this ("You must be born again").

When Jesus was with the Samaritan woman, the Father not only told Jesus what to say to her (that she needed more than what men could give her) he also told Jesus how to communicate it ("living water").

When Jesus had fed the hungry crowds with bread, Abba not only told his Son the truth they needed to hear (that only Jesus would truly satisfy their hunger), he also told him how to say it ("bread from heaven").

Jesus himself is the Word made flesh. He is the Father's perfect and final communication of himself to a lost world. As the Word, Jesus knew all about words. And he communicates perfectly to everyone.

Maybe we need to ask our Abba for the ability to express truth with more grace and beauty in future.

Devotion: *Abba, Father, forgive us as a church that so often we say things in a bland, prosaic and off-putting way. Help us to lean on you more not just for the content of our words but also for the form in which they need to be expressed, in Jesus' name. Amen.*

> *"... whatever I say is just what the Father has told me to say."*
>
> John 12:50

I love the fact that these are the last recorded words that Jesus utters in his public teaching in John's Gospel. From John chapter 13 onwards most of Jesus' words will be spoken to his disciples. A few will be spoken to those who put Jesus on trial. But here, in John 12:50, Jesus makes his final public statement in Jerusalem and his theme is once again his intimate communion with Abba, Father.

Jesus emphasizes one final time that everything he has said up until this moment has been what his Abba in heaven told him to say. At no point did Jesus say something on his own or of his own. Every word, every phrase, every sentence he uttered was uttered first by his Father and then spoken by him. Jesus' mouth was the megaphone through which a perfect Father called out in love to an imperfect world.

So when Jesus spoke to the Jewish leaders in the Temple he was speaking his Father's words.

When he spoke to the crowds in Galilee he was speaking his Father's words.

When he spoke in private to individuals like Nicodemus he was speaking his Father's words.

When he spoke to his own disciples he was speaking his Father's words.

When he speaks to us today he is speaking his Father's words.

Every intonation and inflection, every rebuke and reassurance, every parable and proverb, came first from the heart of the Father.

The last public words of Jesus are about his Abba.

For Jesus, Abba, Father was and is the beginning and end of everything.

He needs to be everything to us as well.

Devotion: *Abba, Father, I pray that you will deepen my intimate communion with you. Make me more like your Son, Jesus Christ. Help me as an adopted child to be like the Son by nature. Give me ears to hear what you're saying, and the boldness to speak it out, in his name. Amen.*

It was just before the Passover Festival. Jesus knew that the hour had come for him to leave this world and go to the Father.

John 13:1

With these solemn words, the whole course of John's story changes. Up until now, John's Gospel has focused on Jesus' ministry of teaching and miracles. John chapters 1 to 12 have described this ministry. There have been at least three Passover festivals (John 2, 6, and 12). Since these were annual feasts held in April we know that the ministry of Jesus must have lasted between two to three years. Now, as John 13 begins, the pace of the story slows down dramatically. From now on, the focus will not be on a period of two to three years. Instead it will be on a period of a few weeks, beginning here in John 13 with Jesus' last supper with his disciples, and ending with Jesus eating breakfast with the disciples a week or so after his resurrection. Everything in John's Gospel has been building up to this final Passover. The time has now arrived. Jesus' last hours on earth have begun. How will he spend his last night?

According to John 13 Jesus chose to have an evening meal with his friends during which he did something very surprising. He got down from the table, removed his outer garments and took a towel and a bowl of water. He stooped and washed each of his disciples' feet – including the feet of the man who would deny him three times and the man who would betray his whereabouts to his enemies. He then put his clothes back on and returned to his seat, saying to his disciples that he has left them an example to follow. Just as he had washed their feet, so they now must wash the feet of others as well.

As I write these devotions, I am constantly amazed by Jesus. Here is the Lord of life about to embrace death. Here is the king of glory taking on the role of the humblest of servants.

If ever someone deserved to be worshipped, it's Jesus. History is littered with stories of men who wanted to become gods. But it tells of only one instance of God becoming a man.

Devotion: *Dear Abba, Father, I thank you that in Jesus you have come to earth as a humble human being and washed our feet. You truly are an extraordinary Dad. Thank you so much that you took on our humanity and modelled true humility, in Jesus' name. Amen.*

Having loved his own who were in the world, he now showed them the full extent of his love.

John 13:1 (NIV)

I remember being told a story about a naughty toddler. He had been misbehaving badly and as a punishment his parents had sent him to bed early. He was in his cot crying, wanting to come downstairs again and be with his brothers and sisters.

The boy's door was open and his grandfather walked past. The toddler, seeing a friendly face, lifted up his arms and cried out. Grandpa came into the room and told him that he wasn't allowed to take him downstairs. He wanted to but he couldn't.

The boy was distraught and continued to cry. So the old man, unable to pick the boy up, climbed into the cot and sat with his grandson cuddling him. The child calmed down and soon fell into a deep and peaceful sleep. The boy wasn't allowed out, so his grandfather climbed in.

John 13 is a glorious episode. It portrays a much loved scene in which Jesus gets down from where he is sitting at the meal table and stoops to perform an extraordinary act of love. He takes a bowl and a towel and he washes all of his disciples' feet.

What a picture this is! Jesus, the Word made flesh and the Son of the eternal Father, serves his followers by performing an act that not even the most menial slave was required to perform.

During these devotional readings in John, we have been constantly looking at the way in which Jesus reveals the fatherly heart of God. Everything Jesus says and does reveals Abba's love.

In this timeless scene, Jesus shows us that our heavenly Father has not remained remote in the heavens but has stooped to our level and exhibited a love that is truly self-giving.

What a perfect Father we have! We couldn't rise to his level to be like him, so he came down to our level and became like us!

Devotion: *Dear Abba, Father, in Jesus you show us just what it means to be a loving, serving Dad. Thank you for the amazing way in which you have washed us and continue to wash us. Thank you for revealing the full extent of your affection for us, in Jesus' name. Amen.*

The evening meal was in progress, and the devil had already prompted Judas, the son of Simon Iscariot, to betray Jesus.

John 13:2

The name Judas has become a byword for betrayal. If someone is described as a "Judas", everyone knows that they are a person who has betrayed someone close to them.

How did Judas come to the place where he could betray the most perfect and loving man who has ever lived? To answer this question we need to look at how Judas' character deteriorates over time.

We first meet Judas at the end of John chapter 6. He is one of the Twelve who has decided to stay with Jesus when others have left. Jesus says that one of them is "a devil" (6:70).

In John 12, we see Judas – along with the other disciples – at the meal held in Jesus' honour in Lazarus' house. Judas, we are told, looked after the money and was helping himself.

Here, in John 13, at another meal, John informs us that Judas has now been "prompted by the devil to betray Jesus". The word "prompted" means that the devil "sent evil thoughts into Judas's heart".

By the end of John 13, Judas's character reaches rock bottom when he eats the bread that Jesus gives him. In verse 27 we are told that when he eats it, "Satan entered into him."

Judas starts off by being greedy. He then helps himself to the common purse. As his love of money increases, he allows himself to be prompted by the devil before finally being controlled by him.

Judas had an orphan heart and was greedy. He had a poverty mindset and he stole money. He reminds us that we must treat finance in a way befitting faithful sons and daughters, not fearful orphans. The Bible teaches that the love of money is the root of all evil. This proves true for Judas Iscariot. His attitude towards money is a warning to all those who sacrifice loyalty for greed.

Devotion: _Dear loving Abba, Father, I pray today that you would help me to trust in you in the area of finance. Help me not to be one who holds and hoards money. Help me to be open-handed and trusting. Keep me from wrong choices in this area, in Jesus' name. Amen._

Jesus knew that the Father had put all things under his power, and that he had come from God and was returning to God... .

John 13:3

Sometimes people make a tragic mistake in their view of Jesus. They think that he was merely a mortal prophet or a great teacher and that he understood himself only in these terms. But that's not what John tells us in his Gospel. Here, John gives us a unique view concerning how Jesus saw himself. He tells us that Jesus knew that he had come from the Father and was now returning to him. He tells us not only that Jesus knew his origin and his destination; he also knew that the Father had placed all things under his power and authority (literally "into his hands"). How can Jesus be just a teacher or a prophet when he knew these things about himself? Jesus is much more than a mere man. He is the Father's one and only Son who travelled from heaven to earth and then from earth to heaven. As the God-Man, he is wholly different from all other men and women who have ever lived. He reigns over all.

When we understand these things about Jesus it makes his journey into the world so much more astonishing. When Jesus was born as a baby, the Word became flesh. The Reason for Everything became a fragile human child. The infinite became an infant. For thirty years, this boy grew up, became a man, and lived in obscurity in a Galilean village. Then, aged about thirty, he was baptized in the River Jordan and began to preach about the Father and his kingdom. He healed the sick, turned water into wine, multiplied bread, raised the dead, and walked on water. After three years of unparalleled acts of kindness and power, he was arrested, tried and brutally abused both verbally and physically. He died a slave's death on a Roman cross outside the walls of Jerusalem and his body was buried in a rich man's tomb. Three days later, he rose from the dead and appeared among his disciples before ascending to heaven, to sit at his Abba's right hand and to rest from his labours.

If ever there was a tale that deserved the title "The Incredible Journey", it's this one. Let's spend time thanking Jesus that he made this journey for you and for me and let's celebrate the pre-eminence of Jesus Christ.

Devotion: *Dear loving, Abba, Father, I worship and praise you because you have placed all things into your Son's hands and you did that because he alone came from heaven and then returned to heaven. Help me always to proclaim the supremacy of Jesus, in his name. Amen.*

... he got up from the meal, took off his outer clothing, and wrapped a towel around his waist. After that, he poured water into a basin and began to wash his disciples' feet, drying them with the towel that was wrapped around him.

John 13:4–5

In Jesus' day, it was customary for people to wash before they left their homes to go to a dinner party. They would then walk over to their host's house. The one part of their bodies that would often become dirty would be their feet. People mostly wore open sandals so it would be very easy for this to happen. For this reason the host would put a bowl of clean water and a towel at the entrance of their home.

The extraordinary thing about Jesus in John 13 is that during supper he lays down his outer clothing and wraps a towel around his waist. He pours water into a bowl – probably the bowl that had been standing at the entrance of the home. One by one he approaches his disciples. He bends down and washes the dirt from their feet. He then removes the towel from around his waist and dries them.

I remember a visiting speaker coming to a church I was leading. On the Monday morning after his Sunday talks, we assembled all the staff of our church and some other church leaders from the area. Without warning, our guest told us to fetch bowls and towels and to get into pairs and wash each other's feet. To this day I don't know which I found harder – washing someone else's feet or having my own feet washed.

I'm guessing the disciples felt awkward too. Here is the High King of Heaven washing their feet. Here is the one who walked on water cleaning their feet with water. They must have been truly startled.

There are many models of leadership in the world today but there is none more striking than the model of servant leadership, uniquely embodied by Jesus of Nazareth.

There are many fine stories about leaders in history but there is none more inspiring than this one – of Jesus washing his followers' feet.

Devotion: *Abba, Father, you have given us all the capacity to lead. When my time comes to exercise this calling, help me to be a Servant Leader. Help me to put others before myself and to be prepared to serve and resource those whom you call me to influence, in Jesus' name. Amen.*

"No," said Peter, "you shall never wash my feet."

John 13:8

Simon Peter is such an odd mixture of good and bad qualities. He is capable of saying really great things to Jesus. For example, in John 6:68–69, He says, "You have the words of eternal life. We believe and know that you are the Holy One of God." That's a really impressive confession of faith. Here, however, Simon Peter says something very foolish. He says "No" and "Never" to Jesus.

If we read other accounts about Peter, we see he has a habit of saying "No" and "Never" to his Lord. When he confesses Jesus as Messiah at Caesarea Philippi, Jesus applauds him. Jesus then goes on to describe what kind of Messiah he is – not a conquering warrior on a white horse but a suffering servant on a Roman cross. Peter takes Jesus aside and rebukes him, saying "Never, Lord!" (Matthew 16:22–23).

After Peter has been baptized in the Holy Spirit at Pentecost, you'd think that he would have ironed out this flaw. However, when Peter has a vision of non-kosher food being lowered in a sheet from heaven, and he hears the Father telling him to eat it, Peter replies (in the KJV), "Not so, Lord" (Acts 10:14). The NIV translates Peter's words as, "Surely not, Lord." Here again we see Peter trying to say "No" and "Lord" all at the same time.

In John 13, Jesus has already begun washing his disciples' feet. He now comes to Simon Peter. Simon Peter reacts with great indignation and refuses Jesus' overtures of loving service. He says, "No" and then adds, "you shall never wash my feet". He says "No" and "Never" to the one he calls Rabbi and Lord (John 13:13).

We need to remember that saying "Lord" cancels out the right to say "Never", and that saying "Never" cancels out the right to say "Lord". And this includes not only those moments when our Father calls us to do tough things. It also includes those times when he wants to bless us and give us good things, as here in John 13.

So let's rediscover the art of saying "Yes" to Abba.

Devotion: Dear Abba, Father, help me to be a son or a daughter who delights in saying "Yes, Lord." When you call me to do something challenging, help me to say, "Yes" and "Always". When you want to bless me, help me to receive cheerfully, in Jesus' name. Amen.

When he had finished washing their feet, he put on his clothes and returned to his place. "Do you understand what I have done for you?" he asked them.

John 13:12

This is a good question. At one level, you'd expect the answer "Yes". Surely the answer was obvious. Jesus has demonstrated that true love means forgetting oneself and giving oneself to others. He has left them an example to follow and indicated that he wants those who will make up the Jesus movement in the future to be a foot-washing community. What could be more obvious than that?

But as so often in John's Gospel, things are not always as simple as they seem. Jesus' actions here are not just a demonstration of self-sacrificial service. They are also a symbolic re-enactment of the whole of his mission – the entire task that the Father gave him.

Let me explain.

When Jesus gets down from the table, this is a symbolic act. It points to his descent from heaven to earth – his journey from the mansions of glory to the manger in Bethlehem.

When Jesus removes his outer garments, this is a symbolic act. It points to his humble acceptance of the call to become a human being, a call that required him to relinquish some of the attributes of divinity.

When he washes his disciples' feet, this too is a symbolic act. It points to the death that he dies at Calvary, a death that makes sinful human beings clean in the sight of a holy Father.

When he puts on his clothes and returns to his seat, this is also a symbolic act. It points to his resurrection from the dead and his ascent into the heavenly realms of glory to rejoin his Abba, his Father.

This is truly a meal with a message and the message has many levels. Jesus asks, "Do you understand what I've just done for you?" Do we understand and appreciate the full extent of what Jesus did for us?

Devotion: Dear Abba, Father, I thank you so much for the self-sacrificial love of your Son, Jesus. I praise you, Jesus, that you were prepared to embrace humiliation so that I could be clean and enjoy Abba's embrace. Give me a deeper understanding and a greater wonder. Amen.

"You call me 'Teacher' and 'Lord,' and rightly so, for that is what I am."

John 13:13

I once published a small book about the spiritual gift of teaching. It seemed to me at the time that one of the gifts of the Spirit that had received the least attention was the gift of teaching, mentioned by the apostle Paul in Romans 12:7. So I wrote this book entitled *The Teacher's Notebook* and I described how a person could excel in the art of communicating God's truth.

In fulfilling this task I spent much of my time examining the teaching of Jesus in the four Gospels. I quoted the maxim that there are really three types of teacher. There are those that you listen to, those you can't listen to, and those you can't help listening to. I described Jesus as the third kind. In fact, I made the claim that he is the finest teacher of truth the world has ever known.

There is a Japanese proverb that goes like this: "Better than a thousand days of diligent study is one day with a great teacher." I am sure that just one day in the presence of Jesus listening to his teaching would have made us happy to address him as "Teacher", as our Rabbi. Even his enemies then called him a great teacher. Even his enemies today are prepared to concede the same.

But Jesus wasn't just a teacher then and he isn't just a teacher now. Jesus was not just teacher, he was Lord. He wasn't just deserving of the title "Rabbi". He was deserving of the title "Lord", a word reserved for God. Jesus was a human being with an unmatched ability to make hard truths simple. But he was also the Son of God, the Lord of heaven, the way and the truth and the life.

Here at the Last Supper, Jesus tells his disciples that they are right to call him both Teacher and Lord. He is worthy of both titles. A true disciple not only sits under his teaching. A true disciple also submits to his Lordship. Let's make sure we call Jesus Lord as well as teacher. Let's always set Jesus apart as "Lord" in our hearts (1 Peter 3:15).

Devotion: *Abba, Father, I thank you so much that your Son Jesus not only teaches me truth in a way that no one else can. I also thank you that he is my Lord and my God. Help me always to confess Jesus as "Lord" in my heart and with my mouth, in his name. Amen.*

> ***Now that you know these things, you will be blessed if you do them.***

John 13:17

There was a time some years ago when my family and I were under serious pressure. I was a busy vicar and our vicarage was situated on the same block of land as the church building itself. The only thing separating our home from the church was a car park. This car park became the magnet for the most troubled and troublesome teenagers in the community. One of them in particular made our lives a complete misery. For more than three years we lived under constant strain from this one person's influence.

Then one Saturday morning something happened. I got up and came downstairs. Looking through the window, I saw this teenager lying in a sleeping bag on the car park. She had clearly been there all night and I remember thinking some not very pleasant thoughts about her. I was still thinking about her as I was making a cup of tea for my wife when the Holy Spirit began to whisper, "What would Jesus do?" I knew the answer straight away though I didn't like it, and for a while – I have to be honest – I resisted it.

Eventually I said "yes" and found a tray. I made a cup of tea, found some of my wife's best muffins, and carried them out to the girl on the car park. I was wearing my dressing gown and slippers and I could feel how cold it was. Compassion began to flow in my heart. As I drew close, she saw it was me and was about to yell the customary abuse when I said, "Hi, I saw you out here and thought you must be hungry and cold so I brought you a hot drink and some breakfast." As I lowered the tray at her head, her mouth opened in shock.

Two things happened as I walked away that day. First of all, the girl's attitude towards me and my family completely changed. We had no more trouble from her or anyone else. Secondly, I felt the blessing of the Father in a way that I had never done before. It reminded me of John 13:17, where Jesus says that we will be truly blessed when we serve other people with acts of surprising kindness, just as he did.

Devotion: *Dear loving, heavenly Dad, I thank you so much for the indescribable blessings that you pour on us when we choose to serve others, especially those who give us grief. Help me to become a radical foot-washer, just like your Son, in his name. Amen.*

After he had said this, Jesus was troubled in spirit and testified,
"Very truly I tell you, one of you is going to betray me."

John 13:21

As the hour of his crucifixion draws near Jesus becomes noticeably more anxious. Here, at the Last Supper with his friends, John tells us that Jesus was "troubled in spirit". The word translated "troubled" is the Greek verb *tarasso*. John has used it twice in the run up to John 13. In John 11:33, he tells us that Jesus was troubled as he saw Mary weeping at the tomb of Lazarus. In John 12:27 Jesus declares that his soul is troubled as he recognizes the arrival of the hour of his death. Here in John 13:21 Jesus is troubled as he contemplates his imminent betrayal.

There are few experiences that create more stress and sadness than the experience of being betrayed by a dear friend. If you have ever been rejected or betrayed by someone you loved very much you will know how unpleasant, shocking, and heartbreaking this is. If that person was your spouse you will have had to endure a particularly devastating pain. You will have known what it is to be troubled in spirit.

How do we cope with the experience of being rejected and betrayed by a good friend – especially one who has walked with us as a brother or a sister in Christ?

The most important thing of all is to remember that Jesus went through this experience too. Here in John 13 we see him deeply troubled by what his friend is about to do. If Jesus experienced this pain, then I know that I have a heavenly Father who has been through what I have been through, a Dad who truly understands. I know that Jesus is a man of sorrows, fully acquainted with the things that grieve and trouble me.

Furthermore, if the most perfect man who ever lived was betrayed by someone, I needn't condemn myself if it happens to me. Yes I must acknowledge any part that I have played and I must repent of my wrongdoing. But I mustn't engage in self-hatred. If it happened to Jesus who was perfect, then it can happen to me.

Devotion: *Dear Abba, Father, I bring to you any friends and loved ones who have betrayed and rejected me. I ask for you to forgive me for any part I played, even as I choose to forgive them. Thank you that Jesus went through this and that you understand, in his name. Amen.*

> *One of them, the disciple whom Jesus loved, was reclining next to him.*

> John 13:23

This is the first time that we meet the disciple whom Jesus loved, or the Beloved Disciple as he is sometimes called. We will meet him again in John 18 when we see him helping Peter gain access into the high priest's courtyard. We will then see him in John 19 at the Cross – the only male disciple who is present at the crucifixion. There Jesus tells him to look after his mother and it is there that this disciple witnesses the flow of blood and water from the wounded side of Jesus. After Jesus' death we will see him again, this time running to the empty tomb with Peter in John 20 and then meeting the risen Jesus in John 21.

Many have tried to identify who this man is. Some have argued that he is Lazarus, others that he is an anonymous disciple who lived in Jerusalem. Most have taken the traditional position, which is that the Beloved Disciple was John the son of Zebedee, and that this Gospel is the eyewitness record deriving from his reminiscences.

We probably won't know with complete certainty the identity of this unnamed man until heaven. What's important in today's passage is not *who* he is but *where* he is. Here we see him lying on a couch at the supper that Jesus is having with his disciples. The Beloved Disciple lies on the right hand side of Jesus and close to his master's heart, just as Jesus is said to be close to the Father's heart in John 1:18. In that position he hears every word that Jesus is saying. While others can't hear because they are further away, the Beloved Disciple can hear even the very heartbeat of his teacher and Lord.

This man became known as the Beloved Disciple because he made friendship with Jesus a priority. In the place of intimacy he received insights that no one else received. In this sacred place of rest, he received revelation that no one else heard.

We need to remember that intimacy with Jesus is the true path to knowing the Father's insights.

Devotion: *Dear Abba, Father, I thank you for this picture of the beloved disciple resting on Jesus' chest. I thank you for the picture of Jesus leaning on your chest. Help me to spend more time enjoying intimacy with you so that I might know your heart better. Amen.*

Then, dipping the piece of bread, he gave it to Judas, the son of Simon Iscariot.

John 13:26

It's impossible to know just how poignant this moment really is unless we have an understanding of Jewish meals during the time of Jesus.

In Jesus' day, meals like this did not involve chairs. They involved couches. Every guest would recline on couches on the floor. They would lean to their left, leaving their right hand free to eat their food. As they inclined this way, it would often involve them actually leaning on the chest of their immediate neighbour.

We know from John 13:21 that the Beloved Disciple was sitting on Jesus' right. He was leaning to his left and in the process resting his head on Jesus' chest, hearing what Jesus was saying. Who then was sitting on Jesus' left? Whose chest was Jesus leaning on during this final supper with his friends?

There can be only one answer. It was Judas Iscariot. For Jesus to speak so personally to Judas, and indeed to hand him a piece of bread, Judas must have been on Jesus' left – the place reserved for an honoured guest.

How did Judas come to be in such a position? Jesus must have invited him. Judas would not have been able to sit there on his own initiative. Jesus, in an extraordinary act of love, asks him to sit next to him.

Furthermore, Jesus gives Judas a piece of bread. This is an extremely significant act. In that culture, it was an act of great affection. It signified that Judas was a special friend.

What love is this! Even at the eleventh hour, just before Judas Iscariot betrays his friend and master, Jesus shows him extreme compassion. To the one who is about to be so unfaithful, Jesus shows great faithfulness. To the one who is about to exhibit such a lack of love, Jesus shows intense love. In Jesus, the Father's love pursues Judas right to the end. He will not let go without a fight.

Devotion: *Dear Abba, Father, I thank you that even when we are rebelling against your love you still invite us to your table and make overtures of undeserved love towards us. Help me to be faithful to you, even as you are relentlessly faithful to me, in Jesus' name. Amen.*

As soon as Judas took the bread, Satan entered into him.

John 13:27

The Last Supper has reached a critical moment. Judas is reclining at the meal table on Jesus' left hand side. He has just heard Jesus speak about being betrayed by one of his friends. He has even felt Jesus' head resting on his chest in this place of special honour. Now Jesus is extending a morsel of bread to him – an act that signified that Judas was a special friend. We don't know if Judas faltered, aware of the fatal choice he was making or the awful hypocrisy of his actions. Whether he hesitated or not, John tells us that as soon as Judas ate this piece of bread from the hand of Jesus, Satan entered into him. Eating this morsel, Judas gave his whole personality over to Satan, the adversary of God.

It is a sobering thing to realize that Judas has had close fellowship with Jesus for two to three years and yet this is still not enough to prevent him from choosing to betray his friend. Judas even receives the undeserved love of being seated in the place of honour yet this is not enough to stop him from committing the most treacherous of acts. Even when Jesus extends his hand to Judas, bearing a special morsel reserved for the closest of friends, Judas still continues unswervingly on his path towards destruction. His heart is corrupt and his will is determined. He will not be deterred from his plan to betray the Father's perfect Son. Even these final unspoken gifts of love are not enough to give him pause.

This scene is extremely poignant. On one side of Jesus we have the Beloved Disciple. He is the very epitome of faithfulness. He follows Jesus to the very end and loves him in the good times and the not so good. Judas is on the other side of Jesus. He is the very epitome of unfaithfulness. He follows Jesus for a while but then deserts him at the end. The Beloved Disciple behaves like a loyal son or daughter of the king. Judas behaves like a disloyal orphan.

Let's resolve to become one of the Beloved Disciples of Jesus. Let's make loyalty and faithfulness some of our core and non-negotiable values. Let's stay true to Jesus all the days of our lives.

Devotion: *Dear Abba, Father, I pray that you would help me to be a loyal person. Increase the virtue of fidelity in me. Help me to be faithful to my loved ones and my friends. Help me to be faithful to my pastors and my church. Help me to be a loyal child, in Jesus' name. Amen.*

And it was night.

John 13:30

Sometimes the deepest truths are uttered in the fewest words.

Judas has just eaten the special piece of bread that Jesus offered him – a morsel that was a great honour in that cultural context. Eating the bread, Judas gives his whole life over to Satan. Having given the enemy an open door of entry through his love of money, Judas now finds that Satan has come through the door and has taken possession of the whole house. Impervious to Jesus' overtures of love, Judas now leaves the intimate setting of the meal table and heads towards the religious leaders in Jerusalem. He has only one thing on his mind. He will tell them where they can find and arrest the man who has demonstrated nothing but love for him, right to the very end.

As Judas leaves the table and then the house, John briefly remarks, "And it was night." As so often in John's Gospel, we can interpret these words at two levels. On the surface of it, John is merely reporting the time of day. Darkness has descended and it is night-time, the evening before Jesus' death. But at a deeper level John is hinting at so much more. Darkness in this Gospel is often a symbol of moral evil and intellectual ignorance. It is the realm in which the spiritually blind dwell. As Jesus says in John 11:9–10, "Are there not twelve hours of daylight? Those who walk in the daytime will not stumble, for they see by this world's light. It is when people walk at night that they stumble, for they have no light."

Judas has no light and is about to stumble and fall. Abandoning the one who is the light of the world, he is now lost in the darkness. He is the epitome of one who walks by night not by day. He is about to betray his Messiah and fall into a place of despair and devastation. For Judas, leaving Jesus is the beginning of an endless night.

"And it was night" says so much more than at first appears. Let's not be a people who live in darkness. Let's be luminous people whose hearts are always filled with the flame of Abba's love.

Devotion: *Dear Abba, Father, I covenant with you today to be a light-bearer not a night-bringer. I don't want to be a child of the night but a child of the light. I want to be someone who changes the atmosphere around me for good, in Jesus' name. Amen.*

"My children, I will be with you only a little longer."

John 13:33

The time for Jesus' departure from the world is drawing very near now. We are within twenty-four hours of Jesus' death on a Roman cross outside the walls of Jerusalem. Jesus begins to prepare his disciples for his return to the Father and he addresses them as "My children".

Actually, this is not a very accurate translation. The word in Greek is *teknion*. It means a "little child". This is a diminutive form of the word *teknon*, which means "child". If *teknon* means a child of any age, *teknion* means an infant or a very small child.

In John 1:12 we read that anyone who welcomes Jesus and chooses to believe in him becomes a child of God. The word translated "child" here is the normal word *teknon*. When Jesus addresses his disciples in John 13:33, he addresses them with the word *teknion*, as little children.

It seems somewhat strange that a man who was probably the same age as the people around him should choose to call his listeners "little children". Maybe if Jesus had been an old man it wouldn't sound so odd. But to call his disciples "infants" sounds alien to our ears.

However, we need to remember the constant message throughout John's Gospel that Jesus only ever says what his Father tells him to say. Jesus reveals the Father. The words Jesus says and indeed the ways in which he says them all reflect the Fatherly heart of God.

When we hear Jesus address his disciples as "little children" we are hearing the voice of Abba, Father. The disciples at this stage are like tiny children; their understanding is limited. But after Jesus has returned, they will no longer be infants. They will be the children of God.

All of us are growing every day as we follow Jesus. As we do, God is not an over-bearing boss who demands our performance. He is a loving Dad who encourages our growth and development. Whether we are children or little children, God is our Abba who is committed to our maturity.

Devotion: *Dear loving, Abba, Father, I thank you so much that following Jesus means that I cannot remain the same as I have been. Thank you that you love me too much to let me stay the same as I was yesterday. As your child, help me to grow to maturity in Christ. Amen.*

> *"A new command I give you: Love one another. As I have loved you, so you must love one another. By this everyone will know that you are my disciples, if you love one another."*
>
> John 13:34–35

Here Jesus gives his disciples a new commandment. The word translated "commandment" reminds us of the "commandments" given to the people of God in the Old Testament. One of those old commandments was to "love your neighbour as yourself" (Leviticus 19:18). Jesus now gives a new commandment, to "love one another as I have loved you". This commandment is not new in the sense that it makes the old redundant. It is new in its scope, its strength and its purpose.

Let's deal with its scope first. Jesus tells his disciples that they must now love one another. The thing that is meant to characterize a local church more than anything else is the love that we have for each other.

Secondly, let's deal with the strength of this commandment. The word translated "love" here is the Greek verb *agapao*. *Agapao* is self-sacrificial love. This is the strongest kind of love. It is Calvary love.

Thirdly, Jesus tells us to love one another so that the world will know that we are truly his followers. This is the hallmark of true Christianity. A true church is a community full of the Father's love.

The other day I was having lunch with an old friend who is attending a lively church in the UK. They have 2,000 members and are growing fast. In fact they now have to extend their buildings to accommodate the rapid growth. I asked her why she thought it was such a vibrant community. She answered without hesitation: "When new people walk in here they are struck by two things: the love people have for each other, and the love they have the poor. They find that irresistible."

I am sure that we would see revival breaking out everywhere if we restored the love commandment to its rightful place in the church today. A loving, united, self-giving fellowship of believers is extraordinarily compelling. It points to Jesus and shows that he is alive.

Devotion: *Dear loving Father, I thank you that love is your primary characteristic. Please restore the Father's love to the Father's house all over the world. Turn local churches into affectionate, caring families so that the world may see how real you are, in Jesus' name. Amen.*

Peter asked, "Lord, why can't I follow you now? I will lay down my life for you." Then Jesus answered, "Will you really lay down your life for me? Very truly I tell you, before the rooster crows, you will disown me three times!"

John 13:37–38

John chapter 13 ends with a conversation between Simon Peter and Jesus. In fact, as we will see, this part of John 13 and much of John 14 describes the interaction that took place between various disciples and their master as he prepared to leave them. In John 13:36–38, Simon Peter is the focus. He has just heard Jesus say, "I will be with you only a little while longer" so Peter asks, "Where are you going?" Jesus answers, "Where I am going you cannot follow now but you will follow later."

What is Jesus referring to here? He is talking about his impending death on the Cross. Jesus is within twenty-four hours of being arrested, tried, tortured and crucified. Simon Peter will try and follow Jesus on this Calvary road but – as we will see in John 18–19 – he will fail. He will end up denying that he even knows Jesus and will be absent at Golgotha when Jesus is crucified. Jesus prophesies that Peter cannot follow him on this road now but that he will later.

Jesus is saying that Peter too will be crucified when he is older. By that time he will be ready to obey the call to become a martyr for Jesus. But now he isn't ready. He hasn't yet received the Holy Spirit and he hasn't yet been refined in the fire of testing and trials. Impatient as he is, Peter says, "Lord, why can't I follow you now?" He adds a rash promise, "I will lay down my life for you." Jesus tells him that he will do no such thing. Before the cock crows, Peter will deny him three times.

Looking back over the course of John chapter 13 we see disciples relating in different ways to Jesus. We see the Beloved Disciple leaning on Jesus and simply listening. We also see Simon Peter making a fine-sounding promise that he will die for Jesus when in fact he will deny Jesus three times. The lesson is quite clear from this. It is better to be like the Beloved Disciple and listen a lot than to be like Peter and say a lot.

Devotion: *Dear Abba, Father, help me not to be a person who makes promises that I'm not ready to fulfil. Please help me to know when to speak and when to listen. And when I speak, let my words be few and let them be sincere, in Jesus' name. Amen.*

"Do not let your hearts be troubled. Trust in God; trust also in me."

John 14:1

As John chapter 14 opens, the final countdown to Jesus' death on the Cross has begun. Jesus is within hours of being arrested and tried, tortured and killed. He knows what's coming. He knows what he is about to face and he knows what the disciples are about to face. His followers are about to feel shock and grief in equal measure. They are about to walk the rocky road of bereavement.

And so, being the good shepherd that he is, Jesus begins to speak words of comfort to his friends. He tells them not to allow their hearts to be troubled. The word translated "troubled" is the same Greek verb that we encountered in John 11:33, 12:27, and 13:21. It is the word *tarasso*, which means "agitated" or "anxious". It is the word used of Jesus feeling troubled as he contemplates his own death.

What we see here is Jesus preparing his followers for the ordeal of bereavement. Those who have lost a loved one will tell you that the path of bereavement is a long and arduous one from feeling the numbness of shock to a sense of acceptance and resignation. They will tell you that without Jesus, this path is almost impossibly hard to take. With Jesus, it is still tough but so much easier.

Jesus helps us in our grief. He helps us to move from being troubled to being trusting. He whispers into our hearts, "Do not be troubled" and in so doing he enables us to cast our troubles on him. He has walked where we walk. He has been troubled by the unwelcome and agonising attentions of death. He has shoulders big enough to carry our troubles. He invites us to send our troubles his way.

In addition, Jesus helps us to come to a place where we can trust. The disciples were going to need to trust. Their world was about to cave in on Good Friday. What they needed to remember is that every Good Friday is followed by an Easter Day. When we face the death of a loved one, we need to trust that there will be an Easter Day for them as well.

Devotion: *Dear loving Abba, Father, I bring you my troubled feelings. Thank you that you are concerned for my anxious heart. I cast my cares upon Jesus today and I ask you to help me to trust that "Dad knows best", in Jesus' name. Amen.*

"In my Father's house are many rooms...".

John 14:2 (NIV)

What did Jesus mean by the word "rooms"? The word translated "rooms" is the word *monai*, which is from the same root as the verb *menein* – a Greek verb that John uses frequently in his Gospel and which means "stay, remain, or abide". It is a word that implies permanent residence rather than a temporary lodging.

What Jesus is saying here in essence is this: "In my Daddy's home there are many places you can stay – and you can stay in them forever."

There are so many things that I find reassuring about this great promise.

First of all, I love the fact that we will have a home in heaven. Many people don't have homes on earth. But they will in glory, if they have put their trust in Jesus.

Secondly, I love the fact that this house is *Abba's* home. It is the place where the greatest Father of all has his residence. This is the royal home of our Daddy in the heavens. Many people have not had dads on earth but they'll live with the perfect Dad in eternity.

Thirdly, I love the fact that there are many rooms in the Father's house. Many homes in our world are over-crowded. Not so in heaven! There's no overcrowding in the Father's house. There will be more than enough room for every person who believed in Jesus during their earthly life.

Fourthly, I love the fact that we are in these rooms permanently not temporarily. This is a home from which we will never be evicted. Once we have been shown to our rooms, we will have them forever.

Finally, I love the fact that the rooms we will occupy are better than anything we could experience on earth. They will not be like rooms in a cheap hotel or a rundown nursing home. They will be the most exquisitely decorated and perfectly adorned rooms we could imagine. They will be the kind of rooms that we will never want to leave!

Devotion: *Dear loving Abba, Father. I thank you so much that I'm going to have a room in your home forever. I am so excited by the prospect of this home and I can't wait to see what you've prepared for me. Help me to get more excited about my eternal home, in Jesus' name. Amen.*

"... if it were not so I would have told you."

John 14:2 (NIV)

I want to dwell on these simple words today. They are so easy to pass over. But they are extremely important and deeply comforting.

Jesus has just been talking about his Father's house. In heaven, there is the most amazing home. No architect will ever have constructed anything as large or as magnificent. No painter will ever have depicted a building or a landscape so vast or exquisite. The Father's house is beyond human imagining. It is so extraordinarily intricate and complex that there are enough rooms for millions, maybe even billions, of people. It is so brilliantly conceived that every room is a masterpiece of interior design and every garden a horticultural triumph. The Father's house is everything we'd want it to be and so much more. It is beyond our wildest dreams and our most cherished stories. It is the place to which every faithful child of God is heading.

And here's the point. Jesus reassures us that this is all real by adding that "If it were not so I would have told you." In other words, "If this was all a myth, I would let you know. But it's not. I am telling you the truth. You have an eternal destiny worth living and dying for. Rest assured; heaven is your home, and it's real!"

I have a friend who was recently diagnosed with cancer. He is a Christian minister. When he received the news, there was understandably a period of shock and adjustment. My friend started to think and imagine the worst. As he did so, he said to me, "I have discovered that I really do believe what I believe." In the time of trial, he knew that his faith was based on facts, not on myths. I am happy to report that my friend was prayed for and completely healed.

Isn't it comforting to know that Jesus was telling the truth when he talked about the Father's house in heaven? Jesus always tells the truth. He cannot and will not lie. What a great hope we have! We are heading for Abba's house in heaven and it's real!

Devotion: *Dear Abba, Father, I thank you that you never lie and that you always speak the truth. In Jesus you have told us that you have a home waiting for us in heaven and have reassured us this is real. Thank you so much for giving us such a wonderful hope, in Jesus' name. Amen.*

> *"And if I go and prepare a place for you, I will come back and take you to be with me that you also may be where I am."*
>
> John 14:3-4

If we are to understand these magnificent words we must first know about Jewish wedding customs because Jesus is using language derived from those customs here.

When a boy wanted to propose to a girl in Jesus' day, he first saw her father, agreed a dowry, and then went to see his bride to be. He poured her a glass of wine. If she drank it, that was her way of saying yes. She would then start to prepare herself by having a special, ritual bath.

The bridegroom, meanwhile, would leave some gifts and then return to his father's house. For a period usually lasting a year or more he would start work building an extension in which he and his bride would one day live. This extension was known as the *chupa*.

When the father decided that the *chupa* was complete, he would give his son permission to return to his bride. The bridegroom's friend would go ahead and blow a *shofar*, a ram's horn. The bride would awaken and gather her bridesmaids together and go out to meet her husband.

The two processions would now become one. Carrying lanterns and singing songs, they would arrive with their friends at the father's house. A great party would begin. Two thrones would be put out and the bridegroom and bride would sit in them, like a king and a queen.

This is the background to what Jesus means when he says to his disciples that there is a "Father's house" in heaven and that he's going on ahead of them to prepare a place for them. Jesus is the bridegroom, the church is the bride. Jesus is telling his friends and followers that he is about to depart from them. He is returning to heaven to his Father's house and there he's going to prepare a place for them so that they can be where he will be. When that happens, the greatest party in history will begin and there will be endless joy and unparalleled celebration.

Devotion: *Dear heavenly Father, I thank you that you are overseeing your Son as he prepares a place for your bride in heaven. I thank you that one day you're going to say, "It's time", and that Jesus is going to come back to us and bring us home. Amen.*

Jesus answered, "I am the way and the truth and the life."

John 14:6

I wonder if you've ever noticed this about Jesus – he isn't worried about offending other people. In fact, he sometimes deliberately says things that are designed to offend the mind so as to reveal the heart.

Today's statement is an example of this. Jesus uses the divine name again. He calls himself the "I am". This is God's name in the Old Testament. Jesus starts by calling himself God!

As if this wasn't bad enough, he then goes on to say he is "the way". He doesn't say he is "a way to God". He says he is "the way". The road to God's heart is found in him alone.

As if this wasn't bad enough, he then goes on to say he is "the truth". He doesn't say he is "a truth about God". He says he is "the truth". The truth about God's name and nature is found in him alone.

As if this wasn't bad enough, he finally adds that he is "the life". He doesn't say he is "a life". He says that in him alone can the life of God be found and experienced.

In a world that values "political correctness", this is offensive! Jesus is unashamedly proclaiming the scandal of his particularity. Jesus will not accept religious pluralism (that all religions lead to God). He will not accept theological relativism (that all religions are relatively true and none absolutely true). He will not accept spiritual consumerism (that all forms of religion and spirituality enhance our lives). Jesus uses the definite article. He says he is *the* way, *the* truth, and *the* life. He is not politically correct; he is prophetically direct.

So often the church is quiet on this issue. Frightened of offending others, we have whispered that Jesus is "a way", "a truth", "a life". But it's time for us to rediscover our confidence in Jesus. It's time for us to rediscover our voice. Yes we can say it with grace, but let's start declaring the truth about Jesus – that he is *the* way, *the* truth, and *the* life.

Devotion: *Abba, Father, please forgive me for those times when I have lost my courage and lost my voice in the process. Encourage me, Abba. Put the courage back in me. And help me to be unashamed about the singularity of Jesus of Nazareth, in his name. Amen.*

"No one comes to the Father except through me."

John 14:6

I was ministering in Israel several months ago, teaching about the Father's love. While I was staying in the Negev desert, I was hosted by a wonderful family whose father was an Israeli-born Jew who had come to know Jesus as his Messiah. His native language is Hebrew not English, and the same is true of his seven children.

During the week I watched with great joy as the smaller children climbed all over the dad. As they did so they uttered one word time and time again. It was the word "Abba".

At the end of the week I went up to the father and asked him a question. I said, "What does the word 'Abba' really mean?" I explained the reason I was asking, that some non-Jewish, Western scholars have argued that "Abba" isn't an intimate word meaning "Daddy" but a formal word meaning "Father". He looked at me as if I was crazy and just kept saying, "Abba is intimate. Abba means Daddy. Not formal, no, not formal. Abba is intimate. Abba means Daddy."

When Jesus taught his disciples about God, he told them God is *Abba*. In Jesus' day as in ours, *Abba* does not mean "Father" in a remote and formal sense. It means "Daddy" in a close and intimate sense. Yes there is a note of respect in the word. But the loudest note of all is the note of relationship. When you think of the word *Abba*, think of "intimacy".

Jesus says in John 14:6 that no one can come to *Abba* except through him. And this is an undeniable truth. In every other religion, God or the gods are remote and your approach to them has to be one of formality and trepidation. In Christianity alone is God portrayed as "Daddy", and only through Jesus can you approach him as such. Only through the Son can we have an intimate child–Father relationship with God.

So let's celebrate the uniqueness of Jesus today. The Son alone reveals Abba, Father. Only through Jesus can we climb upon God's knee and call him "Daddy".

Devotion: *Dear tender, adoring, and playful Daddy, I love you and worship you today because you have shown me who you really are through Jesus. If it wasn't for Jesus I would never have known that you are my Abba. Jesus, I celebrate your uniqueness again today. Amen.*

Philip said, "Lord, show us the Father and that will be enough for us."

John 14:8

Philip's request is an interesting one. His words to Jesus show us that he understands something really important about the revelation of the Father's love. He understands that knowing God as Abba will be sufficient. It will satisfy the hungry heart. It will bring contentment to an anxious, restless, seeking soul. This is why Philip says that the revelation of the Father will "be enough for us".

This is astonishing. Somehow Philip has come to a place of intuiting that the most satisfying reality of all is the reality of Abba's love. If a person can have a direct, personal revelation of the Father, then their hearts will know a peace that the world cannot give. This alone, Philip acknowledges, will bring spiritual satisfaction. This alone will bring serenity to the soul. If a person can stop looking for love in all the wrong places and look to the Father, they will be content.

People today suffer from "love hunger". This love hunger is really a father hunger. It is the intense and heartfelt longing for the unconditional, protective, and affirming love of a father. So many people search for this love through relationships, clothes, money, sex, power, food, drugs, alcohol, and a myriad of other outlets. But it's only in Jesus that we find it. Jesus alone reveals the love of our Abba in heaven.

I wonder if you're enjoying today the inner tranquillity and deep contentment of knowing God as your Abba. You see, Philip got it right. He saw that Jesus was the only one who could reveal God's fatherly heart. So he asked for a revelation of Abba's love because he knew that this is the only thing that leads to satisfaction.

So let me ask you, have you found that satisfaction yet? Have you had a revelation of God as Abba, as Father?

Why not ask Jesus to show you the Father? Ask your heavenly Dad to father you like you've never been fathered before. It is the Father's love that we need.

Devotion: Abba, Father, I thank you for showing me that the revelation of your love brings satisfaction to my life. I need a deeper contentment in my life. So I pray with Philip, "Lord Jesus, show me Abba, Father, that I may be truly and deeply satisfied." Amen.

"Anyone who has seen me has seen the Father."

John 14:9

Philip got so much right when he asked Jesus to show him the Father. He understood that Jesus could reveal God as *Abba* and he also saw that it is the *Abba* revelation alone that brings satisfaction to our restless hearts. In spite of this, there's also something he hasn't understood. He hasn't perceived that this *Abba* revelation has already come. It is not something Philip needs to wait for in the future. He has already been receiving it in the past and he is receiving it right now.

This is why Jesus says, "Anyone who has seen me has seen the Father." In other words, "Philip, you don't need to wait until some future date before discovering the Father. If you've been watching what I've done over the last three years since you started following me you would have seen what *Abba* Father is really like. The Father and I are one. If you take a close look at me, you'll see your God and Father. If you watch me, you'll see your *Abba* in heaven".

What does this actually mean? It means that when Philip saw Jesus turn water into wine, he would have seen that the Father is extravagant.

When Philip saw Jesus speaking words of love to a despised Samaritan woman, he would have seen that the Father is inclusive.

When Philip saw Jesus feeding five thousand hungry people on a mountain, he would have seen that the Father is practical.

When Philip saw Jesus healing a man born blind outside the Temple, he would have seen that the Father is mighty.

When Philip saw Jesus weeping at the tomb of his friend Lazarus, he would have seen that the Father is compassionate.

To see Jesus is to see *Abba*, Father. If you and I want to receive a revelation of the Father's love, the place to start is Jesus. We need to look at what he did in the Bible and ask the Holy Spirit, "What does this reveal about my Father?"

Devotion: *Dear Abba, Father, I want to get to know you better. Help me to study the stories about Jesus with new eyes. Help me to see more clearly what they reveal about your Fatherly heart. Give me spiritual wisdom and revelation as I read so that I might truly know you. Amen.*

> *"Very truly I tell you, all who have faith in me will do the works I have been doing, and they will do even greater things than these, because I am going to the Father."*

John 14:12

I remember a prophet once giving a powerful word at one of my former churches. He is from America and while he was visiting the UK he went on an underground train in London. He heard the repeated announcements to "mind the gap" as people entered and exited the carriages. The Holy Spirit spoke to him and he gave a word to the UK churches that they were to "mind the gap". He pointed out the gap between what we see in the New Testament and what we see so often today. He highlighted miracles in particular and called us to mind the gap between what the early churches saw and what we see. It was a sobering challenge.

In John 14:12 Jesus makes a startling promise. He tells his disciples that anyone who has faith in him will do what he has been doing. Jesus here speaks about his followers doing the same "works" as him. The word translated "works" is the Greek word *erga* and it's used twenty-seven times in John's Gospel. It often refers to miracles. That is why in John 7:3 the New International Version has Jesus' brothers say, "You ought to leave here and go to Judea, so that your disciples may see the miracles you do." The word that is translated as miracles is *erga*. We cannot therefore escape the fact that we are meant to do even greater miracles than Jesus.

In what sense will these miracles be greater? Will they be more extraordinary? *Could* they be? To answer this we must remember that Jesus adds the words "because I am going to the Father." When Jesus returns to the Father he will no longer be physically in one place doing miracles. He will be present by his Spirit in countless believers all over the world, and they will see miracles if they believe. These signs will not necessarily be greater in quality but they will certainly be greater in quantity because Jesus is now with the Father.

Isn't it time for us to bridge the gap between the New Testament experience and our own and press on for "even greater works"?

Devotion: *Dear Abba, Father, I thank you that it was never your intention to stop performing works at the end of the New Testament era. Help me to have a greater faith in your power to save, heal and deliver. Let me see "even greater works" in my life, in Jesus' name. Amen.*

> **"You may ask me for anything in my name, and I will do it."**
>
> John 14:14

This is at first glance a very perplexing promise. On the one hand it sounds immensely comforting. Jesus seems to be saying that if we pray "in his name" it will guarantee a positive answer. On the other hand, this is not what we always see. Sometimes we receive a "no" or a "later" when we ask. How can we square these two things?

We will only really understand what Jesus is saying here if we correctly interpret what Jesus meant when he said "in my name". Did he simply mean that he will do what we ask provided we add the formula "in Jesus' name"? Or is there a deeper meaning?

In Jesus' day, a person's name was far more than just their actual name. It was really an expression of their character as well. In this context, praying in the name of Jesus doesn't just mean using the name "Jesus" when we pray. It means praying in a way that is consistent with his character. When Jesus says, "You may ask anything in my name and I will do it", he means, "You may ask me anything that is consistent with my character, and I will do it."

The key then is to pray for things that look and sound like what Jesus would pray. Sometimes we don't see Jesus doing what we ask because we ask for the wrong things with the wrong motives. This is the point made in James 4:3: "When you ask, you do not receive, because you ask with wrong motives, that you may spend what you get on your pleasures." When we ask for things that are not consistent with the character of Jesus we mustn't be surprised when we don't receive them!

Jesus here encourages us to "ask" in prayer. The word "ask" means "crave, beg, eagerly desire". If there is something you long for today, and it is consistent with the character and the will of Jesus, then believe that help is on the way. Stand on the promises of the Bible, especially this great promise in John 14:13, and trust that your heavenly Abba already knows your request and that he is answering it.

Devotion: *Dear loving Abba, Father, I ask that you would help me to have a better understanding of your Son's character. Help me to be so in tune with Jesus that I ask for the things that he would ask for. Help me to appreciate what it means to pray "in Jesus' name". Amen.*

"If you love me, you will obey what I command. And I will ask the Father, and he will give you another Counsellor to be with you forever – the Spirit of truth."

John 14:15–17 (NIV)

Until the time of Jesus, the Holy Spirit had been absent in the experience of God's people in Israel. In fact, it was stated by the rabbis that there had been a long drought of the Holy Spirit since the time of the last of the Old Testament prophets (a period of about 400 years).

With the coming of Jesus, the long drought of the Holy Spirit comes to an end. At Jesus' baptism the Holy Spirit descends upon him like a dove. From then on Jesus is the man who is filled in an unlimited way by the Holy Spirit (John 3:34).

Now it's the night before his death and Jesus starts to speak to his disciples about the Holy Spirit. He says that if they love and obey him, he'll ask his Father and his Father will give them another "Counsellor". The word translated "Counsellor" in Greek is *parakletos*. It was used of an advocate or attorney who came alongside a person to defend them in a court of law. Jesus promises that the Spirit will come alongside the disciples to help, counsel, encourage, and defend them.

Furthermore, Jesus promises that this will be "another" Counsellor. Why did he say "another"? The answer is because this is what Jesus himself has been doing. For the last two to three years he has been alongside the disciples helping them. This won't stop when Jesus returns to the Father. Jesus promises, "I'm sending another Counsellor, just like me. He'll be unlike me in that he's invisible. He'll be like me because he'll help you."

Finally, this Counsellor will be with the disciples "forever". In the Old Testament era, the Holy Spirit came upon select individuals for certain tasks. Jesus however promises that the Counsellor-Spirit will be with the disciples forever. When he comes, it will not be for a little while or a one-off task. It will be permanently. When we receive the Holy Spirit, this is forever if we continue to love and obey Jesus!

Devotion: *Dear Abba, Father, I thank you so much for the gift of the Holy Spirit. Thank you that at your Son's bidding you sent your Holy Spirit into my life to help and advise me. Thank you that I have the Spirit within me forever, not just for a day, in Jesus' name. Amen.*

> *"... you know him, for he lives with you and will be in you."*
>
> John 14:17

Jesus is still speaking about the Holy Spirit here. He has promised that when he leaves, the Spirit will come. Jesus tells his disciples that they already know the Holy Spirit. The Holy Spirit is already with them but in the future – once he's gone – the Holy Spirit will be in them.

There are several very important truths about the Holy Spirit here.

First of all, we learn that the Holy Spirit is personal not impersonal. This is more obvious in the Greek than in our English translations. In the original Greek, the word for Spirit is *pneuma*. This is a neuter noun. When Jesus uses it, however, he speaks of the Spirit as masculine. He says of this Spirit, "You know *him*". He adds "*he* lives with you". Now this is very odd. How can a word in the neuter be used with a masculine pronoun? Surely Jesus should have said, "You know *it*, for *it* lives with you."

The reason Jesus uses a masculine pronoun is because he knows that the Holy Spirit is a "he" not an "it". The Holy Spirit is personal. He is the third person of the holy and undivided Trinity. He is not some nebulous, impersonal, mystical force field. He is the personal and powerful presence of God. Let's never forget that the Holy Spirit is a divine person.

Secondly, Jesus talks about a transition from the Holy Spirit being *with* the disciples to the Holy Spirit being *in* them. Up until now, the Holy Spirit has been external to them. He has been *with* them because Jesus has been with them and Jesus is filled with the Holy Spirit without limit. However, a time is shortly coming when all this will change. Once Jesus has returned to the Father, the Holy Spirit will be *in* them not just *with* them. He will be an internal reality in their hearts not just an external presence in their lives.

I want to ask, "Do you know the Holy Spirit? Do you know the Holy Spirit as a person? Do you know the Holy Spirit within your heart?" Jesus died and rose again so that we could know the Holy Spirit in this relational and experiential way. So, do you know the Holy Spirit?

Devotion: *Dear Lord and loving Abba, Father, I thank you so much for the gift of the Holy Spirit. I thank you, Jesus, that you died and rose again so that I might know the Holy Spirit personally and powerfully. Holy Spirit, I welcome you in my heart today. Amen.*

"I will not leave you as orphans; I will come to you."

John 14:18

There are many great promises in the Bible but I doubt whether there is a more powerful or important one than this.

The night before he dies, Jesus tells his disciples that he is not going to leave them as "orphans". The word in the Greek is *orphanos*, which means "someone who doesn't have a father". Many of the disciples had fathers so at first sight this is quite confusing. James and John, for example, had a father called Zebedee. Jesus cannot therefore have been speaking literally. He must have been using "orphan" in a spiritual sense.

How then are the disciples spiritual orphans? The answer to this is simple. The disciples, like the rest of humanity, have not yet entered into a personal relationship with Abba, Father. Since the tragic loss of intimacy and innocence in the Garden of Eden, all human beings have been separated from God the Father because of human sin – all bar one, Jesus of Nazareth. Everyone since Adam has been a spiritual orphan.

Now, however, Jesus has come into the world to reveal the Father. Throughout his ministry he has been showing the world that God is the most wonderful Abba in the universe. Through both his words and his deeds, Jesus has revealed that God is the world's greatest Dad, the Father we've all been waiting for.

As he enjoys a last meal with his disciples, Jesus is aware that his death is imminent. He tells them that he's not going to leave them as orphans. He will die, yes, but he will also rise again, and when he rises again he will return to them. When that happens, they will no longer be spiritually fatherless. They will be sons and daughters of Abba, Father.

Jesus' promise in John 14:18 is accordingly one of the great promises in the Bible. Every one of us can celebrate the fact that Jesus died and rose again and in doing so he opened up the way to the Father so that we who were spiritual orphans might become his adopted children. So let's rejoice! We know God as Abba! There are no orphans of God!

Devotion: *Dear loving, heavenly Abba, I thank you so much that because of Jesus I'm no longer fatherless in a spiritual sense. You are my Abba, Father. Thank you, Jesus, for dying and rising again so that I could become an adopted child of God. I worship you. Amen.*

> *"Anyone who loves me will be loved by my Father, and I too will love them and show myself to them."*
>
> John 14:21

One of the worst things we could ever do is separate the revelation of the Father's love from the person of Jesus. The truth is we cannot ever begin to experience the Father's affection until we have first learned to love and obey his Son, Jesus Christ. The Father whose love we so desperately desire does not live alone. He is also related eternally and inseparably to the Son and to the Holy Spirit. The only way we can ever experience the lavish love of the Father is by believing in and obeying Jesus. When we do that we become the adopted children of God and are filled with the Holy Spirit who causes us to cry from our hearts, "Abba, Father" (John 1:12; Romans 8:15). We must therefore never separate the Father from the Son. He is not worshipped and loved in isolation. He is only known when we believe in his Son and receive the promised gift of the Holy Spirit.

As Jesus continues his teaching of the disciples, he tells them that "Anyone who loves me will be loved by my Father". Here Jesus is emphasizing that the Father's love is not some free-floating spiritual experience. He is reminding his followers that loving Jesus is the pre-condition for receiving the Father's love. Anyone who wants to have the deep satisfaction of encountering Abba's love must first choose to love, obey, and follow Jesus. When that happens, we can receive our own, direct, personal revelation of the Father's love.

In addition, not only will we be loved by the Father. We will also be loved by Jesus. In fact, Jesus promises that he will show himself to us. We will not only experience the Father's love in our hearts. We will also have a supernatural encounter with Jesus.

The path to receiving more of the Father's love is the path of loving and obeying Jesus. Let's resolve to grow in our dedication and obedience to the Son so that we may have the inexpressible joy of experiencing the love of the Father – the love of all loves.

Devotion: *Dear Abba, Father, thank you for reminding me that your love is only accessed and encountered through Jesus. Help me to grow in my love for your Son so that I may in turn experience the joy of revelation in my life – the revelation of the Father and the Son. Amen.*

"Anyone who loves me will obey my teaching. My Father will love them, and we will come to them and make our home with them."

John 14:23

You can't separate love from obedience in the teaching of Jesus. If we are disciples of Jesus, then that means we will demonstrate our love for him by doing what he says. Anyone who claims to be a Christian but who does not obey Jesus' teaching is not demonstrating love. Those who truly love Jesus will obey him.

Many of us, reading this, will immediately think, "But it is so tough obeying Jesus. He asks us to do challenging things. He calls us to live in a way that's completely counter-cultural. It costs us to follow Jesus and to do what he asks. I'm not sure I can show this level of love in a world where people's values are so non-Christian."

If you're thinking that right now, be comforted. Jesus knew that it wasn't easy so he didn't leave us to obey his teachings without his help. This is the point behind all the teaching about the Holy Spirit in John 14. The Father gives us the Holy Spirit to remind us of the things that Jesus taught and to help us to obey them. We are not alone!

Furthermore, not only does the Father give us the power to obey Jesus, he also gives us a great incentive. That is why Jesus says that if we obey Jesus' commands, the Father will love us. What an amazingly simple yet extraordinarily profound statement that is. If we obey Jesus, *Abba* will lavish his affections on us.

What will be the mark of this affection? Jesus says that he and his Father will come and make their home in our hearts. What a promise that is! The word translated "home" is the Greek word *monai*, used in John 14:2 of the rooms in the Father's house. The Father and the Son will come and make a permanent home in our hearts if we are obedient.

This is the incentive: the Father and the Son will come and live in our hearts. In the future we will be in the Father's house in heaven. In the meantime the Father has made his home in our hearts on earth.

Devotion: *Dear Lord and heavenly Father, I thank you that those who obey Jesus are people in whom you have made your home. Thank you that my heart is where the Father, the Son, and the Holy Spirit live. Help me always to make you feel welcome, in Jesus' name. Amen.*

> *"The Counsellor, the Holy Spirit, whom the Father will send in my name, will teach you all things and will remind you of everything I have said to you."*
>
> John 14:26 (NIV)

One of the greatest promises in the Old Testament is found in Ezekiel 36:26–27: "I will give you a new heart and put a new spirit in you; I will remove from you your heart of stone and give you a heart of flesh. And I will put my Spirit in you and move you to follow my decrees and be careful to keep my laws." Here God promises that there will come a time when we won't any longer try to obey his laws through human effort alone. Rather, the Holy Spirit will empower us to understand and obey God's commandments. Obedience will therefore no longer be a matter of external observance but of inner motivation.

In John chapter 14 there is a great deal of teaching on the person of the Holy Spirit. Jesus is the man who is filled with the Holy Spirit in an unlimited way. During his last meal with his disciples he begins to prepare them not only for his going but also for the Spirit's coming. In verse 26 he tells his disciples that the Holy Spirit will do two things: he will teach them everything and also remind them of all the things that Jesus said. Let's just focus on the first of these two things – on the promise that the Holy Spirit will be our "Teacher".

There are many diverse ministries of the Holy Spirit in our lives but one of the most important is his teaching ministry. Just as Jesus taught his disciples how to obey the Father, so the Holy Spirit will teach us. In 1 John 2:27, John says to his church, "As for you, the anointing you received from him remains in you, and you do not need anyone to teach you... his anointing teaches you about all things". When a person is truly filled with the Holy Spirit, they are taught how to obey their heavenly Abba. The Spirit of God is their personal trainer.

Consequently, we can't do without the anointing. As Abba's children, we need the Holy Spirit to teach us all things – especially how to live lives that are wholly obedient to the Father.

Devotion: *Dear Abba, Father, I thank you for pouring out the Holy Spirit on all those who follow your Son. Please instruct and inspire me to understand your commandments and to obey your will. Increase the anointing on my life and train me in your ways, in Jesus' name. Amen.*

"Peace I leave with you; my peace I give you. I do not give to you as the world gives. Do not let your hearts be troubled and do not be afraid."

John 14:27

Jesus knows that the disciples are about to be taken on a traumatic journey. They are about to see him betrayed, arrested, interrogated, tried, tortured, and crucified. They are going to need great inner reserves to navigate the storm that is about to break upon them. So Jesus speaks two blessings over them. He tells them, "My peace I give to you", and "Do not be afraid."

What did Jesus mean by "peace"? The word peace is a translation of the Greek word *eirene* and the Hebrew word *shalom*. The gift of *shalom* is far more than just the absence of trouble or anxiety. It describes the state of living at peace with God, at peace with others, at peace within, and at peace with our environment. It is a state of harmony at every level. And it is something that the world can never give us.

Jesus can give us this gift because he is about to die a death that will restore *shalom*. As a result of the Cross, believers will be able to enjoy peace with God, peace with other believers, peace within, and peace with their surroundings. The death and resurrection of Jesus are going to mark a brand new beginning. It will be like the tranquil breeze of the Garden of Eden, where of course we originally lost our peace.

In addition, Jesus says, "do not be afraid". Someone once told me that there are 366 occasions in the Bible where we hear the words "Fear not", or "Do not be afraid." They pointed out that this is one for every day of the year, and one extra for a leap year. Clearly, our loving heavenly Father doesn't want us to live in fear. Jesus tells his disciples not to be afraid and he says the same thing to us today.

Maybe you're facing a major challenge and you feel anxious and afraid. Rest in the Father's arms of love and come to him with child-like trust. Ask him for the presence of peace and the absence of fear. Pray for an extra measure of the Father's *shalom* in your life.

Devotion: *Thank you, Abba, Father, that you give me a peace that the world could never provide. Thank you that your perfect love removes my fears. I pray for a greater measure of your* shalom *and a greater freedom from fear in my heart, in Jesus' name. Amen.*

"... the Father is greater than I."

John 14:28

This is an odd statement. In what sense can the Father be greater than Jesus when Jesus says that he and the Father are one? How can Jesus be both one with the Father and the Father be greater than him?

There are at least two ways that we can interpret this.

The first involves us seeing Jesus in his humanity as in some way or other inferior to the Father. We need to remember what it says in Philippians 2:5–11, that Jesus emptied himself when he became a human being. For example, one of the divine attributes he emptied himself of was his omnipresence. While Jesus was present in a human body he couldn't be present everywhere. He was localized in one place. Therefore, while Jesus was a human being, the Father was greater than him.

The second way is more complicated. It involves us seeing Jesus as subordinate to the Father in terms of his obedience but not in terms of his nature. In other words, Jesus is inferior to the Father in the sense that he can never command the Father to do anything; he can only do the Father's will. But he is not subordinate to his Father in being or in nature because he and the Father are one (John 10:30). He is co-equal and co-eternal with the Father.

When Jesus says "the Father is greater than I" he could mean one or both of these things. He could mean either that the Father is greater because he is not restricted by a human body, as Jesus is (for "God is Spirit", John 4:24). Or it could mean that the Father is greater because the Father can command Jesus to do things, but Jesus cannot command the Father to do anything. Or it can mean both!

For us the implications are really quite simple even if the interpretations are stretching. If Abba, Father was greater than Jesus, who is the Son by nature, then he is certainly greater than us, who are the children of God by adoption. Our Father is greater than us. Let's never forget that.

Devotion: *Dear loving Abba, Father, help me always to celebrate your greatness. You are greater than all things. Even your Son declared that you are greater than he is. We confess that you are far greater than us. We confess that there is no one greater than you, Abba. Amen.*

"... the prince of this world is coming."

John 14:30

Judas has left the building. He is on his way to the religious leaders in Jerusalem to tell them where Jesus can be found. Soon he will have his thirty pieces of silver and the Sanhedrin will have Jesus. With only a few hours to go before his arrest, Jesus warns his disciples that the prince of this world is coming. What does he mean?

In John 10:10 Jesus taught that "The thief comes only to steal and kill and destroy". The word translated as thief is the word *kleptes*, from which we get the word "kleptomaniac". In this context, Jesus is referring to the devil. The devil seeks to steal, kill, and destroy. Jesus on the other hand has come that we might have superabundant life.

In John 12 we see Judas complaining about the expense of the perfume that Mary is pouring on the feet of her Rabbi. He tells everyone that this ointment could have been sold and the money given to the poor. John tells us that Judas didn't really care about the poor. He was a *kleptes*, a thief, who was robbing the common purse (12:6).

John is quite clear here in his Gospel. The devil is a thief and so is Judas. The devil has in fact entered into Judas according to John 13:27. So when Jesus announces that "The prince of this world is coming", he means that Judas and the arresting party are on their way. Darkness is about to envelop them.

Some Christians, when they hear about the devil or about spiritual darkness, can allow themselves to become nervous and even afraid. But we have nothing to fear. The devil may be "the prince of this world" but Jesus has already said in John 12:31, "now the prince of this world will be driven out". At Calvary, Jesus has triumphed!

Remember today that Jesus is Lord and that he who lives within you is greater than he who is in the world. When the devil tries to intimidate and rob you, just remind yourself that Jesus has triumphed!

Devotion: *Dear Abba, Father, I thank you that Jesus is indeed Lord of all. On the Cross he humiliated and disarmed all the evil powers of the universe and today he is seated far above every principality and power in the cosmos. I proclaim, "Jesus is Victor! Jesus is Lord!" Amen.*

"He has no hold over me...".

John 14:30

This is one of the great sayings of Jesus, yet in my thirty-five years as a Christian I have never once heard a sermon on it or – I am sorry to say – given a sermon on it.

What is Jesus really saying here? He has just been talking about the prince of this world. He has told his disciples that the devil is on the way. But then he adds, "He [the devil] has no hold on me".

If you look at the original Greek of this text, it simply says, "On me he has nothing". I love that! Jesus tells his disciples, "The devil's on the way, but don't worry, he's got nothing on me!"

That is one of the greatest statements that Jesus makes in the Gospels. It is a stunning insight into both his healed heart and his pure soul. Jesus says in effect, "I'm not hiding anything. There's no bitterness in my life. There's no secret sin. There are no unresolved hurts, habits and hang-ups. I'm free from all that stuff. Therefore there's nothing that the devil can hook into to get me down and thwart my purpose."

Oh that we could find ourselves in a place where we too could say, "The devil may be prowling around me like a roaring lion, but there's nothing in my life that he can get his claws into. He's got nothing on me."

Most of us are not in this place, if we're honest. There are things in our past that remain unresolved – hurts that have never been healed and sins that have never been confessed. Or there are wounds and failings that we have confronted but which we have not yet relinquished. Maybe we can't let go of the guilt or the shame. Maybe we can't quite believe that we've been healed and totally forgiven.

I believe that Abba, Father wants us to get to such a place of reality and transparency that we can say, "The devil's got nothing on me". So don't let him get his hooks into your past. If you find that the devil keeps troubling you about your history, you just remind him of his destiny!

Devotion: *Abba, Father, I thank you that Jesus could say, "The devil's got nothing on me." I open my heart to you. If there are unhealed wounds please set me free. If there's unconfessed sin please forgive me. I want to be able to say, "The devil's got nothing on me", in Jesus' name. Amen.*

"I am the true vine...".

John 15:1

Jesus has now left the room where he has been sharing a final meal with his disciples. We know this because at the very end of John 14 he says, "Come now; let us leave" (verse 31). As he walks with his friends to the garden where he will be arrested, he continues to teach them. Maybe it's as he passes through one of the vineyards on the edge of the city of Jerusalem that Jesus says, "I am the true vine."

This is the last of the seven occasions in John's Gospel that Jesus uses the phrase "I am". In John 6 he said, "I am the bread of life." In John 8 he said, "I am the light of the world." In John 10 he said, "I am the gate" and "I am the good shepherd." In John 11 he said, "I am the resurrection and the life" and in John 14, "I am the way, the truth and the life." Finally Jesus says in John 15, "I am the true vine".

What did he mean? If we are to understand this saying we must first grasp what the word "vine" denotes. In the Old Testament, the vine was often used as a picture for the people of Israel. The vine was Israel and the branches were the Jewish people. Sometimes Israel, having rebelled against God's love, is compared to a vine that has grown wild. So in Jeremiah 2:21, God says, "I had planted you like a choice vine of sound and reliable stock. How then did you turn against me into a corrupt, wild vine?"

When Jesus says, "I am the vine," he is effectively saying, "I am the fulfilment of Israel's calling. What Israel failed to do, I will succeed in doing." This is why Jesus says, "I am the *true* vine". The word translated "true" can mean "real", "genuine," and "authentic". When Jesus calls himself "the true vine", he is indicating that that he's the true expression of what Israel was called to be.

What this means for us is this: we are called to be as close and connected to Jesus as the branches are to the vine. Jesus is the real vine. We are to be intimately attached to him and to the Father.

Devotion: *Dear Abba, Father, I pray that you will help me to be both a faithful and a fruitful child of yours. Help me to live my whole life in intimate communion with you, and may my growing intimacy lead to growing productivity, in Jesus' name. Amen.*

"... and my Father is the gardener."

John 15:1

My adoptive father was not a keen gardener. In fact, I can never remember seeing him in the garden digging and planting, pruning and watering. The most he ever did was occasionally cut the lawn and trim the edges of the flower beds. Regrettably, I have followed his example. While my wife Alie is a genius in the garden, sowing and growing all sorts of trees, flowers, and vegetables, I have no "green fingers" at all. The magnificent garden that we have at our home is not the work of the father of the house but the mother.

Our heavenly Father is altogether different. He is the greatest gardener in the universe. When Jesus tells us that he is the real vine, he adds "and my Father is the gardener". Jesus is effectively saying this: "My Abba, my dear Dad, is the one who plants, waters, tends, and prunes the vine." How different from my adoptive dad. How different from me. Our Abba in the heavens is the keenest and most creative gardener of all. In his loving hands the vine is magnificently cultivated. In his tender care, the vine is delicately pruned. Abba, Father truly is the gardener.

I don't know how you see God the Father. Maybe you just see him smiling over us and affirming us. This is undoubtedly one aspect of what he does. He delights in us and indeed rejoices over us with singing. But this is not all there is to be said about Abba, Father. He not only embraces us; he also shapes us. If all we ever talk about is the Father's delight we will give a one-sided picture of his nature. As his children, we are called to experience his discipline as well as his delight.

This is why Jesus says, "And my Abba is the gardener." Yes our Father has taken great delight in us, just as a gardener or a farmer takes great delight in his vineyards. But he also disciplines us. He refines us. He strips off our lives those things that hinder our growth and sap our energies. He does this not in order to punish us but to bless us. In this respect, our Father's discipline is one of the most enduring and endearing expressions of his love. We need to learn to welcome it.

Devotion: *Dear loving, heavenly Father, I thank you that you are the perfect gardener and that I am safe in your loving hands. You know what's best for me. Help me to say yes to your seasons of refining. Nurture and shape me, I pray, in Jesus' name. Amen.*

"He cuts off every branch in me that bears no fruit, while every branch that does bear fruit he prunes so that it will be even more fruitful."

John 15:2

There are times when the teaching of Jesus seems really tough. This is one of them. As Jesus continues speaking about life in the true vine, he warns that there are two lifestyles that we can choose. One involves obediently remaining in intimate communion with Jesus and living a fruitful life. The other involves choosing not to remain in relationship with him and living a fruitless life.

In this picture, there are two possible destinies and these are summed up by two words. The first is *airiei* and means "to cut back". The second is *kathairiei* and means "to cut off". These sound similar but they describe vastly different outcomes. The one who chooses to remain in Jesus and live a fruitful life will be "cut back". The one who chooses not to remain in Jesus and live a fruitless life will be "cut off".

What kind of person is "cut off"? The obvious example to think of at this point is Judas Iscariot. Judas had become one of the Twelve and had been given the task of looking after the common purse for the whole group. Then the love of money took hold of him. He started embezzling the funds and after a while his whole life was given over to Satan. He deserted Jesus and was "cut off" by his own choice.

When we think of someone being "cut off", Judas Iscariot is the most obvious example. He shows that you have to go to considerable lengths to be cut off. This is not just about having a bad day as a Christian. We all have those! This is about a consistent choice to rely on something or someone else other than Jesus. To be "cut off" involves far more than momentary failures. It involves consistent rebellion.

If the first outcome is to be "cut off", the second is to be "cut back". What does this mean? It means allowing the Father to remove those things that inhibit our fruitfulness. As sons and daughters, we need to allow our Abba, Father to do this. Those whom he sanctifies, he beautifies.

Devotion: *Dear Abba, Father, I thank you that your call is not just to intimacy but to purity. Help me to say "yes" to those seasons in which you lovingly refine me. Thank you that this is a mark of your great love for me and not a punishment, in Jesus' name. Amen.*

> **"Remain in me, and I will remain in you."**
>
> John 15:4 (NIV)

Throughout John's Gospel we have seen some fall away from Jesus. At the end of John chapter 6 we witnessed the defection of many disciples. They left Jesus because they found his teaching too hard. In John chapter 8 Jesus reserved some of his harshest condemnations for those who had started out on the road of discipleship but then stopped believing in him. Clearly Jesus is not impressed with those who start following him but don't continue to do so. Remaining in fellowship with him is a vital and a very serious value.

As Jesus continues his teaching about the true vine, he tells his disciples that they are like branches and that they are to stay connected to the vine. The word he uses for "remaining" can also be translated as "staying" or "abiding". When a person makes the decision to become a Christian, they choose to enter into a friendship with Jesus. This friendship is not just for a few weeks or a few months. It is for the rest of their lives. Furthermore, this friendship isn't just to be enjoyed from time to time. It is to be enjoyed all of the time and for the rest of time.

It has been said that the world is full of good starters but not so full of good finishers. Jesus wants us not only to start with him. He wants us to continue with him. He wants us to end our lives with him, with his name on our lips as we breathe our last breath. If we do, he promises to remain in us. If we remain "in Christ" then Christ will remain "in us". He, along with his Father, will continue to make his home in our hearts.

All this shows that we are not supposed to sit back and be passive, expecting spiritual growth through some kind of osmosis. We are meant to partner with Jesus. We are supposed to work together with him in the development of our relationship. Let's never forget: we must take responsibility for our own soul care and cultivate a lifelong relationship with the Son and the Father, through the Spirit.

So let's stay in touch.

Devotion: *Dear heavenly Abba, Father, I commit and covenant this day to remain in constant contact with you through your Son, Jesus Christ. I promise to stay connected to you and to abide in your love. Help me to remain faithful to you all my life, in Jesus' name. Amen.*

"... apart from me you can do nothing."

John 15:5–6

One of the greatest obstacles to authentic Christianity is self-reliance and self-sufficiency. When a person believes that they can live without God, or believes that they can live the Christian life without total reliance on God, they are committing the sin of pride. Pride says, "I can live independently from God." Humility says, "I depend on God for everything and in everything."

In his teaching on the true vine, Jesus says that his disciples are like branches. These branches need to remain part of the vine and draw on the sap and the energy of the vine. In other words, those who claim to be followers of Jesus Christ need to live in intimate and consistent communion with Jesus and in an ongoing and humble reliance on the power of the Holy Spirit.

It is a penetrating question for all of us to ask whether our lives are lived in dependence on the Holy Spirit. The truth is this: most of us too easily default to relying on our own resources, especially if we allow our spiritual lives to become routine, predictable and dull. If we are always living in the comfort zone of the familiar and the feasible we will naturally revert to self-reliance.

However, if we are prepared to take risks, then we will find ourselves living more and more in that place of true dependence in which we learn that it is "Not by human might, nor by human strength, but by my Spirit" (Zechariah 4:6, my paraphrase). We will learn to draw on the sap of the Holy Spirit as we step out in faith. As we come to the end of our own resources, we will learn to come to the beginning of God's.

Jesus told his disciples, "apart from me you can do nothing". We will never do anything significant, lasting or productive in the kingdom of God if it is done in our own strength. But if we learn to trust in the power and the leading of the Holy Spirit, we will not only show ourselves to be true daughters and sons. We will also see even greater things.

Devotion: *Thank you, Father, that I can do nothing productive for you if it's done in my flesh. Help me to depend more and more on your resources. Prevent me from ever thinking that I can do things on my own. Make me more God-dependent, in Jesus' name. Amen.*

> *"This is to my Father's glory, that you bear much fruit, showing yourselves to be my disciples."*

John 15:8

It worries me when people talk a lot about simply resting and soaking in the Father's love. Sometimes I get the impression that they think this is all we are supposed to do. The message seems to be this: "Never mind the world outside that needs saving, let's all just stay indoors listening to worship songs and lying in the presence of the Lord."

Now I don't want in any way to undermine the supreme importance of resting in the Father's presence. I do believe we should make time on a regular basis to dial down and soak in his love. This is essential for our well-being as the adopted children of God. We must never forget the supreme value of simply being in his affectionate presence.

Yet all of this should lead somewhere. *Being* should lead to *doing*. Soaking should lead to service. Receiving should lead to giving. If all we're doing is simply "abiding", then we have missed the whole point of Jesus' teaching about the vine and its branches. We have missed the point that abiding must lead to fruit-bearing.

There is accordingly a rhythm of life that each of us needs to learn and each of us will find our own unique way of following it. This rhythm consists of deepening intimacy followed by increased productivity. As Jesus reminds us, we are called to be fruitful. Indeed, Jesus says that it brings Abba great glory when we bear much fruit.

What does fruit-bearing involve? Many Bible teachers assume that it refers to character – particularly to cultivating the fruit of the Spirit in our lives (Galatians 5:22). It means that but it also means reproducing in others the life that the Father has poured into us. It means walking in the Father's love and giving it away, inside and outside of his house.

Jesus tells us that we will prove to be his disciples if we bear fruit in our service. So let's always remember: the deeper the intimacy, the greater the productivity. We are called to be fruitful!

Devotion: Dear Abba, Father, Daddy God, I pray that you will help me to develop a balance of life that is uniquely tailored to who I am. Help me to devote time to abiding and resting in you. But out of this, help me to bring your love, joy and peace to a hurting world, in Jesus' name. Amen.

"I have told you this so that my joy may be in you and that your joy may be complete."

John 15:11

This is a great saying, but to appreciate it fully we must set it in context. Jesus has just said this: "As the Father has loved me, so have I loved you. Now remain in my love. If you keep my commands, you will remain in my love, just as I have kept my Father's commands and remain in his love" (verses 9–10). If we remain in his love then we will receive his joy. If we receive his joy, then our joy will be complete.

The word translated "joy" can also be translated "gladness", "cheerfulness" and "great delight". I wonder if you realize that the Christian life is supposed to be a life of "joy" and of "great delight". I wonder if you realize that the Christian life is not a life of misery and slavery but a life of cheerfulness and freedom. Let's never forget: we were rescued by Jesus in order to be glad not sad!

I remember when I was writing my first book on the Father's love – *From Orphans to Heirs* – I found a great quotation from the nineteenth-century preacher Charles Spurgeon. He said that it was extremely important for Christians to live as the joyful children of a loving Dad. Such "happy saints" are irresistible to lost people. Miserable saints are emphatically not. No one, Spurgeon said, is attracted to a life of slavery.

John 15:11 is the first of seven references to "joy" in John chapters 15–17. The disciples of Jesus are to be joyful, even in trying circumstances. This is one of the great hallmarks of the adopted sons and daughters of God. We live as people who have been set free not as those who are still slaves. We live with the radiant smiles of much loved children not the sad faces of lonely orphans. Our joy is our strength!

One of the greatest incentives for continuing to love and obey Jesus is so that we might have his joy in our hearts and so that our joy might be "complete". Complete means "full to the brim and overflowing". Let's grow in our obedience to Jesus and position ourselves to be surprised by joy!

Devotion: *Dear Abba, Father, I thank you so much that you are the great joy-bringer. You want my life to be so full of your joy that it is overflowing from me to others. Help me to grow in my obedience to Jesus so that I may abound in your gladness, in his name. Amen.*

> **"My command is this: Love each other as I have loved you."**
>
> John 15:12

One of the best pictures for the church is the picture of a family. In this family, God is our loving heavenly Father and Jesus is our perfect older brother. We are the adopted sons and daughters of this affectionate Father, and the younger brothers and sisters of Jesus.

In a family like this, we are called to give each other that same love that we received from our Father and our Brother. We are not called to live like orphans, selfishly and suspiciously. We are called to live like the honoured children of a royal family, generously and trustingly.

In today's reading we hear Jesus reminding his disciples once again of the new love commandment that he gave in John 13:34. He tells them that they are to love each other just as he has loved them. They are to become a family in which love is the defining hallmark.

If we are to love each other in a way befitting the adopted sons and daughters of God then we must look to the one who was the Son by nature, Jesus Christ. Jesus tells us, "Love each other *as I have loved you*." The question then is, "How did the Son love the disciples?"

The answer is he loved them by serving them. Jesus showed his love by selflessly washing his disciples' feet.

There are at least two types of Christian. One type takes hold of a napkin, tucks it into their neck, and says, "Serve me." This kind may be present in God's house but they are living like an orphan. Their whole body language says, "Serve me, feed me, and love me."

Then there are those who take hold of the napkin, drape it over their arm like a waiter, and who say, "How may I serve?" This kind of Christian has learned to put the old orphan nature to death and has chosen to emulate Jesus. Their body language says, "Are you being served?"

It's time for us to behave like sons and daughters not as orphans. It's time to put more emphasis on loving than being loved.

Devotion: *Dear Father, help me to renounce and relinquish all the traits of an orphan and to behave like your royal, adopted child. Give me a greater love for my brothers and sisters in Christ and empower me to show that love through joyful service, in Jesus' name. Amen.*

"Greater love has no one than this: to lay down one's life for one's friends."

John 15:13

My adoptive father went through a great ordeal during World War Two. He was fighting behind enemy lines in the jungle in the Far East and was part of a special force that had to keep on the move. They were told that if any of them were wounded they would be left behind to fend for themselves.

During one particularly bloody action, my father was shot by enemy fire. A bullet went through his chest just missing his heart and came out of his shoulder. The column moved on and he was left behind. The only reason he survived was because a brave and unselfish Gurkha rifleman named Moto volunteered to stay with him and look after him.

Moto dressed Dad's wound every day and foraged in the local villages for food and water to keep him alive. One day, however, Moto did not return. Worried that something bad had happened to him, my father somehow got to his feet and started to limp towards the nearest village. When he arrived, he walked into a clearing. There was a tree directly in front of him and under it were two enemy soldiers resting in the shade, their rifles with bayonets fixed. My father couldn't run away so he shouted out, "Moto, Moto, they've caught me. Get out of here."

But Moto couldn't hear. Later my father learned that enemy soldiers had captured and tortured him. They knew there was a British officer somewhere in the jungle. When Moto wouldn't divulge my father's whereabouts, they shot him dead.

My father was later to say that he felt completely unworthy of Moto's sacrifice and that he would be grateful to his dying day, which he was.

There really is no greater love than this – that someone should lay down their life for their friends. Jesus showed this kind of love at Calvary, more than anyone else in history. We are to show this kind of selfless love towards one another and others. It's time for us to demonstrate the "greater love".

Devotion: *Dear Lord and loving Father, I thank you so much for the "greater love" shown by your Son, Jesus. He has truly shown the world what true love is. Help me to live like your Son. Enable me to put others first and myself last, in Jesus' name. Amen.*

> *"I no longer call you servants, because servants do not know their master's business. Instead, I have called you friends, for everything that I learned from my Father I have made known to you."*

John 15:15

One of the noblest ambitions that a person can have is to be a friend of Jesus. Here Jesus contrasts two states, that of the slave (*doulos* in Greek) with that of the friend (*philos*).

Jesus tells his disciples that he is no longer going to call them slaves or servants but friends. This change in relationship is due to the fact that Jesus is about to die and rise from the dead. When that happens, they will no longer relate to God as Master but as their *Abba*, as their Papa or Dad. They will no longer have the position of a slave but the position of a son. As the hour of Jesus' return to the Father draws near, Jesus says that everything is now changing. They are not to relate to God as slaves any longer but as the friends of Jesus.

What does a friend of Jesus look like? Jesus explains in the second half of this verse. He says, "I have called you friends, for everything that I learned from the Father I have made known to you." "Learned" is a misleading translation because it sounds like Jesus was ignorant. But this is not what Jesus says. Jesus actually says, "everything that I have *heard* from the Father I have made known to you". In other words, "I have received a continuous flow of revelation from Abba's heart and I have passed what I've heard on to you."

Accordingly, a friend of Jesus is someone who has the privilege of knowing God as Abba, Father. This can only happen through Jesus. If we are friends of Jesus we are friends of the Son. If we are friends of the Son, we are friends of the one who has unique access to the Father's heart. We are friends of the one who can introduce us to his Father and who can bring us in to the Father's house. It's as if the Father looks at us and says, "Anyone who's a friend of my Son is a friend of mine."

So which are you? Are you a servant or a friend?

Devotion: *Abba, Father, thank you so much that you are not a master who demands religious servitude. Thank you that I'm a friend of your Son and can relate to you as a child not a slave. Help me to cultivate my friendship with Jesus, now and every day, in his name. Amen.*

"You did not choose me, but I chose you and appointed you to go and bear fruit – fruit that will last."

John 15:16 (NIV)

In today's reading Jesus tells his disciples that they didn't choose him. He chose them. More than that, he didn't choose them simply so that they could go to heaven when they die. He chose them to fulfil God's purposes here on the earth while they lived. In fact, Jesus says that he "appointed" his disciples. The word can mean "ordain" (as in 1 Timothy 2:7) or to "purpose" (as in Acts 19:21). Jesus set his followers apart for a unique assignment, so that they could bear fruit, and fruit that lasts.

I wonder if you realize that you are chosen. When I was adopted in 1961, I didn't choose my father. He chose me. He came looking for me and my twin sister Claire and found us in an orphanage in East London. I was only seven months old at the time. I can therefore safely say that I didn't choose him. He chose me. The same is true in the spiritual realm. When I became a Christian in 1977, I didn't choose God. He chose me. In Jesus, my heavenly Abba came looking for me and brought me out of my spiritual orphanage and into the family of his church. On that day I became "twice adopted"!

I wonder whether you realize what an honour and a privilege it is to have been chosen by the High King of Heaven.

Secondly, I wonder if you realize that you are ordained. That is what Jesus says here in John 15:16. He says that you and I were appointed for a unique assignment. We were purposed, set apart, ordained to complete the Father's task for our lives. We weren't appointed just to sit at the Father's table and feast on his goodness. We were appointed to leave an abiding footprint on this planet.

One of the greatest longings in the human heart is to leave a legacy. We are called to make a lasting impact on other people. Our purpose is to walk in the Father's love and give it away to the people we meet every day. So, are you fulfilling your assignment?

Devotion: *Abba, Father, I thank you so much that you chose me. I was an orphan, but you came into my life and set your affections on me. Not only that, but you chose me for a reason: to fulfil your destiny for my life. Help me to fulfil my purpose faithfully, in Jesus' name. Amen.*

"This is my command: Love each other."

John 15:17

You might feel by now that all this is becoming a little repetitive. All this talk about loving one another has started to become somewhat worn. Perhaps you are becoming bored with it.

One of my favourite stories concerns the old man John – the author of John's Gospel. It is said that when he became very old he would be carried to church where he would be expected to give the sermon during Sunday worship. He was the presiding elder and the founding father of the church so everyone waited with baited breath to hear his words. On one occasion he came to the place of worship and preached the following message: "My little children, will you please love one another." The following Sunday he preached exactly the same sermon. In fact this went on Sunday after Sunday for months and months. In the end, one of the other leaders in the church plucked up the courage to ask him why he kept giving the same address. His answer was simple. He said, "When you all start living it, I'll stop preaching it."

If there is one message that we can never tire of hearing it is this: "Love each other." This is not an optional extra for followers of Jesus. In fact, Jesus says, "This is my *command*". This is something Jesus requires of us.

What kind of love does Jesus mean? The verb translated "love" here is *agapao*. It refers to self-sacrificial love. In fact, it is a word that is used frequently in John's writings for the love that Jesus exhibited when he laid down his life at Calvary. It is a self-forgetting love in which the ego is crucified and the needs of others put first.

The church is not a company of insecure orphans who manipulate and bite each other out of fear and greed. It is meant to be a family of secure sons and daughters who serve and bless one another with generosity and joy. Let's renounce the orphan state and live as loving brothers and sisters in Christ. Let's obey the command to love one another and live in the happy unity of the family of God.

Devotion: *Abba, Father, I bring before you those brothers and sisters in Christ whom I find difficult to love. Help me to obey your command to forget myself and to put them first. May your church be a family of children who relentlessly love each other. Amen.*

"If they persecuted me, they will persecute you also."

John 15:20

I remember being invited to go into a school and give a talk at Halloween. I decided to speak about Christians as children of the light. I asked my wife Alie to bake a large cake and we put a lot of candles on it. These were not ordinary candles. They were the kind of party candles that automatically reignite when you blow them out.

I gave my talk to several hundred children, many of whom were members of the church where I was an ordained minister. I spoke about how many times people had tried to extinguish the light but they'd failed. I pointed out that this was because Jesus is the light of the world. His light is more powerful than the darkness and the darkness cannot overcome it.

I finished by encouraging the children in the school to understand that being filled with the light does not mean a less joyful life. As I cut the cake and started sharing it out I told them that the real party begins when we come to the light.

About a week later I was summoned by the head teacher of the school. She sat me down in front of all her teaching staff (at least twelve people, as I recall) and proceeded to tear my talk apart. She told me that the staff had been offended by my implication that Christians had been persecuted. They argued that I was mistaken. They claimed that Christians have not been persecuted in the past and they are not being persecuted now. Somehow it escaped their attention that they were ironically doing to me the very thing that they said didn't ever happen! But they weren't prepared to be rational about this issue. At the end of the meeting I had been banned from speaking in the school.

In our passage today, Jesus says that if worldly people persecuted him, then they would also persecute us. From time to time we experience hate-filled opposition. One of the most important things for enduring these attacks is the experience of the Father's love. This helps us to say, "I may be rejected on earth, but I'm accepted in heaven."

Devotion: *Dear loving Father, I pray for all those who are being persecuted for their faith in Jesus Christ today. Wherever they are in the world, please strengthen them. Shower them with your love so that they may be truly secure in your affections, in Jesus' name. Amen.*

> **"If I had not come and spoken to them, they would not be guilty of sin; but now they have no excuse for their sin."**
>
> John 15:22

Sometimes people ask, "What about those who have never heard the gospel? Will they be condemned by a loving God?"

This is a good question and in many people's hearts it is a deeply personal and poignant one. So what is the answer?

Jesus tells us in this passage in John 15. He says that it is only those who have heard his words and who have rejected them who will be regarded as guilty. If a person hears the gospel but decides in their heart to deny its truth, then they are guilty of the sin of not believing in Jesus. However, if a person has never heard the gospel, they will not be guilty of this sin. They will be judged by a different standard. They will be judged on the basis of their response to God in creation and in their consciences. They will be judged on the basis of what they do know, not on the basis of what they don't know.

The apostle Paul makes a similar point in his speech in Acts 17. He says in verses 29–30, "we should not think that the divine being is like gold or silver or stone – an image made by man's design and skill. In the past God overlooked such ignorance, but now he commands all people everywhere to repent". Abba, Father has overlooked the ignorance of people prior to the coming of Jesus. Now, however, he calls upon all people to repent of sin and believe in Jesus. This call is heard through the preaching of the gospel. When people hear the message, they have no excuse any more.

In our passage for today, Jesus says, "If I had not spoken to them, they would not be guilty of sin." He adds, "now they have no excuse for their sin." The word translated "excuse" is a word that can mean a "cloak". Once a person hears the gospel and rejects it, they have nothing to cover their sin. However, if a person hears and accepts it, they have a robe of righteousness to cover their sin – the robe of Christ's righteousness.

Devotion: *Dear loving, Abba, Father, send the fire of your Spirit upon your people and give us a great passion for reaching out to the lost in mission and for preaching the Good News of your Son. Let there be a great response to the gospel, in Jesus' name. Amen.*

"Those who hate me hate my Father as well."

John 15:23

In a chapter full of love, Jesus also talks about "hatred". In fact, he uses the word "hate" seven times between verses 18 and 25. The verb translated "hate" is *miseo* in Greek, and it can also mean "detest".

It is beyond my understanding why anyone would ever want to hate or detest Jesus of Nazareth. Was there ever a more perfect human being in the entire course of history? Jesus was the most authentic and compassionate man who has ever lived. He touched and cleansed the lepers. He sat with and blessed the Samaritans. He had meals with the marginalized and parties with prostitutes. He welcomed the poor and embraced the outcast. He supplied wine for the thirsty and multiplied bread for the hungry. He spoke comfort to the fearful and gave peace to the anxious. He showed patience with his followers and affection for his friends. He challenged the religious and he chastised rulers. He adored the children and he honoured women. He taught with authority and he prayed with humility. He was arrested and tried; he was bruised and crucified. He paid the great price and gave his life for us all. He was raised from the dead and broke out from his tomb. He ascended into heaven and now sits in glory – as the Son of God and the Son of Man, the prince of peace and the king of love. There has never been, nor will there ever be, anyone as perfect as Jesus. Why would anyone, in their right mind, ever hate such a man?

The answer is because of what Jesus said back in John 3:20, where the word *miseo* is also used: "All those who do evil *hate* the light, and will not come into the light for fear that their deeds will be exposed." People hate Jesus because they are running scared. They are terrified of being found out. They are petrified by Abba, Father's love, for Jesus says, "Those who hate me hate my Father as well." When you come across this irrational and perverse hatred of Jesus, remember that this is born of fear. Do not respond with fear to fear. Respond in love, for it is the Father's perfect love alone that drives out fear.

Devotion: *Dear Lord and heavenly Abba, I am deeply sorry that there are people in this world who hate your Son, and by extension, you as well. I pray today for those whose antagonism is born of fear. Reach out to them in love and draw them to yourself, in Jesus' name. Amen.*

"When the Counsellor comes, whom I will send to you from the Father, the Spirit of truth who goes out from the Father, he will testify about me."

John 15:26 (NIV)

Who sent the Holy Spirit on the day of Pentecost? In today's verse Jesus says of the Counsellor (the Holy Spirit), "I will send him". This thought will be repeated in John 16:7. Yet in John 14:16 and 26 Jesus teaches that it is the Father who sends the Spirit. So who is it? Is it the Father or the Son? Or is it in some mysterious sense both the Father and the Son who send the Spirit to us?

In John 15:26 Jesus tells us that he will send the Holy Spirit "from the Father". He calls the Spirit "the Spirit of truth" (literally, the Spirit of "the" truth). He describes the Spirit "going out from the Father". This verb is in the present continuous tense. It indicates that the Holy Spirit is constantly going out from the Father's presence. The Spirit didn't come just once at Pentecost. He is always coming to us!

During the history of Christianity some have argued that the Holy Spirit proceeds *from* the Father *through* the Son. It is the Father who sends the Spirit but he does so through the agency of his Son. Others have traditionally argued that the Father and the Son send the Spirit together. The Father doesn't send the Spirit to us via the Son. Rather, the Spirit proceeds from the Father and the Son together.

Although this issue has historically divided the Eastern and the Western churches, we don't need to let it divide us today. The Holy Spirit comes from both the Father and the Son. The Son lives forever at the Father's side. There he asks the Father to give the Spirit to his people. As the Son requests, so the Father sends and the Spirit comes to us. The Spirit proceeds from the Father's heart at the Son's bidding.

What a generous and lavish Father we have! We have a Father who is constantly giving of himself. As his Son asks so he gives and he gives extravagantly of himself, of his Spirit. Abba is truly the most self-giving Father in the universe.

Devotion: *Abba, Father, I thank you that the Holy Spirit is continuously flowing from your heart. I thank you that you and your Son are constantly sending the Holy Spirit to your children. Pour out your Spirit on us again, I pray. Welcome, Holy Spirit, in Jesus' name. Amen.*

"All this I have told you so that you will not go astray."

John 16:1 (NIV)

Jesus continues to warn his disciples that they will face intimidation and persecution from the world. If the world has hated him, then the world will hate them too because he lives within them by the Spirit. He then says that he has told them this so that they will not go astray. What did Jesus mean by that?

The word translated "go astray" is the Greek verb *skandalizo*. Some versions translate this as "offended". "I have told you so that you will not be offended." But this isn't really the sense of the verb, which is very hard to translate into English. Its true meaning is neither to "go astray" or "offend". So what is it?

The noun *skandalethron* was used of a special kind of trap with a spring mechanism. When a person unwittingly activated the device, a spring would be released and the victim would be caught by surprise. When Jesus says that he doesn't want his disciples to be "scandalized", he means that he doesn't want them to be caught off guard.

For many of us it is becoming increasingly difficult to be open about our faith in non-Christian workplaces. There are so many pitfalls, especially in those countries where equality and diversity have become political values enshrined by law. Often this means equality for everyone except committed Christians.

In a context like this we need to be careful not to court or encourage opposition through unwise behaviour and we must also be careful not to become complacent and vulnerable to being caught off guard. The enemy wants to entrap us. We need spiritual discernment and heavenly wisdom to ensure that we steer well clear of his snares.

The Christian life is a life of many challenges, not a life of endless comfort and ease. Jesus tells us what to expect and gives us a warning. This warning is not meant to turn us into silent witnesses. It is meant to help us to be prudent in the way we witness.

Devotion: *Dear Abba, Father, I want to be an ambassador of your love and a witness to Jesus in the places that I inhabit on a daily basis. I know that the enemy will hate this. Give me prophetic insight into his schemes so that I can be wise in my witnessing, in Jesus' name. Amen.*

> *"... I tell you the truth: It is for your good that I am going away. Unless I go away, the Counsellor will not come to you; but if I go, I will send him to you."*
>
> John 16:7 (NIV)

Jesus says something here that must have sounded strange to the disciples' ears. He says that it is to their advantage that he is leaving them. It is for their benefit that he is departing. I'm not sure how much the disciples understood this or were comforted by it at the time but later they would have known exactly what Jesus meant.

Why was it to their advantage for Jesus to leave? Jesus answers the question himself. He says, "Unless I go, the Spirit won't come." In other words, if he doesn't return home to the Father, the Holy Spirit will not be available to all disciples across the world. He will only be available to those who are near Jesus physically.

The point Jesus is making is actually a very comforting one. He is indicating that while he is on the earth in his human body, he could only touch the lives of those that he was with physically. When he returns to the Father, however, all this will change. By the Holy Spirit, Jesus will be able to present to anyone, anywhere, anytime. He will not be restricted any longer by his human flesh. He will now be in heaven before the Father. From there the Father and the Son can pour out the Holy Spirit on any believer anywhere on the planet. By the Spirit, the Father and the Son can make their home in the hearts of people in Africa, Israel, Latin America, anywhere.

So it really was to the disciples' advantage for Jesus to leave and return to the Father in heaven. Jesus left so the Spirit could come. There are absolutely no limitations to the work of the Holy Spirit. He can be anywhere and everywhere, showing people that Jesus is Lord and drawing them into a heart-to-heart relationship with Abba, Father. All this is thanks to Jesus, who was prepared to embrace the journey home to his Father – a journey that would begin with his agonizing death upon the Cross in twenty-four hours' time.

Devotion: *Dear Abba, Father, I worship you for the gift of your Son to this fallen world. But I also praise you for the gift of the Holy Spirit. Thank you that Jesus was prepared to leave so that the Spirit could come. Thank you that all this was for my benefit, in his name. Amen.*

"When he comes, he will prove the world to be in the wrong about sin and righteousness and judgment."

John 16:8

We know that the Holy Spirit impacts the lives of believers. But what about those who don't believe in Jesus? Does the Holy Spirit impact unbelievers too?

According to John 16:8, the answer is an emphatic "yes". Jesus is teaching in John 16 about the future coming of the Holy Spirit. He is referring primarily to the outpouring of the Holy Spirit on the day of Pentecost, described in the Book of Acts (chapter 2). He says that when this happens, the Spirit will convict the world. Note what Jesus says: he says "the world"; he doesn't say "the church".

When I became a Christian, I was nowhere near a church or a preacher. I was walking down a street, and I was far away from God. Halfway down the street the Holy Spirit began to work upon my heart. Within moments I became convinced of my sinfulness and my desperate need of salvation. I became convicted of my wrongdoings and certain that the only one who could help me was Jesus.

Jesus says there's coming a day when the Spirit will impact unbelievers. They will become acutely aware of their guilt in three areas: sin, righteousness, and judgment.

Sin refers to the sin of unbelief, specifically the sin of not believing in Jesus. On the day of Pentecost, those who heard Peter preach the gospel became convicted of this sin. That was the work of the Spirit.

Righteousness refers to the righteousness of Jesus. Jesus was crucified as a common criminal. On the day of Pentecost, thousands would recognize that Jesus was "in the right". That was the work of the Spirit.

Judgment refers to God's judgment of the devil. After Pentecost, people would come to see that evil is condemned. This too would be the work of the Spirit. How we need the Holy Spirit to move like this today!

Devotion: *Dear loving, heavenly Father, I pray that you would pour out your Spirit again upon the world. Let there be a great awakening in my lifetime. I ask that you would convince and convict the hearts of millions of unbelievers, in Jesus' name. Amen.*

"... when he, the Spirit of truth, comes, he will guide you into all the truth."

John 16:13

I have had the opportunity of being very involved in the world of biblical scholarship over the last three decades. At one time I was extremely committed to the British New Testament Society. I was invited to the International Society of Biblical Literature. I taught in one of the leading departments of biblical studies in Europe and was asked to give lectures all over the world on John's Gospel.

Why am I telling you this? I'm telling you because during that time I have met and heard many extremely intelligent scholars and have read and studied a great many of their works. And this is what I've discovered. A person who has many degrees and doctorates but who is unconverted has less understanding about the person and purpose of Jesus than an uneducated person who is born again.

How can this be? How can the most brilliant, unsaved minds have less insight than the least educated, converted minds? The answer is perfectly given (as always) by Jesus in John 16:13. Here he tells his disciples that when the Spirit of truth comes, he will guide them into all truth. Translated literally, Jesus says, "When the Spirit of the truth comes, he will guide you into all of the truth."

What is the truth? The truth is primarily the truth about Jesus. When the Spirit of truth comes into the hearts of believers, he reveals the whole truth about Jesus. He teaches us that Jesus was more than a man, more than a teacher, more than a prophet. He inspires us to understand that Jesus is the Father's only Son, the Word made flesh, the Lord of glory, the Son of Man and the King of Kings.

You can have all the academic qualifications in the world but if you don't have the Holy Spirit your understanding of Jesus will only ever be false at best and deceived at worst. I don't want in any way to undermine scholarship but we must have our hearts illuminated by the Spirit of truth if we are to encounter the real Jesus and our true Father.

Devotion: *Dear loving, Abba, Father, I ask today for more of the Spirit of truth in my life. I want to understand the whole truth about who Jesus is and why he came to earth. Please fill me with the Spirit of truth so that I may know you and your Son more deeply. Amen.*

"... he will tell you what is yet to come."

John 16:13

Yesterday we saw how the Father generously gives the Spirit of truth to those who follow Jesus. When we have the Spirit of truth we move from a world of information to the world of revelation. We move from a world that can be accessed by the natural mind to the world that can only be accessed by the spiritual mind.

In today's reading Jesus tells his disciples that this same Spirit of truth will tell them "what is yet to come". When Jesus says that the Spirit will "tell" the disciples these things he uses the word *angello* (from which we get the word "angel"), which can be translated "show", "declare", "announce", "report" and "speak".

This same verb is used four times in John 16. It is used here in John 16:13. It is used again in John 16:14 where Jesus says that the Spirit will take what belongs to him and declare it to the disciples. It is used in verse 15 in the same way and in verse 25 where Jesus says, "I will tell you plainly about the Father."

In verse 13, the content of what the Spirit of truth will show us is identified as "those things that are still to come in the future". In the immediate context this refers to the imminent death, resurrection, and ascension of Jesus. The disciples will have revelation about what these future events really mean for them and for the world.

In the long-term it refers to the future direction of history. The disciples of Jesus will come to see where the world is heading. They will not be those who say, "Look what the world's coming to." They will be those who say, "Look what's coming to the world." They will understand the end time purposes of God and especially that Jesus is coming back!

So this same John, who wrote the Gospel we are studying, will one day be caught up in the Holy Spirit and taken through an open door in heaven and shown the things that are to come as history draws to its conclusion (Revelation 4:1–2). How we need the Spirit of truth!

Devotion: *Dear loving, Abba, Father, I thank you that you are in sovereign control of the world. Even when I'm not sure of what the future holds, I know who holds the future. Please fill me with more revelation about what is to come, through your Word and your Spirit. Amen.*

"He will glorify me...".

John 16:14

One of the most beautiful attributes of the Holy Spirit is the way in which he draws our attention away from himself and directs our gaze instead towards Jesus. Jesus himself identifies this as a hallmark of the work of the Holy Spirit. Here in verse 14 he says that in the future the Holy Spirit will bring glory to him. The Spirit will exalt, magnify, and honour the person of Jesus Christ.

This has in fact been happening since the day of Pentecost. When the Holy Spirit falls upon the earliest church, they can't stop praising and proclaiming the name of Jesus. Their message is that Jesus is alive and that Jesus is Lord. From time to time their enemies try to silence them, but they won't be gagged. The fire of the Holy Spirit is in their hearts so their mouths cannot stop glorifying Jesus.

How we need a church like this today! What we don't need is a lukewarm church that has lost its passion for the person of Jesus. We need men and women on fire. We need people who are unashamed of the name of Jesus and who are unafraid of saying that he is the Son of God and the Saviour of the World. What we don't need are timid kittens. We need roaring lionesses and lions.

Whenever there is a revival, this is one of the signs of a genuine move of God. Ordinary believers are filled with an extraordinary desire to exalt the name of Jesus. In an authentic awakening, the deepest longing of the heart is to make Jesus famous in a town, a city, a nation. People suddenly fall in love with the person of Jesus and give him all the honour.

Before the Welsh revival broke out in 1904, there was a meeting that many said acted as the primary catalyst for the awakening. During the meeting a shy teenage girl suddenly stood up and shouted in Welsh, "I love the Lord Jesus with all of my heart." The whole atmosphere changed when she said this and soon revival fire was falling.

Sounds like the Holy Spirit to me!

Devotion: *Dear Abba, Father, fill me with a new love for your Son and a greater passion for giving him my praise. I ask you to pour out your Spirit upon me afresh that I may be one who truly exalts the name of Jesus. Please make the name of Jesus famous in our day. Amen.*

"All that belongs to the Father is mine."

John 16:15

Another translation of this would be, "Everything the Father has is mine."

What then does Abba, Father have?

He has complete sovereignty.
He has total freedom.
He has unparalleled wisdom.
He has timeless truth.
He has supreme authority.
He has incomparable power.
He has amazing love.
He has endless grace.
He has absolute purity.
He has radiant holiness.
He has unfathomable depths.
He has unlimited resources.
He has extreme goodness.
And he has all the glory.

Jesus is the only man who has ever lived that could say, "Everything the Father has is mine." As Abba, Father's natural Son, Jesus has the pre-eminence over every teacher, philosopher, saint, guru, prophet, king, general, celebrity, and hero. He is one with the Father and he owns everything that the Father owns too. One day, every eye will see him, every tongue confess him, and every knee bow to him.

So never forget that all that belongs to Abba, Father also belongs to Jesus. The first person of the Trinity shares all that he is and all that he has with the second person. What an extrvagantly generous Father and what an incomparably glorious Son.

Devotion: *Abba, Father, I praise you that everything you have belongs to Jesus too. Truly, Jesus Christ is Lord and God. I consecrate my heart afresh to celebrate the supremacy of your Son on my own in the secret place and in public with my church family, in his name. Amen.*

"In a little while you will see me no more, and then after a little while you will see me."

John 16:16

The time for Jesus' death is drawing very near now. I don't know how he must have felt knowing that the most agonizing death was just a matter of hours away. We know from previous readings that he was "troubled" by the prospect of his impending passion. Whatever was going on in his mind, this much we know: he was far more concerned about the feelings of his disciples than those of his own.

So now, as the good shepherd and the perfect pastor, he prepares his friends for the imminent trauma of their bereavement. He knows what's coming. They don't. So he tells them that in a little while they will not see him anymore. The words "a little while" are a translation of the simple word *mikron*, which means "a little". If this is late Thursday evening, then Jesus means, "in the next twenty-four hours".

Jesus tells the disciples that they will see him no more. He is referring to the early hours of Friday morning when he will be arrested by the Roman soldiers in the garden where he and his friends are now heading. When that happens they will be separated from him as he is tortured and tried, flogged and crucified. Only John will see Jesus at Calvary. The rest of them will have scattered and will be in hiding.

Jesus then adds, "and then after a little while you will see me". Here he is referring to his resurrection. On the third day he will rise again and his tomb will be empty. He will appear first to Mary Magdalene and then to all the disciples apart from Thomas. He will come to Thomas a week after his appearance to the others. Having left on Good Friday, he will be back on the first Easter Sunday.

The disciples lost sight of Jesus for three days. We can lose sight of him too. In the business and distractions of our lives, we can so easily stop focusing on him. Let's make sure that in a little while we see him again, because if we see Jesus, we see Abba, Father.

Devotion: *Dear loving, heavenly Father, help me never to lose sight of Jesus. If I lose sight of him, I lose sight of you too, and you are the greatest Dad in the universe. Help me to focus on you. Don't let me go days without seeing your face, in Jesus' name. Amen.*

*A woman giving birth to a child has pain because her time
has come; but when her baby is born she forgets the anguish
because of her joy that a child is born into the world.*

John 16:21

I have watched my wife give birth to all four of our children. I remember all too well the discomfort she went through as her contractions started. I recall the almost unbearable pain she experienced as the time for the birth of each child drew nearer and nearer. The only comfort she had was gas and air through a mask. At one point, seeing the concern etched all over my face, she pushed the mask into my face and said, "Here! You need this more than I do right now!"

I remember the pain but I also remember the joy as each of our children emerged from the womb. We were both so relieved that they had been safely delivered and that they were all alive and well. We were so overcome by the miracle of new birth and new life. And we were so happy that we had a new addition to our family. Those moments of holding each newborn child, whispering words of welcoming love to them, made all the pain worthwhile.

In John 16:21 Jesus uses the picture of childbirth to describe his imminent death. This is slightly odd to our ears because Jesus is not a woman but a man. But to Jewish ears, the picture is not at all strange. In the Old Testament the prophets had often used the picture of childbirth as a metaphor for the deliverance experienced by God's people after a time of suffering and distress (e.g., Micah 4:9–10). Jesus uses language from this back story to give meaning to his own imminent suffering.

Note Jesus says that a woman in labour suffers pain because her "time" has come. The word "time" is the same word that Jesus uses throughout this Gospel to describe the "hour" of his death. Jesus' hour has now come. But he knows there's great joy ahead. The bolts of pain that Jesus will experience at Calvary will be the contractions of a new creation. The joy of this brave new world will cause him to forget all the pain.

Devotion: *Dear loving, heavenly Father, I praise you for the willingness of your Son to embrace suffering in order that I might breathe the fresh air of a new world. Thank you so much for Jesus. Help me always to appreciate the cost of this new creation, in Jesus' name. Amen.*

"... and no one will take away your joy."

John 16:22

The final words of Jesus to his disciples are drawing to a close. Jesus lovingly warns his friends that there is a time of intense grief approaching. When their master is crucified they will be devastated and distraught. But this sorrow will be short-lived because Jesus will return to them after he has been raised from the dead. Then their grief will turn to heartfelt joy. After the sorrow of Good Friday they will experience the incomparable joy of Easter Day.

Jesus tells his disciples that the joy is coming and he adds, "no one will take away your joy". The words "take away" are a translation of the Greek verb *airio*, used twenty-six times in John's Gospel. It's first used in John 1:29 when John the Baptist announces that Jesus is the Lamb of God who *takes away* the sin of the world. It will be used for the last time in John 20:15 when Mary Magdalene says at the garden tomb that she wants to *take* Jesus' body *away*.

What kind of joy is Jesus referring to here? He is talking specifically about the joy of the resurrection. The disciples will see the risen Lord with their own eyes. Having suffered the agony of knowing he had been crucified, they will now experience the ecstasy of seeing him in his resurrected, glorious, spiritual body. They will have the unspeakable joy of knowing that Jesus has defeated death and conquered the grave. They will know that death has lost its sting and the grave its victory.

When Jesus says, "no one will take away your joy", he is saying that this Easter joy will never be stolen from them. The devil, who of course is a thief, will never be able to steal this unshakable Easter joy from them. Those who hate and persecute them in the future will never be able to rob them of their unshakable happiness that death is not the end and that Paradise awaits. The resurrection of Jesus will change everything. They will live in the endless hope of the new creation. And so will we.

Let's thank Abba, Father for the resurrection joy!

Devotion: *Dear loving Abba, Father, I praise you for the gift of resurrection joy. Thank you that this life isn't all there is to human existence. Thank you that I'm going to be raised from the dead and live forever with you. I rejoice today with Easter joy. Amen.*

"In that day you will no longer ask me anything. Very truly I tell you, my Father will give you whatever you ask in my name."

John 16:23

What is prayer? Prayer is essentially a child-like conversation with the most loving Dad in the universe. Prayer is not complicated. It is not a matter of understanding sophisticated concepts and complex techniques. It is simply coming before God, praising him as "Abba, Father", and asking for our needs to be met and the needs of others too. Prayer is communicating with Abba, Father. It is done through Jesus and in the name of Jesus. And it is done in the power of the Holy Spirit.

Jesus tells his disciples that there's a time coming when he will no longer be physically present in their lives and that when that time comes they will no longer ask him for anything. Instead, they will go straight to the Father. As the Son returns to the Father, he is going to open up the way to heaven. He is going to reconcile lost spiritual orphans with the Father they've been looking for all their lives. When that happens, they will go straight to *Abba* with their requests, not to Jesus.

Prayer is accordingly directed to Abba, Father. If we are not talking to *Abba* in prayer, then we are not living in the full blessings of Calvary. Jesus died and rose again so that we might know the Father. Everything he said and did was about the Father. His whole purpose in coming to the earth was to make the Father known. His reason for dying on the Cross was to enable us to live not as insecure orphans but as confident sons and daughters. For Jesus, it was all about the Father.

It's amazing how fatherless so much Christian prayer is today. Maybe it's because we live in a fatherless world and people no longer feel at ease calling God "Father". Maybe it's because people simply aren't taught to pray to *Abba*. Jesus teaches here that we are meant to come to the Father and ask him for what we need in his name. When that happens we will start to live as sons and daughters. As such we will ask for the kind of things that the Son asks for, and our prayers will be granted.

Devotion: *Dear loving Abba, Father, I pray that you will teach me how to pray. Help me to come to you as a child would approach an affectionate dad. Establish me in my sonship that I may pray the kind of prayers that your own Son prays, in his name. Amen.*

> *"Until now you have not asked for anything in my name. Ask and you will receive, and your joy will be complete."*
>
> John 16:24

Jesus continues to teach his disciples about the radical transformation that is coming to their prayer lives. After Jesus has returned to the Father, they will no longer go to Jesus with their requests. He will, after all, have departed. Instead they will go straight to the Father and ask for whatever they need in Jesus' name. Instead of asking Jesus, they will ask the Father. Instead of making their requests to Jesus' face, they will make their requests in Jesus' name.

We said yesterday that Christian prayer is addressing the Father, through Jesus, in the power of the Holy Spirit. If we are truly the adopted sons and daughters of the Father, we will find prayer to be an exhilarating and inspiring delight. No longer will it be us praying on our own, hoping that God exists, slaving away in prayer in the hope that he will hear us and perhaps grant our request. Prayer will be altogether different. It will be a Trinitarian adventure!

Let me explain. Once Jesus has returned to the Father, everything changes. God will no longer be a distant king and Lord. He will be an intimate Father and friend. Through Jesus, a whole new understanding of God will have been activated. A whole new way of relating to God will have been initiated. Prayer will accordingly no longer be the drudgery of a slave approaching a master. With the help of the Spirit it will be the delight of a child approaching the most generous of all fathers.

Jesus makes everything new, including our prayer lives. Now, when we enter the secret place, we are gathered up into the unending flow of praise and prayer in heaven. In Jesus, we come before the perfect Father in the dazzling and radiant throne room of heaven. As the Spirit of adoption works upon our hearts, we cry out, "Abba, Father" to the ruler of the universe and we begin to pray as Jesus prays.

So let the adventure of true prayer begin!

Devotion: *Dear loving Abba, Father, I praise you for the treasures of the secret place of prayer. Thank you that every time I pray I am lifted up into the prayer life of your Son in heaven. Teach me to pray in the Spirit and in the name of your Son, Jesus Christ. Amen.*

"... the Father himself loves you..."

This is one of the most important sayings of Jesus in John's Gospel. In fact, it's one of the most important statements in the entire Bible. What a wealth of comfort there is in Jesus' words, "The Father himself loves you."

Keep in mind that the word Jesus would have used for "Father" is *Abba* and that this is intimate. It is the word used by an Israeli child even to this day. It is an affectionate word for "father".

The word translated "loves" here is the Greek verb *philein*. In his book, *The Four Loves*, C. S. Lewis spoke about the four different words for love in the Greek language in the time of the New Testament.

Storge love is the nurturing love of a parent. It is the love that a nursing mother shows to her child when she breast feeds, strokes and soothes her baby. It is the practical love of a hands-on father.

Agape love is the self-sacrificial love of someone who forgets themselves and puts someone else's interests before their own. It is the love that a person has when they lay down their life for their friend.

Eros love is sexual love. In the Bible, sex is regarded in the highest possible light as a gift from the Father. It is seen as life-uniting act. As such, it is intended for the life-uniting context of marriage.

Phileia love, finally, is the love between friends. It is a love that expresses itself through demonstrated affection. It is a love that delights in kind words, gift-giving, frequent hugs, and endless fun.

When Jesus says, "The Father himself loves you", he uses the Greek verb *philein*, which is friendship love. Jesus tells his disciples that *Abba* loves them dearly, as a person loves their closest friend.

Every day you can declare, "My Abba in heaven loves me with a demonstrated affection because I am a friend of God." What joy!

Devotion: *Dear loving Abba, Father, I praise you for your intimate and affectionate love. I thank you that the words that Jesus spoke to his disciples he says to me too: "Abba loves me dearly." Help me to revel and rejoice in this revelation today, in Jesus' name. Amen.*

> *"I came from the Father and entered the world; now I am leaving the world and going back to the Father."*
>
> John 16:28

This is the clearest statement of the "incredible journey" that Jesus undertook for us. He tells us where he came from and he tells us where he's going. He tells us that he came from the Father in heaven. He tells us that he's now leaving the world and returning to the Father. This journey is the key to everything – so let's spend a few moments looking at the three great truths in this verse.

First of all, Jesus said he came from the Father. There was a moment in heaven when the Father told Jesus that it was now time to leave the realms of glory and enter a world of space and time. The reason Jesus did this was because of love. The Father couldn't stand to see us living as spiritual orphans any longer. So he sent his only Son on a mission to deal with the sin that separated us from his arms.

Secondly, Jesus says that he entered the world. He who was God in nature took on human form and became flesh. He lived in obscurity for thirty years then called his disciples together. He taught about the Father and performed many miracles. Now, in John 16, he is preparing to leave the world. He will do this not by being transported supernaturally to the glory of heaven. He will do it by being lifted up on the Cross.

Thirdly, Jesus says that he is going back to the Father. Heaven is his home. Jesus belongs in glory. Jesus returns to the majesty of his eternal home through his death, resurrection, and ascension. What a homecoming that will be! What unbridled rapture in the hearts of the Father and the Son! In John 16, Jesus looks forward to this moment when he says that he is "going back to the Father".

From time to time we should ponder what all this cost. It must have hurt the Father and the Son as Jesus left the realms of glory. And it must have cost them both so much as Jesus died on the Cross. Let's never forget the price of our adoption.

Devotion: *Dear loving Abba, Father, I praise you for the incredible journey that your Son made for our sakes. Never was such a vast expanse traversed. Never was such a sacrifice embraced. I can't thank you enough today, in Jesus' name. Amen.*

"You believe at last!"

John 16:31 (NIV)

You can hear the relief in Jesus' voice here! The disciples have not always found it easy to understand Jesus. This is because he has spoken to them in word pictures. The term that they use in verse 29 is *paroimia*, which means a parable, proverb, or riddle. Jesus has been using brief sayings that have been difficult to grasp. He has constantly used the *paroimia* in his teaching. Now however, Jesus has started to speak "plainly". The word the disciples use is *parresia*, which can be translated "openly", "clearly", or "freely". They now understand him. He is no longer speaking figuratively; he is speaking plainly.

What was it that prompted the disciples to understand Jesus? It was the statement we studied yesterday. Jesus says in verse 28, "I came from the Father and entered the world; now I am leaving the world and going back to the Father." As soon as Jesus says this, it is as if the penny finally drops. They understand that Jesus came from heaven and is returning to heaven, that he is the Father's only Son, and they exclaim, "Now you are speaking clearly, without figures of speech." They add that they now realize that Jesus knows everything and they believe that he has come from God. With this Jesus says, "You believe at last!"

It is easy to look down on the disciples at this point but we forget that we have had 2,000 years to reflect on the teaching of Jesus. They were hearing it for the first time! Furthermore, the disciples were in a process of training. They were in a school of discipleship in which they were gradually growing in their understanding of Jesus and the reason why he came to this earth.

A disciple is by definition a "learner" and the truth is, there will always be things that seem mysterious to us, which prompt us to study and pray until we see more clearly. With the help of the Holy Spirit, we too can grow from being confused to being clear. So let's push through until we too can say to Abba, Father, "I understand" and he can say to us, "You believe at last!" Let's never stop learning.

Devotion: *Dear loving, heavenly Father, I thank you for your patience with those who follow Jesus. I thank you that we are all learners and that you are keen for us to understand the things we believe. Help me to see things more clearly, in Jesus' name. Amen.*

"You will leave me all alone. Yet I am not alone, for my Father is with me."

John 16:32

Have you ever experienced rejection or abandonment? Have you ever been deserted by family and friends? If you have, then you will know what Jesus is about to experience. Within a few hours, his followers and friends will have fled. As Jesus is arrested by the Roman soldiers, his disciples will be scattered and will disappear into hiding. Jesus will be alone. He will be dragged before the high priest and interrogated. He will be taken before the Roman governor and subjected to a farce of a trial. He will be flogged within an inch of his life by Roman soldiers and he will be forced to carry the cross beam of his own cross to the Place of the Skull. During all of this, not one of his friends will accompany him. He will be all on his own. Even when he is hanging on the Cross, most of the men that he has spent the last three years with will be nowhere to be seen. There will be one man present, the Beloved Disciple, and a few women (including his mother). The rest will be absent. As Jesus prophesies, "You will leave me all alone."

And yet... I love the word "yet" here. "Yet I am not alone, for my Abba is with me." Though Jesus' friends will be absent, his Father will not. As Jesus is interrogated by Annas, his Father will be supporting and reassuring him. As Jesus is examined by Pilate, his Father will be right by his side, telling him what to say. As Jesus is flogged by the soldiers, his Abba – his Dad – will be there too, watching through teary eyes and whispering his encouragement. As Jesus carries his Cross to Calvary, his Father will be walking with him and speaking peace to his heart. As Jesus suffers and dies at Calvary, his Father will even be there too. His Father will never leave him. He will always be by his side.

Good fathers don't leave their children. They stick with them and are not just physically present during their lives. They are emotionally present too. A good father is always there for you, through thick and thin, come hell or high water. Abba, Father is the perfect Father. He was there for his Son. He will be there for his adopted sons and daughters too.

Devotion: *Dear loving Abba, Father, I thank you that you never left your Son but that you accompanied him on his Calvary road. I thank you that you are with us too and that you never leave us. While some dads walk out on their kids, you never do. I praise you, in Jesus' name. Amen.*

"In this world you will have trouble. But take heart! I have overcome the world."

John 16:33

Jesus wraps up his teaching in John 16 by telling his disciples, "In this world you will have trouble." The chapter started with Jesus warning his followers that "They will put you out of the synagogue; in fact, a time is coming when anyone who kills you will think he is offering a service to God." The chapter now ends with Jesus warning his friends that in the world they will have trouble.

What did Jesus mean by "trouble"? The word refers specifically to persecution. For the disciples, this persecution was to come from two main sources. The first would be from their fellow Jews. The earliest church was composed of Jewish followers of Jesus. Jesus predicts a time when his Jewish disciples will be thrown out of their synagogues and even murdered for believing in him.

The second source was the Romans. When Christians started confessing Jesus as "Lord" and "Saviour", this put them in immediate conflict with Rome because these were titles reserved for the emperor. On the emperor's birthday every Roman citizen was required to confess in a public place "Caesar is Lord and God." Many Christians refused to do this and they paid the ultimate price.

Jesus says, "In this world you will have trouble." But then he adds, "But take heart! I have overcome the world." Jesus is now at the hour of his return to the Father. This is the time of his victory over sin and death through his crucifixion and resurrection. The disciples should therefore be encouraged. If they are threatened with death, Jesus has overcome death! This is the hour of victory!

Whenever we face opposition, we should do so with cheerful hearts. Our enemies, though intimidating, have already been defeated. However much they appear to be in control, they are not because Jesus reigns over all. So never forget, you are on the winning side!

Devotion: *Dear loving Abba, Father, I thank you that even though being a Christian means that I may face opposition, Jesus has overcome the world. I praise you that your Son has conquered the worst that my enemies can throw at me. He truly is the conquering king. Amen.*

After Jesus said this, he looked toward heaven and prayed.

John 17:1

Whenever we are faced with stressful circumstances, we are presented with a choice. We can look down and become fearful and depressed. Or we can look upwards at the Father and recognize that he is in control. Orphans allow themselves to descend into worry as they become preoccupied with the things of this earth. Sons and daughters make a decision to rise up above impending troubles and to set their hearts and minds on their Abba in heaven. Orphans despair in the face of hardship. Sons and daughters abound in faith and hope.

As Jesus finishes his teaching in John 16, he now turns to prayer. In fact, John 17 is the most wonderful insight into the prayer life of Jesus. The disciples had seen him many times withdraw to lonely places in order to enjoy uninterrupted alone times with his Abba. Now they get to hear what he actually prays. They get to hear the Son's conversation with the Father and in the process discover how adopted sons and daughters can talk with their Abba in heaven.

We don't know where Jesus prayed this prayer. All we know is the immediate context. Jesus is about to be arrested, tried, flogged, and crucified. In fact, the time of his suffering is just one quiet time away. If ever there was someone who had good reason to be anxious and troubled, it was Jesus. He knew what was just around the corner. He understood the agony that awaited him. But instead of looking down and feeling sullen, he looks up and becomes hopeful.

Maybe you are facing a difficult time ahead. Maybe you've been told you have to have an operation, or an extended period of intensive treatment. Maybe you've been informed that you're going to lose a job, or there is a threat you might. Whatever challenging circumstances may lie ahead, you and I have a choice. We can either react like orphans or we can respond like sons. We can either choose fear or we can choose faith. We can either look down or we can look up. Let's be like Jesus and trust in our perfect and divine Dad.

Devotion: _Dear loving, heavenly Abba, Father, I stand amazed today at the example of your Son. He knew what was coming yet he chose to look up to you. He chose to worship and to pray. When I face stressful situations, help me to respond like Jesus, in his name. Amen._

"Father, the hour has come. Glorify your Son, that your Son may glorify you."

John 17:1

The moment has at last arrived. This is the time that Jesus has been waiting for. This is the climax towards which this Gospel has been building. Jesus says to his Father, "the hour has come". In other words, the hour of his departure from the world has arrived.

And so Jesus prays, "Glorify your Son, that your Son may glorify you." What does this mean?

Jesus is referring to his departure from the world. He knows that this involves his death on the Cross – a terrible death that is now imminent. Jesus asks his Father to glorify him. He asks that through his death, his Abba in heaven would honour him.

When does Jesus anticipate that he will be honoured by his Father? I believe it is at his resurrection. Jesus is asking his Father to honour him by raising him from the dead. He is asking his Abba to glorify him by raising him to new life on the third day.

In what way will the resurrection honour Jesus? It will honour Jesus by confirming to the world that he really was and is the Son of God. The resurrection will prove that Jesus is different from all other human beings – that Jesus is the Father's only and glorious Son.

Jesus therefore asks that he would be glorified through his resurrection. He goes on to add that he wants to glorify the Father. He wants the honour of being raised by the Father so that he can thereafter glorify and give honour to his Father forever.

One day we will have the great joy of receiving this same honour. One day we too will be raised from the dead when Jesus returns. This moment will be a moment of great honour. It will confirm and reveal that we are the sons and daughters of God.

And from that day we will bring glory and praise to Abba forever.

Devotion: Dear loving Abba, Father, I thank you that you are going to do for us what you did for your Son. You are going to give me the great honour of being raised from the dead. Thank you that this will lead me to give you all my praise forever and ever. Amen.

> **"Now this is eternal life: that they may know you, the only true God, and Jesus Christ, whom you have sent."**
>
> John 17:3

In his prayer to the Father in John 17, Jesus gives us the clearest definition of "eternal life" anywhere in John's Gospel, or anywhere in the entire Bible. He tells us that eternal life consists of knowing the Father, who is the only true or "real" God, and Jesus Christ, the one whom the Father sent to this earth.

As always, "knowing" here is not just a kind of "head" knowledge. It doesn't simply mean giving intellectual assent to a set of beliefs about God. "Knowing" is a much more relational word. The use of the word "know" here shows that eternal life cannot be experienced outside of a personal relationship with the Father and the Son.

What then is "eternal life"? It is really important at this point to recognize that eternal life is more to do with quality than quantity. To some people the idea of living forever might be a nightmare, especially if their picture of immortality is a non-Christian one. If we understand eternal life in terms of duration we may overlook its significance.

Eternal life is more about quality than quantity. If you put the emphasis on the word "eternal" you may miss this. But if you put it on the word "life" you won't. Eternal life means the spiritual, abundant, energizing life that comes from the Father. It means living the life of heaven, the life of the age to come. It means the resurrection power of the Spirit.

If we get to know the Father, through Jesus, then Jesus promises that we will start to live this quality of life in the here and now. We won't have to wait until Jesus returns on the last day (when the dead will be raised). We can start living this super-abundant life now. We can start enjoying heaven's life on earth today.

I like the sound of "eternal life", don't you? Let's deepen our intimate knowledge of Abba, Father, and his Son Jesus, so that we can grow in our enjoyment of heaven's abundance.

Devotion: *Dear loving Abba, Father, I want to know you and your Son more intimately than ever before. Would you give me a deeper revelation of your love so that I may experience a greater measure of your life? Help me to know you better, in Jesus' name. Amen.*

"I have brought you glory on earth by finishing the work you gave me to do."

John 17:4

Nothing matters more to Jesus than giving his Father all the glory he deserves. Jesus lived and died to make his Abba famous. He wanted the whole world to know about Abba, Father. He wanted everyone to honour, exalt, and worship his Father in heaven.

Jesus shows us that there is no higher priority, no greater goal, no more healthy obsession, than bringing glory to Abba, Father.

He made his Father famous by agreeing to be given as the supreme gift of love to this world.

He made his Father famous by living a life that was 100 per cent obedient, from his birth to his death, from the womb to the tomb.

He made his Father famous by speaking about the revelation of the Father's love wherever he went.

He made his Father famous by performing signs and miracles that revealed the Father's mighty power.

He made his Father famous through acts of kindness and mercy, which demonstrated the Father's compassion.

He made the Father famous through offering himself up to death upon the Cross, taking away the sin of the world.

He made his Father famous by rising from the dead and being confirmed and vindicated as the Father's Son.

From the very beginning to the end of his life, Jesus made his Abba famous. Everything he did and said was a revelation of the Father's love. His whole life was a signpost to the Father. He lived and died to bring honour to his Dad. He fulfilled his assignment on earth in order to bring glory to his Father in heaven. What an example the Son is!

Devotion: *Dear loving Abba, Father, I pray that you would help me to consecrate myself to your purposes afresh. I want to fulfil your assignment for my life. I want to live and die to make you famous and to bring you all the honour and glory you deserve, in Jesus' name. Amen.*

And now, Father, glorify me in your presence with the glory I had with you before the world began.

John 17:5

Reading or listening to John 17 is one of the greatest privileges imaginable. What revelation is being imparted to us as we overhear the Son's prayer to his divine Dad! It is as if Jesus is leading us into his secret place of prayer and allowing us to have access to his innermost thoughts and feelings. We should really take off our shoes and bow our knees. We are being invited into the unending flow of love between the Son and the Father. We are being ushered into the royal throne room of heaven to catch a glimpse of how Jesus speaks to his heavenly Abba. What a privilege! We are on holy ground indeed.

What do we overhear? The conversation between Jesus and his Abba may have gone something like this: "My time to be lifted up has now arrived. I ask that you would restore to me that same honour that I enjoyed with you before we worked together, with the Holy Spirit, to bring all things into being. Before we created the heavens and the earth, the whole company of heaven brought their praise to you, Father, and also to me. They shouted, sang, danced, and clapped before us, giving us honour and exalting us in the highest praise. I have missed that while I've been on earth. Now that I'm coming home via Golgotha, please restore it to me. Let me receive glory again in your presence."

It's only a snapshot, but in these brief words Jesus gives us a glimpse of what it must have been like in eternity before the world was created. Before the Father fashioned the universe, through his Son, and in the power of the Spirit, the divine Trinity lived together and loved each other in the indescribable glory of heaven. In a world beyond time and space, the Father and the Son were worshipped, together with the Spirit, by all the angels. They were enamoured, adored, honoured, and praised. In his final prayer, Jesus looks forward to experiencing this again.

Let's never forget what the Son left behind in order to come to earth as a human being. He truly does deserve to be glorified in the Father's presence. No one has ever shown such love before.

Devotion: _Dear loving Abba, Father, I thank you for Jesus, your Son. What love and grace he showed in leaving the majesty of your presence and the honour of the angels in order to come to earth and die for us. Thank you for his humility and his mercy. Amen._

"I have revealed you to those whom you gave me out of the world."

John 17:6

The word revealed is the Greek verb *phanero*. It means to "show forth", "declare", "make manifest". It contains the idea of unveiling something that has been concealed.

Here Jesus addresses his Father and says, "I have revealed you". Actually, the NIV leaves out a word here. The original manuscripts say, "I have revealed *your name*."

What is the name that Jesus has revealed? It is the name *Abba*. As we have seen time and time again, Jesus addressed God as *Abba* – as "Daddy", "Dad", "Father", or "Papa". No one had ever dared to be so familiar with God before Jesus. People called God Lord, king, creator, and the holy one. Jesus brings a new word into our vocabulary and a new name into our theology. He taught us to pray, "Our Abba in the heavens, hallowed be your name." No one had done this before Jesus. But then there's no one else like Jesus. All other religious founders and leaders are mere mortals. But Jesus is the immortal Son of the God who is Abba, Father. He alone reveals the Father's name. In Jesus, our God-image has been transformed forever.

Jesus says, "I have revealed your name to those whom you gave me out of the world." Jesus is saying something momentous again here – that he gave the first disciples the most wonderful privilege of all. He allowed them to be the first people in history to witness a great unveiling – the unveiling of the true name and nature of God. There had been glimpses of the Father heart of God in the Old Testament. But they are the honoured ones. With them Jesus makes explicit what was only implicit before. To them Jesus gives the Father revelation.

Sometimes people talk about the "message" of the Father's love. But it isn't really a message; it's a revelation. Jesus came to reveal the name, *Abba*. As followers of Jesus we are the recipients of this revelation too. We get to see the unveiling of God as *Abba*, Father.

Devotion: *Dear loving, heavenly Abba, Father, I thank you for unveiling who you really are in and through your Son, Jesus Christ. If Jesus had not come, I would never have known that you are my divine Dad. Thank you for revealing your true name to me. Amen.*

> *"I pray for them. I am not praying for the world, but for those you have given me, for they are yours."*
>
> John 17:9

What does Jesus mean by "they are yours?" It means this: though the disciples were chosen by Jesus, they belonged to the Father. Though the disciples have been following Jesus for two to three years, they belonged to the Father. Though the disciples call Jesus "Teacher" and "Lord", they belonged to Abba, Father. They were Abba's children.

When you and I make the decision to follow Jesus Christ, from that moment on our lives are not our own. We belong to Abba, Father. We become the adopted sons and daughters of God. Our lives are under his loving authority and in his tender hands. Everything we are and everything we have is on trust from him.

In the Roman world at this time, the rite of adoption involved two stages. Usually a childless couple would choose to adopt the son of a slave (sometimes within their own household). The first stage of the adoption would involve a symbolic sale. Three times the child would be sold by the natural father to the adopting father.

In the second stage of the adoption process, a Roman magistrate would rule that the boy was now officially the son and heir of the adopting father. From that moment on, all the boy's previous debts were cancelled. He would have a new father, a new family, a new freedom, and a new future. He would be a son not a slave.

One of the effects of this adoption was that that the boy would no longer be under his previous father's authority. He would now be under the authority of his new, adoptive father. In a practical and legal sense, he belonged to his new father.

As we look at our own lives, we too have been adopted into the family of God. We no longer belong to the devil, the father of lies. We belong to Abba, the Father of lights. You and I can say today, "I belong to my heavenly Dad. I'm no longer a slave. I'm his child."

Devotion: *Dear loving, heavenly Abba, Father, I thank you that I belong to you. Like the first disciples, I am yours. I praise you for the great privilege of being rescued from a life of slavery and being placed in the family of God. It's great to know I belong, in Jesus' name. Amen.*

> **"Holy Father, protect them by the power of your name – the name you gave me – so that they may be one as we are one."**
>
> John 17:11

When Jesus says something once, you listen. When he says something twice, you really listen. When he says something four times, you listen like you've never listened before!

On four occasions during his prayer in John 17, Jesus prays to his Father that his followers would be "one". Verse 11 is the first of these. In verse 21 he prays for his followers, and all subsequent disciples, that they may be one. In verse 22 he says that he has given his followers the same honour that the Father has given him "that they may be one as we are one". Finally, in verse 23, he prays that his followers will be "completely one". Clearly Jesus values unity.

Here in verse 11 Jesus prays that we may be one even as he and the Father are one. One of the great attributes of God is his "oneness". The belief that God is one goes back at least as far as Deuteronomy 6:4, "Hear O Israel: The Lord our God, the Lord is one." These words, regularly recited by Jewish people to this day, underline the importance of God's oneness. The Bible does not promote polytheism, a belief in many gods. It promotes monotheism, a belief in one God.

What is intriguing about Deuteronomy 6:4 is the combination of the two words "God" and "one". The word "one" is the Hebrew word *echad*. It is the word used for the numeral "1". But just before it is the Hebrew word *Elohim*, translated "God", which is actually a plural word. So the original version of Deuteronomy 6:4 has a plural word (God) followed by a word denoting singularity (one). Maybe even here the Holy Spirit is pointing to the Trinity – three persons, one God.

The great desire of Jesus' heart is that the family of God will be united. In the Trinity there is a glorious celebration of diversity and unity. That is to be true of us, too. Jesus asks his Father to protect his children from the evil one, who seeks to bring division, so that they may be one.

Devotion: *Father, I pray that you would help me to stay in harmony with my brothers and sisters in Christ. We are all different because you have made us unique. But we are also called to be a united family. Please protect me against division, by the power of your name. Amen.*

None has been lost except the one doomed to destruction so that Scripture would be fulfilled.

John 17:12

It is easy to be troubled by this verse. If we are not to become confused and dismayed, we must remember two things about Judas that John has made clear in his Gospel.

First of all, we must remember that Judas's actions in the last moments of his life were no sudden impulse. They were the end result of a great many wrong choices over the course of his two to three years following Jesus. John in his Gospel gives us the fullest portrayal of Judas. He shows how Judas's character deteriorated over time, as he went from stealing from the common purse to being controlled by an addiction to money. As this addiction reached its peak, Judas allowed Satan to take full control of his life. All this was the consequence of his bad choices.

Secondly, we must remember that Jesus kept offering Judas overtures of love right to the very end. At the Last Supper, just before Judas left to betray him, Jesus offered Judas the place of honour at the meal table – a place reserved for a special friend. Jesus may even have leant against Judas's chest just as the Beloved Disciple leant against his. He certainly gave Judas a morsel of bread – a gesture of love and honour within that cultural context. It was as if the Father was saying to Judas, "You know, you don't have to do this. I love you, Judas."

And so we have a paradox. On the one hand we have Judas choosing of his own free will to betray Jesus, even in the face of great displays of affection. On the other hand we have Jesus saying here that Judas was "doomed to destruction so that Scripture would be fulfilled" (the Scripture referred to here is Psalm 41:9, quoted already in John 13:18). This is a mystery indeed. We may not be able to work out how God's plan and Judas's choices go together. But one thing we can learn: it is a profoundly self-destructive thing to go on rebelling against love.

Let's make sure we choose wisely and respond positively to Abba's love.

Devotion: *Abba, Father, I pray that you will help me to be vigilant in the area of my personal choices. Help me to realize that wrong choices can end up being destructive, not just to me but to my relationships. Help me to be obedient and wise, in Jesus' name. Amen.*

"I am coming to you now...".

John 17:13

I do an awful lot of travelling for my work on behalf of the Father's House Trust. Sometimes this involves flying to other countries. At other times it involves driving to destinations within my own country. While I love going to meet new people and discover new places, I have to be honest and say that the best moment of all is when the meetings are all over and I can head home. Homecoming is one of the most precious experiences I have. In fact, getting into my car and pressing the button that says "home" on my satellite navigation system is one of my favourite moments. I know that it will only be a matter of hours before I'm at my front door, just seconds away from my welcoming wife and delighted Labrador! There is truly no feeling like coming home.

As Jesus prays to his Father the night before his death, he knows that the hour of his return has arrived. Within twenty-four hours he will have died at Golgotha, the Place of the Skull and will be buried in a tomb. Within four days he will be resurrected by the glorious power of his eternal Father. About forty days later he will ascend to the heavens and be seated at the right hand side of his Father in glory. He must have experienced extreme joy over his anticipation of going home, even if there was anxiety about what his departure would entail.

Jesus knows that it is the hour of his homecoming. He has spent thirty-three years on the earth. Born in Bethlehem, he grew up in obscurity in a carpenter's shop in Nazareth, being mentored by his adoptive father, Joseph. Then, at the age of thirty, he went to the River Jordan where he was baptized in water and the Holy Spirit. There followed two to three years of preaching and teaching, healing and deliverance, mercy and kindness. Now he has been betrayed by one of his friends and he is about to be arrested and tried, tortured and crucified.

Knowing that his time has come, Jesus presses the "home button" and tells his Father, "I am coming to you now". You can hear the excitement even within these very few words.

Devotion: Dear loving Abba, Father, I thank you that Jesus was so excited about coming home. When my time comes, help me to be like Jesus. May my excitement about the destination override any concerns I may have about the route, in Jesus' name. Amen.

"My prayer is not that you take them out of the world but that you protect them from the evil one."

John 17:15

In heaven we will one day discover that our Father has rescued us many times from serious trouble, harm, and even death. We will be amazed when we see how often an unseen angel has stopped us from crossing a road, or driving into a ditch, or saying something that would have had catastrophic consequences. We will be astonished as we see our lives replayed and we recognize all these moments – from those months in our mother's womb, right up to the very day of our homecoming – when the Father stepped in and kept us from disaster.

Jesus says in John 17:15, "My prayer is not that you take them out of the world but that you protect them from the evil one." Jesus doesn't pray that we will be removed from this world the moment we are reborn. He prays that we would remain on the earth to fulfil the assignment that Abba, Father has in mind for each one of us.

In undertaking this assignment, he knows we will be in a conflict. On the one hand we will be helped by the Holy Spirit and indeed angels – celestial spirits whom the Father has commanded to minister to us as we seek to obey him. On the other hand we will be insidiously opposed by Satan and his demonic, unholy spirits.

As we embark on the epic adventure that is the Christian life, Jesus knows that we are in a war zone. The enemy is a defeated foe but like all defeated foes he is fighting a fierce and final rearguard action. In this battle we need protection. We need air cover and prayer cover. We need someone watching over us at all times.

Isn't it a comfort to know that our lives are covered by the greatest intercessor in history? In heaven, Jesus our Great High Priest prays continuously for Abba, Father to protect us. If we have this kind of support, why should we ever be afraid? If our God is for us, then who can stand against us?

Devotion: *Mighty Father, Lord and king, I thank you that Jesus is constantly praying for my protection in the spiritual battles I face here on earth. Thank you for the deliverances that I'm not aware of. Thank you for the ones I am, in Jesus' name. Amen.*

"Sanctify them by the truth; your word is truth."

John 17:17

As Jesus begins to draw his great prayer to a close, he asks his Father to sanctify his disciples by the truth.

What did Jesus mean by the word "sanctify"?

In relation to believers, the word "sanctify" means to make holy. It refers to the lifelong process by which we become more and more like Jesus and less and less like the world. It refers to the gradual transformation of our character into the likeness of God's Son.

There are two views of sanctification. The first is what I call the passive view. This view sees sanctification as solely the work of the Holy Spirit. As disciples, it is the Holy Spirit who makes us holy. We just need to sit back and let him do the work.

The other view is what I call the active view. This view sees sanctification as primarily the work of the believer. As disciples, it is our job to fight the good fight against sin, the world, and the devil. We must take responsibility and actively set ourselves apart from the world.

The truth is this: sanctification is both our work and the work of the Holy Spirit. We cooperate and partner with the Holy Spirit as we intentionally seek to die to the things of this world and become more like Jesus. Sanctification is both-and not either-or.

How then is a believer "sanctified"? Jesus tells us in this verse. He says that we are sanctified by the truth and he defines the truth as God's Word. As we play our part by reading and studying the Bible, the Holy Spirit plays his part by helping us to be obedient to its teaching.

Abba, Father wants us to read his Word. The Bible is our Father's book. It tells us how he thinks and shows us what he wants. It teaches us what to believe and encourages us how to behave. As his sons and daughters, we cannot disregard the Word. Abba's Word sanctifies us.

Devotion: *Dear loving Abba, Father, I thank you that you are in the process of shaping and moulding me into the likeness of your Son. Help me to play my part by revering and reading your Word. Help me to submit to its truth and apply its teaching, in Jesus' name. Amen.*

"My prayer is not for them alone. I pray also for those who will believe in me through their message, that all of them may be one, Father, just as you are in me and I am in you."

John 17:20–21

The great heart cry of Jesus before his Father is that all those who believe in him would be one. Unity is foremost in his mind as he prays. His longing is that all subsequent believers would live in unity and that this would be a reflection of the harmony within the eternal family of the Godhead. Today Jesus is still praying the same prayer – that we would be one even as he and the Father and the Spirit are one.

It saddens me when I travel to cities and countries and discover that churches are so often made up of people of one particular colour, age, background, or race. I am absolutely convinced that this was never the Father's plan. He sent his Son into the world so that people of every kind of racial, economic, and social profile could live together as a united family. Jesus died that we might be one.

When I read John 17 I am certain that we are not meant to divide into black and white congregations, Jewish (or "messianic") and Gentile churches. Jesus prayed that we would be one and that this would be a sign to the world. He prayed that we wouldn't be segregated but that we would be integrated, and that this would cause every observer to realize the power and efficacy of the gospel.

Happily, there are churches that I visit and speak to that have become an answer to Jesus' prayer in John 17. Recently I was speaking in a church in the UK where there were forty-five different nationalities represented. It was exciting and exhilarating to see such a multicultural, inter-generational mix of believers living as a family and worshipping the Father with such freedom and passion.

Jesus died to break down every dividing wall that separates us. He died to create a level of unity between people that the world could never create. So let's start pursuing authentic, radical unity.

Devotion: *Dear loving Abba, Father, I pray that you would continue to build your church on the earth and that this church would increasingly reflect the diversity and unity within the Trinity. May this unity delight your heart and convict the world, in Jesus' name. Amen.*

"I have given them the glory that you gave me, that they may be one as we are one."

John 17:22

If we're going to plumb the depths of this verse we must first understand what Jesus meant by the word "glory". The word "glory" is the Greek word *doxa*, which can be also be translated "honour". It is used nineteen times in John's Gospel. On at least some occasions it is best translated as "honour". So for example in John 5:41, Jesus says "I receive not honour from men" (KJV).

In John 17:22 "honour" seems to me to fit better than "glory" might. Jesus says to his Father, "I have given them the *honour* that you gave me, that they may be one as we are one".

We know that Jesus received honour at his baptism, when the Father said, "You are my beloved Son and i am fully pleased with you" (Mark 1:1, NLT). Now Jesus says that he has passed that same honour on to those who have chosen to believe in him. They too receive the Father's honour. In fact, every follower of Jesus can rest in the knowledge that Abba, Father loves and honours them. Every child of God can know the Father's sense of value and significance for them as individuals.

Jesus adds that he has given this gift so that they may be one as he and the Father are one. Unity is the by-product of the Father's gift of honour. If we honour one another in the family of God – even as the Father, the Son, and the Spirit honour one another in the eternal family – then we will be united. In a culture of honour it is not easy to fall out with your brother or your sister. If you know you're valued by the Father, then you will want to value your brothers and sisters too. Receiving the gift of honour leads to us giving that honour to others.

We need to learn to live under Abba's honour and create a culture of honour. If the Father treats us as honoured sons and daughters, then we should esteem one another highly. That way we will build a strong defence against the enemy's desire to divide us.

Devotion: *Abba, Father, I thank you that you have given me the same honour that you gave Jesus. You love me as a son, as a daughter, and you cherish me. Help me freely to give away what I have freely received. Help me to honour others as you honour me, in Jesus' name. Amen.*

"May they be brought to complete unity...".

John 17:23 (NIV)

There are different levels of unity within churches. In some there is a very strong sense of unity. People honour one another as brothers and sisters in Christ. They work towards the same goals. They love to socialize with each other and enjoy having feasts and fun. You can always tell when you're in a church like this; people take ages leaving the building after the church meetings have finished. Often they can stay several hours after a service has finished.

Then there are churches where the enemy has robbed them of unity. In these churches there is division. People work against a common vision, either actively or unconsciously. Division is "Di –Vision" – it is at least two visions competing with other. When division comes, there is usually a mistrust of authority and an undermining of others. In these churches, people do socialize but it tends to be with people that have formed into like-minded enclaves.

Jesus doesn't want us to be weak on unity; he wants us to be very strong. One of his many requests to the Father in John 17 is that his followers will be brought to "complete" unity. The word "complete" means "finished", or "fulfilled". When it comes to unity within the church, Jesus prays that we would make unity a primary value and that we would seek to attain a harmony that's real and complete. He's looking for a unity that reflects the unity within the Trinity itself.

In the final analysis, the devil isolates, but Jesus integrates. The devil is constantly at work trying to make us think like orphans and become independent. But Jesus is constantly at work encouraging us to think like sons and daughters and become interdependent.

Our attitude to unity is like a barometer for testing whether we are behaving like orphans or behaving like sons and daughters. So are you isolated or integrated? Do you value independence or interdependence? Do you want partial unity or complete unity?

Devotion: Dear loving Abba, Father, I pray that you will give me a greater longing for unity within the family of God. Heal the orphan tendencies in me and in others so that we can relate to one another as your honoured children, in Jesus' name. Amen.

"Righteous Father...".

John 17:25

What a wealth of significance there is in these two words. First of all, Jesus calls God "Father". This speaks of his intimate affection. Time and again in this book I have shown how this word denotes a very close relationship, such as a child has with a kind and good father.

Secondly, Jesus calls his Father "righteous". This speaks of God's moral perfection. It tells us that our Father is holy. *Abba* never does or says anything wrong. He always excels in moral purity. There are no shadows in him; he is undiluted light.

There are two essential qualities for a good father. The first is affection. Good dads express their love for their children. They do this through hugs, affirmation, time, gifts, play, instruction, and so on. Indeed, there are many love languages which a father can use.

The second essential quality of a good father is authority. A good dad exercises authority. This authority is not abusive or controlling; it is tender and loving. A good father will give correction to their children – a correction which is for their protection.

Abba, Father embodies the very best of both of these qualities. He first of all expresses affection for us. This comes through his Word and his Spirit. It comes to us through encountering Jesus and through experiencing the power of the Spirit of adoption.

Secondly, he expresses his authority over us. Our Daddy is the King of Kings and the King of Kings is our Daddy. He is perfectly holy and always in the right. He is infinitely wise and he knows what is best for us. Consequently, he corrects and disciplines us in love.

We cannot have a picture of God that stresses one of these attributes at the expense of the other. Abba, Father is both righteous and intimate. He exercises authority and he expresses affection. We must always make sure that we see him as our "righteous Father".

Devotion: *Holy and righteous Abba, Father, you are truly perfect in holiness and perfect in compassion. Thank you for being the greatest Dad in the universe. Thank you that I can welcome you when you hug me and trust you when you correct me, in Jesus' name. Amen.*

"I have made you known to them, and will continue to make you known...".

John 17:26

As Jesus concludes this wonderful prayer, he tells his Father two things. First of all, "I have made you known to them". He is referring to his disciples here. Jesus says, "I have made you known as 'Father' to those whom you gave me as my followers."

It is important at this point to pause and remind ourselves once again that the word "know" does not just refer to intellectual knowledge. We tend to understand the idea of "knowing" in a Western, Greek way. In the Greek mindset, knowledge is abstract and conceptual. It really refers to propositional knowledge. However, Jesus was not a Greek with a Greek mindset. He was a Jew with a Hebraic mindset. Jesus didn't approach the idea of knowledge from a Western perspective but from an Eastern one. In the Hebraic mindset, knowing is not so much abstract and conceptual as relational and personal. "Knowing" in the Jewish world of Jesus' day meant knowing something or someone personally – even intimately – not just academically and clinically.

When Jesus says, "I have made you known to them", he is saying that he has made the Father known to his disciples in this intimate sense. Thanks to Jesus, the disciples now have the opportunity of knowing God as Abba in an affectionate, direct, profound way. Not only will they know him as Father in their heads. They will know him as Father in their hearts. God will therefore no longer be remote; he will be relational. He will be the Father they've been waiting for.

The second thing Jesus says is "I will continue to make you known". What a great promise that is! Jesus tells us that the revelation of the Father was not just something that his immediate disciples would enjoy. All disciples, throughout all history, in all places, will have this revelation. Jesus will continue to make God known as *Abba* to those who follow him. He will continually impart the Spirit of adoption to those who choose to believe in him. And that means us too!

Devotion: *Almighty God, I thank you so much that I can know you as my Abba, my "Daddy". Jesus made you known as Father 2,000 years ago and for 2,000 years he has continued to make you known. Help me to know you more dearly as my Dad. Amen.*

"... that the love you have for me may be in them and that I myself may be in them."

John 17:26

Why does Jesus make the Father known to those who follow him? The answer is given in the final words of one of the greatest prayers ever prayed. Jesus says that he makes *Abba* known that the love the Father has for the Son might be in the adopted sons and daughters too. What a thought that is! We are meant to receive the same love in our hearts that Jesus received from the Father.

Do you realize that if Jesus – by the Holy Spirit – has made God known to you as *Abba*, it is so that you might have the same experience of the Father's love that Jesus enjoyed?

Remember: at the River Jordan, the heavens opened, the Spirit descended upon Jesus and the Father said, "This is my beloved Son, my chosen one, the delight of my life." Jesus already knew that he was the Father's Son so this was not an adoption. This was an affirmation of an already existing position. But it was more than that. It was an unprecedented moment in Jesus' human, earthly life. It was a deeply heartfelt experience. The Father spoke these words with intense affection and the Son received them with joy in his heart. In fact this must have been a mighty moment. His heart must have burst with joy. "I'm loved by the greatest *Abba* in the universe. I'm accepted and affirmed by the perfect Dad. I'm adored by a Father who takes great delight in me just simply for who I am."

Jesus says in John 17 that he makes the Father known to us and he makes him known intimately not just intellectually. The reason why he does this is so that we too may stand in the river, under an open heaven, and be lavished by the same divine and fatherly affection that Jesus received. As the adopted sons and daughters of God, we too can know with joy that the Father loves us. We too can know this love as an internal reality within our hearts. We can have Jesus in our hearts, yes. But we can also have the Father's love as well.

Devotion: *Dear loving, heavenly Abba, Father, I thank you so much that you have the same affection for me that you had for Jesus when he was here on the earth. I want to receive more of your love into my heart. Speak to me as you spoke to your Son, in his name. Amen.*

When he had finished praying, Jesus left with his disciples and crossed the Kidron Valley. On the other side there was an olive grove, and he and his disciples went into it.

John 18:1 (NIV)

The prayer in John 17 has now concluded. Jesus gathers his disciples and leads them across the Kidron Valley to an olive garden – the place where he will be arrested by his enemies.

Let's examine this brief journey.

Jesus and his disciples left through one of the city gates and walked down a steep hill into a valley where the Kidron brook flowed. The water in this stream would very likely have had a distinctive colour in the light of the full Passover moon. At this time, thousands of lambs were being slaughtered in the Temple for the Passover festival. Maybe as many as a quarter of a million lambs were killed in the Court of the Priests. What did the priests do with all the blood? Through a deft piece of engineering, they had created a channel that allowed the blood to flow from the altar of sacrifice into the Kidron brook. This means that as Jesus crossed the stream, it would almost certainly have been red with the blood of the lambs.

How would Jesus have reacted to that? Most likely his mind would have gone back to that moment several years before when John the Baptist said of him, "Look, the Lamb of God, who takes away the sin of the world" (John 1:29, NIV). Seeing the blood of the lambs would have reminded him of his own imminent sacrifice – a sacrifice that would make all animal sacrifices redundant.

John 18:1 describes a journey that's brief in length but deep in significance. Let's celebrate the fact that Jesus is the perfect Passover lamb who has been sacrificed once and for all for us. This was Jesus' destiny. He shed his blood so that our sin would be taken away and the barrier between us and Abba, Father removed. Let's thank God for the blood of Jesus today.

Devotion: *Dear loving, heavenly Abba, Father, I thank you so much that Jesus' blood has been shed and that my sin has been removed from me. I can't thank you enough for the blood of your Son. Thank you that I can now know you as Abba, in Jesus' name. Amen.*

Now Judas, who betrayed him, knew the place, because Jesus had often met there with his disciples. So Judas came to the garden, guiding a detachment of soldiers and some officials from the chief priests and the Pharisees. They were carrying torches, lanterns and weapons.

John 18:2–3

After crossing the Kidron brook, Jesus arrives at a garden. Three things can be said about this garden. First of all, since its location was on the Mount of Olives we know that it would have been filled with olive trees. Secondly, we can also surmise that it was the private property of someone known to Jesus. In those days, people couldn't have gardens in Jerusalem because the city was too small for that. Wealthy people therefore had private gardens and allotments on the slopes of the Mount of Olives. Thirdly, this garden was a favourite location used frequently by Jesus and his band of disciples. They must have had permission to use it whenever they needed it. The owner had most likely given them a key and they spent time there whenever they could.

Why does John mention this garden? It is because this is the vital piece of information that Judas has in his possession – the secret meeting place of Jesus and his followers. Judas sells this information to the chief priests who then summon their Temple officers. They secure the assistance of a large company of Roman soldiers from their barracks in the Antonia Fortress – no doubt selling the lie that Jesus was a threat to public order during the tense time of Passover. John tells us that a "detachment" was sent. The word can be translated "maniple" – a company of about 200 Roman troops. These men arrived, carrying torches, lanterns, and weapons, led by Judas. There were 200-plus men who had come to arrest one Galilean preacher with a tiny group of disciples!

I love the idea that Jesus often met with his friends in a secret garden. That thought intrigues me. They must have rested, talked, eaten, laughed, cried, and encouraged one another many times in the shade of the olive trees. Parks and gardens are great places for encountering the presence of God. If you haven't already, try and find somewhere in the great outdoors where you can hang out with Abba and talk with him.

Devotion: *Abba, Father, I thank you that I can find your presence anywhere, any time. I particularly thank you that I can encounter your love outdoors, in the beauty of your creation. Help me to find mountains and groves where I can meet with you. Amen.*

> *Jesus, knowing all that was going to happen to him, went out and asked them, "Who is it you want?"*
>
> John 18:4

When I was in my late twenties, I chose John chapters 18 and 19 as the focus for my PhD dissertation. One of the new insights that the Holy Spirit gave me was into this particular scene involving Jesus, his disciples, the walled garden, and those who came to arrest him in John 18.

In today's verse we see Jesus going out of the entrance of the garden and asking his enemies, "Who are you seeking?" Jesus already knew the answer because he knew all things. But he wanted to hear them identify him because he wanted them to take him and him alone.

When I was studying this for my PhD, I found parallels between this episode and Jesus' teaching on the good shepherd. In John 18, Jesus goes in and out of the garden just as the shepherd and the sheep go in and out of the sheepfold in John 10. Jesus stands at the entrance of the garden just as the shepherd guards the gate to the sheep pen in John 10. Jesus protects his disciples just as the good shepherd protects his sheep in John 10 – even to the point of giving his life for them.

I also found that Judas acts out a part from John 10. In John 10, Jesus says that "thieves" seek to get into the fold to steal the sheep. John describes Judas as a "thief" in John 12:6. Here we see Judas bringing a detachment of soldiers to the garden. He is clearly playing the part of the thief from John 10. He has come to steal, kill, and destroy.

In John 18 we see Jesus practising what he preaches. He has preached earlier in the Gospel that he is the good shepherd who gives his life for his sheep. Now he actually lives this out.

There is so often a gap between our beliefs and our behaviour. Jesus teaches us the importance of living a life in which what we say and what we do line up. So let's make sure we walk the talk, not just talk the talk. Let's raise the bar on our authenticity as Abba's children.

Devotion: *Dear loving, heavenly Abba, Father, help me to be a person of integrity, like your Son. Cause my behaviour and my beliefs to come into closer alignment. Help me to be like Jesus and practise what I preach. Help me to live a truly selfless life, in Jesus' name. Amen.*

"I am he," Jesus said.

John 18:5

This is a truly dramatic moment in the unfolding drama of Jesus' last hours on this earth. The temple officers and the Roman soldiers have come to the olive garden where Jesus and his disciples are resting. There are over 200 of these soldiers with lanterns and torches, swords and spears. Jesus, seeing and hearing their arrival, goes to the entrance of the garden and identifies himself with the words, "I am he." According to verse 6, all the officers and guards fell to the ground when they heard these words.

What was it about Jesus that caused this intimidating company to shrink back as he spoke? Was it the dignity and gravitas of his character? Was it the presence of warrior angels behind him? John doesn't tell us. The only hint we have is in the original Greek text of this incident. There we read that Jesus simply says the two words "I am." This is what floored his enemies. It wasn't Jesus' personality, though that was extraordinary. It wasn't the presence of angels, though we can imagine they were there. It was the simple statement, "I am."

As we have read previously (see John 4:25–26) "I am" is the divine name. It is God's name – the name that the Father divulges to Moses and the name he declares to the nations. In Exodus 3:14, we read, "God said to Moses, "I am who I am. This is what you are to say to the Israelites: 'I am has sent me to you.'" In Isaiah 48:12, God says "Listen to me, O Jacob, Israel, whom I have called: I am he; I am the first and I am the last." "I am" is God's name. When Jesus stands at the entrance of the garden, he says "I am" and with that his enemies are momentarily disarmed.

The words "I am" show that Jesus wasn't just a great human being, he was God incarnate. He was Yahweh in a human body. No emperor, president, prime minister, or monarch has ever had the authority he had then and he has now. So never forget, Jesus is the great I am. No power of hell or troop of men has higher authority than Jesus. One day, every knee will bow before him to the glory of Abba, Father.

Devotion: *Dear loving, heavenly Abba, Father, help me always to proclaim that Jesus has the name above every name. Help me to know that one day everyone who has ever lived will be on their faces on the floor, bowing before his glorious majesty, including me. Amen.*

(And Judas the traitor was standing there with them.)

John 18:5

This is the last time we will hear of Judas in John's Gospel. We know that he had gone to the religious leaders in Jerusalem in order to sell information about where Jesus could be found. He passed this information on for thirty pieces of silver. Now Judas arrives with the arresting party at the olive garden where he used to spend many hours with Jesus and the other disciples. He plays no part in the arrest itself other than to lead the temple guards and the detachment of Roman soldiers to the entrance of the garden. In an aside, John briefly states that Judas the traitor was standing with them.

What a wealth of suggestion there is in just those few words. "Judas was standing with them." When the time of decision came, Judas chose to stand with the enemies of Jesus. He sided with the darkness, not the light. He stood with the world, not with Jesus.

As we have seen in our readings of John 12 and 13, Judas was a man whose weakness was the love of money. In this regard he had what I call an orphan heart. Instead of resting and trusting in Abba, Father's love, he lived in a constant fear of poverty and with a secret addiction to money. However small this may have started, it grew and grew until Judas was completely ensnared by his greed. He put the temporary rush of having more money above the permanent peace of having Abba's love. He became a man whose addiction completely controlled him. Jesus wasn't his master anymore. Money was.

In the end, Judas made his choice. Judas chose to stand with the darkness rather than the light.

The last thing John says about Judas in his Gospel is that he was standing with the enemies of Jesus. What a desperate epitaph. When people come to speak of us in the future, let it be said that we loved the Father as his sons and daughters, not the world as orphans and slaves. Let it be said that we stood with the light, not the darkness.

Devotion: *Dear loving, heavenly Abba, Father, I pray that it would always be very clear where I stand. Especially when it comes to material things, help me to trust you like a child, not grab and hoard like an orphan. Help me always to be a faithful child, in Jesus' name. Amen.*

Jesus commanded Peter, "Put your sword away! Shall I not drink the cup the Father has given me?"

John 18:11

Jesus is now standing outside the olive garden. His disciples are behind him; the soldiers are in front of him. Peter steps forward and whips out a dagger from underneath his robe and attacks one of the high priest's servants, a man called Malchus. This act results in Malchus losing the lobe from his right ear. As soon as Jesus sees this, he reprimands Peter and tells him to put his little sword away. He then asks, "Shall I not drink the cup the Father has given me?"

What was this "cup"? It was the cup of the Father's wrath, the Father's holy anger. This wrath was not anger with his Son; it was anger over our sin. The Father's wrath is his holy indignation over sin, evil, and injustice. This was the cup that Jesus volunteered to drink.

If we are to understand this we must always remember that there are two main aspects to Abba, Father's character. There is his matchless love and extreme kindness, on the one hand. Then there is also his unparalleled holiness and perfect justice, on the other.

When Adam and Eve sinned in the Garden of Eden, God's holiness and justice decreed that they – and indeed all of us – should suffer the death penalty. But God's love and kindness meant that he couldn't stand to see human beings live and die as spiritual orphans.

The only solution was for the Son to volunteer to take our punishment. As Isaiah prophesied, "he was pierced for our transgressions, he was crushed for our iniquities; the punishment that brought us peace was upon him, and by his wounds we are healed. We all, like sheep, have gone astray, each of us has turned to his own way; and the Lord has laid on him the iniquity of us all" (Isaiah 53:5–6).

Peter's way was the way of violence. Jesus' way was the way of suffering. On the Cross, the Father's love and justice meet. Jesus voluntarily drank the cup so that we could be rescued from our orphan state.

Devotion: *Dear loving Abba, Father, thank you that you were not angry with your Son at Calvary, you were angry with our sin. Thank you that mercy triumphed over judgment and that I am now no longer under any judgment or condemnation, in Jesus' name. Amen.*

They bound him and brought him first to Annas, who was the father-in-law of Caiaphas, the high priest that year.

John 18:12–13

Annas was an extremely wealthy, powerful, and infamous individual in Jerusalem during the time of Jesus. From AD 6 to AD 15 he was the high priest during the Roman occupation of Judea – a position he had attained through bribery and corruption.

Much of Annas's wealth came from taxing the Jewish pilgrims who came to the Temple. He gained a great deal of income from selling animals for sacrifice and exchanging currency in the Court of the Gentiles. This area of the Temple turned into a bazaar from which Annas profited.

After Annas's reign ended, four of his sons became high priest, followed by his son-in-law Caiaphas. A Jewish book known as the Talmud makes this telling indictment of them all: "Woe to the house of Annas! Woe to their serpent's hiss! They are high priests; their sons are keepers of the treasury; their sons-in-law are guardians of the Temple; and their servants beat the people with staves."

Annas loved money and power more than God the Father. This is a warning. The idols of money and power have always had the capacity to entice and entrap people. As God's children we are not to bow down to them. We must love our Father, not the things of this world.

In his first letter, John said this: "Do not love the world or anything in the world. If you love the world, love for the Father is not in you. For everything in the world – the cravings of sinful people, the lust of their eyes and their boasting about what they have and do – comes not from the Father but from the world" (1 John 2:15–16).

As Abba's children, we must allow our hearts to be seized by an affection that supersedes all others – the divine love of Abba, Father. The Father's love must always eclipse any love for the world. Abba's love is the only antidote to the Annas syndrome.

Devotion: *Dear loving, heavenly Abba, Father, fill me with the holy fire of your love again today. Let the love of the Father replace the love of the world in my life. I confront and destroy every idol in my life and choose to love you above all other things, in Jesus' name. Amen.*

Simon Peter and another disciple were following Jesus.
Because this disciple was known to the high priest, he went
with Jesus into the high priest's courtyard, but Peter had to wait
outside at the door.

John 18:15–16

Jesus has been led bound into Annas's house. Most of the disciples scatter and return to their own homes. But two of them decide to follow Jesus to the courtyard of the high priest's house. One is Simon Peter. The other is described as "another disciple".

There has been much discussion about the identity of this mysterious disciple. The most likely solution is that this is the disciple known as the "disciple whom Jesus loved", or "the Beloved Disciple", first mentioned in John 13:23 at the Last Supper.

The reason for this is because the Beloved Disciple is sometimes seen together with Simon Peter in John's Gospel. Perhaps the most obvious example is in John 20 where the two men run to the empty tomb on the first Easter Day.

Not only are the two paired together, the Beloved Disciple is sometimes presented in a more favourable light. So, at the Last Supper, he leans close to Jesus and hears what he says. Peter meanwhile has to ask the Beloved Disciple what Jesus is saying.

So it seems likely that the unnamed disciple in John 18:15 is the Beloved Disciple. He can freely enter and exit the courtyard of Annas's home because he is said to be "known" to the high priest himself.

Peter on the other hand cannot. He has to wait outside until the Beloved Disciple returns to persuade the woman at the gate to let him in. Peter only gains access to where Jesus is because of the Beloved Disciple.

John tells us "Simon Peter and another disciple were following Jesus." Are you like Peter or like the Beloved Disciple? Do you depend on others to gain access into the presence of Jesus? Or do you make your own way to Jesus?

Devotion: *Dear heavenly, loving Abba, Father, help me to mature into a person who has their own intimate relationship with you. Thank you for the help of others on the journey. But help me now to enjoy my own access to the heart of your presence, in Jesus' name. Amen.*

> **"You are not one of his disciples, are you?" the girl at the door asked Peter. He replied, "I am not."**
>
> John 18:17 (NIV)

Up to this point, Simon Peter has been courageous. In stark contrast to all the other disciples, Simon Peter has sought to defend Jesus with his little sword in the garden and has followed him into the high priest's courtyard. None of the others tried to help Jesus at his arrest. Nor did any other than the Beloved Disciple follow Jesus this far. Simon Peter was extremely brave and went further than his peers.

But at the very moment when we are tempted to praise him, he falters. A servant girl in the courtyard spots Simon Peter. Maybe she hears his northern, Galilean accent. She asks him, "Aren't you one of his disciples?" And Simon Peter replies, "I am not." The man who showed no fear in the presence of the temple guards and the Roman soldiers now cowers under the interrogation of a servant girl.

Notice what Peter says: "I am not." This is a very striking phrase in the context of John chapter 18. A few verses earlier, when the detachment of soldiers came to the olive garden, they state that they are seeking Jesus of Nazareth. Jesus identifies himself with the words "I am" in the Greek. Now, when the servant girl asks Simon Peter if he is a disciple of Jesus, he replies, "I am not."

Simon Peter is such a mixture. How is it that he can be so strong in the garden and yet so weak in the courtyard? The answer is because Jesus is still with Peter in the garden whereas he is no longer with him in the courtyard. In the garden, Jesus is with Peter and Peter can see him. In the courtyard the opposite is true: Jesus is in Annas's house and Peter can no longer see him.

If we are to be strong in the face of intimidation, we must stay close to Jesus. As soon as we wander from his presence, we become vulnerable. So let's draw close to Jesus. Through him, let's draw near to our Father, whose love drives out all our fears.

Devotion: *Dear loving Abba, Father, I pray that you will help me to be courageous when I am put on the spot and asked intimidating questions about my faith. Help me to be so close to you and so full of your love that I am unashamed and unafraid, in Jesus' name. Amen.*

It was cold, and the servants and officials stood around a fire they had made to keep warm. Peter also was standing with them, warming himself.

John 18:18

This is one of the most poignant moments in the whole of John's Gospel. Simon Peter has just denied that he is a follower of Jesus. Now John reports that Peter stood with the high priest's servants and officials, keeping warm by a charcoal fire.

One of the finest gifts that John has as a storyteller is his ability to say a great deal in a very few words. He does this more by suggestion than intrusion. Here is a great example. John the storyteller suggests a lot about Peter without ever intruding in the story and telling his readers what to think. He lets highly evocative details speak for themselves and in the process creates rich layers of meaning.

Let's look at two examples in this one verse.

First of all, John tells us that Simon Peter was standing with the servants and officials in Annas's courtyard. Who are these servants and officials? They are the people serving the high priest Annas. These men and women accordingly represent the darkness and John says that Peter "stands with" them. He doesn't stand *with* Jesus. He doesn't stand *for* Jesus. He stands with Jesus' enemies. That speaks volumes.

Secondly, John says that Simon Peter was keeping warm by a charcoal fire. This again is very suggestive. People who live in darkness depend upon artificial light and worldly ways of keeping warm. Those who follow Jesus, on the other hand, follow *the* light. They are comforted and strengthened by the warmth of his radiance. Simon Peter accordingly chooses a man-made fire rather than the light of the world.

There are seasons in our Christian lives when we come under pressure and need to choose to stand with Jesus. When we do, we will be warmed and comforted by the fire of Abba's love. Let's resolve to prefer the Father's love to all counterfeit, worldly affections. In his presence our hearts are truly ignited and emboldened.

Devotion: *Dear loving, heavenly Abba, Father, help me always to stand with and to stand for Jesus. He is the light of the world and your love is what truly warms my heart. Give me strength to reject love for the world and choose instead love for my Abba, Father, in Jesus' name. Amen.*

> *Meanwhile, the high priest questioned Jesus about his disciples and his teaching.*
>
> John 18:19

The high priest in question here is Annas. As I stated in an earlier study, he was a most unpleasant man, notorious for his corruption in the Temple and his collusion with the Romans. It is Annas who is now interrogating Jesus, specifically about his disciples and his teaching.

Why is Annas questioning Jesus? It is because Annas wants to hold on to power in Jerusalem. He is concerned that Jesus now poses a threat to his own security. He isn't bothered about Jesus' innocence. He is only concerned to stop this potential threat to his status and stability.

Furthermore, the way Annas conducts these proceedings is at best illegal. Jewish law at the time decreed that no question could be posed to a prisoner that might in any way incriminate him. Yet here we see him questioning Jesus about his disciples and his teaching.

It is this issue that Jesus highlights. In the verse that follows he points out that he has spoken very openly in the public domain and he adds that others can be brought forward to testify about his character and his teaching. He then adds, "Why are you questioning *me*?"

There are accordingly two things wrong with Annas's informal, night-time trial. First of all his motivation is wrong – he only cares about preserving his own status. Secondly his method is wrong – he interrogates Jesus in a way that violates the law.

Now let's keep in mind that Jesus reveals the Father. According to John's Gospel, Jesus and the Father are one. Anyone who's seen or heard Jesus has seen or heard the Father too.

That being the case, this incident should be of great comfort to anyone who has been the victim of a false arrest, an unjust interrogation, or a farce of a trial. It shows that in Jesus, our Father has experienced these things too. He knows how we feel. He truly understands.

Devotion: *Dear loving, heavenly Abba, Father, thank you that you understand what it is like to be on the receiving end of injustice. I pray for victims of injustice in our world that they would know that Abba, Father has walked where they walk, in Jesus' name. Amen.*

"Why question me? Ask those who heard me. Surely they know what I said." When Jesus said this, one of the officials nearby struck him in the face. "Is this the way you answer the high priest?" he demanded.

John 18:21–22

Today I'd like to show you how brilliant John is at storytelling.

John 18:15–27 is a very good example of this. Here John gives us a new storyline in verse 15. Verses 15–18 describe Simon Peter's behaviour outside Annas's house in the courtyard. A servant girl asks Peter if he is one of Jesus' disciples, and Peter replies, "I am not."

A second section then runs from verses 19–24. Now we are inside Annas's house, witnessing the illegal proceedings conducted against Jesus. These verses contain our reading for today, in which Jesus asks his interrogators to question those who have heard his teaching (i.e. his disciples).

A third and final section begins in verse 25 and continues until verse 27. We are once again outside Annas's house in the courtyard. Peter is asked two more times whether he is a disciple of Jesus. Both times he says no. And then John reports, "a rooster began to crow".

Notice the two-stage effect here. Jesus is inside the house responding courageously to his interrogations. Peter is outside responding in a cowardly way to his. Jesus tells his accusers to question his disciples, while Simon Peter fails to respond to the questions posed to him.

Why am I sharing all this? It's because I want to show you that John is a masterful storyteller. I want to show you that John was not just inspired in what he said. He was also inspired in the way he said it. The form of his storytelling is as inspired as the content.

Do you know that your heavenly Father is the greatest storyteller in the universe? When the stories known as the Gospels came to be written, he inspired their authors to tell them beautifully not just truthfully. He has been inspiring storytellers ever since.

I think it's time for the storytellers to arise, don't you?

Devotion: *Dear loving, heavenly Abba, Father, I thank you that you love stories. Teach me how to communicate your truth in creative ways, especially through story. Help me to tell stories of Abba's love in my generation, in Jesus' name. Amen.*

One of the high priest's servants, a relative of the man whose ear Peter had cut off, challenged him, "Didn't I see you with him in the garden?" Again Peter denied it, and at that moment a rooster began to crow.

John 18:26–27

Cast your mind back a few days ago in our readings. In the olive garden, Peter had struck a man called Malchus. Leaping to Jesus' defence at the time of the arrest, he cut off the lobe of Malchus' right ear.

Now Simon Peter is in the courtyard of the high priest's house. Jesus is inside being interrogated. Peter is outside, also being interrogated. He has already denied Jesus twice. Now he is about to do it again.

While Peter is warming himself by the fire in the courtyard, one of the high priest's servants comes up to him. He is a relative of Malchus. Indeed, he was with Malchus when Peter attacked him.

This man looks at Peter and asks, "Didn't I see you with Jesus in the olive garden?" Peter's answer is immediate. He denies being there even though this is Malchus' cousin he's talking to.

At the moment Peter denies Jesus for the third and final time, John reports that a rooster began to crow. Jesus had prophesied that this would occur in John 13:38. Now it happens.

Was this a literal rooster? The answer is probably no. There was a law at the time that roosters could not be kept in the city of Jerusalem. In such a densely populated city, you can imagine why!

It is possible that the rooster wasn't a literal rooster but a trumpet call known as the *gallicinium* – the cock crow. This was sounded by the Romans at the changing of the guard at 3.00 a.m.

If this is correct, then the cock crow would in fact have been the trumpet call from the Roman garrison. When Simon Peter heard it he would have truly experienced a wake-up call – the wake-up call of repentance.

Devotion: *Dear loving, heavenly Abba, Father, help me always to be unashamed about my faith in your Son, Jesus Christ. Pour out your Spirit upon me today and give me boldness to speak about my faith in him and my love for you, in Jesus' name. Amen.*

> *Then the Jewish leaders led Jesus from Caiaphas to the palace*
> *of the Roman governor. By now it was early morning, and to*
> *avoid ceremonial uncleanness they did not enter the palace,*
> *because they wanted to be able to eat the Passover.*
>
> John 18:28

Throughout John's Gospel we have seen that the greatest conflict has always been between Jesus and the Pharisees. This confrontation is between reality and religion. Jesus represents reality – indeed, he is *the* truth, *the* reality, in our midst. The Pharisees meanwhile represent religion. They are extremely negative, often judgmental, highly critical, and blatantly hypocritical.

Nowhere is this hypocrisy perhaps more obvious than in our passage for today. For here we see the religious leaders taking Jesus from Caiaphas's house to the palace of the Roman governor, Pontius Pilate, in Jerusalem. John tells us that it was early morning and that the Jewish leaders did not enter Pilate's residence. The reason given is that they didn't want to become unclean.

Now what's the real issue here? The religious leaders believed that "the houses of the Gentiles are unclean". This was part of their law. Pontius Pilate was one of the *goyim*, the pagans. He was a Latin-speaking Italian, not a Hebrew or Aramaic-speaking Jew. His headquarters were therefore "unclean" because he was a Gentile.

Furthermore, as part of the preparations for Passover, the Jewish leaders would have searched their own homes for leavened bread in order to remove it. This was part of the ceremonial cleansing that precedes Passover even to this day. Pilate's house would have contained leavened bread so they won't enter.

Here we see the hypocrisy exhibited by these religious leaders. On the one hand they are fastidious about being ceremonially clean. On the other hand they don't care at all that they are putting the Son of God to death. They majored on minors and completely lost their moral compass.

Devotion: *Dear loving, heavenly Abba, Father, please help me to embrace reality over religion. I don't want to become judgmental and hypocritical. Help me always to see myself as you see me and to live a life of integrity. Help me to be live a life of authentic sonship, in Jesus' name. Amen.*

So Pilate came out to them and asked, "What charges are you bringing against this man?" "If he were not a criminal," they replied, "we would not have handed him over to you."

John 18:29–30

The trial of Jesus before Pontius Pilate is now in full swing. The Jewish leaders won't go into the governor's house because they are frightened of becoming ceremonially unclean. This means that Pilate has to keep going in and out of his headquarters. He speaks to Jesus inside the house. He then goes to speak to the religious leaders outside the house.

Pilate hasn't yet spoken to Jesus so he goes out to the Jewish leaders and asks what criminal charges they are bringing. The leaders don't answer that question at all. They merely and quite rudely state that they wouldn't have handed Jesus over to Pilate had he not been a criminal (literally, a "wrongdoer").

Why don't the leaders bring an explicit, precise accusation against Jesus? The answer is because the real charge won't wash with Pilate. In fact, it would have had no weight at all in Roman law. Their charge was that Jesus was a blasphemer. They wanted to kill Jesus because he claimed to be equal with the Father.

In John 10:31–33, we read this: "Again the Jews picked up stones to stone him, but Jesus said to them, 'I have shown you many great miracles from the Father. For which of these do you stone me?' 'We are not stoning you for any of these,' replied the Jews, 'but for blasphemy, because you, a mere man, claim to be God.'"

The Jewish leaders just don't get it. The very charge they wanted to bring – but which they couldn't – was that Jesus claimed to be Abba's Son. But the very thing they wanted to bring as a charge against him was the very thing that could be stated in his defence!

Jesus truly is the Father's only Son. Let's never be ashamed of stating that to anyone. And let's celebrate that we are sons and daughters of the same Father by adoption.

Devotion: *Dear loving, heavenly Abba, Father, I honour Jesus of Nazareth as Abba's one and only Son by nature. I honour Jesus for being equal and one with you, Father. I celebrate the uniqueness of Jesus and I thank you for my adoption as your child, in Jesus' name. Amen.*

Pilate said, "Take him yourselves and judge him by your own law." "But we have no right to execute anyone," they objected. This took place to fulfil what Jesus had said about the kind of death he was going to die.

John 18:31–32

The religious leaders in Jerusalem have brought Jesus from Caiaphas to Pilate. They won't tell Pilate the real charge they want to make against Jesus because they know Pilate will regard it as a purely religious matter, which they can settle themselves. So they state that Jesus is merely a wrongdoer, hoping that Pilate will condemn him for that.

But the very thing they are trying to avoid now occurs. Pilate bats the whole issue back to them, saying "Go and judge him by your own law." At this point the religious leaders reveal their true hand. They remind Pilate that they don't possess what the Romans called the *ius gladii*, the right to the sword (i.e. the authority to execute).

The interesting thing here is that technically they could have executed Jesus. In Leviticus 24:16 we read that the whole congregation of Israel is to stone a blasphemer to death. Deuteronomy 17:7 says the witnesses of this blasphemy are to be the first people to raise their hands and cast their stones, with the whole congregation then following.

The Jewish leaders could have therefore stoned Jesus, but they won't. What is holding them back? John says that it's because Jesus' words about the kind of death he was going to die had to be fulfilled. Jesus had prophesied that he would be "lifted up". For this to happen, his enemies would have to get Pilate to condemn and then crucify him.

So the authorities in Jerusalem think they are in control, whereas in reality the Father is. As Peter later declares, "Herod and Pontius Pilate met together with the Gentiles and the people of Israel in this city to conspire against your holy servant Jesus, whom you anointed. They did what your power and will had decided beforehand should happen" (Acts 4:27–28).

Let's remember, when life seems most out of control, our God still reigns!

Devotion: *Dear loving, heavenly Abba, Father, I thank you that you are the sovereign Lord and king of the universe and that no authority on this earth has power or authority over you. You are truly in control of everything, and I worship you, in Jesus' name. Amen.*

Jesus said, "My kingdom is not of this world. If it were, my servants would fight to prevent my arrest by the Jewish leaders. But now my kingdom is from another place."

John 18:36

There are two kingdoms in conflict at this moment in the trial: there is God's kingdom and there is the Roman empire. In the Roman empire, Caesar was given the titles "Son of God", "Lord" and "Saviour of the World" by his subjects. His ambition was to bring the whole world under Roman rule through the might of his army. When that happened, *pax Romana* – Roman peace – would be established.

The kingdom Jesus represents is wholly different. Jesus is the true Son of God, Lord and Saviour of the World. God has given him these titles, not the world. Furthermore, Jesus wants his people to bring the peace that comes from the gospel to every creature on this fallen planet, not through the power of violent force and military might but through the power of the Father's love and kindness.

Jesus tells Pilate here that his kingdom is not a kingdom like the one Pilate serves. If it were, then the 200 soldiers Pilate sent to the olive garden would not have been met by unarmed disciples (with the notable exception of Peter, of course) but by an army of rebels with shields and swords. These rebels would have fought off the arresting party and there would have been many casualties.

But this is precisely what they didn't do. And the reason for that is because the kingdom of Jesus is "from another place". It is from heaven and heaven is the atmosphere of the Father's love. Jesus' kingdom therefore advances through non-violence not violence. It proceeds through love not power. It is extends the peace of the Father rather than the peace of Rome.

As Napoleon Bonaparte once said, "Alexander, Caesar, Charlemagne, and I have founded empires. But on what did we rest the creation of our genius? Upon force. Jesus Christ founded His empire upon love; and at this hour millions of men would die for Him."

Devotion: *Dear loving, heavenly Abba, Father, help me always to prefer the power of love to the love of power. When it comes to extending your kingdom on the earth, may my methods reflect your methods, not the world's, in the name of Jesus, the prince of peace. Amen.*

> *"... the reason I was born and came into the world is to testify to the truth. Everyone on the side of truth listens to me." "What is truth?" retorted Pilate.*

John 18:37–38

In our passage today, Jesus is standing before Pontius Pilate. He tells Pilate that the reason why he was born, the reason he came into the world, was to testify to the truth. He adds that all those who are on the side of truth listen to him.

What was the truth that Jesus came to reveal? It was the truth about the Father's love. It was the truth summed up in John 3:16 where we read that "God so loved the world that he gave his one and only Son that believing in him we should not perish but have eternal life."

Jesus came to declare that God is the most loving Abba, Father. He came to tell us that he himself is the one and only Son of God. He came to reveal that we are all desperately in need of salvation. He came to tell us that eternal life comes simply through believing in him.

Jesus came to tell the Father's truth. Everything he said was true. Everything he did was true. In fact, in Jesus, truth became a human being, which is why Jesus can say, "I am the way and the truth and the life" (John 14:6). Jesus is the living testimony of true truth.

What is Pilate's response to this? It is to make one of the most tragic statements in the Gospels. He looks at Jesus and asks, "What is truth?" This betrays such a sad lack of understanding, for Pilate is of course looking at the truth.

There are many people in our world today who are asking, "What is truth?" There are many who don't believe in objective or absolute truth any more. For those who are born again, Jesus is the truth in person.

So don't be melancholy and despairing like Pilate. Be like Jesus. Understand that one of the reasons why you are on the earth is to testify to the truth, even if some doubt whether truth exists at all.

Devotion: *Dear loving, heavenly Abba, Father, I thank you that in Jesus truth has become a person. I thank you that Jesus is the true truth about who you are. Thank you for showing me the truth about your Father heart, in Jesus' name. Amen.*

> *"But it is your custom for me to release to you one prisoner at the time of the Passover. Do you want me to release 'the king of the Jews'?" They shouted back, "No, not him! Give us Barabbas!" Now Barabbas had taken part in an uprising.*
>
> John 18:39–40

Pontius Pilate knows that Jesus is an innocent man. Desperate to extricate himself from the injustice that is about to follow, he appeals to a Passover amnesty. This amnesty allowed for one prisoner to be released by the Roman authorities during the Passover festival.

Pilate now brings two prisoners before the crowds and asks them to choose which one will be freed. On one side is Jesus, whom Pilate calls "the king of the Jews". On the other is a man called Barabbas, who had been involved in a revolt against the Romans.

When the crowd looks at these two prisoners, their response is loud and uniform. They point at Jesus and exclaim, "No, not him!" Then they turn to Barabbas and shout, "Give us Barabbas!" Pilate is now forced into condemning an innocent man and releasing a terrorist.

I don't know if you've ever thought about this but it is fascinating to ask what the name "Barabbas" actually means. In the Hebrew language "Bar" means "son". "Abbas" means "father" (as in *Abba*). Barabbas's name literally means "son of the father".

As Pilate sits on his judgment seat, he points to two men. One is the true Father's Son, who is innocent of all charges. The other is a man called "son of the father", and is guilty of his charges.

Furthermore, the true Son of the Father came to release us from the tyranny of sin by dying for us. Barabbas on the other hand rose up to release his nation by killing the Romans.

The crowds choose a man whose name means "son of Abba" when they could have chosen Abba's only Son. In the process, they released a dangerous criminal and condemned their true liberator.

Devotion: *Dear loving Abba, Father, I thank you that Jesus alone is your Son by nature. He is truly and uniquely Abba's Son. Thank you that he came to liberate us not through killing but through dying. Help me always to choose Jesus as the first in my heart, in his name. Amen.*

Then Pilate took Jesus and had him flogged.

John 19:1

Pilate now resorts to drastic measures. Caught in a situation that is quickly spiralling out of his control, he has an innocent man flogged. He has tried to push this case back to the Jewish leaders, arguing that it is not a criminal matter. That didn't work. So he then tries appealing to the Passover amnesty. That didn't work either; in fact, Pilate succeeded only in liberating a bandit who was a real threat to the peace. Now Pilate has Jesus flogged, hoping that this will prove enough to satisfy the Jewish leaders. As we will see in the next few days, this doesn't work either. At every turn, Pilate shows poor judgment and a lack of strong leadership. In trying to keep the religious leaders happy he ends up torturing an innocent man within an inch of his life.

And that's what would have happened. Pilate would have had Jesus taken from his residence to a public courtyard of the Antonia Fortress. There Jesus would have been stripped of all his clothes and tied to a post. Soldiers who were trained for precisely this kind of torture would have taken hold of short handled whips with tiny leather balls and animal's teeth at the end of them. At least two soldiers would have administered the punishment, lacerating their victim's back, buttocks, and legs. It would have been indescribably and unimaginably painful.

It's hard to even begin to imagine the agony that Jesus experienced as he was beaten within an inch of his life. Great shock waves must have reverberated through his body and soul. In fact, they must have reverberated throughout the father heart of God as well. How else could it have been? The Father forever adores his Son and now has to watch the pride of his life suffer indescribable torment. It must have been a terrible ordeal for Jesus. But it must have also been a terrible ordeal for Abba, Father too. No loving dad ever wants to see his child suffer. Our Heavenly Father didn't want his Son to suffer either. But for our sakes the Son offered up his life and the Father tearfully received it. This truly is love, vaster than any ocean.

Devotion: Dear loving Abba, Father, today I stand amazed at the depths of your suffering love. You gave up your only Son for me. Jesus, you gave up your life for me. Thank you for the lengths to which you were prepared to go so that spiritual orphans could become your children. Amen.

> **When Jesus came out wearing the crown of thorns and the**
> **purple robe, Pilate said to them, "Here is the man!"**
>
> John 19:5

Jesus has been brutally beaten and cruelly mocked by the Roman soldiers on duty in the Antonia Fortress. His back is covered in blood and bruises. The flesh is peeling off his skin and he is numb with shock. There are small rivulets of blood pouring down his face from where the thorns from a makeshift crown have punctured the skin on his clotted head. He is almost unrecognizable.

Jesus stands before Pilate with a robe given by the soldiers to mock his kingship. They had shouted repeatedly at him, "Hail, king of the Jews", and punched him in the face. Now Jesus wears a crown of thorns and a purple robe. He is brought before the crowd that has been whipped into an irrational frenzy by their religious leaders. Pilate says to them in his native tongue, *Ecce homo*, "Behold the man."

What a statement that is! "Here is *the* man". Not any man, but "the" man. It is emphatic in the Greek text. Pilate uses the definite article. He calls Jesus *ho anthropos*, literally "*the* human being". What Pilate meant by this is not hard to guess. He meant, "Behold the innocent man you want me to crucify." He hoped that the spectacle of this brutalized man would cause them to see reason.

Hundreds of years before this moment, the prophet Isaiah had foreseen the sufferings of this Servant of Yahweh. He had declared of him, "there were many who were appalled at him – his appearance was so disfigured beyond that of any man and his form marred beyond human likeness" (Isaiah 52:14). Isaiah saw prophetically what Pilate saw with his own eyes. He saw the man who was disfigured and marred.

"Behold the man" means all this. But it also has a deeper meaning. Jesus was not just the greatest moral teacher, preacher, prophet and King. He was also the God-Man. He was fully God and fully man. He was God with skin on. He was and is truly *the Man*.

Devotion: *Dear loving, heavenly Abba, Father, I thank you that Jesus is the most perfect man who has ever lived. As I look at the self-sacrificial love of your Son, help me to understand that self-forgetful love is what makes me truly human in your eyes, in Jesus' name. Amen.*

When Pilate heard this, he was even more afraid, and he went back inside the palace. "Where do you come from?" he asked Jesus, but Jesus gave him no answer.

John 19:8-9

What is it that has made Pilate "even more afraid"? The answer is found in the verses leading up to this. In John 19:6–7 we see how Pilate is trying to remain neutral and avoid passing judgment upon Jesus. He knows that Jesus is innocent and so he tells the religious leaders, "You take him and crucify him. As for me, I find no basis for a charge against him." Here Pilate is desperately trying to remain neutral. But the leaders reply by saying, "We have a law, and according to that law he must die, because he claimed to be the Son of God."

This claim to be "Son of God" makes Pilate "even more afraid" – or better still, "exceedingly afraid". At one level, Pilate is afraid because this constitutes a direct challenge to the authority of Caesar Augustus. As we have seen, in the Roman empire, Caesar was treated as a god and indeed was given divine titles, such as "Lord", "God", "Saviour of the World", and indeed *divii filius,* "Son of God". Hearing that Jesus has claimed this of himself causes Pilate to become even more afraid. He now suspects that Jesus is a direct threat to the emperor's authority.

So at one level, Pilate's fear is political. But at another, it is also spiritual. We know from other sources that Pilate was a superstitious man. Matthew says this in his Gospel: "While Pilate was sitting on the judge's seat, his wife sent him this message: 'Don't have anything to do with that innocent man, for I have suffered a great deal today in a dream because of him'" (Matthew 27:19). Pilate's fear is accordingly spiritual not just political. He senses that there is something other-worldly about Jesus, which is why he asks Jesus where he comes from. But Jesus remains silent.

Pilate actually ends up asking the most important question of all – the question of Jesus' origins. Jesus comes from heaven, from the presence of Abba, Father. Indeed, he is the Father's only Son. To see that is to see everything. But Pilate ends up seeing nothing.

Devotion: *Dear loving, heavenly Abba Father, I pray that you will make a person of true faith rather than superstitious fear. Help me to see clearly who Jesus really is and to acknowledge that he alone is worthy of the title, the "Son of God", in his name. Amen.*

"You would have no power over me if it were not given to you from above. Therefore the one who handed me over to you is guilty of a greater sin."

John 19:11

Pilate has just made a comment about his authority to release or condemn Jesus. He asks Jesus, "Don't you know I have the power to set you free or to have you crucified?" He says this because Jesus has refused to answer his earlier question, "Where do you come from?" Jesus tells Pilate that he would have no power unless it had first been given "from above". He then adds a curious statement, "Therefore the one who handed me over to you is guilty of a greater sin."

What did Jesus mean? First of all, we must understand what Jesus is saying about Pilate here. He is saying that Pilate is exercising an authority that he has been given "from above". In one sense this refers to the fact that Pilate has been given his position by his superior, Caesar Augustus. Caesar was "above" him. In another sense it refers to the fact that he has been given this position from the highest authority – from the Father himself. God is above and over Pilate.

In Romans 13:1, Paul says, "Let everyone be subject to the governing authorities, for there is no authority except that which God has established." This is what Jesus is effectively saying here. He is telling Pilate that he only has his position because it has been established and given by God. In conducting this trial, Pilate is guilty of the lesser sin because he is merely exercising a legal authority that God has given him to exercise. This authority is from above.

Who, then, are the ones that are guilty of the "greater sin"? They are those who handed Jesus over to Pilate. This can only refer to the chief priests. While Pilate is using his power legally, they are using the power of Rome to secure an unjust sentence. This makes them guilty of a far greater sin than Pilate. Pilate's sin was really the sin of trying to remain neutral about Jesus. The sin of the religious leaders was the sin of deicide – putting God's Son to death.

Devotion: *Dear loving, heavenly Abba, Father, thank you for showing me that no one has authority in this world unless you have decreed that they do. Help me always to respect the position you give to people, even when it is hard to respect the people themselves, in Jesus' name. Amen.*

*From then on, Pilate tried to set Jesus free, but the Jews kept
shouting, "If you let this man go, you are no friend of Caesar.
Anyone who claims to be a king opposes Caesar."*

John 19:12

When a person becomes enslaved to a religious system, they almost
always end up engaging in manipulation in order to preserve and
protect that system, especially if they are leaders.

This is what is happening here. The chief priests are only concerned
about maintaining their position and preserving their religious system.
They know how to press Pilate's buttons to achieve this.

The chief priests understood that Pontius Pilate was under Caesar's
direct oversight. This is because his province required the presence
of Roman troops (about 3,000 of them), and all such provinces were
directly accountable to the emperor. Pilate's province was accordingly
an imperial province. The eyes of Caesar Augustus were upon it and
Pilate was both aware and fearful of that. And the chief priests knew
it too.

Pilate had taken control of this troubled and volatile region in
AD 26 and would remain in power for just under ten years. If there was
one thing he was deeply concerned about it was not being reported to
Caesar. This could easily happen. If Pilate failed in his duties, then the
people he was governing could file a report to the emperor. This would
lead to him being either demoted or moved to another province.

As Pilate prevaricates at Jesus' trial, the chief priests play their
final card. They say that if he lets Jesus go he will prove that he is no
friend of Caesar because Jesus is claiming to be a king. See how they
press Pilate's buttons! It is sheer manipulation. And their behaviour is
a lasting warning to all of us. It is a timeless picture of the controlling
and destructive power of religious slavery and abusive structures.

If you are in leadership, lead like a son or a daughter, not like a
slave or an orphan. Don't build oppressive, abusive religious structures.
Build places of controlled release and released control.

Devotion: *Dear loving, heavenly Abba, Father, I pray that you will help me
to be completely free from religious slavery and controlling behaviour.
Heal any parts of my heart that are prone to manipulation and make me
a person who releases rather than oppresses others, in Jesus' name.
Amen.*

> *"Shall I crucify your king?" Pilate asked. "We have no king but Caesar," the chief priests answered.*

John 19:15

We reach now the very end of the trial of Jesus as the religious leaders utter the most awful statement of all, "We have no king but Caesar." This was the worst of all their duplicitous comments to Pilate. One of the great cries of the Jewish people at Passover was, "We have no king but God." Now the chief priests use this same expression to confess not Yahweh but Caesar as their king. The person they hated most in the world – a pagan emperor who was responsible for the occupation of their land and the restriction of their freedoms – is the very person they now declare to be their ruler. If ever there was a betrayal of one's beliefs, it is right here at the climax to the trial of Jesus of Nazareth.

What we see in these verses is the way in which hatred can cause people to lose all sense of reason. The chief priests begin by refusing to go into Pilate's residence, preferring to remain ceremonially pure rather than morally upright. They then make sure that they present their charge against Jesus in such a way that Pilate is forced to act even if he doesn't want to. Their charge is in reality one of blasphemy – that Jesus claimed to be equal with God. But they present it as a charge of political rebellion, implying that Jesus is a threat to peace. Now they end up denying the thing that in earlier times they had shed blood to defend – that God alone is king, Caesar is not.

It is an awful thing when an intense hatred takes hold of a person's soul. It grows and grows until all rationality disappears. Hatred is like a disease; it gnaws away at human reason until all sense of perspective is gone and the person whose heart has been poisoned is capable of almost any betrayal, either of people or principles.

The human heart is hopelessly corrupt. All of us need to guard our hearts against hatred and bitterness. It is truly toxic to our relationship with the Father and indeed other people. Let's choose to have our hearts filled with Abba's healing love, not with hatred.

Devotion: *Dear loving, heavenly Father, please help me to guard my heart against bitterness, anger, hatred and lies. Heal any orphan tendencies in my life and help me to be a person of love, joy and peace, not hatred, misery, and aggression, in Jesus' name. Amen.*

Carrying his own cross, he went out to the place of the Skull (which in Aramaic is called Golgotha). Here they crucified him, and with him two others – one on each side and Jesus in the middle.

John 19:17–18

All the Gospel writers are extremely brief in what they say about the manner of Jesus' death. John here simply states "they crucified him".

From many other sources – both historical and archaeological – we know what Jesus must have gone through. After carrying the *patibulum* or crossbeam to Golgotha, he would have been forced on his back. This simple act must have caused him great pain because of the lacerations caused by the whipping he had received earlier. Nails of about six inches in length would then have been hammered through his wrists into the crossbeam. The soldiers would have been careful to avoid arteries because this would have caused severe blood loss and a quick death. They knew from experience how to keep victims alive for as long as possible and in as much pain as possible. Great bolts of agony must have passed through Jesus' body as nerves were severed.

After this, Jesus would have been lifted up on an upright post called the *stipes*. Four soldiers would have been required for this task. Jesus' feet were nailed to the lower front part of the *stipes*, again avoiding arteries but penetrating major nerves. From this point on normal respiration was impossible. The weight of his body bearing down on his chest would have fixed intercostal muscles in an inhalation state. Breathing would have become shallow. Muscle cramps would have quickly set in. No bodily movement would have been able to ease the pain, especially since any attempt to do so would result in the wounds on the back scraping against the upright post. The inevitable result would eventually be death by exhaustion, shock, dehydration, or asphyxia.

John simply says, "they crucified him". But in this one simple statement, something truly profound is visible, for the crucifixion of Jesus is without doubt the greatest demonstration of the divine love in human history. It is God's "I love you" to an orphaned planet.

Devotion: *Dear loving, heavenly Abba, Father, words fail us as we read this brief statement about your Son, "they crucified him". All we can say is thank you. Thank you, Abba, for giving up your Son. Thank you, Jesus, for giving up your life. Amen.*

Pilate had a notice prepared and fastened to the cross. It read: Jesus of Nazareth, the King of the Jews.

John 19:19

When I was a young Christian I remember going to a Pentecostal church and listening to a preacher deliver an inspiring message entitled, "The Gospel of Christ's Enemies". In it he went through all those occasions in the four Gospels when the opponents of Jesus proclaim the truth about who he is! He included demons because even they end up telling everyone that Jesus is the Holy One of God!

In John 19:19 we see one of the classic examples of this. Pontius Pilate, the Roman procurator of the region, has interrogated Jesus. Even though he has found no fault in him, Pilate has Jesus flogged and now crucified. Before his soldiers lead Jesus led to Golgotha – to the Place of the Skull – he has a placard made. He orders the execution detail to take this to the scene of the crucifixion and to nail it to the top of the Cross.

This sign reads, "Jesus of Nazareth, the King of the Jews" – not "a king" but emphatically "the" king. Pilate himself didn't believe this, of course. In all likelihood he resented being manipulated by the religious leaders into torturing and executing an innocent man so he sought to enact some revenge by writing something that he knew would bate them. In the process, one of Christ's enemies proclaimed the gospel!

In John 19:20 we learn that this profession was written in three different languages – in Aramaic (the language of the Jews), Latin (the language of the Romans) and Greek (the language of many of the Gentiles in Judea). These were the three main languages spoken in the ancient world. Pilate wanted everyone to know what he'd written about Jesus.

One day, every politician who has ever governed, every president who has ever been in office, every monarch who has ever reigned, will kneel before Jesus and say, "You're the King of Kings." Pilate's ironic declaration is a foretaste of this great day when even Christ's most powerful enemies will have to concede that he is Lord!

Devotion: _Dear loving, heavenly Abba, Father, I pray today for political leaders all over the world, especially for those who oppose the Christian faith. Would you cause their hearts to be open to the truth about who Jesus really was and is, in his name. Amen._

> *When the soldiers crucified Jesus, they took his clothes,*
> *dividing them into four shares, one for each of them, with the*
> *undergarment remaining. This garment was seamless, woven*
> *in one piece from top to bottom.*
>
> John 19:23

I remember a friend of mine going to his father's funeral. After the service, all the family retired to the house to have some food. While he was mingling with the relatives, my friend overheard a cousin asking, "How much did he leave?" My friend gave the answer. "How much did he leave? He left everything."

Many people spend their whole lives accumulating more and more money and possessions. In today's consumer-oriented world, people cannot really disassociate who they are from what they have. We forget in the process that none of these things lasts and that we can't take any of it when we die. Indeed, we leave everything.

Jesus was the richest man in history and yet when he died he left only the clothes that he was wearing. Jesus was the Son of God and the King of Kings. No human being has ever owned more or had more influence and significance. Yet when he died he didn't leave mansions and money. He left only the clothes on his back.

So here we see the execution squad of four Roman guards dividing up Jesus' last possessions. It was customary for soldiers in an execution detail to share the belongings of the crucified victim. Here they haggle over some clothes left by Jesus. That wasn't very much for one whose Father owns the cattle on a thousand hills.

One item of clothing gets a special mention – a seamless garment woven from top to bottom. Why does John mention this? We may never know this side of eternity but it is worth noting that the high priest was said to wear a seamless garment, especially on the Day of Atonement. Maybe John is pointing to the fact that Jesus is our Great High Priest.

Whatever the case, let's follow Jesus' example. When it comes to possessions, we leave everything. So let's hold them all very lightly.

Devotion: *Dear loving, heavenly Abba, Father, I pray that I would sit very lightly to money and possessions. Help me to remember that your Son did not store up treasure on earth but rather treasure in heaven. Give me grace to value spiritual realities above material things. Amen.*

When Jesus saw his mother there, and the disciple whom he loved standing nearby, he said to her, "Woman, here is your son," and to the disciple, "Here is your mother." From that time on, this disciple took her into his home.

John 19:26–27

This is one of the most touching scenes in the Gospels. As his life ebbs away, Jesus gives thought to his mother. She is one of four women standing at the foot of the Cross. Nearby is the Beloved Disciple, whom many identify as John the son of Zebedee, one of the Twelve.

As Jesus looks at his mother and his friend, he first addresses his mother. He says to her, "Behold, your son." He then turns his head towards John and says, "Behold, your mother." The Gospel writer then adds that from this hour, the mother of Jesus lived with John.

What is the message in this extraordinarily poignant scene? At a purely practical level, Jesus is here portrayed as someone who is eager to put his house in order before he dies. He is being a good first-born son. He is seeing that his mother has an earthly provider.

At a deeper level, however, what we witness here is a kind of adoption. At the Cross, Jesus tells his mother that the Beloved Disciple is now part of their family. He is Mary's son and Jesus' brother. Similarly, he tells the Beloved Disciple that he has a new, adoptive mother.

Here then we see the fulfilment of Jesus' promise to his disciples in John 14:18, "I will not leave you as orphans". By adopting the Beloved Disciple into his own family, Jesus shows how his death brings a new family into being – the family of the church.

And this is the whole point. The church that Jesus died for is a family in which God is our Father, Jesus is our perfect older brother, and we are adopted brothers and sisters. What an amazing privilege!

Let's give thanks to the Father today that the church is not a cold institution but a loving and warm family.

Devotion: *Dear loving, heavenly Abba, Father, help me always to appreciate the wonder of the Cross. Thank you that at Calvary your Son made it possible for me to be adopted in your family. Thank you that you set the lonely in families of faith, in Jesus' name. Amen.*

Jesus said, "It is finished."

John 19:30

Over the next three days we are going to look at this great statement from three different angles. You may ask, "Why are we doing this?" The answer is because these are among the most important words ever uttered. What Jesus said in his dying breath has literally history-making and earth-changing ramifications. These are Jesus' last words and they require special attention and indeed profound reverence.

So let's begin by looking at what Jesus said. John 19:30 uses a form of the verb *teleo* meaning "to finish", "to accomplish", and "perform". It is a word used only one other time in John – just a few verses earlier in verse 28: "Later, knowing that all was now *completed*, and so that the Scripture would be fulfilled, Jesus said, 'I am thirsty.'" When Jesus died on the Cross, he was completing, accomplishing, and fulfilling his mission.

And in doing that, Jesus finished well. He performed the task that his Abba, Father had given him. He completed his assignment.

When Jesus said "It is finished", this was accordingly not a statement of defeat but a declaration of victory. Often we speak of Jesus' triumphal entry, referring to the way he came into Jerusalem a week before he died. Jesus' death suggests that we can use another, contrasting phrase – "triumphal exit". Jesus' death on the Cross was a victorious exit from this world. It was a moment of unprecedented triumph.

In a world that is full of good starters but not so full of good finishers, Jesus shows us how to finish well. Finishing well means fulfilling everything that our heavenly Father wants for our lives. It means beginning well when we are born again. It means continuing well as we follow Jesus. It means ending well by finishing our lives with an undiminished affection for Abba.

As adopted brothers and sisters of the one who said "It is finished", let's make it our aim to finish well.

Devotion: *Dear loving, heavenly Abba, Father, I thank you so much that you have a perfect plan and a unique assignment for my life. Help me to be like Jesus. Help me to know what my task is and to be able to complete it and say, "It is finished", in his name. Amen.*

Jesus said, "It is finished."

John 19:30

As we saw yesterday, just before Jesus breathes his last, he says, "It is finished." What was he referring to? He was referring to the assignment that his heavenly Father had given him to fulfil.

On a number of occasions in John's Gospel Jesus has spoken about his Abba's "task" or "work". In John 4:34, Jesus says, "My food is to do the will of him who sent me and to finish his work." In John 5:36 Jesus says, "the very work that the Father has given me to finish, and which I am doing, testifies that the Father has sent me." In John 17:4 Jesus says, "I have brought you glory on earth by completing the work you gave me to do." The whole of Jesus' life was focused on fulfilling his Father's work. As the Father's Son, Jesus was passionate and intentional about completing the assignment that was his and his alone.

What was this assignment? In John 3:16–17 we read, "For God so loved the world that he gave his one and only Son, that whoever believes in him shall not perish but have eternal life. For God did not send his Son into the world to condemn the world, but to save the world through him." Jesus' unique assignment was to save the world from sin. As the Lamb of God, his mandate was to take away our sin at Calvary.

As his life ebbs away on the Cross, Jesus turns his eyes heavenward to the Father and says, "It is finished." He knows that he has taken the sin of the world into his body on the Cross. He knows that he has paid the penalty for our sin and that he is moments away from dying the death that we deserved. Looking up to his Abba he declares, "It is finished." Not "I am finished", but "It is finished."

Aren't you glad that it is finished? Our good works could never secure our salvation. But Christ's great work at Calvary could! Christianity is therefore not a "big do"; it is a "big done". All we need to do is put our faith and trust in the finished work of the Cross.

Hallelujah! It is finished!

Devotion: *Dear loving, heavenly Abba, Father, I thank you that I don't have to climb a thousand hills or cross a hundred oceans to earn your salvation. I thank you that Jesus has done everything necessary at Calvary. Thank you so much for the Cross, in Jesus' name. Amen.*

Jesus said, "It is finished."

John 19:30

In our third and final look at "It is finished" we're going to go a bit deeper into the meaning of these magnificent words. Actually, in the original Greek text, it's only one word that is used. Our English translations have three words – "It is finished." But the Greek manuscript simply has Jesus saying one word, *tetelestai*.

Yesterday we saw how this word can mean "perform", "complete", "fulfil", and "accomplish". Jesus completed the Father's assignment for his life. And that was truly exceptional. The Bible tells the stories of over 500 leaders, but only thirteen of them finished well, the greatest of whom was Jesus of Nazareth.

That said, there's an even deeper significance to the word *tetelestai* than this. It doesn't only mean "complete" or "perform". It also means "pay". When Jesus used this word, he was saying, "It's over. The debt has been paid. The bill has been met in full!"

In the Roman era, if someone couldn't pay a bill, they would usually be thrown in prison. However, on rare occasions, mercy was extended, especially to those who could never pay what they owed. Then the Roman authorities would stamp the word *tetelestai* on the bill, "Paid in full."

On the Cross, Jesus declared, "*tetelestai*". What a great statement that is! At one level it means, "I've done it! I've completed your assignment, Abba". At a deeper level it means, "Paid in full. The debt of human sin has been cancelled. I've paid the price."

What a miracle the Cross is! We owed a debt to the Father that we could never have paid. But Jesus Christ paid the bill in full, so now we are no longer in debt because of our sin but in credit because of his righteousness.

Let's celebrate God's amazing grace today. Let's remember that Grace means "God's Riches At Christ's Expense".

Devotion: *Dear loving, heavenly Abba, Father, I'm humbled and amazed by your grace. I didn't deserve to be set free from the debt that I owed, but in Jesus the price has been paid in full and my debt to you has been cancelled forever. Hallelujah! What a Saviour!*

With that, he bowed his head and gave up his spirit.

John 19:30

As so often in John's Gospel, this statement can be interpreted at both a literal and a spiritual level.

At the literal level, John's words refer to the last breath that Jesus exhales in his physical body here on the earth. As his weary and bleeding head falls down upon his chest, Jesus emits a last breath from his tortured body. His friends and family at the foot of the Cross would have heard this. Through tear-stained eyes they would have seen their beloved die. No doubt there was a strange mixture of grief and relief in their hearts – grief that their loved one was gone but also relief that his excruciating agony was now over.

So there is a purely physical, literal, and medical meaning to the words, "Jesus gave up his spirit." But then there's also a deeper, spiritual meaning.

At the spiritual level, this statement refers not just to the breath that Jesus uttered. It also refers to the Holy Spirit whom Jesus now gives or "hands over" to the world. John had told us that the Holy Spirit would not be given until Jesus had been glorified (John 7:39). Jesus is being glorified here. He is being "lifted up", both literally and figuratively. This is therefore the moment when the Holy Spirit begins to be released. Accordingly, Jesus didn't just give up his last breath. He activated the release of his Spirit, the Holy Spirit.

In the church today, there are many who value the work of the Cross, but who neglect the work of the Holy Spirit. There are conversely also many who value the work of the Holy Spirit but neglect the work of the Cross. John 19:30 reminds us that we cannot have the Cross without the Spirit or indeed the Spirit without the Cross. The Holy Spirit was only given because Jesus died for our sins at Calvary. So let's be champions of the both-and! Let's revere both the work of the Cross and the work of the Spirit.

Devotion: *Dear loving, heavenly Abba, Father, I thank you that the Holy Spirit was released into our lives as a result of your Son's atoning death upon the Cross. I commit to being a Christian who always keeps the Cross and the Spirit together, in Jesus' name. Amen.*

Now it was the day of Preparation... .

John 19:31

When it comes to God's plans, there are no coincidences. There are only "God-incidences" – extraordinary moments in which events converge and coincide in a miraculous way. Maybe you've experienced such moments in your life. When such "synchronicity" happens, I am tempted to quote the refrain from the old TV series called *The A-Team*: "Don't you just love it when a plan comes together?"

That is precisely what is going on here. John reports that Jesus' death took place on "the day of Preparation". Keep in mind that in the Bible a day runs from 6 p.m. one day to 6 p.m. the next. In other words, a day begins in the evening. This is quite unlike the Western world of today where a day begins in the morning. This is an important point to remember as we look at the timing of Jesus' death.

What then was "the day of Preparation"? It was the day on which every father brought a one-year-old, unblemished lamb to the Temple courts. This was done as part of every family's preparations for the Passover. The priests would take this lamb and slit its throat. This effectively turned the Temple into an abattoir and the blood of the lambs flowed from the Temple through a channel into the Kidron ravine.

The sacrifice of these lambs was performed in accordance with the requirements of Exodus 12 and done in memory of the first Passover, in which the Hebrew slaves were told to kill a lamb and daub the lintels and doorposts of their homes with its blood. That way, when the Angel of Death visited Egypt, he would "pass over" those homes protected by the blood of these lambs.

Jesus' death took place on the day of Preparation. At precisely the moment when lambs were being slaughtered in the Temple, Jesus was paying the price for our sins at Golgotha. Jesus is truly the Lamb of God who takes away the sin of the world. His death reminds us that Abba's perfect plan was coming together.

Devotion: *Dear loving, heavenly Abba, Father, I thank you that even in history's most devastating moments, you are still on your throne, reigning as the sovereign Lord of all creation. Thank you that even when your Son died, your perfect plan was being fulfilled. Amen.*

... one of the soldiers pierced Jesus' side with a spear, bringing a sudden flow of blood and water.

John 19:34

I don't know if you've ever noticed this, but there's a great deal of water in John's Gospel.

In John chapter 2, Jesus turns 180 gallons of water into wine.

In John 3, John is baptizing people in Aenon where there's a lot of water.

In John 4, Jesus talks to the Samaritan woman about "living water".

In John 5, Jesus heals a man by a pool of water.

In John 6, Jesus walks on water.

In John 7, Jesus tells everyone who is thirsty to come to him and drink.

In John 9, a blind man gets healed when he washes his eyes in a pool.

In John 13, Jesus washes his disciples' feet using a bowl of water.

There really is "plenty of water" in John (John 3:23)!

Here at the Cross, we see yet more water. This time a soldier thrusts a spear into Jesus' chest and water immediately flows out of the wound, as well as blood.

Whatever medical explanation one may give of this, in John's eyes this is miraculous. Jesus had prophesied in John 7:38 that streams of living water would flow from his belly. John had added, "By this he meant the Spirit, whom those who believed in him were later to receive. Up to that time the Spirit had not been given, since Jesus had not yet been glorified."

On the Cross, water flows from the wounds of Jesus as he is lifted up and glorified. This water is the Holy Spirit. Thus we see once again the inseparability of the work of the Cross and the work of the Spirit. It is because of the Son's passion that we receive God's power. It is because of Christ's death that we receive the Spirit's life.

Devotion: *Dear loving, heavenly Abba, Father, I thank you for the Cross again today. I thank you especially that it was through the death of your Son that I received the life of your Spirit. Thank you so much for the amazing sacrifice you made, Lord Jesus, in your name. Amen.*

Nicodemus brought a mixture of myrrh and aloes, about seventy-five pounds.

John 19:39

Nicodemus is such an enigmatic character. If you remember, we first met him in John chapter 3 when he came to Jesus at night-time so that he wouldn't be seen by his colleagues from the Sanhedrin. There he acknowledged that Jesus was a teacher sent by God. But he also failed to see that he had to be born again if he wanted to enter the kingdom of God. So his understanding at this stage was limited.

Then in John chapter 7 Nicodemus appeared again. This time the chief priests and the Pharisees were angry with the temple guards for failing to arrest Jesus. Nicodemus stood up for Jesus and told his peers that their law did not condemn anyone without first giving them a fair hearing. The chief priests silence Nicodemus by telling him that they don't need to hear Jesus. He couldn't be from God because he came from Galilee.

In John 19, Nicodemus appears one final time, alongside a wealthy man called Joseph of Arimathea who has petitioned Pilate for Jesus' body. Pilate agrees and Joseph, accompanied by Nicodemus, takes Jesus' corpse to a brand new tomb in a garden nearby. This tomb belongs to Joseph. Joseph provides a place for Jesus to be buried; Nicodemus provides the customary spices and oils for the embalming of Jesus' body.

And look how much Nicodemus brings! He brings 75lb worth! This is the kind of quantity required for the burial of a king.

Joseph and Nicodemus may have been secret disciples during Jesus' ministry (for fear of their fellow Jewish leaders), but at the end of Jesus' life they give him a burial fit for a king.

Little did they know that Jesus was borrowing the tomb only for a while. They didn't know that Jesus would leave it on Easter Sunday, abandoning the burial clothes in which Nicodemus and Joseph had lovingly wrapped him. Then they would no doubt worship Jesus not only as their King but as their risen Lord.

Devotion: *Dear loving, heavenly Abba, Father, I want to thank you that you are prepared to wait so patiently while we move from misunderstanding to understanding, especially about your Son. Thank you that you are such a faithful, patient Dad, in Jesus' name. Amen.*

> **At the place where Jesus was crucified, there was a garden, and in the garden a new tomb, in which no one had ever been laid.**
>
> John 19:41

These verses mark the end of what is traditionally known as John's "Passion Narrative". The word "passion" means "suffering" in this context. This narrative begins with the first verse of John 18 and ends with the final verse of John 19. It begins with Jesus' arrest in the olive garden. It ends with Jesus' arrest in another garden – a garden where there was a brand new tomb, belonging to Joseph and waiting for Jesus.

All this talk of gardens would no doubt have triggered significant memories in the readers of John's day. They were altogether more familiar with the Old Testament than we are and they would have gone back in their minds to the very beginning of the Hebrew Bible and the opening chapters of the Book of Genesis. There, in a garden called Eden, Adam and Eve had sinned and fallen from grace.

Now, in another garden, Jesus Christ is laid in a brand new tomb. Here, on the first Easter Sunday, there will be the greatest miracle in history. Abba, Father will send resurrection power from heaven into the uncorrupted body of his Son and – in the twinkling of an eye – Jesus will be raised to life. He will burst forth from the grave as a second Adam, and his resurrection will usher in a brand new creation!

So the garden in which Jesus is buried has some special resonances. What was done in the Garden of Eden will be undone in this garden. What was marred by the sin of the first Adam will be redeemed and restored here by the second Adam. Through the death and resurrection of Jesus Christ, paradise that was lost will now be regained – and paradise means literally "a beautiful garden".

Never forget that you and I are part of the Father's brand new creation. Through Jesus' death and resurrection, the old has gone and a brave new world has come. Truly, our Father makes all things new!

Devotion: *Dear loving, heavenly Abba, Father, I worship you that you are truly the God of new beginnings. Even here, when all seemed lost as Jesus was buried, a brave new world was about to explode into life. How I praise you that you are the God of the second chance. Amen.*

Early on the first day of the week, while it was still dark, Mary Magdalene went to the tomb and saw that the stone had been removed from the entrance.

John 20:1

It is now very early on Sunday morning, sometime between 3 a.m. and 6 a.m. Mary Magdalene is the first person to arrive at the tomb of Jesus. She would have gone earlier but for two reasons: first, it was the sabbath day before this and walking to the tomb would have constituted work and therefore a sabbath infringement. Secondly, it would have been dark both on Saturday evening and Sunday in the very early hours. Mary therefore goes to the tomb at the earliest possible opportunity, when the sabbath is over and a new dawn is breaking.

When Mary gets to the tomb she finds that the heavy stone has been wheeled away and that the tomb is empty. At this stage she doesn't know what has happened; she thinks that someone has removed the body. She is yet to realize that Jesus has been raised from the dead. This will come, but for now Mary is confused and distressed.

As we look at John's great story of the resurrection, we can be confident that we are dealing with history and not with fiction. Let me offer two reasons for trusting the historical reliability of John's account.

First of all, notice how it is Mary who sees that the tomb is empty. This is significant. In John's day, the testimony of a woman was regarded as worthless. If John had been writing a fictional story he would hardly have had Mary as the first witness to the resurrection.

Secondly, notice how John emphasizes it was Sunday. In the earliest church, Sunday became the most important day of the week. Something radical must have occurred to cause Jewish believers to make this their most important day. It did! Jesus was resurrected on Sunday!

The Christian faith is based on history not myths. As we look at John's resurrection story, you can be confident that Jesus lives!

Devotion: *Dear loving, heavenly Abba, Father, thank you that on the third day you sent your glorious power from heaven into the tomb where your Son lay. Thank you that you raised him from the dead and wheeled the stone away. Thank you that this is fact! Hallelujah! Amen.*

> *... she came running to Simon Peter and the other disciple, the one Jesus loved, and said, "They have taken the Lord out of the tomb, and we don't know where they have put him!"*
>
> John 20:2

Mary Magdalene is devastated. She had come to the tomb to pay her respects to Jesus, but she finds when she gets there that his body has been removed. She runs as fast as she can through the streets of Jerusalem until she arrives at the location where the disciples are hiding. She finds Simon Peter and the Beloved Disciple. She tells them that the body of Jesus has been removed. Notice she says, "*we* don't know where they have put him". The use of the word "we" shows that Mary Magdalene was not alone. She was evidently accompanied by other women when she went to the tomb. While John doesn't mention them, the other Gospels do. John wants to focus on Mary Magdalene in his account.

Yesterday I wrote about the compelling, historical truthfulness of John's report. I offered two important pieces of evidence. First, I argued that John would never have had a woman as the first witness if he had been writing fiction. A woman's testimony lacked credibility and validity in a Jewish court of law. Second, John shows that it was on the first day of the week that this happened. This focus on Sunday shows that something momentous has occurred. For the earliest Jewish believers in Jesus, the highlight of the week has moved from sabbath to Sunday. The only good reason for this is because the earliest Christians knew that Jesus had been raised on a Sunday morning.

Today let me offer a third very strong piece of evidence in favour of John's historical reliability. He stresses that the tomb was empty. Now this may seem obvious but it is immensely significant. In the time of Jesus, disciples of a great rabbi would visit his tomb every year on the anniversary of his death. This practice of tomb veneration was very common. What is very interesting about the tomb of Jesus is this: the disciples only visit his tomb on this one day. They don't go back every year thereafter. There can only be one explanation: they knew that Jesus was no longer in the tomb and that he was alive! And he is!

Devotion: *Dear loving, heavenly Abba, Father, I praise you that my faith is not based on the shifting sands of myth and legend but on the solid ground of history and truth. Help me to grow in my confidence that the tomb was empty because Jesus was and is alive, in his name. Amen.*

Peter and the other disciple started for the tomb. Both were running, but the other disciple outran Peter and reached the tomb first.

John 20:3–4

There's a curious thing going on throughout John's Gospel. It seems almost as if Peter and the Beloved Disciple are in some kind of competition with each other. Let's look at some examples.

First of all, in John chapter 13, notice how it is the Beloved Disciple who is next to Jesus at the Last Supper. He leans against Jesus' chest and hears everything his master is saying, especially about the imminent betrayal. At one point in the Supper, Peter asks him what Jesus has just said. Peter needs the Beloved Disciple to access Jesus' words here.

Secondly, in John 18, notice how it is the Beloved Disciple who is well known to Annas and who can go in and out of the courtyard to the house where Jesus is being interrogated. Peter can only gain access when the Beloved Disciple tells the gatekeeper to let him in. Here again Peter seems to be cast as someone who needs the Beloved Disciple.

Thirdly, notice here in John 20 how Peter and the Beloved Disciple run to the tomb and how the Beloved Disciple arrives first. This could be because he was a younger man. But it also could be because he had a greater passion to meet Jesus again. Peter had denied Jesus three times. His longing would have been tempered by that.

Why is the Beloved Disciple portrayed so positively in these episodes? It is because he has something of priceless value – he has a longing to be near to Jesus. At the Last Supper he leans on Jesus' chest. At the interrogation, he ensures that he is as near to Jesus as possible. Even at the Cross, the Beloved Disciple is close to Jesus.

If we want to become Beloved Disciples, we need to prioritize friendship with Jesus and intimacy with the Father. It is these characteristics above all others that mark us out. It is these that qualify us to become Beloved Disciples. So let's pray, "Draw me close to you, Jesus."

Devotion: *Dear loving, heavenly Abba, Father, I pray today for a closer friendship with your Son and a deeper intimacy with you. Pour out the holy flame of your love upon my heart today. Make me a true friend of Jesus and a loving child of God, in Jesus' name. Amen.*

> *Then Simon Peter came along behind him and went straight into the tomb. He saw the strips of linen lying there, as well as the cloth that had been wrapped around Jesus' head.*
>
> John 20:6–7

Although the Beloved Disciple arrives at the tomb first, he doesn't enter. He just stoops and looks through the opening. Simon Peter on the other hand goes right into the tomb as soon as he catches up with his running partner. He sees two things – the grave cloths that had been wrapped around Jesus' whole body and the turban-like cloth that had covered Jesus' head.

As we continue to consider the historical truthfulness of John's account, let's pause today and consider several other pieces of evidence.

First of all, notice the detail about the cloth bands that had covered Jesus' body. And here we find something very intriguing. For the way John describes them leaves the reader in no doubt. They are left unwrapped in the tomb. They are not in an untidy heap or stretched out in a long trail inside and outside the tomb. They are exactly as they had been when they had been around Jesus' body. In other words, these grave cloths lay in such a way that the reader is left thinking only one thing – nobody unwrapped Jesus from this mummified state; rather, he emerged from these bands as if they weren't even there!

Secondly, notice how economical John is in his report of all this. He leaves so much unsaid. He doesn't include any description of the actual moment when the power of God came from heaven, the stone was rolled away, and Jesus broke free from his grave clothes. There is absolutely none of this. If I had been constructing a fictional story of the resurrection, I would have gone to great lengths to boost the authority of my hero by having him portrayed in a mystical, super human light. But this is precisely what John does not do. His storytelling is a masterpiece of restraint. He lets the facts speak for themselves.

What a great comfort it is to know that our faith is based on solid facts.

Devotion: *Dear loving, heavenly Abba, Father, I worship and praise you that what I'm reading in John 20 is the truth, the whole truth and nothing but the truth. In a world full of myths and lies, it is so good to know that what I believe is based on true truth, in Jesus' name. Amen.*

The cloth was folded up by itself, separate from the linen.

John 20:7 (NIV)

John is not known for including details in his descriptions of scenes and events in his Gospel. He tends to tell stories in a very brief and general way, not lingering over the nuances of peoples' voices, or the niceties of their physical appearances. John's Gospel is not a modern novel, full of precise descriptions of places and times. It is a first-century biography of Jesus, told with remarkable and artistic economy.

Except, that is, in the case of John 20:7! For here we see John including what at first sight seems to be an entirely redundant and unexpected piece of information. He mentions that Jesus had left his head cloth in a separate place from the linen that had wrapped his body and that *it was neatly folded*. Why does John include this detail about the folded napkin? What is so important about that?

The answer comes from what may seem a rather random and left-field source – from first-century Jewish meal customs. If you were invited to someone's house for dinner in Jesus' day you would say yes and go and share fellowship with them. If you enjoyed the meal and the company, you would take hold of your napkin, crumple it, and leave it at your place. That was code for, "I have enjoyed this and I'm coming back."

Now here's the important thing. If you had *not* enjoyed the experience, you would do the exact opposite. Instead of crumpling up your napkin and leaving it where you had been reclining, you would fold it up and leave it at your seat before departing. This also was code. It said this: "I have not enjoyed this experience one little bit. The hospitality has been lousy and the company shoddy. I am *not* coming back!"

When the risen Jesus leaves his folded napkin in the tomb, this would have conveyed to a Jewish mind only one thing – that Jesus had not enjoyed the experience he'd been through. It would have sent the signal that Jesus is never going back to that place again – that he would never have to die again! He is truly alive for evermore!

Devotion: *Dear loving, heavenly Abba, Father, I thank you that Jesus was raised immortal and that he is the firstborn from the dead of those who follow him. Thank you that one day we will leave our folded napkins behind and we will never have to die again, in Jesus' name. Amen.*

> *... the other disciple, who had reached the tomb first, also went inside. He saw and believed.*

John 20:8

In his excitement and curiosity, the Beloved Disciple outruns Simon Peter and arrives at the tomb first. Simon Peter catches up and goes into the tomb before him. After Peter has seen the tomb, he comes out and it's now the turn of the Beloved Disciple. He goes inside and sees what Peter sees. The big difference between him and Peter is this: when the Beloved Disciple sees the empty tomb he is said to believe.

What is it that the Beloved Disciple believes? There can only be one answer. He believes that Jesus has burst through the grave clothes and risen from the dead. He believes on the basis of the evidence of the empty tomb that his Lord is alive for evermore. He knows that his Redeemer lives!

The word "believe" is one of John's favourites in his Gospel. He uses it 100 times. He never uses the noun *pistis* (meaning "faith" or "belief"). He always uses the verb *pisteuein*, which means to "believe" or "to put one's trust in something or someone". The use of the verb form shows that in John's eyes faith is always active.

Sometimes John uses this word in the sense of believing *that* something is true. In John 20:31 John says, "These things are written that you may believe *that* Jesus is the Christ, the Son of God, and that by believing you may have life in his name."

At other times John uses this word in the sense of believing *in* someone, specifically believing in Jesus and the Father. So for example in John 12:44 Jesus says, "Those who believe *in* me do not believe *in* me only, but *in* the one who sent me."

In John 20:8, the Beloved Disciple believes. He believes that Jesus is alive. If we want to be Beloved Disciples, we too must believe that Jesus has been raised from the dead and is Lord of all.

Devotion: *Dear loving, heavenly Abba, Father, I want you to know that I believe in my heart that your Son Jesus Christ was raised from the dead on the first Easter Day and is alive for evermore. I want to confess with my mouth that Jesus is Lord, in his mighty and matchless name. Amen.*

> *As she wept, she bent over to look into the tomb and saw two angels in white, seated where Jesus' body had been, one at the head and the other at the foot.*
>
> John 20:11–12

Mary Magdalene stoops over the entrance over Jesus' tomb and peers into the space where Jesus' body should have been. She sees the slab of rock but there is nothing there. Before she has time to grieve, she sees something else which takes her breath away. There are two angels, one either end of the empty slab. They are dressed in white. One of them is positioned where Jesus' head would have been, the other where his feet would have rested.

If we are to understand this scene we need to appreciate some Old Testament background. When Moses came to build the tabernacle during the wilderness wanderings, he was told to create an inner room called the Holy of Holies. This area was to be separated from the Holy Place by a veil and the only person who was allowed there was the high priest on the Day of Atonement. This was where the Ark of the Covenant was kept. It was the earthly counterpart of God's throne in heaven.

Since the Most Holy Place was the place of God's throne on earth, it had to be guarded. In the Holy of Holies it was the *cherubim* that guarded the throne. There were two of these angels, carved in gold, and they were positioned over the throne-like ark with their wings draped over its sacred contents. They were the guardians of the presence, and they stood one at each end of the Ark (Exodus 25:17–22).

When Mary looks into the tomb of Jesus, she finds the slab guarded by two angels, one at each end. To anyone steeped in the Old Testament, this can only mean one thing. Heaven has invaded this place of gloom. Death has lost its grip on planet earth. The devil has lost his authority over the world. Our God reigns!

This was truly a tomb with a view. Through Mary's eyes we can see that the resurrection means that our Father rules on the earth!

Devotion: *Dear loving, heavenly Abba, Father, thank you so much for raising your Son through your mighty and glorious power. Thank you that heaven invaded the tomb where your Son lay and that angels guarded it. I praise you that you reign over all things, in Jesus' name. Amen.*

> **At this, she turned around and saw Jesus standing there, but she did not realize that it was Jesus.**
>
> John 20:14

It is a curious thing that Mary Magdalene didn't recognize Jesus. She has come to the tomb with thoughts only for him. She has loved him since she first met him – not with a worldly, carnal love but with a pure and tender affection. If there was one face that she knew and revered more than any other it was the face of her Rabbi, Jesus of Nazareth. But here she fails to see that it is in fact Jesus speaking to her at the entrance of his own tomb.

Why did Mary Magdalene not recognize Jesus?

There are two likely reasons. The first has to do with Jesus' physical appearance. Jesus has been resurrected by the Father's glorious power and he has a new, spiritual body. This body is incorruptible and perfect. Consequently, there must have been something different about the way Jesus looked. To be sure, this new body is continuous with the old one. But it is also a resurrected body. Jesus must have looked more radiant and alive than ever!

The second has to do with the intensity of Mary's grief. Mary is still in the first stage of bereavement – in the disorienting numbness of shock. She has been through an indescribable trauma. She has seen Jesus die the most horrible execution that human beings have ever devised. She is accordingly traumatized. Her eyes are red with crying. Her mind is clouded with confusion. Her whole being has been destabilized. No wonder she didn't recognize Jesus.

When we are in deep grief, the greatest need we have is for Jesus to come to us. What we need more than anything else is a supernatural encounter with the death-defeating and grave-conquering Lord. Only this can begin to dispel the mists of confusion, shock and pain.

If you are grieving today, pray not only that Jesus would come to you but also that you'd recognize him when he does.

Devotion: *Dear loving, heavenly Abba, Father, I praise you that you are very close to the broken hearted and that you comfort those who mourn. Manifest your supernatural and healing presence in the lives of those who grieve and reveal your compassion. I ask in Jesus' name. Amen.*

"Who is it you are looking for?"

This is one of the great questions of the Fourth Gospel.

Jesus has been raised from the dead. He is now walking in the garden where he was buried in Joseph's tomb. Now Mary Magdalene is weeping outside the entrance of the tomb. Jesus comes up to her and asks her why she is weeping and then who it is that she is looking for.

The word translated "looking for" is a verb that John uses over thirty times in his Gospel. It is the Greek word *zetein*, which means to "seek". The first time John uses this is right at the beginning of his Gospel when Jesus asks the same question of two of John the Baptist's disciples: "Turning around, Jesus saw them following and asked, 'What do you want?'" (John 1:38).

Here Jesus literally asks, "What are you seeking?" Now at the end of the Gospel Jesus asks Mary, "Who are you seeking?"

There is a lot of talk these days about "seeker sensitive Christianity". Those who believe in this model of church argue that we should make our churches as "seeker friendly" as possible. In other words, we should make sure our services are designed to attract unbelievers.

Whether this is right or wrong is not my concern here. What Mary Magdalene demonstrates in John 20:15 is the importance of Christians seeking Jesus. Mary Magdalene was looking for Jesus. Her quest was the presence of the Lord.

In reality, it is Jesus Christ who is "seeker sensitive". He is acutely sensitive towards those who seek him with all their heart. If we truly want revival, we must revere God's presence more highly than our programmes. Like Mary, we must weep for his presence.

Let's be more like Mary Magdalene – relentless and passionate seekers after the presence of the Risen Lord.

Devotion: *Dear loving, heavenly Abba, Father, stir up in me a passion for your presence. Make me more like Mary; create a holy hunger for the cloud of your glorious presence in my life. I want to encounter the Spirit of Jesus in my life, in his name. Amen.*

Jesus said to her, "Mary." She turned toward him and cried out in Aramaic, "Rabboni!" (which means "Teacher").

John 20:16

To understand the profound importance of this moment we need to go back to John chapter 10. At the beginning of that chapter, Jesus spoke about sheep and their shepherd:

> The man who enters by the gate is the shepherd of his sheep. The watchman opens the gate for him, and the sheep listen to his voice. He calls his own sheep by name and leads them out. When he has brought out all his own, he goes on ahead of them, and his sheep follow him because they know his voice.

So much of what Jesus says about the shepherd and the sheep acts as a telling background to what happens in this beautiful moment that he shares with Mary Magdalene in John 20.

Up until now, Mary hasn't recognized Jesus. Looking at him through tear-stained eyes, she thinks he is the gardener. But when Jesus mentions her name, suddenly she realizes who it is. This is her Rabbi.

In this little episode we see Mary Magdalene fulfilling much of Jesus' teaching about the shepherd and the sheep. Like the sheep in John 10, Mary Magdalene listens to and knows Jesus' voice.

At the same time, Jesus enacts the part of the shepherd from John 10. After all, the shepherd knows all his sheep by name. Jesus knows Mary's name and utters it here in the garden in John 20.

And so it is by hearing and not by seeing that Mary Magdalene comes to recognize her risen Lord. As she listens to her master's voice uttering her name, her heart leaps. She cries out "My Teacher."

We can take comfort from the fact that even though we cannot see him, Jesus knows us by name and speaks to us still through the Word and by the Spirit.

Devotion: *Dear loving, heavenly Abba, Father, please help me to hear what you're saying with greater clarity. Make the Bible live to me. Speak to me personally through its pages and teach me how to listen to what the Holy Spirit is saying to me, in Jesus' name. Amen.*

Jesus said, "Do not hold on to me, for I have not yet returned to the Father."

John 20:17 (NIV)

As Mary Magdalene realizes that it is not the gardener but Jesus who is speaking to her she cannot refrain from reaching out to her master to embrace him. She has had a special and holy affection for him ever since he set her free from the oppression of seven demons that had been afflicting her for years. She had followed him on his journeys through Judea and the surrounding countries. She had hung on every word that he said and watched with awe every sign that he performed. She had faithfully followed him to Golgotha and been at the foot of the Cross when he died. She had been devastated – forlorn beyond words – at the suffering and death of her beloved Rabbi. Now he is alive again and she has heard him speak her name. She cannot hold back. She throws her arms around him.

And Jesus then says something strange. Literally, he says, "Don't keep holding on to me." This shows that he wasn't telling Mary not to touch him (as so many medieval and Renaissance painters of this scene thought); he was telling her to let go because she had already grabbed hold of him. Why did he do this? The answer Jesus gives is "I have not yet returned to the Father." We may not know until heaven the full significance of these words but at the very least they seem to suggest this: that the time for relating to Jesus as she had been is now over for Mary Magdalene. She will no longer be able to see, hear, and touch him in the way that she had while he was in his earthly, incarnate body. Now Jesus is going home to the Father and Mary Magdalene will need to learn a different and better way of showing her devotion and love.

Jesus was therefore not being rude or cruel to Mary. He was pointing to the whole purpose of his death and resurrection. From now on, Mary will worship the Father and she will do this through Jesus and in the Spirit. From now on, Mary will find her heart's true home as she approaches her heavenly Father in intimate worship. She must let him go so that this better way can come.

Devotion: *Dear loving, heavenly Abba, Father, thank you so much that Jesus has opened up the way into your arms and that we can hold on to you forever. Help me to draw closer to you and to experience the fullness of your divine embrace, in Jesus' name. Amen.*

> *"Go instead to my brothers and tell them, 'I am returning to my Father and your Father, to my God and your God.'"*
>
> John 20:17 (NIV)

The risen Jesus gives Mary Magdalene two great privileges. The first is that she is the first person to see the Lord alive after the crucifixion. The second is that she is sent by Jesus to go and tell the disciples that Jesus is alive and that he is returning to the Father. She is sent to the apostles, "apostles" meaning "the sent ones". For centuries she has therefore been described as "the apostle to the apostles".

The message that Jesus actually gives Mary to send has history-making implications. He tells her to tell the brothers, "I am returning to my Father and your Father, to my God and your God." The message is clear. They can now relate to God as Jesus has been relating to God – in other words, intimately, personally, and relationally.

This is momentous. Jesus is saying here that something has changed dramatically in the disciples' relationship with God. Thanks to the events of Good Friday and Easter Day, human beings will no longer be spiritual orphans, alone and afraid in a hostile cosmos. They will be able to call God "My Father, my God."

It is hard to exaggerate the seismic shift that has now occurred. Thanks to his atoning death and mighty resurrection, Jesus has removed the partition of sin between humanity and God and made a road home into the Father's arms. Now Jesus can tell us that God is "my Father and your Father, my God and your God".

We are now accordingly a family! In this family, God is our loving Abba, Father. Jesus is the Father's unique Son. Those who put their trust in Jesus are the adopted sons and daughters of God who can call God "my Father". Jesus is our perfect older Brother and we can be referred to as "the brothers" and indeed "the sisters" of Jesus.

As a church, let's be family. In a fatherless world, people are looking for the Father and they are looking for family.

Devotion: *Dear loving, heavenly Abba, Father, I thank you that through his death and resurrection, Jesus has made it possible for me to know you personally as "my Father". Help me to grow in my appreciation and understanding of what it means to call you my Abba. Amen.*

On the evening of that first day of the week, when the disciples were together, with the doors locked for fear of the Jewish leaders, Jesus came and stood among them and said, "Peace be with you!"

John 20:19

Here are the disciples behind locked doors. Having seen the cruel way in which the religious leaders have treated their master, they are now afraid that they will be subject to a similar ordeal. So they lock the doors of the house they're in and they bunker down.

What they haven't taken into consideration is the fact that Jesus has been raised from the dead. They know from the reports of Simon Peter and the Beloved Disciple that the tomb is empty and that the body of Jesus has gone. But they haven't until this moment met the risen Lord.

Now Jesus comes to them. The locked doors are no obstacle to him. In his new, resurrected, spiritual body, he is not subject to the same restrictions that he experienced in his earthly, physical body. He has unlimited access to any place he wants, even those that are locked.

So John reports that he came to the disciples and stood among them. John doesn't say how Jesus entered the room – whether it was by passing through the closed doors or by materializing in the room. He simply comes and stands among them!

This must have been a moment of extreme emotions for the disciples. Some of them were no doubt terrified. If they were frightened about what was outside the house before, they are terrified of what's in it now. Others must have been elated – weeping with joy.

So what is the risen Jesus' first word to his disciples? It is the word "peace", *shalom* in the Hebrew language. If there was one thing these disciples needed to experience, it was the divine *shalom*. As the good shepherd, Jesus knew what his followers needed.

If it's peace we're looking for, then it's in Jesus that we'll find it. So pray for an encounter with the risen Lord and receive his *shalom*.

Devotion: *Dear loving, heavenly Abba, Father, I thank you for your divine* shalom. *It is your peace that truly makes us feel secure and complete. I pray for those I know who are afraid and uncertain. Give them the healing balm of your heavenly peace, in Jesus' name. Amen.*

The disciples were overjoyed when they saw the Lord.

John 20:20

I remember when I was training for the ordained ministry going somewhat reluctantly to a compulsory college chapel service. I was extremely busy and had a lot to do and didn't really want to be there. However, there was a visiting preacher who had been involved in the translation of the Bible into the language of the Inuit people. He said something in his message that I've never forgotten. He told us that when the translators came to this particular verse of John 20 they were stumped. Their language doesn't deal in abstract concepts so it was a challenge to find a verb that conveyed the idea of being "overjoyed". John reports that the disciples were "overjoyed" when they saw the risen Jesus. The word for "overjoyed" is *chairo* in Greek, which means "to be cheerful" or "happy". The preacher told us that the Inuit people have no such verb in their language.

What were the translators to do? They prayed about it and then one of them hit upon a perfect solution. He had noticed how the Inuit men were inseparable from their husky dogs. When these men got up in the morning, they went to their dogs to let them out and then to pull their sleighs. When the dogs saw them they were so overjoyed that they wagged their tails with great delight. The translator suggested that they used this idea in the Inuit Bible translation of John 20. So that was what was agreed. In that translation, it reads, "The disciples wagged their tails when they saw the Lord."

I don't know if you like dogs, but I love them. All through my life I have lived with dogs. Since we have been married, Alie and I have had three black Labradors, all of them the most faithful friends. The one I have today is called Molly. Every time I come home from a ministry trip, she is waiting for me and when I come home she does a merry dance of joy, wagging her tail furiously.

The disciples were that happy when they saw their master – the risen Lord Jesus. They wagged their tails with glee!

Devotion: *Dear loving, heavenly Abba, Father, I am so overjoyed that death couldn't hold your Son down and that he rose again on the third day. I cannot contain my happiness that death has been defeated and that the grave has lost its sting – glory to God, in Jesus' name. Amen.*

"As the Father has sent me, I am sending you."

John 20:21

Throughout our readings in John's Gospel we have seen how important the word "send" is. Jesus is often described as the one "sent from the Father". Jesus is the Son sent by the Father and indeed from the Father. He is sent into the world with the mission of proclaiming the Father's love and bringing spiritual orphans into relationship with their perfect Abba, Father. His mandate was to help us become the children of God through believing in and obeying him.

In John 20:21 the risen Lord turns to his disciples. He tells them that they too are going to be "sent" people. Just as the Father sent him, so Jesus is sending them to proclaim the Father's love. The disciples are not to hide behind closed windows and locked doors, living in fear and insecurity. They are to be sent out into the world enjoying that perfect love that drives out all fear – the perfect love of the Father, given through the power of the Spirit.

We should never forget this. We are not called to live in fear and insecurity like mistrustful orphans. We are called to break out of the four walls of our churches and to take the Father's love to the fatherless. And we are called to do this locally, regionally, nationally, and globally. As followers of Jesus, we are called to emulate the Son. If the Son by nature was a "sent one", then Jesus wants us to understand that the sons and daughters by adoption are "sent ones" too.

Very often the word translated "send" in John's Gospel is *apostellein*. This is the word from which we get "apostolic". If there is one thing we need to rediscover it is the apostolic call upon the church. We are not supposed to stay in one place and tell the world to "come to us". Rather, we are called to move out and "go to them". Indeed, a true church is not measured by its seating capacity. It is measured by its sending capacity.

Are you a part of a church that is living in the apostolic impulse of John 20:21? Are you a "Come to us" Christian or a "Go to them" one?

Devotion: *Dear loving, heavenly Abba, Father, I recognize that what your Son said to the original disciples he is saying to us today. It is time to go into the world to share the Father's love. Help me to rediscover the adventure of being a "sent one", in Jesus' name. Amen.*

... he breathed on them and said, "Receive the Holy Spirit."

John 20:22

At the very dawn of time, Abba, Father created a perfect garden known as Eden. He created Adam and Eve to live in this garden and to enjoy intimacy with him, walking and talking with him every day. He created Adam first and then Eve afterwards, out of one of Adam's ribs.

When Abba, Father created Adam, he first of all formed him out of the dust of the earth. The name Adam in Hebrew is *Adam* – a word that sounds like *Adamah*, used of the dust of the earth from which he was made. Calling him Adam was like calling him "Dusty".

But God doesn't just form Adam, he also fills him. Having made Adam's physical frame, Abba, Father breathes into his nostrils the breath of life and he becomes a living being. The first thing Adam would have seen was his heavenly Father's face, close to his.

Tragically, this face-to-face intimacy with the Father didn't last. After Eve had been created, Satan tempted her and our first parents sinned. That original innocence and intimacy was lost. Adam and Eve had to leave the Father's presence as the gates of Eden slammed shut.

Now, many centuries later, Jesus comes to undo the effects of this great fall from grace. He dies on the Cross for our sins and is raised from the dead through the glorious power of our heavenly Father. Now in John 20 he has come to his disciples. What will he do?

John reports that Jesus breathed on them and said, "Receive the Holy Spirit." The word "breathed" clearly echoes Genesis 2:7 where God breathes into Adam's nostrils. Jesus comes to give his disciples a brand new start. It is as if a new creation has begun.

Whenever anyone comes to Jesus, they receive the Holy Spirit. When that happens, they are born again and become brand new creations. Jesus wants all of us to come to the Father so that we can be filled with the life of the Holy Spirit. He is truly the one who makes all things new.

Devotion: *Dear loving, heavenly Abba, Father, thank you for Jesus, especially for the way he died and rose again so that we might receive the Spirit and become brand new creations in him. Breathe on me, Abba, Father, today I pray. Make all things new in me, in Jesus' name. Amen.*

"If you forgive the sins of anyone, their sins are forgiven; if you do not forgive them, they are not forgiven."

John 20:23

In this great verse Jesus gives his disciples the authority to pronounce forgiveness. This means that we have the right to proclaim God's forgiveness to any sinner who is remorseful, and to withhold that forgiveness if they are not. It also means that we have the ability to forgive or indeed not to forgive those who sin against us.

Do you realize that the power to forgive others is within your grasp? Jesus has given you authority to forgive those who have sinned against you. You don't need to live in a state of unforgiveness and bitterness any longer. You can choose to release mercy. You can take responsibility and rise out of the victim state and become a victor.

Many believers live with deep-rooted bitterness towards other people. In fact, it has been said that unforgiveness is one of the most debilitating diseases in the body of Christ today. The devil has brought many into captivity through causing a root of bitterness to grow within their hearts. He has robbed them of abundant, spiritual life in the process.

What the risen Jesus said to the disciples he says again to us. We have the power to forgive others and we also have the power not to forgive them. If we choose to forgive, however hard that decision may be, Jesus promises that he will give us the grace to give others a gift they don't deserve – the gift of our unconditional forgiveness and blessing.

Very few of us manage to enter adult life unhurt. And when we become adults, even fewer go through their lives without being wounded in a severe way. When this happens we have a choice. We can either live in the low ground of judgment, tormented by the enemy. Or we can live in the high ground of mercy, enjoying the freedom of Abba's love.

If there is someone you need to forgive, take hold of the promise in John 20:23. With the help of the Spirit, give that person the gift of your forgiveness. You will feel so free when you do.

Devotion: *Dear loving, heavenly Abba, Father, I thank you that I can speak your words of forgiveness over others – both those who sin against you (and who are penitent) and those who sin against me (whether penitent or not). Give me grace to do this I pray, in Jesus' name. Amen.*

> *"Unless I see the nail marks in his hands and put my finger where the nails were, and put my hand into his side, I will not believe."*

John 20:25

I have a theory about Thomas, who said these words. I don't believe that Thomas really doubted that Jesus had appeared to the other disciples and was therefore alive. I believe that Thomas doubted that Jesus would ever appear to someone like him.

Let's consider Thomas's life for a moment. We don't know much about him. But one thing we do know is that he was never referred to by his real name but by the name *Didymus*. This is the Hebrew version of the Aramaic name *Thomas* which means "twin".

I don't know about you but I feel sorry for Thomas! I am a twin myself and I can feel Thomas's pain here. A twin doesn't want to be known as a twin. They want to be known as a separate human being. They want to be known by name.

What happens to a twin whose uniqueness and separateness is not valued? They can go one of two ways. They either become overly passive or they become overly active. They either become subsumed into the group or they seek to rise above the group.

Thomas chooses the latter. In John 11, when Jesus is talking about returning to Judea to visit Lazarus, Thomas says that they all should go to Judea and die with Jesus. Thomas didn't really mean this. This was his attempt to rise above the parapet and be seen.

So here we are now in John 20. Jesus has appeared to the group but not to Thomas. I don't think Thomas doubted that Jesus had appeared to them. He doubted that Jesus would appear to him. He doubted that Jesus would value his individuality to appear to him.

If there is a root of worthlessness and shame in your heart, remember this: Jesus loves you for who you are. He celebrates your unique individuality. He knows you by name.

Devotion: *Dear loving, heavenly Abba, Father, I praise you that you have known me from the time when I was in my mother's womb. I thank you that my life is not an accident and that you know me by name. Please release me from all shame and help me to receive your honour. Amen.*

Then he said to Thomas, "Put your finger here; see my hands. Reach out your hand and put it into my side. Stop doubting and believe."

John 20:27

John tells us what no other Gospel writer tells us – that eight days after Jesus appeared to the disciples, he came and made an appearance for Thomas. Eight days after his appearance to ten men, he comes and makes an appearance for just one man. If ever there was a Gospel story that highlighted the Father's love for us as individuals, it is this one.

Let's remember what I wrote in the devotional note yesterday. Thomas was given a label not a name. As we saw in John 11:16, his label was *Didymus*, meaning "the twin". This label must have stuck. This nickname must have hurt. Even if other people meant it only as a descriptive phrase, in Thomas's heart it felt like a curse. It robbed him of his unique individuality.

Consequently, Thomas's great problem was not so much that he doubted that the risen Jesus had appeared to the others. It was that he doubted that the risen Jesus would appear to him personally. So he gives voice to his pain and tells the others that he won't believe unless he sees and feels Christ's wounds for himself.

And here we see yet another example of the Father's kindness. His Son comes to the house where the disciples are staying. It is eight days after he appeared to all of them, bar one of course – Thomas. Now Jesus comes and stands among the disciples again but this time he is only interested in seeing Thomas.

Jesus is always doing this in the Gospels. Jesus is not one of those preachers who love crowds but hate people. He loves both. And indeed, he will stop a whole crowd for just one person. He will interrupt what he's doing with a crowd in order to reveal Abba's compassion to just one person. His behaviour towards Thomas just confirms this.

Maybe you feel like everyone else is having a spiritual experience but you've been left out. Don't doubt yourself and don't doubt Jesus. Position yourself to receive the honour of a personal encounter.

Devotion: *Dear loving, heavenly Abba, Father, I thank you for this amazing aspect of your character – that you stop everything for just one person. You are such a kind and compassionate Dad. Please give me a personal experience of your love I pray, in Jesus' name. Amen.*

Thomas said to him, "My Lord and my God!"

John 20:28

We are coming to the end of the story of Thomas now. Keep in mind what I've been proposing in the last few notes – that Thomas was a wounded soul and that he suffered from shame. This came from the fact that he was constantly being labelled as "the twin" rather than celebrated for who he really was. Consequently, when the other ten disciples saw the risen Lord, Thomas was upset when they told him. He didn't doubt that Jesus had appeared to them. He doubted that Jesus would ever make an appearance to someone like him.

But Jesus does. He's kind like that. When he left the city of Jericho followed by a great crowd, he stopped the procession to minister healing to a blind man called Bartimaeus. When he was preaching to a crowd in Peter's house, he stopped the sermon to minister healing to a paralyzed man who was lowered on a stretcher from the roof by his friends. When Jesus was walking through a crowd and a woman touched him – causing power to go from him and heal her – he stopped everything to find her. Jesus was always treating people as unique individuals.

Jesus is the human embodiment of the Father's unparalleled kindness and compassion. He reveals the Father's great love for us as individuals. And here with Thomas, Jesus makes a special appearance. He tells Thomas to put his finger in the wounds in his body. As he does so, Thomas begins to get in touch with the sufferings of his master. He sees that Jesus knows what human pain is like. He sees that Jesus has been labelled too. He sees that Jesus is a man of sorrows who is intimately acquainted with his grief. He sees and he says, "My Lord and my God!"

Notice the little word "My". Thomas has had a personal encounter. This is not a group encounter. It is Thomas's very own encounter. And it is carefully designed to reinforce Thomas's individuality and to heal his shame. No wonder Thomas says that Jesus is "My Lord and my God" – the most profound declaration of Jesus' divinity in the Gospels. What a wonderful transformation we see in Thomas. What hope there is for us all!

Devotion: *Dear loving, heavenly Abba, Father, I praise you for the greatness of your healing love. You truly know how to displace our shame and replace it with honour. You are my Lord and my God. You are my Abba, Father and I love you, in Jesus' name. Amen.*

"... blessed are those who have not seen and yet have believed."

John 20:29

Thomas has just confessed Jesus as "My Lord and my God." No one in any of the Gospels makes such a high and exalted confession of Jesus as this. And this is a very bold declaration in his world. At that time, there was already someone else who had these titles – Caesar. As part of the imperial cult, the emperor was confessed as *dominus et deus*, as "Lord and God". Thomas begs to disagree. Now he has had his own personal encounter with the risen Jesus, he confesses him as "My Lord and my God." He proclaims that Jesus is Lord and Caesar is not. Jesus is divine and Caesar is not.

Jesus tells Thomas that he has seen him with his own eyes and this is why he has come to believe such great truths about who he really is. But he then adds, "Blessed are those who have not seen and yet have believed." What did he mean by this?

Thomas has seen and therefore believed. But this is not the way it will be once Jesus has returned to the Father in heaven. After that happens, Jesus will no longer be visible to our physical eyes. We will therefore have to put our trust in someone who is invisible.

Here is the great difference between the way the world works and the way the kingdom of God works. The people of the world say, "I'll believe it when I see it." The people of the kingdom say, "I'll see it when I believe it." This is faith and faith is being certain about what you can't see.

The Thomas episode ends with what we might call a "Beatitude". In Matthew's Gospel, Jesus gives a number of sayings beginning with the word "Blessed" (Matthew 5:1–12). Here we find another one – "Happy are those who have not seen yet who believe."

There are many things that we can't see yet which we believe are real – such as the wind. We see their effects, but we don't see them. The same is true of Jesus. We believe he is real even though we cannot see him. We believe he is our all-powerful Lord and God and this makes us blessed.

Devotion: *Dear loving, heavenly Abba, Father, even though I cannot yet see you, I know that you exist and that you love me. Thank you that I am truly blessed by believing this. Thank you that one day I will receive the reward of my faith – seeing the one in whom I have believed. Amen.*

> *Jesus did many other miraculous signs in the presence of his disciples, which are not recorded in this book. But these are written that you may believe that Jesus is the Christ, the Son of God, and that by believing you may have life in his name.*
>
> John 20:30–31 (NIV)

This is some thought! John tells us here that Jesus did many other miracles than the ones recorded in his Gospel. In other words, John tells us that he's been selective. He could have told us about many other things that Jesus had done – healings, resurrection miracles, and of course exorcisms – but he's chosen to record just seven great signs:

The transformation of water into wine (John 2)

The healing of the royal official's son (John 4)

The healing of the man at the Pool of Bethesda (John 5)

The feeding of the five thousand (John 6)

The walking on the water (John 6)

The healing of the man born blind (John 9)

The raising of Lazarus (John 11).

So John settles on seven signs out of all the many that he could have recorded. And he includes these seven for one main purpose – to encourage the reader to believe that Jesus is the Christ and God's Son.

It is vital to remember that in John's eyes, miracles are not supposed to be enjoyed and revered for their own sakes. Rather, they are "signs". They point away from themselves to the glorious and divine personality of Jesus. As soon as we become preoccupied with miracles for their own sakes we have lost the point. Miracles are messages and the message is this: that the miracle-worker is the Messiah of Israel, the Saviour of the World and the Son of God. So let's not become focused on the miracles. Let's stay focused on the miracle worker!

Devotion: *Dear loving, heavenly Abba, Father, keep me from becoming obsessed with supernatural wonders for their own sakes. Help me always to worship the giver not the gifts. Help me to worship the King and not the bling, in Jesus' name. Amen.*

"I'm going out to fish," Simon Peter told them ....

John 21:3

You could be forgiven for thinking that the Gospel of John had ended with the closing of chapter 20. John sounds like the author is finishing when he mentions the purpose of writing his book. But now a new chapter begins. Why is chapter 21 needed when chapter 20 seemed to be such a resounding and fitting finale?

The answer is because there is one major piece of unfinished business in John's story and this has to do with Simon Peter. We know that Peter denied Jesus three times in the courtyard of the high priest's house in Jerusalem. One question remains: What will happen to Simon Peter after such a failure of nerve?

John 21 opens on the edge of the Sea of Galilee. There are seven men on the shore: Peter, Thomas, Nathanael, James, John, and two unnamed disciples. Simon Peter turns to his companions and tells them that he is going to go out to fish. It is night, the optimum time for net fishing. His friends tell him that they're coming too.

Why does Simon Peter react to his failure by fishing? It is because this is what he was doing before he met Jesus. Before Peter accepted the call to become a disciple, he had been in the fishing business by the Sea of Galilee. Peter had now lost his way so he figured the best thing to do was to retrace his steps to the place where he had begun.

Simon Peter goes back to the place of his call as he processes what he's done in denying Jesus. What he is going to discover in John 21 is that Jesus is going to make him confront his failure, not in order to destroy or humiliate him but in order to heal and liberate him. We are going to see a great example of restoration in the Father's love.

John 21 is necessary because it tells us about Peter's healing and also because it shows us that the call is bigger than the fall. We all fail from time to time as we follow Jesus. But John 21 reveals that our Father God is the God of the second chance.

Devotion: *Dear loving, heavenly Abba, Father, I thank you so much that the call is bigger than the fall. Help me to accept your process of healing and restoration in those areas where I have failed you. Keep me in alignment with the call and destiny upon my life, in Jesus' name. Amen.*

Jesus called out to them, "Friends, haven't you any fish?"

John 21:5

Simon Peter and his six friends have gone out on a nocturnal fishing trip. This was the best time to go fishing yet they have caught nothing. They are now weary and it is early in the morning. The risen Jesus appears on the shoreline and stands on the beach. He is unrecognized by the disciples and shouts out to them, "Friends, haven't you caught anything yet?"

The New International Version doesn't do justice to what Jesus actually says. Jesus does not address the seven men as "friends". He addresses them as "little children". The word in Greek is *paidia* and it has been used twice before in John's Gospel. The first time is when John describes the royal official's son as "a little child" in John 4:49. The second time we find it is in John 16:21: "A woman giving birth to a child has pain because her time has come; but when her *baby* is born she forgets the anguish because of her joy that a child is born into the world."

The word translated "baby" here is *paidia*.

When the risen Jesus appears by the Sea of Galilee, he addresses his disciples as "little children" or "infants". This is the word used in Matthew 18:3–4 where Jesus says, "I tell you the truth, unless you change and become like little children [*paidia*], you will never enter the kingdom of heaven. Therefore, whoever humbles himself like this child is the greatest in the kingdom of heaven."

Why does Jesus call grown men "little children"? It is because Jesus reveals the Father. Everything Jesus says and does is a window onto Abba Father's heart. When Jesus calls his followers "little children", we are hearing the Father's voice. The Father wants the disciples to enjoy a child–Father intimacy with him. He wants us to as well. They – and we – are small children in the loving hands of a great Father.

Devotion: *Dear loving, heavenly Abba, Father, help me to relate to you in the humble simplicity of a trusting child. Help me to hear you addressing me as your son or your daughter and to know you more intimately as my Abba, Father, in Jesus' name. Amen.*

*He said, "Throw your net on the right side of the boat and you
will find some." When they did, they were unable to haul the net
in because of the large number of fish.*

John 21:6

Peter and his six companions have been out fishing all night and have
caught nothing. They are exhausted; their little fishing expedition has
yielded no benefit to them whatsoever. Now it's time to come into the
shore with nothing to show for all their efforts.

Before they set sail for the beach, the risen Jesus appears by the sea.
They don't at first recognize him as he calls out, "Haven't you any fish?"
They simply answer no. Then Jesus tells them to throw their nets out
on the right side of the boat.

What happens next is extraordinary. As soon as the net is in the
water they can see fish everywhere. There are fins splashing furiously
on the right side of the boat and suddenly there is an abundant catch.
The disciples move from exhaustion to elation in a few seconds.

What's the message in this story? I think it's this. When we come
to the end of ourselves we find the beginning of God. In other words,
when our own human resources run out, we discover the Father's divine
resources. We experience his power in our weakness.

Peter is learning a vital lesson for the rest of his life here. From now
on he will remember this moment. He will not seek to work in the flesh.
He will seek to be led by the Spirit. He will not rely on his own strength.
He will rely on the Father's strength.

And the same needs to be true for us, too. All of us are called to catch
fish – not literal fish, but people. We are all called to put out the net of
the Father's love and draw lost people into the safety of his embrace.
We are all called to bring spiritual orphans to the Father. But if we are
to see an abundant catch, then we must learn to rely not on our human
strength and power but on the Spirit of God (Zechariah 4:6). His power
is more important than our programmes.

Devotion: *Dear loving, heavenly Abba, Father, help me to rely on your
divine power rather than on my own human strength as I seek to win
others to Christ. Give me that grace that is sufficient – that power that is
made perfect in my weakness, in Jesus' name. Amen.*

Then the disciple whom Jesus loved said to Peter, "It is the Lord!"

John 21:7

We have seen time and again in John's Gospel how the Beloved Disciple and Simon Peter are paired together in many scenes, from the Last Supper right up to this story of the fishing trip in John 21. Often when this is the case, the Beloved Disciple is presented in a more positive light – as the disciple who stays close to Jesus and who sees and hears things that Peter doesn't. This isn't any different in John 21.

The two men are on board a fishing boat on the Sea of Galilee. The risen Jesus appears on the shoreline and shouts to them. He tells them to cast their nets on the right side of their boat. When they do they catch a huge haul of fish. At this the Beloved Disciple realizes the identity of the stranger on the beach. He turns to Peter and tells him, "It is the Lord." Once again the Beloved Disciple sees more than Peter does.

I wonder if you've noticed something about the stories John tells from chapter 20 through chapter 21. They are mostly what you might call "recognition scenes". The primary example in John 20 involves Mary Magdalene. At the empty tomb she meets Jesus. Only she doesn't recognize him at first. She thinks he's the gardener. But then he speaks her name and she recognizes his voice.

In John 21 it is now the Beloved Disciple's turn. Jesus appears on the beach but at this stage the Beloved Disciple doesn't know who it is. John points this out in verse 4: "Early in the morning, Jesus stood on the shore, but the disciples did not realize that it was Jesus." This lack of recognition may have been because of a lack of visibility. Or it may just have been a matter of distance. Either way, no one recognized Jesus.

Until, that is, he started to speak to them. Mary Magdalene doesn't recognize Jesus until he speaks – and the same is true of the Beloved Disciple. From the resurrection onwards, we will all have to learn to relate to Jesus not by seeing but by hearing. As Jesus said in John 10:4, the sheep recognize the good shepherd's voice.

Devotion: *Dear loving, heavenly Abba, Father, help me to remember that I have to walk by faith and not by sight. And teach me continually that faith comes to me by hearing – through your Word and by the Spirit. Help me to recognize your voice more quickly, in Jesus' name. Amen.*

When they landed, they saw a fire of burning coals there with fish on it, and some bread.

John 21:9

Jesus is truly the most wonderful Counsellor. He knows exactly how to lead us through the healing of hurtful memories. He is gracious, gentle, trustworthy, and kind. When it is time for life's hurts to be healed, we simply couldn't be in safer hands.

We have reached the point in John 21 when Simon Peter has arrived at the shore where his risen Lord is waiting for him. Now is the moment of truth for Peter. He has denied his master three times in the run up to Jesus' crucifixion. What kind of welcome will he receive?

When Peter and the others get to the shore they find that Jesus has prepared a fire for them. He is cooking fish for their breakfast and has fresh bread to boot. The risen Lord – the conqueror of sin and death – is barbequing a meal for his disciples.

That alone is a thought – heaven's eternal champion is providing a fry-up for his followers. But there is more to this moment than even that, for the word that John uses here for "a fire of burning coals" is a very distinct one. It is a word we have already met once before in John's Gospel.

In John 18:18, we read this: "It was cold, and the servants and officials stood around a fire they had made to keep warm. Peter also was standing with them, warming himself." The word translated "fire" here is the Greek noun *anthrakia*, meaning "charcoal fire".

This rare word is used only twice in the entire New Testament. It is used of the fire made up of charcoal in the courtyard where Peter denied Jesus. And it is used one more time, here in John 21:9, of the charcoal fire where Peter will have to confront his painful past.

Notice then how carefully Jesus recreates the atmosphere, even the smell, of Peter's denials in order to take him through the healing process. Jesus truly is the wonderful Counsellor and the Prince of Peace.

Devotion: *Dear loving, heavenly Abba, Father, I thank you that you heal our wounded memories. You know how to help us to confront them. You know how to help us find our freedom. There is no one like you. Thank you that I can trust you in the healing process, in Jesus' name. Amen.*

Simon Peter climbed aboard and dragged the net ashore. It was full of large fish, 153, but even with so many the net was not torn.

John 21:11

So much ink has been spilled over the number "153"! Many commentators have tried to suggest that there is some secret symbolism here. For example, one of the earliest theologians of the church suggested that the number is a composite of three things – the number 100, which symbolizes the full number of Gentile people that will come to Christ; the number 50, which symbolizes the number of Jewish people who will confess Jesus as Lord; the number 3, which stands for the three persons of the Holy Trinity.

I'd like to suggest a different interpretation. The 153 fish don't symbolize anything. I believe it's an eyewitness detail that is meant to be taken literally. There were simply 153 fish and this was a massive haul by any calculations. When you take into account that all these fish were large in size then the real point isn't any symbolic meaning of the number but the simple fact that the nets didn't break. That's what interests John. Not that 153 stands for something, but that in spite of this abundance the nets stayed intact.

I don't know if you've ever noticed, but John doesn't like things being broken. When he describes the multiplication of the loaves in John 6, he says that Jesus took, blessed, and distributed the bread, but he never says he broke it. At the Cross in John 19, the seamless robe of Jesus is not torn into four pieces by the soldiers on duty; rather, they throw dice so that one soldier can own the whole garment. A little later we see a Roman soldier breaking the legs of the crucified men either side of Jesus; but he does not break Jesus' legs.

John doesn't like things torn or broken. And here's the hidden message of John 21:11: Jesus wants us to bring great numbers of people into the orbit of his love and he wants this to happen in nets that don't get broken. He wants a united church to contain and clean new converts. If we prepare strong nets, he will produce a great catch.

Devotion: *Dear loving, heavenly Abba, Father, I thank you that your desire is for us to engage in a lifestyle of fishing for men and women. Help us to know your strategy for net building and give us your blueprint for an effective mission-shaped church in this age, in Jesus' name. Amen.*

When they had finished eating, Jesus said to Simon Peter, "Simon son of John, do you love me more than these?"

John 21:15

It's now time for Simon Peter's restoration. Peter has been sitting nervously with his six friends in the presence of the risen Jesus. They have all eaten the barbequed fish cooked for them over a charcoal fire. The smell of the burning coals has possibly stimulated Peter's memory of his three denials even more sharply. After all, it was while he was warming himself next to a charcoal fire that he had claimed not to know Jesus three times.

Now Jesus turns to Peter. No doubt up until this moment the conversation has been general – for everyone's ears. But after the meal has ended Jesus addresses Peter personally. And he asks him a question that begins, "Simon son of John". Notice that Jesus doesn't say "Peter". Peter literally meant "rock" and the name meant "Rocky". But Simon has not been a rock. He has not been strong and steadfast. Jesus therefore uses his old name for now.

And now here comes the question. "Do you truly love me more than these?" What did Jesus mean? He could have meant, "Do you love me more than you love these friends?" He could have meant, "Do you love me more than these men do?" Or, "Do you love me more than these things – the materials needed for your fishing business?"

There is no way of knowing for sure but I lean towards the last. Jesus challenges Peter. Does he want to be Simon, son of John or does he want to be Simon Peter? Does he want to go fishing for fish or does he want to go fishing for men and women? Does he want to go back to his old life or does he want to embrace the new life of following Jesus?

This is a question for us too. Do we love Jesus more than we love our possessions? Have our hearts been captured by the greatest love of all – the Father's love? And does this love eclipse all other loves in our lives?

Devotion: *Dear loving, heavenly Abba, Father, I want to confess to you that sometimes I love the things of this world more than I love you. Help me to love you more than all the other people and things in my life. Please arrest my heart with the love of all loves, in Jesus' name. Amen.*

Jesus said, "Take care of my sheep."

John 21:16

We are right in the middle of a painful process. Peter has denied Jesus three times. Now Jesus has been raised from the dead. Peter and his six friends have come to the beach and had breakfast with him. They have seen him with their own eyes. They have watched as he ate the fish he cooked and they know he is truly alive in a resurrected body. Now they are listening to him as he speaks. In particular, Peter is listening as he is asked the question, "do you truly love me more than these?"

How does Peter answer this question? He says, "You know that I love you." With that, Jesus says, "Take care of my sheep." Why "Take care of my sheep"?

To understand this we need to go back to John chapter 10 where Jesus had taught about the sheep, the shepherd, and the sheep pen. There we heard Jesus say that he is the good shepherd who gives his life for the sheep. This is something that the seven men on the beach have seen vividly fulfilled at Calvary.

But in John 10 Jesus also spoke about the hired hand who doesn't really care about the sheep and who runs away in the hour of danger, leaving the sheep unattended. Simon Peter had graphically fulfilled this role in his behaviour before and after the crucifixion. He had effectively run away and allowed the sheep to scatter.

But now it's restoration time. It's time for Simon to become Peter (the rock). It is time for the hired hand to become the shepherd. It is time for Peter to put on the mantle of "shepherd" in the earliest church.

Whenever we are dismantled by our heavenly Father it is for one reason and one reason alone – so that we might be re-mantled. It is so that we might move from the fall back to the call.

Never forget this. When it comes to the restoration of sinners, God is a kind and compassionate Dad. He is not an angry and condemning boss. Isn't it time the church embraced Abba's methods of restoration?

Devotion: *Dear loving, heavenly Abba, Father, I can't thank you enough for your mercy and grace over the years. You have been so kind to me when I have fallen. You have forgiven me for my history and reminded me of my destiny. You are truly an awesome Dad. Amen.*

Peter was hurt because Jesus asked him the third time, "Do you love me?" He said, "Lord, you know all things; you know that I love you."

John 21:17

There is a poignant beauty about the restoration of Simon Peter after the fry-up by the Sea of Galilee. Notice how Jesus uses a meal as the context for Peter's healing. He allows Peter to relax with him during breakfast before he turns to the painful issues of Peter's past.

I think we can learn a lot from that. I remember how one of my early mentors would buy fish and chips for me on a Monday evening. He would sit and eat with me. At the end of the meal he would sometimes very gently challenge me about an area of weakness that he'd seen in my life, especially something that had been exhibited the day before as I'd ministered in church on the Sunday. He was brilliant at making me feel safe in his presence. Even the hard things were easier to hear because of the careful way he prepared my heart to receive.

I think this is what's happening to Peter here. Jesus has cooked a meal of fish and bread and Peter has sat with the others enjoying it. I am guessing that a breakfast cooked by God is going to taste just that bit better than the ones we normally eat! Peter is now feeling full and has been reassured by the accepting heart of his Master. Now Jesus asks Peter the same questionabout whether Peter loves him three times. As he asks the third time, Peter feels hurt. He wasn't hurt the first time or the second. It was the third time that Peter felt it.

And of course the reason why is obvious. Peter had denied Jesus three times in Annas's courtyard next to a charcoal fire. Now he has been asked to affirm Jesus three times on a beach next to a charcoal fire. As Peter says, Jesus truly knows all things. He knows everything about Peter and he knows exactly how to draw the pain out too.

And the same is true for us. Jesus knows everything about our lives and – if we let him – he can very tenderly draw the pain out of our past. He truly is the wonderful Counsellor! We are safe in his loving hands.

Devotion: *Dear loving, heavenly Abba, Father, I thank you that you create a safe place for me to confront the unsafe issues of my life. You truly are the most gentle and wonderful Counsellor. I trust you to draw the pain out of my heart I pray, in Jesus' name. Amen.*

> **"Very truly I tell you, when you were younger you dressed yourself and went where you wanted; but when you are old you will stretch out your hands, and someone else will dress you and lead you where you do not want to go."**
>
> John 21:18

As Peter's restoration comes to an end, Jesus turns from Peter's past to Peter's future. He prophesies that Peter will have to face a great trial when he is very old. One day he will stretch out his hands and be dressed by someone else and taken to a place he doesn't want to go. John adds that this showed the kind of death that Peter was going to die – a death that would bring glory to God.

The New Testament doesn't describe Peter's death. But we know from the theologians and leaders of the early church what may have happened to him. In the year AD 64, there was a great fire that destroyed much of the city of Rome. The emperor Nero blamed Christians for this disaster and had them rounded up and barbarically killed. It seems very likely that Peter was one of these martyrs.

Early tradition has it that Peter was fleeing from Rome at the time of these persecutions. As he left, he had a vision of Jesus heading towards the city. Peter asked Jesus *"Quo vadis?"* In Latin this means, "Where are you going?" Jesus told him that he was going to Rome to be crucified again. Peter was so challenged by this that he went there to die too.

And so it was that Peter's arms were stretched out on a cross. Tradition has it that Peter felt so unworthy of dying as his master had that he asked to be crucified upside down. This is very possibly true. The Jewish historian Josephus tells us that the Romans were extremely cruel and would crucify their victims in different positions.

Whatever may be said about Peter's failings, when it came to his death he was faithful. His death did indeed bring glory to God. And when Peter died the Father cried. For as it says in Psalm 116:15, "Precious in the sight of God is the death of his saints."

Devotion: *Dear loving, heavenly Abba, Father, I don't know what the future holds, but I do know who holds the future. You do! And I trust you. I trust that it is my destiny to finish well and to bring glory to you. Help me to be faithful and true, as Peter was, in Jesus' name. Amen.*

This is the disciple who testifies to these things and who wrote them down. We know that his testimony is true.

John 21:24

Jesus has finished speaking to Simon Peter. There is a solemnity about this scene now as Peter reflects on the words of destiny that his master and Messiah has uttered. Peter now knows the end game of his life. One day he is going to be forced to go somewhere he doesn't want to go. One day he is going to die for the cause of Christ.

As Simon Peter looks at his six friends around the charcoal fire his eyes are drawn towards the man whom Jesus called the Beloved Disciple. Peter has always felt particularly close to this brother. He has just been fishing with him. Several weeks before, he ran to the tomb with him. Before that he went to the high priest's house with him.

In these last few weeks, Peter and the Beloved Disciple have often done things together. Now Peter looks at his friend and becomes curious. If his own destiny is to be martyred, what will the Beloved Disciple experience? Will this man also be led where he doesn't want to go to face a death that he doesn't want to die?

Jesus' response is to tell Peter that his friend's destiny is not his concern. If Jesus wants the Beloved Disciple to be alive when he returns on the last day of history then that is his business not Peter's. Peter is to be focused on his life and on the great goal of finishing well. The Beloved Disciple's future is the Beloved Disciple's focus.

And with that the Gospel writer addresses us – the readers – directly. He tells us that this Beloved Disciple is the same man who witnessed the things described in this Gospel and indeed who wrote them down. He adds that he and his community know that his testimony is true.

As we come to the end of John's Gospel, we can be confident that the Beloved Disciple's testimony is historically accurate and theologically true. The written Word is true, just as the incarnate Word is true. The Gospel of John is true truth. We can be greatly reassured by that.

Devotion: *Dear loving, heavenly Abba, Father, I thank you for the witness of the Beloved Disciple. I thank you that he bore witness to the truth and that his testimony is true. Help me to be a beloved disciple and to proclaim the truth about your Son in my generation, in his name. Amen.*

Jesus did many other things as well. If every one of them were written down, I suppose that even the whole world would not have room for the books that would be written.

John 21:25

If there were a competition for the best ending to a book then the final verses of John's Gospel would be my winner. For here John concludes his magnificent account of the life of Jesus by telling us that the whole earth could not contain the number of books that could have been written about Jesus of Nazareth. He ends, in short, by telling us that he has really only just begun.

When it comes to Jesus, you and I will never be able to map the contours of his limitless personality. To describe him with any degree of finality would be to reduce him to a mere mortal. But he was and is far more than that. No man or woman has ever left such a profound and lasting mark on the world's stage as Jesus. If John could not give a final, definitive account of him, then we certainly can't.

John tells us here that he has been selective in writing his book. He assures us that there were countless other things that Jesus did which have not been recorded. John has necessarily had to omit many episodes and teachings. If all that John knew had been written down in a series of books then all the libraries in the world would not have had room on their shelves for them.

I don't know about you, but I sometimes imagine what the Father's house is like in heaven. When I do I picture the largest library in the universe – with bookshelves as high as the clouds and as wide as the oceans. One day we're going to roam with our Dad in those hallowed halls and read those precious books of his. We're going to feast our eager eyes on all the stories that the Gospel writers didn't tell.

And we will find that what John said here is true, that the end of his Gospel was not the end at all, but just the beginning – the beginning of the most epic adventure... our eternal journey with the perfect Father.

Devotion: _Dear loving, heavenly Abba, Father, I thank you so much for this beautiful Gospel about your Son. As I end this year and prepare to begin a new one, please give me a deeper hunger for your Word and a greater passion for your truth, in Jesus' name. Amen._

I Am Your Father
by Mark Stibbe

Mark Stibbe is convinced that
our society has been deeply
damaged by absent, apathetic
or abusive fathers. The church
can offer a solution – a
healing relationship with our
Heavenly Father – but many
Christians have been poorly
fathered and are still bound
by the legacy of this wound.
I Am Your Father is designed
to help Christians find
healing in a fatherless world.

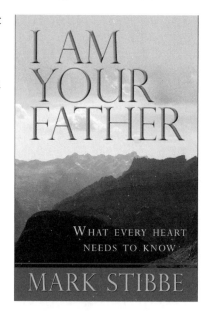

"*Important and profound.*"

Bill Johnson, Bethel Church, Redding, California, USA

"*A masterpiece of excellent scholarship, heart-moving storytelling and compelling vision.*"

Ed Piorek, Author and speaker

ISBN 978-1-85424-937-1 £9.99 UK / $14.99 US

www.lionhudson.com/monarch

MONARCH

The 100 Verse Bible
by Mark Stibbe

Through the Bible runs an incredible story; that of God the Father and His love for humanity.

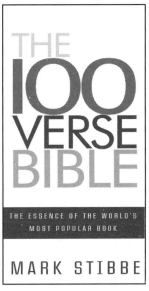

To highlight this, Mark Stibbe chooses 100 verses, 50 from the Old Testament and 50 from the New. Each illustrates an aspect of God's love, and together they tell the big story of His fatherhood. Mark Stibbe explains each verse simply and succinctly, bringing stories, characters and ideas to life.

"... Mark Stibbe has attractively illuminated the character of Our Father ...."
— Jonathan Aitken

"For me this book has changed the way I look at God, my life and my faith. Groundbreaking and skilful inkmanship of the highest order."
— **G.P. Taylor,** New York Times bestselling author
of the *Shadowmancer* Saga

ISBN 978-1-85424-933-3 £3.99 UK / $6.99 US

www.lionhudson.com/monarch

MONARCH